ZAGATSURVEY

1995

NEW YORK CITY RESTAURANTS

Published and distributed by
ZAGATSURVEY
4 Columbus Circle
New York, New York 10019
212 977 6000

Third Printing

ISBN 1-57006-008-8

Contents

Introduction   4
Foreword   5
Explanation of Ratings and Symbols   6
New Yorkers' Favorite Restaurants   8
Traffic Report   9
Top Ratings
   • Top Food and by Cuisine   10
   • Top Decor, Rooms, Views, Service   13
Best Buys   15
ALPHABETICAL DIRECTORY
   • Names, Addresses, Phone Numbers,
     Ratings and Reviews.   21
INDEXES
   • **Types of Cuisine** 168
   • **Neighborhood Locations** 183
   • Breakfast, Brunch and Buffets 196
   • BYO 197
   • Coffeehouses and Dessert Places 197
   • Dancing/Entertainment. 197
   • Delivers/Takeout 199
   • Dining Alone 199
   • Fireplaces. 199
   • Game in Season 200
   • Health/Spa Menus. 200
   • Hotel Dining. 200
   • "In" Places 201
   • Late Late – After 12:30 202
   • Meet for a Drink. 204
   • Noteworthy Newcomers and Closings. 204
   • Offbeat 206
   • Old New York. 207
   • Outdoor Dining 207
   • Parties/Private Rooms. 208
   • People-Watching and Power Scenes 208
   • Pre-Theater and Prix Fixe Menus 209
   • Pubs/Bars/Sports. 210
   • Quiet Conversation 211
   • Romantic Spots. 211
   • Saturday/Sunday – Best Bets. 212
   • Senior Appeal 214
   • Singles Scenes 214
   • Sleepers and Teflons 215
   • Smoking Prohibited 216
   • Teas 217
   • Teenagers and Other Youthful Spirits 217
   • Visitors on Expense Accounts 218
   • Winning Wine Lists. 219
   • Young Children 219
Wine Chart. 220

Introduction

Here are the results of our *1995 New York City Restaurant Survey* covering more than 1,500 restaurants in what we believe is the best and most varied restaurant scene in the world.

By annually surveying large numbers of regular restaurant-goers, we think we have achieved a uniquely current and reliable guide. We hope you agree. Nearly 11,500 people participated in this *Survey*, eating some 1.9 million restaurant meals, an average of over 1,000 meals per restaurant surveyed. Since the participants dined out an average of 3.12 times per week, this *Survey* is based on over 5,000 meals per day (10 times what a single critic eating two meals a day, five days a week could cover in a year.)

We want to thank each of our participants. They are a widely diverse group in all respects but one – they are food lovers all. This book is really "theirs."

Of the surveyors, 52.7% are women, 47.3% are men; the breakdown by age is 18% in their 20s, 28% in their 30s, 23% in their 40s, 19% in their 50s and 12% in their 60s or above.

To help guide our readers to NYC's best meals and best buys, we have prepared a number of lists. See, for example, New Yorkers' Favorites (page 8), Top Ratings (pages 10–14), Best Buys (pages 15–18) and Prix Fixe Menus (pages 19–20). We are also including for the first time a Traffic Report (page 9) listing the restaurants most frequently visited by our surveyors in the past year. On the assumption that most people want a "quick fix" on the places at which they are considering eating, we have tried to be concise and to provide handy indexes.

We invite you to be a reviewer in our next *Survey.* To do so, simply send a stamped, self-addressed, business-size envelope to ZAGAT SURVEY, 4 Columbus Circle, New York, NY 10019, so that we will be able to contact you. Each participant will receive a free copy of our *1996 NYC Restaurant Survey* when it is published.

Your comments, suggestions and even criticisms of this *Survey* are also solicited. There is always room for improvement – with your help!

New York, New York   Nina and Tim Zagat
November 14, 1994

Foreword

This has been a year of dramatic change in the New York restaurant industry. Last month, Andre Soltner sold his Lutèce to the Ark Restaurant Group. Earlier, the food world was shaken by the untimely death of Gilbert LeCoze, owner of Le Bernardin. Those events were widely reported as marking the end of an era – but that era had already ended, as reflected in this *Survey* over the past several years. Lutèce, which had been No. 1 in overall popularity from 1983 to 1989, ranks 8th this year. Le Bernardin, the survey's 3rd most popular restaurant in 1990, is 11th this year.

Neither Lutèce nor Le Bernardin experienced a major decline in food ratings; rather, they were eclipsed by such culinary modernists as Bouley, Aureole, Union Square Cafe and Gotham Bar & Grill, all helmed by dynamic, young American chefs. Thus, the recent changes at Lutèce and Le Bernardin simply serve as a coda for the fundamental transition that had already taken place at the top of the industry.

Other forces reshaping the dining landscape:

- An explosion of restaurant openings, which outpaced closings by a survey record of 196 to 69. Major newcomers such as Gramercy Tavern and Nobu reflect the continuing Americanization and ethnic diversification of local dining.

- The *Survey's* average cost of dinner with one drink dropped below $30 for the first time since the early '80s. This year's average cost, $29.38, is down 2.7% from last year and 12.9% from three years ago.

- There was continued strong growth among casual, low-cost places designed to meet the needs of the typical '90s household, a phenomenon we call "BATH", i.e. "better alternative to home." Of the 196 newcomers, the majority are BATH Spots.

Overall restaurants have never offered greater efficiency, quality or value. Thus, as we approach the 50th anniversary of the United Nations in October 1995, we can truly call New York City both the political and culinary capital of the world.

New York, New York   Nina and Tim Zagat
November 14, 1994

Key to Ratings/Symbols

This sample entry identifies the various types of information contained in your Zagat Survey.

(1) Restaurant Name, Address & Phone Number

    (2) Hours & Credit Cards

        (3) ZAGAT Ratings

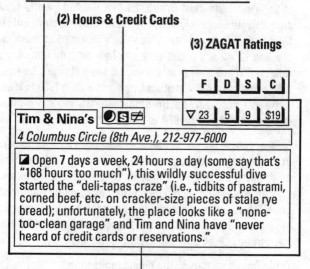

	F	D	S	C
Tim & Nina's ◑ S ⊄	▽ 23	5	9	$19

4 Columbus Circle (8th Ave.), 212-977-6000

◪ Open 7 days a week, 24 hours a day (some say that's "168 hours too much"), this wildly successful dive started the "deli-tapas craze" (i.e., tidbits of pastrami, corned beef, etc. on cracker-size pieces of stale rye bread); unfortunately, the place looks like a "none-too-clean garage" and Tim and Nina have "never heard of credit cards or reservations."

(4) Surveyors' Commentary

The names of restaurants with the highest overall ratings and greatest popularity are printed in **CAPITAL LETTERS**. Addresses and phone numbers are printed in *italics*.

(2) Hours & Credit Cards

After each restaurant name you will find the following courtesy information:

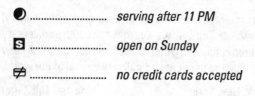

◑ .... *serving after 11 PM*

S .... *open on Sunday*

⊄ .... *no credit cards accepted*

(3) ZAGAT Ratings

Food, **Decor** and **Service** are each rated on a scale of **0** to **30**:

F	D	S	C

F .... Food
D .... Decor
S .... Service
C .... Cost

23	5	9	$19

0 - 9	*poor to fair*
10 - 19	*good to very good*
20 - 25	*very good to excellent*
26 - 30	*extraordinary to perfection*

▽ 23	5	9	$19

▽ .... *Low number of votes/less reliable*

The **Cost (C)** column, reflects the estimated price of a dinner with one drink and tip. Lunch usually costs 25% less.

A restaurant listed without ratings is either an important **newcomer** or a popular **write-in**. The estimated cost, with one drink and tip, is indicated by the following symbols.

–	–	–	VE

I	....	*below $15*
M	....	*$16 to $30*
E	....	*$31 to $50*
VE	....	*$51 or more*

Occasionally, a restaurant's numerical ratings and comments are based on our *1994 Survey,* as indicated by a **(94)** following the restaurant's name.

(4) Surveyors' Commentary

Surveyors' comments are summarized, with literal comments shown in quotation marks. The following symbols indicate whether responses were mixed or uniform.

◨ .... *mixed*
◼ .... *uniform*

7

New Yorkers' Favorite Restaurants

Each of our reviewers has been asked to name his or her five overall favorite restaurants. The 50 spots most frequently named, in order of their popularity, are:

1. Bouley	26. Aquavit
2. Aureole	27. Rainbow Room
3. Union Square Cafe	28. Jo Jo
4. Gotham Bar/Grill	29. Montrachet
5. Four Seasons	30. Capsouto Frères
6. Cafe des Artistes	31. Les Celebrités
7. Chanterelle	32. Sparks
8. Lutèce	33. La Reserve
9. Peter Luger	34. Trattoria dell'Arte
10. La Cote Basque	35. La Caravelle
11. Le Bernardin	36. Palm
12. Le Cirque	37. Vong
13. Lespinasse	38. Smith & Wollensky
14. La Grenouille	39. Alison
15. One If By Land	40. March
16. Mesa Grill	41. Docks Oyster Bar
17. Sign of the Dove	42. Periyali
18. River Cafe	43. Le Chantilly
19. Daniel	44. Felidia
20. Il Mulino	45. An American Place
21. Manhattan Ocean	46. Le Madri
22. Carmine's	47. Da Umberto
23. Hudson River Club	48. Le Perigord
24. Park Ave. Cafe	49. Terrace
25. Arcadia	50. Arizona 206

It's obvious that most of the above restaurants are expensive, but New Yorkers also love a bargain. Fortunately, our city has an abundance of wonderful ethnic restaurants and other inexpensive spots that fill the bill. Thus, we have listed over 200 "Best Buys" on pages 15–18, and identified Prix Fixe and Pre-Theater Bargains at some of the city's major restaurants on pages 19–20.

Traffic Report

The Traffic Report indicates the number of our surveyors who visited each restaurant in the last year one or more times. The 50 spots most often visited are:

3,459	Cafe des Artistes	1,835	La Cote Basque
3,430	Union Square Cafe	1,783	Russian Tea Room
3,328	Bouley	1,771	Bice
3,242	Carmine's	1,739	Le Cirque
3,163	Gotham Bar/Grill	1,703	Dallas BBQ
2,926	Carnegie Deli	1,697	Manhattan Ocean
2,723	Four Seasons	1,687	Palm
2,669	Sfuzzi	1,666	Lutèce
2,639	Docks Oyster Bar	1,639	Benny's Burritos
2,594	Arizona 206	1,629	Ollie's
2,465	Tavern on Green	1,629	China Grill
2,441	Aureole	1,622	Houlihan's
2,285	John's Pizzeria	1,614	Le Bernardin
2,277	Sarabeth's	1,607	Second Ave. Deli
2,258	Smith & Wollensky	1,591	American Festival
2,196	EJ's Luncheonette	1,585	Hudson River Club
2,165	Peter Luger	1,578	Vong
2,146	Cafe Un Deux Trois	1,578	Cafe Luxembourg
2,024	Jackson Hole	1,569	TriBeCa Grill
1,986	Sign of the Dove	1,563	Rainbow Room
1,933	Aquavit	1,504	Chanterelle
1,915	America	1,499	T.G.I. Friday's
1,914	Mesa Grill	1,485	Park Ave. Cafe
1,894	Trattoria dell'Arte	1,468	Oyster Bar
1,878	Brasserie	1,448	River Cafe

The above numbers represent simple volume: i.e. the number of our reviewers who have gone to these places. Since the average person visited each restaurant 6.7 times, the number of meals eaten in the above listed restaurants is enormous. For example, if the 6.7 visits figure holds true for Cafe des Artistes, then our surveyors dined there 23,175 times in the past year – that's 63 people a day.

It's obvious that these restaurants are not high traffic spots solely for their food; many of them have either been bashed by the professional food press or simply ignored; however, the above numbers reflect that other features such as ambiance, convenience and value usually determine where New Yorkers eat.

Top Ratings*

Top 50 Food Ranking

29 Bouley	Le Chantilly
28 Aureole	Oceana
Lespinasse	Sparks
La Grenouille	River Cafe
27 Peter Luger	Terrace
Chanterelle	**25** Felidia
Union Square Cafe	Patsy's Pizza/Bklyn
Le Cirque	Sonia Rose
Lutèce	Cucina
La Cote Basque	Il Nido
Le Bernardin	Periyali
Les Celebrités	Da Umberto
March	Hasaki
Four Seasons	Park Ave. Cafe
Daniel	Seryna
Gotham Bar/Grill	Mesa Grill
Sushisay	Primavera
Il Mulino	Mark's
La Caravelle	Parioli Romanis.
26 Le Perigord	San Domenico
Montrachet	Hudson River Club
Manhattan Ocean	Alison
Arcadia	Rao's
Le Regence	Raphael
La Reserve	Il Giglio

Top Spots by Cuisine

Top American
- **28** Aureole
- **27** Union Square Cafe
  March
  Gotham Bar/Grill
- **26** Arcadia
  River Cafe

Top American Regional
- **25** Mesa Grill/SW
  Hudson River Club/NY
- **24** An American Pl./NE
- **23** Tropica/FL
- **22** Pearson's/BBQ
- **21** Miracle Grill/SW

Top Breakfast
- **25** Mark's
- **24** Carlyle Dining Rm.
- **23** Cafe Pierre
  Cafe Botanica
- **22** 57, 57
- **21** Regency

Top Brunch
- **26** Le Regence
  River Cafe
- **25** Park Ave. Cafe
  Hudson River Club
- **24** Cafe des Artistes
  Sign of the Dove

---

* Excluding restaurants with low voting.

Top Cafes
27 Union Square Cafe
Gotham Bar/Grill
26 River Cafe
25 Park Ave. Cafe
24 Cafe des Artistes
Sign of the Dove

Top Chinese
24 Shun Lee Palace
Canton
Chin Chin
23 Chiam
22 Szechuan Kitchen
Wong Kee

Top Continental
27 Four Seasons
25 Mark's
One If By Land
Petrossian
24 Box Tree
Restaurant 222

Top Delis
21 Second Ave. Deli
20 Carnegie Deli
18 Pastrami King
17 Stage Deli
16 Katz's Deli
15 Wolf's Deli

Top French
29 Bouley
28 Lespinasse
La Grenouille
27 Chanterelle
Le Cirque
Lutèce

Top French Bistros
26 Montrachet
25 Alison
Raphael
24 Jo Jo
La Bouillabaisse
23 Chez Michallet

Top "Gen X"
22 Blue Ribbon
21 Pó
Kin Khao
Pisces
20 Park Avalon
18 Benny's Burritos

Top Greek/Mideast
25 Periyali
24 Elias Corner
21 Karyatis
Turkish Kitchen
Gus' Place
20 Pamir

Top Hotel Dining
28 Lespinasse/St. Regis
27 Le Cirque/Mayfair
Les Celebrités/Essex
Daniel/Surrey
26 Le Regence/Plaza Ath.
25 Mark's/Mark

Top Indian
24 Dawat
22 Jackson Hts. Diner
Jewel of India
21 Darbar
Haveli
20 Mitali East/West

Top Italian Overall
27 Il Mulino/Aquila
25 Felidia/Trieste
Cucina /Florence
Il Nido/Lucca
Da Umberto/Florence
Primavera/Arezzo

Top Italian Regional
25 Parioli Romanis./Rome
San Domenico/Bologna
Rao's/Naples
Il Giglio/Rome
24 Il Tinello/Trieste
Pic. Venezia/Venice

Top Japanese
27 Sushisay
25 Hasaki
Seryna
Hatsuhana
Iso
27 Sushi Zen

Top Mexican/Tex-Mex
23 Zarela
22 Mi Cocina
Rosa Mexicano
19 Orig. Cal. Taqueria
Fresco Tortilla
18 Benny's Burritos

11

Top Newcomers/Rated
24 La Bouillabaisse
Morton's Chicago
23 Patría
Matthew's
Christer's
Bolo

Top Newcomers/Unrated
Cafe Centro
Campagna
C.T.
Gramercy Tavern
Monkey Bar
Nobu

Top Old New York
27 Peter Luger/1897
25 Rao's/1891
Palm/1925
24 Cafe des Artistes/1914
23 Oyster Bar/1913
21 Rainbow Room/1934

Top Outta Boros
27 Peter Luger (Bklyn)
26 River Cafe (Bklyn)
25 Cucina (Bklyn)
24 Pic. Venezia (Qns)
Elias Corner (Qns)
La Bouillabaisse (Bklyn)

Top People-Watching
28 La Grenouille
27 Le Cirque
Four Seasons (lunch)
22 Le Colonial
21 Regency (breakfast)
44 (lunch)

Top Pizza
25 Patsy's Pizza/Bklyn
23 Patsy's Pizza/NY
22 Mario's
Mad. 61
John's Pizzeria
20 Vinnie's Pizza

Top Private Rooms
28 La Grenouille
27 Le Cirque
Lutèce
La Cote Basque
Le Bernardin
Les Celebrités

Top Pub Dining
25 Rao's
23 Oyster Bar
22 Wollensky's Grill
21 Frank's
Docks Oyster Bar
20 Bridge Cafe

Top Seafood
27 Le Bernardin
26 Manhattan Ocean
Oceana
24 Elias Corner
Wilkinson's
23 SeaGrill

Top Steakhouses
27 Peter Luger
26 Sparks
25 Palm
24 Post House
Smith & Wollensky
Morton's Chicago

Top Tasting Menus
29 Bouley
28 Aureole
27 Chanterelle
Le Cirque
Les Celebrités
March

Top Thai
23 Thailand Rest.
Vong
22 Jai Ya Thai
21 Pongsri Thai
Kin Khao
20 Thai House Cafe

Top Trips to the Country*
29 Xaviar's at Piermont, NY
28 La Panetiere, Rye, NY
27 Jean-Louis, Greenwich, CT
Mirabelle, St. James, LI
Harrald's, Stormville, NY
Saddle River Inn, NJ

Top Wild Cards
25 Sonia Rose/Eclectic
23 Solera/Spanish
Aquavit/Scandinavian
Patría/Latin
Christer's/Scandinavian
22 Le Colonial/Vietnamese

---

*See *Zagat Tri-State Survey* for reviews.

Top 50 Decor Ranking

28 Bouley
   Lespinasse
   Rainbow Room
   Les Celebrités
   La Grenouille
   River Cafe
27 Four Seasons
   Le Regence
   Aureole
   Terrace
   La Cote Basque
   Sign of the Dove
   Le Bernardin
   Cafe des Artistes
   Hudson River Club
   One If By Land
   Carlyle Dining Rm.
   Cafe Botanica
26 Edwardian Room
   Water's Edge
   Palio
   Box Tree
   View
   Tavern on Green
   Mark's

   La Caravelle
   March
   Chanterelle
   La Reserve
   Le Cirque
   Temple Bar
   Water Club
   Cafe Pierre
   Nirvana
25 Le Chantilly
   Palm Court
   Aquavit
   Adrienne
   Tse Yang
   Oak Room
   Lutèce
   Gotham Bar/Grill
   Petrossian
   Daniel
   SeaGrill
   Parioli Romanis.
   Jezebel
   Oceana
24 Halcyon
   Union Square Cafe

Top Gardens

American Festival
Aureole
Barbetta
Barolo
Boathouse Cafe
Casanis
Hulot's
Manhattan Plaza
Miracle Grill

One If By Land
Palm Court
Provence
Remi
River Cafe
SeaGrill
Sumptuary
Tavern on Green
Water Club

Top Romantic

Arcadia
Aureole
Black Sheep
Bouley
Box Tree
Cafe des Artistes
Cafe Nicholson
Chez Josephine
Chez Michallet
La Grenouille
Le Colonial
Les Celebrités

March
Mark's
One If By Land
Rainbow Room
Raphael
River Cafe
Sign of the Dove
Temple Bar
Terrace
Vivolo
Water Club
Water's Edge

Top Rooms

Aureole
Bouley
Cafe Botanica
Cafe des Artistes
Carlyle Dining Rm.
Edwardian Room
Four Seasons
Hudson River Club
La Caravelle
La Cote Basque
La Grenouille
La Reserve
Le Bernardin
Le Chantilly
Le Regence
Les Celebrités
Lespinasse
Lutèce
March
Mark's
Metronome
One If By Land
Palio
Rainbow Room

Top Views

American Festival
Boathouse Cafe
Edward Moran
Harbour Lights
Hudson River Club
Le Pactole
Nirvana
Rainbow Room
River Cafe
SeaGrill
Sequoia
Tavern on Green
Terrace
Top of the Sixes
View
Water Club
Water's Edge
World Yacht

Top 50 Service Ranking

27 Lespinasse
Les Celebrités
Aureole
Bouley
La Grenouille
26 Four Seasons
Chanterelle
Le Regence
La Cote Basque
March
Le Bernardin
Lutèce
La Caravelle
25 Union Square Cafe
Le Perigord
Carlyle Dining Rm.
Terrace
Leopard
La Reserve
24 Mark's
Le Cirque
Le Chantilly
Gotham Bar/Grill
Cafe Pierre
Oceana

Il Tinello
Arcadia
River Cafe
Montrachet
One If By Land
Sonia Rose
Box Tree
Raphael
Manhattan Ocean
Adrienne
23 Rainbow Room
Hudson River Club
Sign of the Dove
Alison
Tempo
Daniel
Erminia
Cafe des Artistes
San Domenico
Montebello
Petrossian
Tse Yang
Park Ave. Cafe
Palio
Cafe Botanica

Best Buys

Top 100 Bangs For The Buck

This list reflects the best dining values in our *Survey*. It is produced by dividing the cost of a meal into the combined ratings for food, decor and service.

1. Seattle Bean Co.	51. Patsy's Pizza/NY
2. Gray's Papaya	52. El Pollo
3. Papaya King	53. Kaffeehaus
4. Ess-a-Bagel	54. Old Town Bar
5. Vinnie's Pizza	55. Marnie's Noodle
6. Veniero's	56. Bar and Books
7. Fresco Tortilla	57. Pink Tea Cup
8. Cafe Lalo	58. Fez
9. Barnes & Noble	59. Manganaro's
10. Orig. Cal. Taqueria	60. Jackson Hts. Diner
11. Taq. de Mexico	61. Veselka
12. City Bakery	62. Nha Trang
13. Prime Burger	63. Passage to India
14. Amir's Falafel	64. Tea Box
15. Rose of India	65. Wong Kee
16. Moustache	66. Moonrock Diner
17. Patsy's Pizza/Bklyn	67. Book-Friends Cafe
18. Freddie & Pepper's	68. Bo Ky
19. Caffe Reggio	69. T Salon
20. Angelika Film Ctr.	70. Kings Pl. Diner
21. Cupcake Cafe	71. Taco Taco
22. Windows on India	72. Whole Wheat
23. Gandhi	73. Harry's Burritos
24. California Pizza	74. Atomic Wings
25. Stingy Lulu's	75. Eighteenth & 8th
26. Corner Bistro	76. Mr. Souvlaki
27. Life Cafe	77. Viand
28. Chez Brigitte	78. Arturo's Pizzeria
29. John's Pizzeria	79. Haveli
30. Angelica Kitchen	80. Chicken Chef
31. Orologio	81. Westside Cottage
32. McSorley's	82. Dojo `
33. Cafe Con Leche	83. Mee Noodle Shop
34. Benny's Burritos	84. EJ's Luncheonette
35. Totonno Pizzeria	85. Caffe Rafaella
36. Little Poland	86. Lupe's East L.A.
37. Szechuan Hunan	87. Kwanzaa
38. Two Boots	88. Serendipity 3
39. Kelley & Ping	89. Good Enough to Eat
40. Bertha's Burritos	90. Hunan Garden
41. Silk Road Palace	91. Kiev
42. La Taza de Oro	92. Aggie's
43. KK Restaurant	93. Pho Pasteur
44. Anglers & Writers	94. Lum Chin
45. Tacomadre	95. Frutti di Mare
46. Bell Caffe	96. Pandit
47. O'Casey's	97. Cucina del Fontana
48. Barking Dog	98. Ear Inn
49. Szechuan Kitchen	99. Thailand Rest.
50. Big Wong	100. La Bouillabaisse

BANG FOR BUCK – RANKED BY CUISINE

American
Stingy Lulu's
Anglers & Writers
O'Casey's
Book-Friends Cafe

Bar-B-Q
Zacki's BBQ
Pearson's BBQ
Virgil's BBQ
Brothers Bar-B-Q

Breakfast
City Bakery
Caffe Reggio
Cupcake Cafe
Viand

Brunch
Barking Dog
EJ's Luncheonette
Aggie's
Popover Cafe

Burgers & Dogs
Gray's Papaya
Papaya King
Prime Burger
Corner Bistro

Burritos
Benny's Burritos
Bertha's Burritos
Harry's Burritos
Calif. Burrito Co.

Cafes
Angelika Film Ctr.
Life Cafe
Bell Caffe
Cafe S.F.A.

Cajun/Creole
Two Boots
Baby Jake's
Great Jones Cafe
Levee

Caribbean/So. American
Caribe
Boca Chica
Vernon's Jerk
Island Spice

Cent./Eastern Europe
Veselka
Little Poland
KK Restaurant
Kiev

Chicken
El Pollo
Atomic Wings
Chicken Chef
Pudgie's

Chinese
Szechuan Hunan
Kelley & Ping
Silk Road Palace
Szechuan Kitchen

Coffeehouses
Seattle Bean Co.
Veniero's
Cafe Lalo
Barnes & Noble

Delis
Ess-a-Bagel
Bloom's Deli
Second Ave. Deli
Katz's Deli

Diners/Coffee Shops
Cupcake Cafe
Moonrock Diner
King's Pl. Diner
Eighteenth & 8th

Family Dining
Szechuan Hunan
Arturo's Pizzeria
Ollie's
Carmine's

French
Chez Brigitte
La Bouillabaisse
La Chandelle
Cafe St. John

Greek
Mr. Souvlaki
Papa Bear
Telly's Taverna
Karyatis

Health Food
City Bakery
Angelica Kitchen
Whole Wheat
Souen

Hotels
Sarabeth's/Wales
Edison Cafe/Edison
J. Sung Dynasty/Lexington
Bistro 790/Sheraton NY

Indian
Rose of India
Windows on India
Gandhi
Jackson Hts. Diner

Italian
Orologio
Brunetta's
Ci Vedeamo
Mappamondo

Japanese
Menchanko-tei
Tea Box
Sapporo East
Avenue A

Mexican/Tex-Mex
Fresco Tortilla
Orig. Cal. Taqueria
Taq. de Mexico
Benny's

Middle Eastern
Amir's Falafel
Moustache
Afghan Kebab Hse.
Khyber Pass

Newcomers
Taq. de Mexico
Angelika Film Ctr.
Kaffeehaus
Kwanzaa

Noodle Shops
Marnie's Noodle
Mee Noodle Shop
Menchanko-tei
Honmura An

Pastarias
Frutti di Mare
Cucina del Fontana
Cucina Stagionale
Ecco-La

Pizza
Vinnie's Pizza
Patsy's Pizza/Bklyn
Freddie & Pepper's
California Pizza

Pubs
Bar and Books
Manhattan Brewing
Telephone Bar
Gramercy Watering

Sandwiches
Manganaro's
Shopsin's
Bloom's Deli
Merchants N.Y.

Seafood
La Bouillabaisse
Cucina di Pesce
Fish
Oriental Pearl

Southern/Soul Food
Pink Tea Cup
Kwanzaa
Ludlow St. Cafe
Sylvia's

Spanish/Cuban
Cafe Con Leche
La Taza de Oro
La Caridad
Cafe Español

Steakhouses
Embers
Moran's
Wollensky's Grill
Rusty Staub's

Teens
Bendix Diner
Planet Hollywood
Hard Rock Cafe
Harley Davidson

Thai
Thailand Rest.
Pongsri Thai
Thai House Cafe
Regional Thai

Vietnamese
Kelley & Ping
Nha Trang
Pho Pasteur
New Viet Huong

100 More Good Values
(A bit more expensive, but worth every penny)

Afghan Kebab Hse.
Andalousia
Avenue A
Baby Jake's
Bella Donna
Bendix Diner
Bloom's Deli
Bright Food Shop
Brothers BBQ
Brunetta's
Bubby's
Burger Heaven
Cafe S.F.A.
Cafe St. John
Caffe Buon Gusto
Calif. Burrito Co.
Carnegie Deli
Casanis
Chat 'n' Chew
Chef Ho's
Ci Vedeamo
Cloister Cafe
Copeland's
Cucina di Pesce
Cucina Stagionale
Danal
Diwan Grill
Dok Suni
Ecco-La
Elephant & Castle
Ellen's Stardust
Empire Diner
Fanelli
Friend of Farmer
Georgia Diner
Goody's
Great Jones Cafe
Hakata
Hard Rock Cafe
Harpo
Hasaki
Hourglass Tavern
Hunan Balcony
Indian Cafe
India Pavilion
Jekyll & Hyde
Jing Fong
John's of 12th
Khyber Pass
La Caridad

Lamarca
Levee
Lipstick Cafe
Mandarin Court
Manhattan Plaza
Mappamondo
Marti Kebab
Menchanko-tei
Merchants N.Y.
Mingala Burmese
Mitali East/West
Mr. Tang's
New Viet Huong
Panchitos
Papa Bear
Pearson's BBQ
Pedro Paramo
Picolo Angolo
Pizzeria Uno
Planet Hollywood
Pongsri Thai
Popover Cafe
Pudgie's
Rancho Mexican
Regional Thai
Rocking Horse
Ruppert's
Sapporo East
Second Ave. Deli
Shanghai Manor
Shopsin's
Souen
Spring St. Natural
Spring St. Rest.
Sukhothai West
Taci Int'l
Takahachi
Temple Bar
Teresa's
Thai House Cafe
Three of Cups
Tibetan Kitchen
Tien Fu
Tortilla Flats
Trattoria Pesce
Urban Grill
Virgil's BBQ
Walker's
Westside Cafe
Zacki's BBQ

Prix Fixe Menus Below $40
At Major Restaurants†

• Lunch •

Adrienne	$30.00	L'Ecole	$15.99
Akbar	13.95	Leopard, The	36.00
Ambassador Grill	19.95	Le Perigord	32.00
Aquavit	29.00	Le Pistou	19.95
Arqua	19.95	L'Ermitage	15.95
Aureole	32.00	Les Pyrenees	19.00
Becco	16.00	Levana	19.95
Bouley	35.00	Lutèce	38.00
Cafe Beulah	18.95	Mark's	19.95
Cafe Botanica	22.00	Montrachet	19.95
Cafe des Artistes	19.50	Oceana	28.00
Cafe Luxembourg	19.95	Odeon, The	14.50
Cafe Pierre	26.00	Opus II	29.95
Capsouto Frères	19.95	Palio	39.00
Carlyle Dining Room	29.50	Palm	19.95
Chanterelle	33.00	Peacock Alley	27.50
Chin Chin	19.95	Petrossian	29.00
Christ Cella	29.95	Picholine	18.00
Daniel	31.00	Quatorze Bis	11.95
Darbar	19.95	Russian Tea Room	25.00
Da Silvano	20.00	San Domenico	27.50
Duane Park Cafe	19.95	Sardi's	25.95
Gage & Tollner	19.95	Sel et Poivre	12.95
Girafe	17.50	Shaan	12.95
Gotham Bar/Grill	19.95	Sign of the Dove	19.95
Gramercy Tavern	28.00	Solera	32.00
Halcyon	19.95	Sonia Rose	21.00
Harry Cipriani	19.95	Tavern on Green	19.95
Hudson River Club	24.95	Terrace	25.00
Jean Lafitte	19.95	Toscana	19.95
JoJo	25.00	TriBeCa Grill	19.95
J. Sung Dynasty	20.00	Trois Jean	19.95
La Caravelle	35.00	Truffles	19.95
La Cote Basque	31.00	Tse Yang	23.75
La Mediterranée	21.00	21 Club	19.95
La Reserve	31.00	Vong	25.00
La Tour D'Or	19.95	Water Club	19.95
Le Chantilly	26.00	World Yacht	27.50
Le Cirque	33.75		

---

†This list shows the lowest prix fixe menu available; there may be higher-priced options. Since prix fixe prices may change or be canceled at any time, check on them when reserving. Virtually every Indian serves an AYCE (all-you-can-eat) buffet lunch for $15 or less.

• Dinner •

Adrienne*	$32.00	Le Beaujolais	$21.00
Algonquin Hotel, The*	25.00	Le Chantilly*	28.00
Ambassador Grill	24.95	L'Ecole	17.89
American Festival	22.95	Le Colonial*	24.00
Anche Vivolo**	18/13	Le Comptoir*	24.00
Aquavit*	39.00	L'Ermitage	29.00
Arcadia*	29.95	Les Pyrenees	26.00
Aria*	19.95	Levana	19.95
Arqua	19.95	March	39.00
Assembly*	24.75	Metronome*	29.00
Barbetta*	39.00	Michael's*	29.50
Brasserie	24.00	Mi Cocina*	15.00
Cafe Botanica**	26/29	Montebello*	26.75
Cafe Crocodile*	18.50	Montrachet	28.00
Cafe des Artistes	32.50	Oak Room and Bar*	39.00
Cafe Luxembourg	28.50	Opus II	29.95
Cafe Pierre*	34.00	Palio*	35.00
Caffe Bondí	35.00	Pen & Pencil	27.95
Charlotte*	32.50	Petrossian	35.00
Chez Michallet*	19.95	Pó	25.00
Christer's*	34.00	Rainbow Room*	38.50
Cinquanta	23.95	Raphael*	29.00
Cité*	34.50	Regency*	28.50
Cité Grill	31.50	Restaurant 222*	29.50
Darbar*	26.95	Russian Tea Room*	39.75
Edwardian Room*	38.00	San Domenico*	29.50
Ferrier*	19.95	San Martin's	19.95
44*	36.00	Sardi's*	35.95
Four Seasons Grill	26.50	Sfuzzi	29.95
Gage & Tollner	22.95	Shaan*	19.95
Gascogne*	25.00	Shanghai 1933	38.00
Grifone	35.00	Sign of the Dove*	30.00
Halcyon**	30/35	Snaps	19.95
Hudson River Club*	29.95	Sonia Rose	33.00
Il Menestrello	32.50	Symphony Cafe*	30.00
Indochine*	19.50	Table d'Hôte*	19.95
Jean Lafitte	25.50	Tatou*	22.50
J. Sung Dynasty	30.00	Tavern on Green*	24.95
JUdson Grill*	29.95	Terrace	36.00
La Boite En Bois**	28/30	Thomas Scott's*	21.95
L'Acajou*	26.00	Toscana	22.00
La Caravelle*	38.50	Trois Jean**	24/35
La Mediterranée	24.00	Truffles	35.00
La Scala	25.00	21 Club*	29.00
La Tour D'Or	26.95	View	39.95
Le Bar Bat*	19.95	Zinno	16.95

*Pre-theater only.
**Prices divided by a slash are for pre-theater and normal hours.

Alphabetical Directory of Restaurants

F **D** **S** **C**

Abby
`14` `11` `13` `$24`
254 Fifth Ave. (bet. 28th & 29th Sts.), 212-725-2922
🔲 A "lively young" "Downtown" coterie applauds this American's "great burgers" and calls lunch "a nice change from coffeehouse fare" in an "area that's desperate for a decent meal", but others are put off by "poor management" and "spacey" service.

Acadia Parish (Brooklyn) 🆂
`17` `8` `14` `$21`
148 Atlantic Ave. (bet. Clinton & Henry Sts.), 718-624-5154
🔲 "It's not New Orleans" but this "family-run", Zydeco-playing, jambalaya joint "ain't bad for Cajun-starved Brooklyn"; just BYOB and don't expect much "Southern hospitality."

Acappella
`–` `–` `–` `E`
1 Hudson St. (Chambers St.), 212-240-0163
In the attractive space that once housed One Hudson Cafe, this Italian newcomer has set up shop with a surprisingly old-fashioned and pricey menu; although it's too new to call, it seems too old to believe.

Acme Bar & Grill ◗🆂
`–` `–` `–` `I`
9 Great Jones St. (bet. B'way & Lafayette), 212-420-1934
Tabasco and beer are the complementary themes of this "garagelike" NoHo Dixie dive that specializes in white-trash cooking for the young.

Adoré, The 🖂
`–` `–` `–` `M`
17 E. 13th St. (bet. 5th Ave. & University Pl.), 212-243-8742
Only a few know about this "charming" "second-story" Village newcomer, but those few adore it for "romantic" and "reasonably priced", casual Eclectic "dining in the treetops."

Adrienne 🆂
`23` `25` `24` `$49`
The Peninsula Hotel, 700 Fifth Ave. (55th St.), 212-903-3918
⬛ In a "posh" and "gracious" Midtown hotel dining room that's "always emptier than it deserves to be", one can enjoy "beautiful and beautifully served" New American food with a "healthy" slant; N.B. pre-theater dinner and prix-fixe lunch are both bargains.

Afghan Kebab House
`17` `6` `13` `$16`
764 Ninth Ave. (bet. 51st & 52nd Sts.), 212-307-1612 🖂
1345 Second Ave. (bet. 70th & 71st Sts.), 212-517-2776
155 W. 46th St. (bet. 6th & 7th Aves.), 212-768-3875
🔲 "It even smells like Afghanistan" at these "marvelous" "third-world" "dives" where the easily affordable grilled kebabs are "savory" and "spicy" and the beer is whatever you bring; service ranges from "friendly" to "just back from the jihad."

Aggie's 🆂 🖂
`17` `8` `11` `$15`
146 W. Houston St. (MacDougal St.), 212-673-8994
⬛ "There's always a line" at this "hip" and "funky diner" where the "resident" cats roam the room and "service depends on Aggie's mood"; enthusiasts exclaim over the "wonderful", wallet-friendly "comfort food", while sour palates shrug it off as a "greasy spoon."

Ahnell ◗🆂
`18` `19` `17` `$35`
177 Prince St. (bet. Thompson & Sullivan Sts.), 212-254-1260
⬛ "It's fun to watch the mannequins munch" at this "throbbing" SoHo magnet for "models" and assorted "Downtown beautiful people"; most find the Italian fare "consistently good", the service "fine" and the room "woody and warm", but a few say "just another pretty face."

Ah Umakatta

– | – | – | I

201 Prince St. (bet. Sullivan & MacDougal Sts.), 212-353-3099
Mostly take-out but this simple SoHo Japanese has a very '90s flavor of efficiency and good value; it's not worth a special trip, though most Japanophiles would love to have it around their corner.

Akbar S

19 | 18 | 18 | $29

475 Park Ave. (bet. 57th & 58th Sts.), 212-838-1717
☑ The faithful call this "upscale" Indian a "cozy", "romantic" "jewel on Park", praising its cuisine as "solid" and "lovingly prepared", but some see signs of slippage, calling it "grey", "uninspired" and "badly in need of renovation"; to decide for yourself, check out the $13.95 prix fixe lunch.

Albuquerque Eats ◐ S (94)

13 | 14 | 13 | $22

375 Third Ave. (27th St.), 212-683-6500
☑ But for the facts that it makes a mean margarita and has good music, this youthful, high-vibe Southwestern food mill would bite the dust.

Al Bustan S

18 | 16 | 17 | $31

827 Third Ave. (bet. 50th & 51st Sts.), 212-759-8439
■ Midtown aficionados of midpriced Middle Eastern food are thrilled to find Lebanese fare "that would please a shepherd" served by a "friendly", "obliging" staff in an "airy", "upscale" room that's bright enough for brain surgery.

Algonquin Hotel, The ◐ S

14 | 20 | 17 | $38

The Algonquin Hotel, 59 W. 44th St. (bet. 5th & 6th Aves.), 212-840-6800
■ This Theater District landmark of the literary Round Table is "held together by nostalgia" – most often, "dining with the deceased" means "airplane food" served by "waiters avoiding eye contact", but the handsome wood-paneled lobby is "perfect for meeting people over tea or for a liquid dinner" followed by "great cabaret."

ALISON ON DOMINICK STREET S

25 | 22 | 23 | $49

38 Dominick St. (bet. Varick & Hudson Sts.), 212-727-1188
■ The consensus is that new chef Daniel Silverman is "holding up well" creating French bistro "food that lives up to the romantic ambiance" at this "classy" West SoHo "hideaway" where "Alison makes you feel like you're her special guest"; a small minority terms the place "precious" and "not what it used to be."

Allegria ◐ S

15 | 16 | 14 | $28

66 W. 55th St. (6th Ave.), 212-956-7755
☑ A "handy" Midtown location with "airy European decor" and "sunny" "sidewalk tables" makes for a busy lunch hour at this bustling trattoria; while some praise the pasta, others call the whole experience "marginal."

Alley's End S

19 | 19 | 17 | $27

311 W. 17th St. (bet. 8th & 9th Aves.), 212-627-8899
■ "Marked only by a neon knife and fork", this comfortable "surprise at the end of a nondescript alley" yields the "hidden treasure" of an "inner garden" where savvy seekers are rewarded with "terrific", "reasonably priced" American bistro food.

Alva ◐ S

– | – | – | E

36 E. 22nd St. (bet. Park Ave. S. & B'way), 212-228-4399
As in Thomas Alva Edison, this electric green-and-black New American bistro has lots of bright ideas: sophisticated food, utilitarian swank decor, a sleek, settle-in bar and a terrific photo collection.

F | D | S | C

Amarcord ◐ [S] 22 | 21 | 20 | $46
7 E. 59th St. (5th Ave.), 212-935-3535
◪ While some call Pino Luongo's latest East Side venture "the most interesting Italian restaurant in years", others are put off by the mural depicting women's legs ("Pino, please!") and by high prices; most, however, say Amarcord is "as much fun as the Fellini film."

Ambassador Grill [S] 21 | 21 | 20 | $39
Hyatt U.N. Park Plaza Hotel, 1 U.N. Plaza (bet. 1st & 2nd Aves.), 212-702-5014
■ Diplomats from the nearby U.N. favor this "cushy", "hi-tech" "Hall of Mirrors", and while cynics view the room as "too touristy", most enjoy the Continental dining, especially the "excellent brunch" and "sumptuous" Friday night seafood buffet, both prix-fixe bargains.

Ambrosia Tavern (Queens) ◐ [S] ▽ 17 | 15 | 14 | $26
192-02 Northern Blvd. (192nd St.), Bayside, 718-357-7463
■ Although its ratings slipped, most surveyors take the "spotty" service in stride and find this "bright", "crowded" Astoria Greek taverna "a pleasant surprise".

America ◐ [S] 13 | 14 | 12 | $23
9 E. 18th St. (bet. 5th Ave. & B'way), 212-505-2110
◪ Come to this "soccer stadium" of a restaurant "with earmuffs and kids"; the "huge menu" offers "something mediocre for everyone" with service that's "friendly" but "slow"; whether you find this "yuppie circus" "fun" or "hell" is your call.

American Festival Cafe [S] 15 | 20 | 15 | $31
20 W. 50th St. (Rockefeller Skating Rink), 212-246-6699
◪ Even if this handsome Rockefeller Center rinkside American cafe is a "tourist trap" with variable service and an "upscale TGIF menu", it's still "so very NY" to "watch the skaters on a winter's evening" or enjoy "the quintessential alfresco" lunch in summer; but why Restaurant Associates doesn't upgrade the food is hard to fathom.

American Renaissance – | – | – | E
American Thread Bldg., 260 W. Broadway, 212-343-0049
This new TriBeCa restaurant and cafe in the historic American Thread Building has been handsomely redecorated for a first-class chef, Eric Blauberg (ex Colors); given the amount of talent and money that has gone into this place, it should be a good bet; P.S. we've been assured the TVs in the men's room are not two-way and the mirror in the ladies' room is not see-through.

Amici Miei ◐ [S] 14 | 15 | 13 | $28
475 W. Broadway (Houston St.), 212-533-1933
◪ Lots of "Euro-types" and "beautiful people" chow down on "passable Italian food" at this "so-hip-it-hurts" SoHo watering hole; some say the "snooty staff" favor those who "wear black clothes."

Amir's Falafel [S] 🚫💳 15 | 4 | 11 | $9
2911-A Broadway (bet. 113th & 114th Sts.), 212-749-7500
A&S Plaza, 901 Sixth Ave. (bet. 32nd & 33rd Sts.), 212-594-2667
■ Both branches of this popular falafateria qualify as "cheap", "quick", "healthy" places to "eat not dine" on "tasty", "reliable" Middle Eastern fare; ergo, they're popular with the young.

Amsterdam's ◐ [S] 14 | 10 | 13 | $23
428 Amsterdam Ave. (bet. 80th & 81st Sts.), 212-874-1377
■ This "West Side classic" remains a "comfortable", "noisy", "kid-friendly" "standby" for "yummy spit-roasted chicken" and "great french fries" at modest prices; every neighborhood needs one.

AN AMERICAN PLACE 24 | 21 | 21 | $44

2 Park Ave. (32nd St.), 212-684-2122

■ Larry Forgione's "civilized", "handsomely appointed" Midtown cafe continues to draw kudos for "generous portions" of "wonderful" "dishes from Maine to New Mexico" as well as for servers who "treat you right"; Forgione makes many feel "proud to be American."

Anarchy Cafe ◐ [S] ▽ 14 | 20 | 13 | $24

27 Third Ave. (bet. St. Marks Pl. & 9th St.), 212-475-1270

◪ "Generation Xers with nose-rings" frequent this noisy, "hippie-ish" East Village Eclectic where "the only chaos is the decor" – which is "plush" and vaguely "modern" "Turkish"; most find the fare "decent" but "not revolutionary" with brick-oven pizza a good bet.

Anche Vivolo ◐ 19 | 17 | 18 | $33

222 E. 58th St. (bet. 2nd & 3rd Aves.), 212-308-0112

■ Well-priced early-bird and "late-bird" dinners make this "tastefully decorated" East Side "modern Northern Italian" a "consistent" choice for "very good food" with "no surprises", which sits well with the generally "well-heeled", "older crowd."

Andalousia ◐ [S] ▽ 19 | 12 | 16 | $22

28 Cornelia St. (bet. Bleecker & W. 4th Sts.), 212-929-3693

■ Ignore this Villager's "dark", "slap-dash" "Arab bazaar decor" and tuck into "authentic" Moroccan couscous, tajine, salad and mint tea; the staff is "smiling and friendly", the fare easily fared.

Angelica Kitchen [S] ⇏ 18 | 12 | 14 | $17

300 E. 12th St. (bet. 1st & 2nd Aves.), 212-228-2909

■ "You'll need your Birkenstocks to stand on line" at this East Village oasis for "imaginative", "haute healthy" "Vegetarian food that could convert carnivores"; service is "friendly" and everything is strictly "PC."

Angelika Film Center Cafe [S] ⇏ 13 | 11 | 10 | $11

18 W. Houston St. (Mercer St.), 212-995-1081

◪ Sort of like "Dean & DeLuca go to the movies", this "convenient", "artsy" movie-house cafe has pre-film munchies, focaccia sandwiches, cappuccino and desserts – as ratings show, not all is angelic.

Angelo's of Mulberry St. [S] 18 | 11 | 15 | $30

146 Mulberry St. (bet. Hester & Grand Sts.), 212-966-1277

◪ Is this "living legend" of "pasta", "red sauce" and "garlic" the best in Little Italy, or is it just a "loud, tacky", "past-its-prime" joint for "tourist Italian" food? – our surveyors are split, so you must decide.

Angel's ◐ [S] 17 | 11 | 13 | $20

1135 First Ave. (bet. 62nd & 63rd Sts.), 212-980-3131

■ "A bit of heaven on First Avenue" where folks elbow in for monstrous portions of "awesome pasta" and "bread to live and die for" at pittance prices; come early and wear white cotton earplugs.

Anglers & Writers [S] ⇏ 17 | 22 | 17 | $22

420 Hudson St. (St. Luke's Pl.), 212-675-0810

■ In a "quaint", "flower-filled", "sun-drenched" West Villager, discover "English comfort food with a Wisconsin twist" – chicken pot pie, tea and home-baked desserts; it's a "great place to catch up with friends" or just "relax with a book on how to relax."

Annabelle ◐ [S] – | – | – | E

890 Second Ave. (48th St.), 212-486-2560

Attractive new East Midtown Asian-accented Contemporary French with a well-regarded chef from Lespinasse and a charming Manet mural dominating its decor; it's too new to call, but appears promising.

Annie Beneau [S] ▽ 15 | 16 | 14 | $25
1490 Second Ave. (bet. 77th & 78th Sts.), 212-988-5300
■ Upper Eastsiders find this "welcome newcomer" nothing more – or less – than an "easy", "casual" spot for "hearty American bistro" fare; "reasonable prices" make it all the more "comforting."

Antico Caffee ◐ [S] ⇏ 16 | 12 | 11 | $19
1477 Second Ave. (77th St.), 212-879-4824
■ "Cheap", "tasty" pasta draws the young and the restless to this "hip" "goldfish bowl" on "the 2nd Avenue strip" where alfresco "people-watching" can fill a summer's evening, if not a stomach.

Aperitivo 19 | 15 | 19 | $39
29 W. 56th St. (bet. 5th & 6th Aves.), 212-765-5155
◪ Fans of this "old-world Italian" standby rave about the "big veal chops" served by "attentive waiters", but although it might be "mom's favorite" and "dad's home away from home", younger restaurant-goers see the place as "old hat."

Appetito ▽ 18 | 15 | 17 | $31
47 W. 39th St. (bet. 5th & 6th Aves.), 212-391-5286
■ "For the Garment District, it's good" say business-lunchers who like the "small" Italian menu, don't mind the "crowded" room and laud the "efficient", "professional" service; it closes by 9 PM.

Apple Restaurant [S] 13 | 11 | 12 | $18
17 Waverly Pl. (bet. Greene & Mercer Sts.), 212-473-8888
◪ With "high ceilings and low prices" this Village "natural food" place offers "something for both vegetarians and carnivores" (plus a "karaoke room in back"); critics say waiters and food are "sleepy."

AQUAVIT 23 | 25 | 22 | $50
13 W. 54th St. (bet. 5th & 6th Aves.), 212-307-7311
◪ This "sophisticated Scandinavian still works" says a charmed majority, citing the "dazzling", "coolly elegant" architecture, the "calming waterfall", "wonderful" Nordic cuisine ("fish from heaven") and "professional service"; a disenchanted minority calls it "cold", "overrated" and "losing its edge"; N.B. the upstairs cafe is "less formal and less expensive" and prix-fixe deals are a bargain.

ARCADIA 26 | 24 | 24 | $55
21 E. 62nd St. (bet. 5th & Madison Aves.), 212-223-2900
■ In "charming" "townhouse" digs of "cramped elegance", highlighted by a wraparound landscape mural, star chef Anne Rosenzweig continues to serve "innovative" and "delicious" New American food, and despite a few gripes about "snotty" service, NYers still find it all "delectably" "romantic."

Arcimboldo ◐ [S] 16 | 19 | 17 | $31
220 E. 46th St. (bet. 2nd & 3rd Aves.), 212-972-4646
◪ "Mama mia!", another "Italian newcomer" – this one's a decorator's dream in peach and, if some say "the food's not as creative as the trompe l'oeil walls", things seem to be "improving."

Area Code Cafe ◐ [S] – | – | – | I
510 Sixth Ave. (13th St.), 212-924-3799
A new American cafe with a gimmick: there's a phone on each table and you can call anyplace in the US for 25¢ – if your food bill reaches $5.

Argentine Pavilion ◐ [S] 16 | 12 | 15 | $29
32 W. 46th St. (bet. 5th & 6th Aves.), 212-921-0835
■ Order a "good juicy steak" and "feel like a gaucho around the charcoal fire" at this elemental Midtown eatery that's "not quite a trip to Buenos Aires", but a "pleasant" experience and a "great value."

Aria [S] — 20 | 18 | 20 | $37

253 E. 52nd St. (2nd Ave.), 212-888-1410

■ Our surveyors agree that this East Side Italian is a "comfortable", "quiet", "friendly" and "consistently good" spot that's a standout "in an area that's overrun with pseudo Italians."

ARIZONA 206 AND CAFE ◐ [S] — 21 | 18 | 17 | $33

206 E. 60th St. (bet. 2nd & 3rd Aves.), 212-838-0440

■ "Always crowded", "always delicious", "always fun", this SW "pioneer" wins hearts with its "eclectic", "upbeat" fare, but isn't without complaints regarding "uncomfortable chairs", "noise" and "poor service"; the less serious adjoining cafe is a "better buy."

Arlecchino ◐ [S] **(94)** — 19 | 16 | 19 | $28

192 Bleecker St. (bet. 6th Ave. & MacDougal St.), 212-475-2355

■ Sitting by the window at this jaunty Mid-Village trattoria is like eating in the middle of a circus; happily, there are no clowns in the kitchen, but there may be on the street.

Armadillo Club ◐ [S] — ▽ 13 | 12 | 13 | $21

2420 Broadway (W. 89th St.), 212-496-1066

◪ At this "neighborhood sleeper" for "good, greasy Mexican junk food", the chef "might not always be consistent" but the scene is usually "fun"; some people would rather eat armadillo than eat here.

Arqua [S] — 23 | 19 | 20 | $41

281 Church St. (White St.), 212-334-1888

■ Most diners rhapsodize about this "pristinely" "beautiful space" in TriBeCa for its "divine", "delectable" Venetian fare and Italian-hill-town feel; however, some cite off-putting service.

Arriba Arriba ◐ [S] — 11 | 8 | 11 | $18

1463 Third Ave. (bet. 82nd & 83rd Sts.), 212-249-1423
484 Amsterdam Ave. (bet. 83rd & 84th Sts.), 212-580-8206
762 Ninth Ave. (51st St.), 212-489-0810

◪ These "twentysomething" East and West Side "hangouts" specialize in "annihilator margaritas", after a few of which the "cheap" "fill-'er-up" "Mexican eats" may seem, er well, "not bad."

Arté [S] — – | – | – | E

21 E. Ninth St. (bet. University Pl. & 5th Ave.), 212-473-0077

Village newcomer (in the former Arcobaleno space) boasting a romantic setting with an intimate back garden; its Mediterranean cuisine with seafood dishes from France to Portugal is a bit pricey but worth a try.

Artepasta [S] 🚫💳 — – | – | – | M

81 Greenwich Ave. (bet. 7th Ave. & Bank St.), 212-229-0234

Just another pasta place offering Villagers a chance to eat out less expensively than at home – and without cleaning the dishes.

Arturo's Pizzeria ◐ [S] — 18 | 8 | 11 | $15

106 W. Houston St. (Thompson St.), 212-677-3820

◪ A "moody, authentic old-world Italian" Village favorite for "great", "crisp", "coal-oven pizza" and "cool live jazz"; there's also a limited menu, but regulars advise: "stick to the pizza or you'll sing the blues."

Asia [S] — 17 | 19 | 17 | $29

1155 Third Ave. (bet. 67th & 68th Sts.), 212-879-9888

◪ All enthuse about the "mesmerizing fish tanks" at this "elegant" pan-Asian Eastsider; while some say the food is "wonderful", others call it merely "ordinary"; service, too, can vary.

Assembly, The — 17 | 15 | 19 | $38
Rockefeller Center, 16 W. 51st St. (bet. 5th & 6th Aves.), 212-581-3580
■ "Working hard for a comeback", this "warm", "family-run" Rockefeller Center steakhouse is "holding its own" serving "great steaks" (the "garlic steak is a must") in a "relaxing atmosphere."

Atomic Wings ◐ [S] ≠ — 17 | 5 | 9 | $13
1649 Third Ave. (bet. 92nd & 93rd Sts.), 212-410-3800
1446 First Ave. (bet. 75th & 76th Sts.), 212-772-8400
2180 Broadway (77th St.), 212-877-1010
179 W. 4th St. (bet. 6th & 7th Aves.), 212-627-9500
■ It's a perpetual "frat party" at these "dive bars" where "suicidally" spicy wings and "yummy waffle" fries seem designed to make binge drinking a necessity.

Au Bon Coin ◐ [S] ≠ — – | – | – | M
85 MacDougal St. (bet. Bleecker & Houston Sts.), 212-673-8184
Not much to look at, but this new Village storefront bistro is turning out authentic, unpretentious French regional cooking at moderate prices (aided by an initial BYOB policy).

Au Cafe ◐ [S] — 13 | 12 | 11 | $20
1700 Broadway (53rd St.), 212-757-2233
■ Theatergoers like the "convenience" of this "civilized outdoor place" for a "pleasant" but "predictable" "light bite"; service is "amateurish" and prices "reasonable" for the West Midtown area.

Au Mandarin [S] — 19 | 17 | 17 | $27
World Financial Ctr., 200-50 Vesey St. (West St.), 212-385-0313
◪ Wall Streeters praise this "elegant" WFC Mandarin, but say the "in-house dining" is "priced to include the rent", making this a rare "expense-account" and "business-meeting" Chinese; Sunday brunch is a "best buy."

Aunt Sonia's (Brooklyn) [S] — 18 | 13 | 16 | $28
1123 Eighth Ave. (12th St.), 718-965-9526
◪ "The closest thing to innovative dining in Park Slope", this "homey", "reasonably priced" Eclectic can be "festive" – especially for Sunday brunch – but our surveyors see signs of "inconsistency."

AUREOLE — 28 | 27 | 27 | $64
34 E. 61st St. (bet. Madison & Park Aves.), 212-319-1660
■ "Grand" and "gorgeous", Charlie Palmer's "romantic" duplex townhouse and garden are the backdrop for "some of the most memorable meals" in NY – his "sublime" cuisine is "food as art", especially the "architectural", "fairy-tale" desserts; service is "attentive" and "professional", and the sole complaint is that "smokers are rewarded with the best seats"; the $32 prix fixe lunch is a steal.

Automatic Slim's ◐ [S] ≠ **(94)** — 13 | 14 | 13 | $21
733 Washington St. (bet. Bank & Bethune Sts.), 212-645-8660
◪ A funky, "zany" late-night West Villager that's best for drinks and socializing since the American food makes a good case for staying slim.

Au Troquet [S] — 21 | 20 | 19 | $39
328 W. 12th St. (Greenwich St.), 212-924-3413
◪ "Cozy", "lace-curtained" West Villager evoking "a quaint Paris bistro", but what some say is "fine", "solid French cooking", albeit pricey, others call "just average."

Avanti [S] — 20 | 17 | 17 | $28

700 Ninth Ave. (48th St.), 212-586-7410

■ "A find in Hell's Kitchen", this Italian yearling has won a following for its "inventive" cookery including "excellent" pastas and desserts; "huge", "well-priced" portions don't hurt either.

Avenue A ◐ [S] — 19 | 14 | 14 | $22

103 Avenue A (bet. 6th & 7th Sts.), 212-982-8109

■ This "hip hop" "sushi haven" in a "funky" East Village brownstone draws Gen Xers who say it's "like eating in a dance club with friends."

Awoki [S] — ▽ 20 | 15 | 20 | $37

305 E. 46th St. (bet. 1st & 2nd Aves.), 212-759-8897

◪ Japanese suits seek out this "serene spot" near the U.N. for "traditional" cuisine and "consistently good" sushi served by "kimono-clad waitresses"; it's little known to gaijin and often empty at night.

Azzurro [S] — 18 | 16 | 16 | $35

245 E. 84th St. (bet. 2nd & 3rd Aves.), 212-517-7068

◪ "A notch above the typical East Side Italian", this "gourmet Sicilian" delights with "home cooking" in an elegant, "relaxed atmosphere"; critics cite service (too little) and prices (too high).

Baalbek [S] — ▽ 17 | 15 | 16 | $29

1484 Second Ave. (bet. 77th & 78th Sts.), 212-249-3000

◪ Top-notch traditional Lebanese cuisine, "gracious" service and pleasant surroundings make this moderately priced Eastsider a "delightful" outing for many; some, finding the servings small and "mediocre", ask "what's the big deal?"

Baby Jake's ◐ [S] — ▽ 17 | 10 | 13 | $18

14 First Ave. (bet. 1st & 2nd Sts.), 212-254-BABY

■ Funky East Village Cajun joint that's serving up "fresh New Orleans–style food" (e.g. andouille, crab cakes, po' boys, muffaletta, fried fish) in "small and crowded" coffee shop-with-theatrical- lighting quarters; you'd have trouble beating these prices down on the bayou.

Bachué Café [S] ≠ — ▽ 19 | 9 | 15 | $17

36 W. 21st St. (bet. 5th & 6th Aves.), 212-229-0870

◪ What fans call "a dream come true" – "healthy food that actually tastes like something" – is merely a "normal vegetarian" for others, with the ambiance of a "cramped, tacky broom closet."

Baci ◐ [S] ≠ — 18 | 14 | 15 | $29

412 Amsterdam Ave. (bet. 79th & 80th Sts.), 212-496-1550

◪ Most diners agree that "consistency is the key" at this recently redecorated West Side Italian where well-prepared pasta is the draw, but even admirers decry cramped tables best suited for a "lilliputian" clientele; detractors say that standards have slipped.

Back Porch [S] — 11 | 10 | 12 | $23

488 Third Ave. (33rd St.), 212-685-3828

◪ This Murray Hill Continental elicits little enthusiasm even among its supporters; outdoor seating, location and price are its attractions; though ideal for "cocktails and munchies on a summer evening", "if you live in the neighborhood, fine, if not, why bother?"

Bali Burma — 14 | 10 | 14 | $19

651 Ninth Ave. (bet. 45th & 46th Sts.), 212-265-9868

■ Though it's "slipped a little" and can be "uneven", this Indonesian-Burmese in the Theater District wins praise as a "fun, tasty surprise" offering "cheap eats" and a wide selection of lunch specials; if you have romantic expectations of either Bali or Burma, it's a letdown.

Ballato's 🄂
55 E. Houston St. (bet. Mott & Mulberry Sts.), 212-274-8881
☑ It's "getting overhyped by the hip" and has "gone downhill", but this reasonably priced Italian storefront standby has a luncheon menu and late-night prix fixe that maintain a loyal following.

| 17 | 10 | 15 | $28 |

Ballroom, The ●
253 W. 28th St. (bet. 7th & 8th Aves.), 212-244-3005
☑ Despite "service with attitude" and a "pricey" menu ("bring lots of dinero"), most surveyors say that this Chelsea Spaniard has "first-rate" tapas, a lunch menu that is "one of the best deals around" and "super cabaret entertainment" at night.

| 17 | 16 | 15 | $37 |

Baluchi's ●🄂
193 Spring St. (bet. Sullivan & Thompson Sts.), 212-226-2828
■ A new Indian that offers "expertly spiced" fare at a reasonable price served by an attentive staff in "pleasing, pseudo-exotic" surroundings; a few critics say it's "overrated, overpriced."

| ▽ 20 | 17 | 16 | $28 |

Bamiyan 🄂
358 Third Ave. (26th St.), 212-481-3232
■ "For a good kebab experience" try this affordable new Downtown Afghani, which "brings spice to an otherwise dull area"; to a few, it's "disappointing" and "mediocre."

| ▽ 17 | 14 | 15 | $23 |

Bangkok Cuisine ●🄂
885 Eighth Ave. (bet. 52nd & 53rd Sts.), 212-581-6370
■ An "old standby", this Westsider is still "reliable" (some say the "best Thai in NY"), but the "cheesy decor" is in "bad need of a face-lift."

| 18 | 12 | 15 | $23 |

Bangkok House 🄂
1485 First Ave. (bet. 77th & 78th Sts.), 212-249-5700
■ This East Side Thai continues to win raves for "food spicy enough to make you beg for mercy" and staff who will do their best to grant any request; even supporters say the decor is "getting Thai-ered."

| 20 | 11 | 16 | $25 |

Bar and Books ●🄂
1020 Lexington Ave. (73rd St.), 212-717-3902
889 First Ave. (50th St.), 212-980-9314
636 Hudson St. (bet. Horatio & Jane Sts.), 212-229-2642
■ "Great for a date" and "conducive to lucid conversation", these "very romantic", moderately priced bars provide a "classy, comforting" ambiance, but look elsewhere if you're hungry.

| 11 | 22 | 17 | $20 |

Baraonda ●🄂⇗
1439 Second Ave. (75th St.), 212-288-8555
■ A "scene of dressed-in-black wanna-bes", this stylish East Side Italian is great for people-watching and "surprisingly good" food, but the service can be "awful"; "fake Italian accents get you a table fast" as do long legs and short skirts.

| 18 | 17 | 11 | $34 |

Barbetta ●
321 W. 46th St. (bet. 8th & 9th Aves.), 212-246-9171
☑ "Breathtaking" formal decor, a "wonderful garden" and reliably good food make this Theater District Italian "always an enjoyable experience", or almost always: a few critics say that "the setting deserves better food"; "it could be heaven with some help."

| 18 | 23 | 18 | $44 |

Barking Dog Luncheonette 🄂⇗
1678 Third Ave. (94th St.), 212-831-1800
☑ "Outstanding mashed potatoes and gravy" and a "cozy, friendly" atmosphere that's "great for kids" are the draws for this East Side concept restaurant, where lunch and brunch are favorites; some find it "ruff around the edges" and suggest trying "a real diner."

| 15 | 15 | 15 | $18 |

F | D | S | C

Barnes & Noble Cafe S⊘
675 Sixth Ave. (bet. 21st & 22nd Sts.), 212-727-1227
2289 Broadway (bet. 82nd & 83rd Sts.), 212-362-8835

12 | 13 | 11 | $11

■ Welcome additions to Chelsea and the West Side doing double duty as "relaxing places for java and a book" and new hangouts "for the pickup set", making B&N a social, as well as a literary, center.

Barney Greengrass S⊘
541 Amsterdam Ave. (bet. 86th & 87th Sts.), 212-724-4707

21 | 5 | 11 | $19

■ "Oy, what fish" say fans of this "soulful Jewish brunch" "institution"; the decor is "tacky, tacky, tacky", the service can be "atrocious" and "the lines – oh my gawd", but who's complaining?

Barocco ◗S
301 Church St. (bet. Walker & White Sts.), 212-431-1445

20 | 16 | 15 | $35

■ "Trendy but not snobby", this TriBeCa "Euro-trash hangout" serves "solid" Italian food that has built a loyal following; "spacey servers" are a weak point, but not a turnoff.

Barolo ◗S
398 W. Broadway (bet. Spring & Broome Sts.), 212-226-1102

18 | 22 | 15 | $39

☑ Expensive, modern SoHo restaurant serving consistent Piedmontese fare; though food and service "could use a lift", the courtyard garden in back is what dazzles most diners.

Bar Pitti ◗S⊘
268 Sixth Ave. (bet. Bleecker & Houston Sts.), 212-982-3300

17 | 13 | 13 | $22

☑ Compensating for "erratic", "slow" service, this casual South Village Tuscan provides "a real trattoria experience"; look for "simple Italian food" "without pretense" and "relaxing" ambiance.

Bar Six ◗S
502 Sixth Ave. (bet. 12th & 13th Sts.), 212-645-2439

14 | 17 | 13 | $27

☑ Give this "hip" new French bistro "an 'A' for attitude"; "definitely a scene but not a scary one", it delivers decent food, drinks and celebrity sightings; though some are turned off by "middle-aged skirt-chasers", others are turned on by the "skirt" and "frat boy" crowd.

Basco S
1049 Lexington Ave. (bet. 74th & 75th Sts.), 212-535-8400

▽ 15 | 13 | 12 | $31

■ "The old Cafe Mimi with new paint" and the same "simple" fare; "it's a good neighbor" but consistency is a problem and service could easily be improved.

Basta Pasta
37 W. 17th St. (bet. 5th & 6th Aves.), 212-366-0888

17 | 14 | 17 | $25

☑ Some find this mid-priced Japanese-Italian hybrid a "novel idea that works", but the unimpressed say that despite an "immaculate" setting and service "like clockwork", "you can make better pasta at home."

Bayamo ◗S
704 Broadway (bet. E. 4th St. & Washington Pl.), 212-475-5151

13 | 15 | 12 | $22

☑ "Fun and young", this NYU-area "Chino-Latino fusion" is "a great place to take tourists" for a "change of pace", but not for food.

Beach Cafe ◗S
1326 Second Ave. (70th St.), 212-988-7299

11 | 10 | 12 | $23

☑ "Honest", "adequate", "all right" are among the kindest views on this good-value East Side bar/burger joint; if "uninspired", it's "inoffensive."

31

Becco ◐ 🅢
20 | 16 | 19 | $32

355 W. 46th St. (bet. 8th & 9th Aves.), 212-397-7597

■ This "warm", "attractive" Theater District Italian is "a smash hit" with the Broadway crowd who love its "amazing prix fixe", "affordable wines" and "generous" servings.

Beer Bar
– | – | – | M

MetLife Bldg., 200 Park Ave. (45th St. & Vanderbilt Ave.), 212-818-1333

The perfect commuter's pit stop or luncher's leitmotif, this new Restaurant Associates Grand Central neighbor has it all – a good, simple American menu, stylish quarters and, naturally, a great choice of beers.

Beijing Duck House 🅢
19 | 8 | 13 | $26

144 E. 52nd St. (bet. Lexington & 3rd Aves.), 212-759-8260
22 Mott St. (Pearl St.), 212-227-1810

■ "Nobody does duck better" than this Chinese chain but "there are better places for most other things": the decor is "dated", service "marginal" and the consensus is this is a "one-trick pony."

Beit Eddine 🅢
– | – | – | M

308 E. 49th St. (bet. 1st & 2nd Aves.), 212-888-7726

A midpriced Middle Eastern with "very good" food and a reasonable lunch buffet, but the atmosphere is "gloomy" and service can be "slow."

Bella Donna ◐ 🅢 ⇗
18 | 8 | 13 | $19

307 E. 77th St. (bet. 1st & 2nd Aves.), 212-535-2866
1663 First Ave. (bet. 86th & 87th Sts.), 212-534-3261

■ Set out early for these East Side Italian storefronts since space is at a premium for "the best pasta deal in town"; "you keep coming back", even if you end up "sitting in your neighbor's lap."

Bella Luna 🅢
18 | 15 | 16 | $25

584 Columbus Ave. (bet. 88th & 89th Sts.), 212-877-2267

☑ "A good neighborhood standby", this spacious, lunar-themed West Side Northern Italian pleases with a "first-rate" if "low-risk" menu; "hellacious" noise and "snooty" service can be drawbacks.

Bell Caffe ◐ 🅢
▽ 12 | 17 | 12 | $16

310 Spring St. (bet. Greenwich & Hudson Sts.), 212-334-BELL

■ It's a "one-of-a-kind" SoHo hangout featuring an Eclectic menu "for nonmeat-eaters who are hungry at 4 AM"; but don't let the food distract you, the main fare is "funky" '90s Bohemia.

Bello
21 | 17 | 20 | $34

863 Ninth Ave. (56th St.), 212-246-6773

■ With "generous portions" and "reasonable prices", this West Side Northern Italian is "a surprising find"; it's "consistent" enough and good enough to be "always crowded."

Ben Benson's 🅢
22 | 17 | 19 | $45

123 W. 52nd St. (bet. 6th & 7th Aves.), 212-581-8888

■ It may not be the best steakhouse in NY, but this "Midtown man's place" serves up "a fine steak" and fixings that satisfy most diners; still, this "real meal for a real man" may be too "noisy" and "gruff" for some – the litmus test is whether you agree with the formula: "steak, cigar, cognac – heaven."

Bendix Diner ◐ 🅢 ⇗
12 | 8 | 10 | $15

219 Eighth Ave. (21st St.), 212-366-0560

☑ People love or hate this "bizarre" Thai-Mex-Jewish Chelsea combo; many swear it offers "reliable diner food", "terrific variety" and "fun"; others think it "tries too many things and gets nothing right."

Benihana of Tokyo [S] — 15 | 14 | 18 | $29

120 E. 56th St. (bet. Park & Lexington Aves.), 212-593-1627
47 W. 56th St. (bet. 5th & 6th Aves.), 212-581-0930

■ The food cooked on teppenyaki grills can be "fine", but "go for the show" of samurai chefs dicing and slicing your meal; the spectacle is best enjoyed with a group of far-out-of-towners or young kids.

Benito I [S] — – | – | – | M

174 Mulberry St. (bet. Grand & Broome Sts.), 212-226-9171

Benito II [S] ⊄

163 Mulberry St. (bet. Grand & Broome Sts.), 212-226-9012

Separately owned, but for good, old-fashioned red-sauce fare at a fair price either of these crowded Little Italy storefronts will do fine.

Benny's Burritos ◐ [S] ⊄ — 18 | 8 | 11 | $14

93 Avenue A (6th St.), 212-254-2054
113 Greenwich Ave. (Jane St.), 212-727-3560

◪ "Awesome", "gut-busting" burritos at "amazing prices" and "killer" margaritas keep the lines long, the youthful crowds large and the "people-watching" first-rate; no one much cares that the service is "miserable"; "go early and wait anyway" – it's that popular!

Benvenuti Ristorante — ▽ 17 | 12 | 16 | $33

162 W. 36th St. (bet. 7th Ave. & B'way), 212-736-0178

◪ A haven in the "fast-food" Garment District, this Italian serves "mammoth portions" of "good traditional food", but critics say it's deservedly "dark" and advise bringing someone else's credit card.

Bertha's Burritos ◐ [S] ⊄ — 17 | 11 | 11 | $15

2160 Broadway (76th St.), 212-362-2500

◪ A "yuppie" Upper West Side "clone" of Benny's, this burrito joint is "the best for fun, prices and the food", but if you're over 30, it can make you "feel l'ke grandma."

Between the Bread — 17 | 10 | 13 | $19

141 E. 56th St. (bet. Lexington & 3rd Aves.), 212-888-0449

■ With "A-1 sandwiches and soups" this lunch outlet is "old reliable", though the prices ("expensive if you're paying") and "cafeteria-style" service leave some grumbling; it also caters.

Bice ◐ [S] — 21 | 21 | 17 | $44

7 E. 54th St. (bet. 5th & Madison Aves.), 212-688-1999

■ The "hip" clientele of this "still buzzing" Midtown Milanese ranges from "Chanel wearers" to "Eurotrash", but "that's what makes it fun"; go "for lunch on a good hair day" or "when you're in the mood for flash"; don't be surprised by "haughty" service and prices, just remember "the sum is greater than the parts" here; "encora!, encora!"

Bienvenue Restaurant — 16 | 12 | 15 | $28

21 E. 36th St. (bet. 5th & Madison Aves.), 212-684-0215

■ A "timeless" French bistro that's "getting a little old" and "tired", but is "homey" and tastes "the way French food should."

Big Cup ◐ [S] ⊄ — – | – | – | I

228 Eighth Ave. (bet. 21st & 22nd Sts.), 212-206-0059

New, funky "'40s modern" tea, coffee and sandwich house in Chelsea; it's a semi-gay, low-budget "experience."

Big Sur ◐ [S] — – | – | – | M

1406 Third Ave. (80th St.), 212-472-5009

High-stylish new East Side lounge with a limited American menu; it's worth seeing – especially the model maitre d's.

F | D | S | C

Big Wong [S] 🚫 — 20 | 2 | 7 | $11

67 Mott St. (bet. Canal & Bayard Sts.), 212-964-0540

■ "If you can stand the surroundings" visit this Chinatown deep "dive" for its "superb and cheap" congee, roast pork and spare ribs; brush up on your Chinese – "waiters speak little or no English."

Bill Hong's ◐ [S] — 19 | 13 | 17 | $32

227 E. 56th St. (bet. 2nd & 3rd Aves.), 212-751-4048

◪ Some say this "stable, dependable" 1970s-style, fancy "chow-mein-and-egg-roll" Chinese is "a cut above the rest"; others consider it "a bit pricey for ordinary" food and outdated decor.

Bill's Gay 90's — 11 | 13 | 14 | $29

57 E. 54th St. (bet. Madison & Park Aves.), 212-355-0243

◪ "No longer 'gay', just a place to go for drinks" after work or for "a decent lunch", this atmospheric 1890s pub/restaurant simply cries out for 1990s management, and a good cook.

Billy's ◐ [S] — 16 | 12 | 16 | $33

948 First Ave. (bet. 52nd & 53rd Sts.), 212-753-1870

◪ "Classic watering hole" that's a "comfortable" place for "relaxed" meals from a "hearty" menu of steak and fish; there are so many regulars on hand that it's like an "extended family" with paternal "no-nonsense" waiters; to critics, "classic" translates as "old and tired."

Bimini Twist ◐ — 14 | 12 | 13 | $25

345 Amsterdam Ave. (bet. 76th & 77th Sts.), 212-362-1260

◪ "Undergoing an identity crisis", this "quirky" Eclectic Westsider can be "imaginative", "relaxing" and "grown-up" on one visit and "blah", "seems to have lost its way" on the next.

Bimmy's [S] — ▽ 14 | 14 | 11 | $11

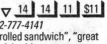

21 E. 8th St. (bet. 5th Ave. & University Pl.), 212-777-4141

■ "Generation X" seems to enjoy the "unique, rolled sandwich", "great music" and "'70s setting" at this "groovy", nostalgia-driven restaurant, despite bad vibes from the tourists and "B & T crowd."

Birdland ◐ [S] — 14 | 17 | 15 | $26

2745 Broadway (105th St.), 212-749-2228

■ Most say "go for the music" at this jazz club on the Upper West Side, where the Southern-style food gets mixed reviews; critics say it's "too expensive for so-so food and usually so-so music."

Biricchino — ▽ 19 | 13 | 17 | $30

260 W. 29th St. (8th Ave.), 212-695-6690

■ A "best bet" before a night at the Garden, this "undiscovered jewel" may be crowded and the ambiance lacking, but the "wonderful" homemade sausages won't disappoint.

Bistro Cafe [S] — ▽ 19 | 14 | 16 | $25

538 Third Ave. (bet. 35th & 36th Sts.), 212-686-6660

■ "Good food", "good prices", "good portions" – "what's not to like?" about this Murray Hill Italian; it's fast becoming a "neighborhood standby", and deservedly so.

Bistro du Nord ◐ [S] — 19 | 17 | 16 | $37

1312 Madison Ave. (93rd St.), 212-289-0997

◪ This "very French" Upper East Side jewel box is a "refined retreat from NYC clamor", with "dependable" food; on the downside, the lovely, tiny space is near "claustrophobic" and "service is a bit chilly."

Bistro 790 S
15 | 14 | 14 | $27
Sheraton Manhattan Hotel, 790 Seventh Ave. (51st St.), 212-621-8537
■ A "good pit stop before a B'way show", this American Midtowner is also not bad for "a casual business lunch"; however, beware of "waiters on another planet" and "mediocre" food.

Bistro 36 (Brooklyn) S
 ∇ 18 | 14 | 18 | $33
36 Joralemon St. (Columbia Pl.), 718-596-2968
■ "A homey little French miracle where you hardly expect it" wins praise for generous portions and "friendly" service; it might be "nothing special" in Midtown, but it's good news in the Heights.

Black Sheep, The S
19 | 19 | 17 | $36
344 W. 11th St. (Washington St.), 212-242-1010
■ A "lovely, relaxing" French-Italian in the West Village that's "almost too romantic"; though there's probably no better place for a "cozy brunch on a cold winter's day", critics note that it's "slipping fast" and "way too pricey for what and where it is."

Bloom's Delicatessen S
12 | 10 | 12 | $15
350 Lexington Ave. (40th St.), 212-922-3663
■ "It doesn't compare to NY's great delis", but it "serves a need in a neighborhood (Grand Central) where it's tough to find anything decent"; critics sniff "maybe great in DC or Texas but not here."

Blue Moon Mexican Cafe ◑ S
– | – | – | M
150 Eighth Ave. (bet. 17th & 18th Sts.), 212-463-0560
1444 First Ave. (75th St.), 212-288-9811
Handy but uninspired Tex-Mexicans that are good neighbors for easygoing, young dining and drinking.

Blue Ribbon ◑ S
22 | 17 | 17 | $33
97 Sullivan St. (bet. Prince & Spring Sts.), 212-274-0404
■ "Deserving a blue ribbon", this "tiny" SoHo Eclectic is so popular that it's "hard to turn around"; besides an "excellent raw bar" there's "deeply satisfying", "creative" "comfort food" that's "priced right" and justifies the inevitable wait; it's one of the few "after-hours" "hot" spots where there's "no attitude", and so good that "other chefs hang out."

Blu Restaurant S
20 | 20 | 18 | $30
254 W. 23rd St. (bet. 7th & 8th Aves.), 212-989-6300
■ Fans say that this Chelsea newcomer is a "real discovery", providing a "tranquil setting", "lazy music", a "vest-pocket garden" and "creative" Eclectic eats; critics are simply "blu" about it all.

Boathouse Cafe S
12 | 22 | 13 | $30
Central Park Lake, East Park Dr. & 73rd St., 212-517-2233
■ An "unbeatable location" on Central Park Lake combines with "Chef Boyardee" food and "uncaring service" to make political activists wonder about the city's franchising process and more philosophical types settle for "drinks and view."

Boca Chica S
18 | 12 | 13 | $21
13 First Ave. (1st St.), 212-473-0108
■ The secret's out on this "lively" East Village Latino, where "dazzling tastes", "potent drinks", "saucy atmosphere", a salsa band and "low prices" produce a "zesty" experience.

Bo Ky S ⊅
18 | 2 | 7 | $12
80 Bayard St. (bet. Mott & Mulberry Sts.), 212-406-2292
■ "Close your eyes, plug up your ears and slurp the superb noodle soups"; this "cheap" Chinatown noodle shop is "ugly but authentic", providing a "soup-er" meal if you overcome the "language barrier."

Bolo ◐Ⓢ   23 | 21 | 20 | $42 |
23 E. 22nd St. (bet. Broadway & Park Ave. S.), 212-228-2200
■ Chef Bobby Flay (also of Mesa Grill) "has done it again", producing "assertive", "garlic-intensive" Spanish food that's "busting with flavor" in "festive", "noisy" quarters that some call "the best new place this year"; its few critics say garlic and olives are too plentiful and that "inconsistency keeps it from being outstanding."

Bombay Palace Ⓢ   17 | 15 | 16 | $27 |
30 W. 52nd St. (bet. 5th & 6th Aves.), 212-541-7777
☑ The buffet lunch is the "best value" at this mid-priced Midtown Indian, which serves "consistently good" but "pedestrian" fare; it's "not as good as it used to be" and "the interior needs a make-over."

Book-Friends Cafe Ⓢ   13 | 19 | 15 | $19 |
16 W. 18th St. (bet. 5th & 6th Aves.), 212-255-7407
☑ You "walk into another world" at this Chelsea bookstore; "warm and inviting", it's a "bibliophile's paradise"; "stick to the books", tea and snacks since anything else can be "overpriced" and "ordinary."

Boom ◐Ⓢ   16 | 16 | 12 | $35 |
152 Spring St. (bet. Wooster St. & W. B'way), 212-431-3663
☑ Some say this "boom box" for the black-bedecked "Euro/SoHo crowd" is "completely unworth it", but what brings them here is not the "weird" International food, "dark", pseudo "rain forest" decor or "sedated service", but the intense "sexy scene" at the bar.

Boonthai Ⓢ   14 | 11 | 15 | $22 |
1393-A Second Ave. (bet. 72nd & 73rd Sts.), 212-249-8484
☑ "Sturdy" but "pedestrian" East Side Thai that's "inexpensive but nothing special"; "go only if you happen to be in the neighborhood."

Bora   ▽ 22 | 12 | 20 | $33 |
179 Madison Ave. (bet. 33rd & 34th Sts.), 212-725-3282
■ A good-old-feeling Italian in Murray Hill that's a "reliable place" for "delicious" food and "helpful service" "in an area where either is hard to find"; only the "sterile" setting holds it back.

Borsalino   18 | 14 | 16 | $28 |
255 W. 55th St. (bet. B'way & 8th Ave.), 212-246-0710
■ Convenient to Carnegie Hall, this Italian is "acceptable", even "very good", with a "homey" atmosphere and a favorable "food-price ratio"; but even fans concede it's "not memorable."

Bos ◐Ⓢ   ▽ 16 | 5 | 11 | $13 |
930 Eighth Ave. (55th St.), 212-582-8887
■ "Cheap" dumplings, noodle soup and Chinese BBQ are the upside at this Midtown Westsider; the downside is small, bright Formica space and "staff that can't get your order right."

Boston Chicken (Queens) Ⓢ ⊟   – | – | – | I |
23-90 Bell Blvd. (23rd Ave.), Bayside, 718-224-1747
It's no wonder that this rotisserie chicken chain is so popular – it can outcook 90 percent of NYC's moms at a lower price; so why eat at home?

Boulevard ◐Ⓢ   12 | 12 | 13 | $22 |
2398 Broadway (88th St.), 212-874-7400
☑ This inexpensive Westsider is a "casual" place with a "basic" "diverse" menu, including BBQ and the full cuisines of the NAFTA nations; "take the kids, not the grandparents" since it can be "frenetic" and "you can grow old waiting for service"; critics stick to drinks and watching the B'way traffic.

BOULEY
29 | 28 | 27 | $70

165 Duane St. (bet. Greenwich & Hudson Sts.), 212-608-3852
■ Over 3,000 surveyors agree: "it doesn't get any better in NY"; this TriBeCa organic French for the third year in a row ranks No. 1 in both popularity and food, defining "everything a restaurant should be"; from the food (especially the tasting menu) to the setting, it represents a "feast for the eyes, nose and mouth"; though you must "prepare to drop a lot of cash", the $35 prix fixe lunch offers the same experience for a lot less; the main problems are getting reservations and waits for a table even with them.

Boxers ◗ S
13 | 13 | 13 | $20

190 W. 4th St. (bet. 6th & 7th Aves.), 212-633-BARK
■ An "atmospheric", "old" "Village standby" that's exactly what it looks like – a "cozy pub" that's "perfect for hanging with friends"; on weekends it's "a zoo."

Box Tree, The S
24 | 26 | 24 | VE

The Box Tree, 250 E. 49th St. (bet. 2nd & 3rd Aves.), 212-758-8320
◪ "Romance" is the main attraction at this "elegant", antique-filled art nouveau Midtown townhouse, and most say its French-Continental food is also "very good"; to critics, however, the "limited menu" is "about as lively as the antiques" and, at $86 prix fixe, almost as costly.

Brasserie ◗ S
16 | 14 | 15 | $29

100 E. 53rd St. (bet. Park & Lexington Aves.), 212-751-4840
■ "Filling a real niche" in Midtown, this "old, reliable", 24-hour "insomniac heaven" of a French coffee shop feeds soup, omelets and well-priced specials to office workers and lovers late at night, while providing handy business breakfasts, lunches and dinners throughout the day; if "a bit worn", it gets lots of use.

Bridge Cafe S
20 | 15 | 18 | $32

279 Water St. (Dover St.), 212-227-3344
■ "Leave your tie at home" and enjoy the "consistently good" seafood at this "intimate", "unpretentious" "NY classic" near City Hall; the waterfront dive setting makes the experience even more of a treat; Democrats, Republicans and even Ed Koch like it.

Bright Food Shop S ⌁
18 | 8 | 13 | $18

216 Eighth Ave. (21st St.), 212-243-4433
◪ Though some can't grasp this Chelsea Sino-Mexican luncheonette with "strange hours" and "spacey" help, most are impressed by its "healthy", "creative" food and a room so clean it "lives up to" its name.

Brighton Grill ◗ S
15 | 13 | 15 | $30

1313 Third Ave. (bet. 75th & 76th Sts.), 212-988-6663
■ The truth about this East Side "grill" can best be discerned in its "good, solid food", "casual setting" (promoting "real conversation") and "excellent value"; neighbors treat it as a second home.

Brio ◗ S
19 | 16 | 17 | $33

786 Lexington Ave. (bet. 61st & 62nd Sts.), 212-980-2300
■ Most are impressed by this stylish "storefront" Italian; "bordering between intimate and cramped" and with a menu of "inexpensive, consistent" pasta, it's just the place for a light meal near Bloomies.

Briscola ◗
▽ 19 | 15 | 18 | $36

65 Fourth Ave. (bet. 9th & 10th Sts.), 212-254-1940
◪ The "upgraded" version of the location's predecessor, Siracusa, has 100 percent better decor and "excellent" Sicilian food, but the trade-off is higher prices and more "attitude"; ergo, it's often empty.

Broadway Diner 🅂 ⇗
13 | 8 | 11 | $17

590 Lexington Ave. (52nd St.), 212-486-8838
1726 Broadway (55th St.), 212-765-0909

☑ These upscale diners are "a cut above the average egg-and-toast joint" and, at the B'way outlet, there's always the chance of sitting next to David Letterman; skeptics add up "so-so food" and service and conclude: "a diner is a diner is a diner."

Broadway Grill ◑
14 | 12 | 14 | $26

Holiday Inn Crowne Plaza, 1605 Broadway (49th St.), 212-315-6161

☑ This Eclectic grill remains a "sensible pre-theater choice", serving "great" pizza and other consistent fare at a "reasonable" price; naysayers suggest that it's just "a glorified coffee shop."

Broome Street Bar ◑ 🅂
13 | 11 | 12 | $19

363 W. Broadway (Broome St.), 212-925-2086

■ Though only "one step above a dive", you could do a lot worse; with "old-world atmosphere", "delicious juicy burgers" and "good sandwiches" this SoHo pub is "a slice of Downtown life."

Brother Jimmy's BBQ 🅂
15 | 9 | 11 | $18

1461 First Ave. (76th St.), 212-288-0999

☑ "A bit of N. Carolina in NY", this "pork shrine" has fans who say it's "good, cheap and authentic" with "nuclear-powered" hot sauce; it also may resemble a "frat party" where "Beavis and Butt-head hang out."

Brothers Bar-B-Q ◑ 🅂
15 | 10 | 12 | $18

228 W. Houston St. (bet. 6th Ave. & Varick St.), 212-727-2775
2182 Broadway (77th St.), 212-873-7364

☑ This may be the "closest to Southern BBQ you'll find in NYC" with "giant portions" having "a week's worth of cholesterol, but what a way to go!"; then again, these may be "shallow, noisy, money machines"; either way, they're "not for the timid."

Bruce Ho's Four Seas ◑ 🅂
18 | 15 | 19 | $31

116 E. 57th St. (bet. Park & Lexington Aves.), 212-753-2610

☑ "An aging dowager" that still offers "reliable Cantonese" and "very friendly" service, but even supporters groan at Midtown prices and admit it's "not like it used to be."

Brunetta's 🅂 ⇗
20 | 10 | 16 | $20

190 First Ave. (bet. 11th & 12th Sts.), 212-228-4030

☑ Though little known, this East Village Italian dive is an "amazing value" for "well-prepared" food and a "charming garden"; dissenters say "cute and cozy" is "claustrophobic."

Bruno Ristorante ◑
20 | 19 | 20 | $42

240 E. 58th St. (bet. 2nd & 3rd Aves.), 212-688-4190

■ You get two for one at this "classy" Italian – a quiet downstairs and a "lively bar" upstairs; "good, consistent food and service" "make you feel at home", but the prices make this "an expense-accounter."

B. Smith's ◑ 🅂
18 | 17 | 16 | $34

771 Eighth Ave. (47th St.), 212-247-2222

■ "For a quiet lunch or bustling pre-theater dinner", this "Southern-flavored" buppie hangout "is always dependable"; it's an "upbeat" experience with a good bar scene, spacious, "relaxing" dining room and large, upstairs private-party space.

Bubby's [S] — 17 | 10 | 12 | $17

120 Hudson St. (N. Moore St.), 212-219-0666

■ A "homey", "unpretentious TriBeCa haunt" that delivers "good, reliable American home cooking" (pancakes, soups, salads, pies, brownies "to live for") despite spacey service; look for lunchers and brunchers such as JFK Jr. and Harvey Keitel, and low prices.

Bull & Bear ◐ [S] — 16 | 18 | 17 | $39

Waldorf-Astoria, 301 Park Ave. (49th St.), 212-872-4900

◪ The "guys love" this "old boys' club" and its reliable surf and turf, but reserve strictly for business lunch – "the food isn't good enough for a personal dinner"; bears report that it's "stodgy to the bone."

Burger Heaven — 12 | 4 | 10 | $12

804 Lexington Ave. (62nd St.), 212-838-3580
536 Madison Ave. (bet. 54th & 55th Sts.), 212-753-4214
9 E. 53rd St. (bet. 5th & Madison Aves.), 212-752-0340
20 E. 49th St. (bet. 5th & Madison Aves.), 212-755-2166
291 Madison Ave. (bet. 40th & 41st Sts.), 212-685-6250

◪ "When you need a grease fix" it's comforting to know that one of these "fast and efficient", coffee shop–style joints is not far away; though "not heaven", it sure as hell "beats McDonald's et al."

Burritoville ◐ [S] ≠ — – | – | – | I

1489 First Ave. (bet. 77th & 78th Sts.), 212-472-8800
451 Amsterdam Ave. (bet. 81st & 82nd Sts.), 212-787-8181
1606 Third Ave. (bet. 90th & 91st Sts.), 212-410-2255
148 W. 4th St. (bet. 5th & 6th Aves.), 212-505-1212
141 Second Ave. (bet. 8th & 9th Sts.), 212-260-3300
36 Water St. (Broad St.), 212-747-1100

Fast, fresh and affordable is the formula that this new mini-chain has ridden into town with; look for burritos, fajitas and quesadillas at south-of-the-border prices, but "no lard, no preservatives and no cans in the kitchen."

Busby's ◐ [S] — 15 | 14 | 14 | $32

45 E. 92nd St. (Madison Ave.), 212-360-7373

◪ If you're "in the neighborhood" this "too-Waspy-for-words" Carnegie Hill American may be for you; though some find it "uptight", "noisy" and "not worth the money", just as many consider the fare "dependable", even "delightful" for "a quick lunch or dinner."

Byblos — ▽ 18 | 12 | 17 | $26

200 E. 39th St. (3rd Ave.), 212-687-0808

◪ "Authentic" Lebanese with "tasty" food, "friendly" atmosphere and music and dancing (at night), all at a "reasonable price"; even those who consider it "bland" and a "waste of time" admit that you're at little risk with a prix fixe dinner for $21.

Cabana Carioca [S] — 16 | 8 | 13 | $23

123 W. 45th St. (bet. 6th & 7th Aves.), 212-581-8088

■ The "party atmosphere" at this colorful Theater District Brazilian brings in followers for an annual ritual of indulgence: "mondo portions" of "decent food" and "mucho value"; so what if it's "unrefined", the service "surly" and "could be cleaner."

Cafe Andrusha [S] — 17 | 11 | 17 | $27

1742 Second Ave. (bet. 90th & 91st Sts.), 212-360-1128

■ A "charming" "little Russian place" with "delicious", "authentic Slavic and Balkan offerings"; "cozy" if small, it's a "romantic" and "affordable" stop before or after the 92nd Street Y.

Cafe Baci
▽ 17 | 14 | 15 | $24
136 W. 31st St. (bet. 6th & 7th Aves.), 212-967-7755
◨ Waiters who "don't have a clue" struggle to keep up with diners' demands at this Garment District Italian; though capable of "good, basic pasta", the kitchen "can't handle more than 10 dinners at once."

Cafe Beulah S
20 | 20 | 17 | $33
39 E. 19th St. (bet. B'way & Park Ave. S.), 212-777-9700
◨ "Here's a winning, down-home, good food, great idea place"; "upscale" Soul Food "south of 125th Street" makes this "one of the best racially integrated restaurants in NYC"; a few complain that the vittles are too "low-key" and service "amateur."

Cafe Botanica S
23 | 27 | 23 | $42
Essex House, 160 Central Park S. (bet. 6th & 7th Aves.), 212-484-5120
■ "Floral and festive", this "gardenlike" room across from Central Park wins bouquets for its "imaginative" Contemporary French-American food, "comfortable", "spacious" setting and "charming" service; don't miss the "sumptuous" buffet brunch or "superb" prix fixe menus ("a steal"); if you don't know it, you should.

Cafe Cento Sette S ⊅
– | – | – | M
107 Third Ave. (bet. 13th & 14th Sts.), 212-420-5933
"A nice addition to a barren" East Village block offering "good cafe food", java and desserts in a "sunny, exposed-brick" setting; the menu may be "unremarkable", but the parade passing by isn't.

Cafe Centro
– | – | – | M
MetLife Bldg., 200 Park Ave. (45th St. & Vanderbilt Ave.), 212-818-1222
This grand cafe features handsome, muralled quarters and an attractive open kitchen that produces French, American and Moroccan classics that keep the crowds coming at all hours; it has the potential to be NYC's La Coupole – put it on your list to try!

Cafe Con Leche ◑S
16 | 11 | 14 | $15
424 Amsterdam Ave. (bet. 80th & 81st Sts.), 212-595-7000
◨ "A million cabbies, rollerbladers and cops can't be wrong" – follow their lead and "cram into" this "funky" West Side luncheonette for hearty Cuban sandwiches, the "best cafe con leche" and other "bargain", "soulful" Latino food.

Cafe Crocodile
20 | 17 | 20 | $38
354 E. 74th St. (bet. 1st & 2nd Aves.), 212-249-6619
■ "It feels good" sums up Eastsiders' views of Charles and Andrée Abramoff's Mediterranean bistro; "wonderfully original" cooking, a "lovely townhouse" setting and "caring" service explain why; the menu is limited and "not cheap", but the prix fixe is a "good value."

Cafe de Bruxelles ◑S
21 | 17 | 18 | $34
118 Greenwich Ave. (W. 13th St.), 212-206-1830
■ If it's Tuesday (or any other day) "it must be Belgium" at this cozy, triangular Village cafe; "fab frites", marvelous moules, "exotic beers", lace curtains and a zinc bar add to the authenticity.

Cafe de la Paix ◑S
– | – | – | E
St. Moritz Hotel, 50 Central Park S. (6th Ave.), 212-755-5800
Suffering from delusions of adequacy, this touristy American cafe is a waste of a great location; only the outside seats on a balmy day justify its appeal to unwitting tourists.

F D S C

Cafe de Paris ◐ [S] — 17 | 15 | 17 | $34
924 Second Ave. (49th St.), 212-486-1411
◪ "Nothing special", just a "simple" East Midtown bistro that's "been around forever" serving good steak frites, salads and pasta; newly installed French doors are a plus, "waiters on automatic pilot" a minus.

CAFE DES ARTISTES ◐ [S] — 24 | 27 | 23 | $49
1 W. 67th St. (bet. CPW & Columbus Ave.), 212-877-3500
◪ "As romantic as they come", this "ageless" "grand cafe" seduces surveyors with its "elegant, old-world" ambiance, "delicious" French cuisine and "magical" setting featuring lush flowers and murals of lusty nymphs; to most NYers this is the No. 1 "place to fall in love" and as close to "heaven" as the West Side gets.

Cafe des Sports ◐ [S] — 16 | 14 | 17 | $32
329 W. 51st St. (bet. 8th & 9th Aves.), 212-581-1283
◪ "Tried and true" Theater District standby that owes its longevity to "solid" French bistro food and "good prices"; it's not big on excitement or looks, but most find it "cozy" and "friendly."

Cafe du Pont [S] — ▽ 18 | 14 | 19 | $29
1038 First Ave. (bet. 56th & 57th Sts.), 212-223-1133
■ "What a find", this tiny, affordable East Side "neighborhood sleeper" has "terrific" Eclectic food, "enthusiastic" service, "romantic" ambiance and a prix fixe dinner that's a "best buy."

Cafe Español ◐ [S] — 20 | 12 | 17 | $25
172 Bleecker St. (bet. MacDougal & Sullivan Sts.), 212-505-0657
63 Carmine St. (7th Ave.), 212-675-3312
■ "No one goes home hungry" from these "bustling" old Village Spaniards thanks to "huge portions" of garlic-laden food (try the lobster) at low prices; they're "always crowded" and "noisy", but "friendly service" and "free-flowing sangria" help ease the pain.

Cafe Europa [S] — 16 | 13 | 14 | $25
205 W. 57th St. (7th Ave.), 212-977-4030 ◐
1177 Sixth Ave. (46th St.), 212-575-7272
◪ A cross between an "upscale cafeteria" and a "chichi" cafe, these "airy" Midtowners are usually jammed thanks to a "simple but creative" menu of salads, sandwiches, pizzas and desserts; "don't look for comfort here", but they're fine for a "quick bite" or coffee break.

Cafe Greco [S] — 17 | 15 | 16 | $29
1390 Second Ave. (bet. 71st & 72nd Sts.), 212-737-4300
◪ Early-bird crowds flock to this "friendly" East Side Mediterranean for its "real steal" of a prix fixe deal; it "doesn't pretend to be gourmet, but it's good", generous and comfortable; critics contend only "the Geritol set" could like such "tired" food.

Cafe Lalo ◐ [S] — 19 | 16 | 11 | $13
201 W. 83rd St. (bet. Amsterdam Ave. & B'way), 212-496-6031
◪ "A chocolate cake for every mood" plus other "scrumptious" desserts and coffees are the draws at this atmospheric West Side cafe; but the price you pay (aside from calories) includes "airhead service", "zero elbow room", noise and lines; afternoons are calmer.

Cafe Loup ◐ [S] — 19 | 18 | 18 | $34
105 W. 13th St. (bet. 6th & 7th Aves.), 212-255-4746
■ Typifying the "perfect neighborhood bistro", this "unassuming" yet stylish West Villager has it all: "honest food at reasonable prices", "good wines by the glass", an "artistic ambiance" plus "a rare find – space between tables"; what a few find "boring", others call "reliable."

Cafe Luxembourg ◐Ⓢ

200 W. 70th St. (bet. Amsterdam & West End Aves.), 212-873-7411

☒ The "atmosphere still clicks" at this ever-hip West Side bistro where a "stylish crowd" digs into "satisfying" French food in a "sleek", "retro" setting; critics say it's "cramped" and "you need to be named Fabio" to get service; P.S. kill the ads or improve the buttocks.

Cafe Melville Ⓢ

110 Barrow St. (Washington St.), 212-924-0110

☒ We get mixed reports on this West Village Continental: "better than usual" food in a "soaring", "dramatic" setting vs. "waste of a beautiful space" with "forgettable" fare and "forgetful" service.

Cafe Metairie Ⓢ

1442 Third Ave. (82nd St.), 212-988-1800

☒ "Decent" French food served in a "cute", countrified setting makes this a popular East Side standby, especially for a "bargain" brunch or pre-theater dinner; however, not everyone's charmed: "pedestrian", "too precious", "this duck laid an egg."

Cafe Nicholson

323 E. 58th St. (bet. 1st & 2nd Aves.), 212-355-6769

☒ Unquestionably "offbeat" (it's open only at John Nicholson's whim), this "unique" East Side American is also "a secret paradise" with "stage-set decor", "caring" staff and "excellent chocolate soufflés" that can make wives feel like mistresses and vice versa.

Cafe Nosidam ◐Ⓢ

768 Madison Ave. (bet. 65th & 66th Sts.), 212-717-5633

☒ Spell the name backwards to reveal this Italian's main asset: a prime address affording "glamorous" people-watching from sidewalk seats; since the food's "not bad", the setting "attractive" and the staff "obliging", it's a "pleasant" way to see what's in fashion.

Cafe Pierre ◐Ⓢ

The Pierre Hotel, 61st St. & Fifth Ave., 212-940-8185

■ "One of NY's most sophisticated rooms" where it's easy to "feel like royalty" over a "power breakfast", "lovely afternoon tea" or "quiet" dinner; fine French cuisine, "opulent" decor, "gracious service" and, alas, "killer prices" are all part of this "class act."

Cafe S.F.A. Ⓢ

Saks Fifth Ave., 611 Fifth, 8th fl. (50th St.), 212-940-4080

■ A "haven for weary shoppers" and "ladies who lunch – well", this "delightful" cafe provides "terrific salads and breads", a "spacious, restful" art deco setting and a view of St. Pat's that even the Cardinal would envy; it's a "lunchtime dream" marred only by long lines.

Cafe St. John Ⓢ

500 W. 110th St. (Amsterdam Ave.), 212-932-8420

■ An answer to the prayers of Morningside Heights locals: a "cozy", "low-key" bistro serving "hearty" fare at "moderate" prices just "steps from the cathedral"; a few heretics complain of "slow" service and "lame" food, but overall it's a "refuge" in a dining wasteland.

Cafe Tabac ◐Ⓢ

232 E. 9th St. (bet. 2nd & 3rd Aves.), 212-674-7072

☒ "Not over yet", this East Village "scene" is still filled with "anorexic models", celebs ("isn't that Francis Coppola?"), "posers" and "smoke"; there's debate over the bistro food ("decent" vs. who cares "if you're planning to throw it up anyway?"), but most agree the staff's "annoying" and upstairs is the place to be.

Cafe Trevi ◐ [S] — 22 | 18 | 22 | $40
1570 First Ave. (bet. 81st & 82nd Sts.), 212-249-0040
■ What makes this Upper East Sider "stand out from a long list" of Northern Italians is its "hospitable owner", Primo Laurenti, and staff – "nowhere in NY will you feel more welcome"; add "fine food" and it's clear why patrons call it a "home away from home."

Cafe Un Deux Trois ◐ [S] — 15 | 13 | 14 | $31
123 W. 44th St. (bet. B'way & 6th Ave.), 212-354-4148
◪ "Easy as 1, 2, 3" for Theater District dining, this "spirited" French bistro is as "big as Grand Central" and just as manic pre-curtain; the bistro food is "not fantastic" but it's fast and affordable.

Café Word of Mouth [S] — 18 | 11 | 13 | $24
1012 Lexington Ave., 2nd fl. (bet. 72nd & 73rd Sts.), 212-249-5351
◪ The word is mostly good on this "cute" little cafe perched above the East Side catering shop of the same name; people love its "interesting" salads, sandwiches and light meals, but aren't so wild about its "gold-plated prices", cramped tables or staircase.

Caffe Biondo ◐ [S] 🚫 — ▽ 17 | 14 | 15 | $26
141 Mulberry St. (bet. Grand & Hester Sts.), 212-226-9285
◪ To admirers, this brick-walled Little Italy storefront dessert specialist is "NY's most authentic Sicilian", a "nice place" to linger over pastry and cappuccino, especially in the pleasant garden; but to critics it's merely a place for "decent pastry at inflated prices."

Caffe Bondí — 20 | 18 | 18 | $32
7 W. 20th St. (bet. 5th & 6th Aves.), 212-691-8136
■ "A bit different", this Flatiron cafe/restaurant serves "heavenly desserts" plus a "panoply of Sicilian delights" including "dishes not found elsewhere"; though some call it "a bit pricey and precious", to most it's a "hidden treasure" complete with "romantic garden."

Caffe Buon Gusto ◐ [S] — 19 | 10 | 15 | $21
236 E. 77th St. (bet. 2nd & 3rd Aves.), 212-535-6884 🚫
151 Montague St. (bet. Clinton & Henry Sts.), 718-624-3838
◪ When "looking to keep it cheap" look no further than these priced-right pastarias; "tasty", "mix 'n' match" pastas and sauces and "terrifically friendly" service generate crowds, noise and waits; critics yawn "you can do better at home."

Caffé Carciofo (Brooklyn) [S] 🚫 — ▽ 19 | 16 | 15 | $26
248 Court St. (Kane St.), 718-624-7551
■ "They take chances with food and usually win" at this Cobble Hill Italian; even when the kitchen misses, there's always the "airy" setting and "congenial" service to compensate; try it "on a beautiful spring evening" when it opens onto the sidewalk.

Caffe Cielo [S] — 19 | 17 | 17 | $32
881 Eighth Ave. (bet. 52nd & 53rd Sts.), 212-246-9555
◪ It seldom soars despite its sky motif, but this West Side Northern Italian maintains a cruising altitude with "dependable", "respectable food", "easy prices", an "attractive", "airy" setting and proximity to theaters; aka "the Cravath lunchroom."

Caffe di Nonni ◐ [S] — ▽ 18 | 16 | 16 | $22
104 Grand St. (Mercer St.), 212-925-5488
◪ "Good brunch" and "reasonable prices" are among this SoHo Italian's many assets; however, an "inconsistent" kitchen may make it a cafe no-no on occasion.

F | D | S | C

Caffe Grazie [S] 19 | 15 | 17 | $28
26 E. 84th St. (bet. Madison & 5th Aves.), 212-717-4407
■ "Fresh, vibrant", "a gem" are typical accolades for this "small" but "very sweet" East Side Italian yearling; with "very good" food and "cozy-chic" decor, it's "lovely for a bite before or after the Met."

Caffe Lure ◐ [S] – | – | – | M
169 Sullivan St. (bet. Bleecker & Houston Sts.), 212-473-2642
A touch of Montmartre comes to NoHo at this instantly busy, midpriced Continental newcomer specializing in seafood, brick-oven pizzas and interesting desserts; the main drawbacks are cramped quarters, no waiting space and no reserving.

Caffe Rafaella ◐ [S] 🚫 ▽ 16 | 19 | 13 | $20
134 Seventh Ave. S. (bet. 10th & Charles Sts.), 212-929-7247
Rafaella Ristorante [S]
381 Bleecker St. (bet. Perry & Charles Sts.), 212-229-9885
■ "Cozy, funky, friendly" hybrids that function as both coffeehouses ("bring a book" and "linger forever" over "great desserts") and as restaurants ("good pasta", "excellent veal"); "lovely" decor and sidewalk seating help atone for "lackluster" service.

Caffe Reggio ◐ [S] 🚫 ▽ 15 | 18 | 11 | $15
119 MacDougal St. (bet. W. 3rd & Bleecker Sts.), 212-475-9557
■ "Dark and smoky, but with great character" as befits a "funky", old-time Village coffeehouse where you can "sip a cappuccino for a couple of hours" while enjoying simple "cafe fare"; it's "not a poser place", but even so there's "good people-watching."

Caffe Rosso ◐ [S] ▽ 20 | 19 | 19 | $29
284 W. 12th St. (W. 4th St.), 212-633-9277
■ West Villagers take a rosy view of this "simple but stylish" Italian "hideaway"; it's "cozy and romantic" with "terrific food" at fair prices and the staff makes you "feel at home."

Caffe Vivaldi ◐ [S] 🚫 (94) 16 | 19 | 15 | $15
32 Jones St. (bet. Bleecker & W. 4th Sts.), 212-929-9384
◪ A romantic, "European"-feeling Village cafe that specializes in "classic desserts and classic music" best enjoyed in winter by the fire.

Cajun [S] 16 | 12 | 14 | $25
129 Eighth Ave. (bet. 16th & 17th Sts.), 212-691-6174
◪ "Ok Cajun-Creole at better-than-ok prices with much-better-than-ok music" sums up this Chelsea "party spot"; its "tacky riverboat decor" and "deafening" live bands may send you down river.

Cake Bar & Cafe, The – | – | – | M
22 E. 13th St. (bet. 5th Ave. & University Pl.), 212-807-1313
This straightforward (modern '90s) pastry bar ain't just a piece of cake, it also has soups, salads, sandwiches, pastas and daily specials; if chef-owner Susan Povich looks familiar, that's because she's Maury's daughter; if co-owner Jude Quintiere looks familiar, you may have met her at the French Culinary Institute, where both studied.

California Burrito Co. 12 | 4 | 8 | $11
172 Seventh Ave. (bet. 20th & 21st Sts.), 212-727-7888 [S] 🚫
885 Ninth Ave. (bet. 57th & 58th Sts.), 212-977-8484 [S] 🚫
456 Hudson St. (bet. Barrow & Morton Sts.), 212-727-2626 ◐ [S] 🚫
1343 Second Ave. (bet. 70th & 71st Sts.), 212-288-2929 [S] 🚫
447 Sixth Ave. (bet. 10th & 11th Sts.), 212-647-0734 [S] 🚫

California Burrito Co. (Cont.)
1530 Third Ave. (bet. 86th & 87th Sts.), 212-987-6056 ◐ [S] ⇏
4 World Financial Ctr., 250 Vesey St., 212-233-6800
609 Second Ave. (bet. 33rd & 34th Sts.), 212-689-7280 [S] ⇏
◪ Burrito buffs battle over this Cal-Mex mini-chain: "fast", "filling", "fresh" and "flavorful" vs. "gives California a bad name"; "Speedy Gonzalez" delivery compensates for "zero" decor and "pathetic" teenage service; P.S. quality quesadillas too.

California Pizza Oven [S] ⇏ — 17 | 10 | 11 | $14
122 University Pl. (bet. 13th & 14th Sts.), 212-989-4225
◪ This Villager's "designer", thin-crust pizzas with a zillion "interesting" toppings are quite "good", even if "laid-back" West Coast service isn't.

Cal's [S] — 20 | 19 | 18 | $35
55 W. 21st St. (bet. 5th & 6th Aves.), 212-929-0740
◪ A handsome, "airy" setting plus an "original", "well-executed" menu (including one of the "best burgers" around) have won this Chelsea American a steady following; service glitches and highish prices turn some off, but to most it's a pure "pleasure."

Campagna ◐ [S] — – | – | – | E
24 E. 21st St. (bet. B'way & Park Ave. S.), 212-460-0900
At the heart of the jumping new Gramercy restaurant scene, chef Mark Strausman's (ex Coco Pazzo) unpretentious, warm and handsome new "flavorful country Italian" restaurant is so popular it makes one ask: "is anyone still eating on the Upper East Side?"

Campagnola ◐ [S] — 21 | 18 | 19 | $41
1382 First Ave. (bet. 73rd & 74th Sts.), 212-861-1102
◪ Regulars consider this East Side Italian standby "a joy", crowding in for "terrific antipasti" and other "carefully prepared" fare served in a "comfortable" setting by an "accommodating" staff; but to cynics it's "overpriced" for "nothing new."

Can [S] — 20 | 20 | 18 | $38
482 W. Broadway (Houston St.), 212-533-6333
◪ An "intriguing" fusion of French-Vietnamese cuisine in a "starkly" "pretty" SoHo setting makes for often "excellent" dining; but high prices and inconsistency lead critics to sigh: Can can't.

Canastel's ◐ [S] — 17 | 17 | 15 | $33
233 Park Ave. S. (19th St.), 212-677-9622
◪ The granddad of lower Park Avenue hot spots is, "like the Energizer bunny, still going strong" thanks to "better-than-average" Italian food, an attractive pastel, postmodern setting and lively ambiance.

Cantina ◐ [S] — 9 | 8 | 11 | $21
221 Columbus Ave. (70th St.), 212-873-2606
◪ The food may be "Mexican glop" that "peaks with the salsa" ("oh, the heartburn"), but low prices, potent margaritas and sidewalk views explain why this wilted Westsider is "still alive."

Canton [S] ⇏ — 24 | 11 | 20 | $32
45 Division St. (bet. Bowery & Market Sts.), 212-226-4441
■ For one of NY's best Chinese meals "simply order what the house suggests" and then enjoy "absolutely wonderful" Cantonese fare; prices are high for Chinatown, but the decor is "pleasant", the waiters "speak English" and owner Eileen "takes care of patrons."

F | D | S | C

Canyon Road ◑Ⓢ
20 | 18 | 16 | $28
1470 First Ave. (bet. 76th & 77th Sts.), 212-734-1600
■ There are "creative ideas at work" in the kitchen of this "upscale" East Side Southwestern, yielding "tasty" fare served in a setting resembling "Ralph Lauren's ranch"; affordable prices and "frozen drinks with a punch" help make it "perfect for the yuppie first date."

Capriccio
18 | 16 | 18 | $37
33 E. 61st St. (bet. Madison & Park Aves.), 212-759-6684
☑ Despite "good quality" food and a "nice garden room", many feel that this "pleasant" East Side Italian is "not special" and "overpriced."

CAPSOUTO FRÈRES Ⓢ
23 | 23 | 22 | $43
451 Washington St. (Watts St.), 212-966-4900
■ "Wonderful in every way", this "hidden" TriBeCa "treasure" rewards those who find it with "fine" French food, "caring" service and a "lovely", high-ceilinged, brick-walled setting; it's a delight from brunch to "romantic dinner" – just "get directions" first.

Captain's Table, The
19 | 15 | 17 | $39
860 Second Ave. (46th St.), 212-697-9538
☑ "Fish so fresh it almost flaps on your plate" is served amidst "kitschy" decor at this Midtowner where diners select their seafood from a display; some praise its "old-fashioned excellence", but critics harpoon its high prices.

Caribe Ⓢ
15 | 16 | 13 | $21
117 Perry St. (Greenwich St.), 212-255-9191
■ "A trip to Jamaica, minus sunburn", complete with "ear-splitting music", "knockout rum drinks", "cheap, spicy" grub and enough tropical vegetation to thrill Tarzan; so what if the food's not terrific, this "funky" Villager beats Prozac as a "mood-lifter."

Carino Ⓢ
20 | 11 | 18 | $28
1710 Second Ave. (bet. 88th & 89th Sts.), 212-860-0566
■ There's nothing slick about this East Side Italian: it's "tiny", "homey" and "family-run" with "hearty" Sicilian food "cooked by mama" and served with a "low price tag"; the "elbow-to-elbow" seating only adds to the feel of "eating at an Italian friend's house."

Carlyle Dining Room Ⓢ
24 | 27 | 25 | $54
The Carlyle Hotel, 35 E. 76th St. (Madison Ave.), 212-744-1600
■ Exhibiting "real class and style", this "civilized" hotel dining room is a "place of refuge" that's "always satisfying"; the French food isn't always inspired but it's "beautifully served" in one of NY's "most elegant" settings and the "sumptuous brunch" is hard to top; "heaven can wait, as long as this place is open."

CARMINE'S Ⓢ
18 | 14 | 16 | $25
2450 Broadway (bet. 90th & 91st Sts.), 212-362-2200
200 W. 44th St. (bet. B'way & 8th Ave.), 212-221-3800
☑ To best enjoy these wildly popular, family-style, pseudo-turn-of-the-century Southern Italians, "bring an army, Rolaids and earplugs", "arrive on Wednesday to be seated by Friday", "order half what you think you need", "stuff yourself silly", "wake up with a garlic hangover" and "eat leftovers for days"; there's no reserving for under six and critics call them "profoundly mediocre", but Roseanne would love 'em.

F	D	S	C

CARNEGIE DELI ◑ [S] 💳̸ 20 | 6 | 10 | $19

854 Seventh Ave. (bet. 54th & 55th Sts.), 212-757-2245

◪ "The deli of your dreams" and a "true NY experience": "rushed", "raucous" and Runyonesque with cramped seating and service from the "whaddyawant, slam, bang" school; but tourists and natives alike line up for its "awesome" hot pastrami and "jaw-stretcher" sandwiches.

Carnegie Hill Cafe [S] 17 | 11 | 13 | $23

1308 Madison Ave. (93rd St.), 212-534-7522

◪ A "quaint", little, "Europeanesque" Carnegie Hill cafe that's "a family favorite for light lunch" and for "fresh", "well-presented" food; service needs polish, but it's a "lunchtime bargain" and "a good place to hang out and read alone"; critics say "ok, but just ok."

Casa Di Pre [S] ▽ 14 | 11 | 16 | $24

283 W. 12th St. (4th St.), 212-243-7073

◪ "The old Village as it was in the '50s" lives on in this Northern Italian; to regulars it's a "soothing" "home away from home" with good, "simple" food, but to critics it has "seen its day."

Casa La Femme ◑ [S] 14 | 20 | 12 | $33

150 Wooster St. (bet. Houston & Prince Sts.), 212-505-0005

◪ When reviewers refer to this SoHo Mediterranean's "excellent surroundings", it's hard to tell if they mean its "sensuous" decor or the "models" everywhere; "don't go on a bad hair day" if you want to fit in and don't go hungry, since it's "the scene" that counts.

Casalone ◑ [S] 16 | 20 | 13 | $31

1675 Third Ave. (bet. 93rd & 94th Sts.), 212-369-1944

◪ "Go for the garden view" at this "pretty barn" of an Upper East Side Tuscan; the pizzas and pastas, though palatable, don't live up to the "lovely" setting and the staff should try "waiter's school"; the front of the restaurant has been made into a sports bar, no cause for optimism.

Casanis ◑ [S] ▽ 20 | 17 | 15 | $28

54 First St. (First Ave.), 212-777-1589

■ A bit of "offbeat Paris in offbeat NY" with "honest bistro food" and "great decor" that "transports you" out of the East Village and onto the Left Bank; it's "small and crowded", but the crowd includes lots of "artistic types" and there's a nice garden.

Cascabel 23 | 19 | 19 | $43

218 Lafayette St. (bet. Spring & Broome Sts.), 212-431-7300

■ A "winning newcomer", the Zaccaro (as in Geraldine Ferraro) family's SoHo American is even more "exciting" under new chef Tom Valenti (ex Alison); an "innovative" menu, "striking" red decor, "savvy" crowd and "personal" service make it a "scene" "restaurant for the '90s."

Castellano [S] 22 | 18 | 21 | $43

138 W. 55th St. (bet. 6th & 7th Aves.), 212-664-1975

■ Facing City Center, this "upscale" Venetian offers "well-prepared (if not well-priced) pasta", fish and meats in an "elegant but not stuffy" setting; though it's not well-known, "one often sees well-known faces here" enjoying the "refined" fare and service.

Castillo de Jagua [S] 💳̸ – | – | – | I

125 Avenue D (9th St.), 212-254-6150

"Good, cheap Spanish food and a loud jukebox" explain why there's "always a crowd" at this "wonderful old joint" in Alphabet City.

Caterina's
_ | _ | _ | M

213 E. 38th St. (bet. 2nd & 3rd Aves.), 212-922-3609

"Good goulash" and other Hungarian food "just like mom cooked" draw a "big lunch crowd" to this ethnic newcomer; decor and service are more East European than East Midtown but so are prices; still, critics say "from hunger, not Hungary."

Caviarteria S
_ | _ | _ | E

Delmonico Hotel, 502 Park Ave. (59th St.), 212-759-7410

This modern East Side caviar specialist has added a few tables in the shop to go with the black eggs and golden bubbles.

Cedars of Lebanon S
16 | 11 | 15 | $25

39 E. 30th St. (bet. Madison & Park Aves.), 212-679-6755

M – It's "undeniably shabby", but this Midtown Lebanese "old-timer" is still appreciated for its "bargain" lunch specials and "authentic" fare; you may even enjoy the weekend bands and belly dancing.

Cent'Anni S
24 | 15 | 20 | $40

50 Carmine St. (bet. Bleecker & Bedford Sts.), 212-989-9494

■ "A simple setting for superb Tuscan dining"; this "minor classic" in a Village storefront is small and "not cheap", but it's "honest, consistent, authentic, delicious and low-key", with "expert" service; surveyors "hope it's around for another 100 years."

Century Cafe ◑
17 | 14 | 15 | $29

132 W. 43rd St. (bet. 6th Ave. & B'way), 212-398-1988

☑ "Interesting food" at "reasonable prices" in an "unconventional" setting make this California-style grill a popular Theater District choice; the high-tech, "loftlike" space can be noisy and is "filled with B'way casts between shows."

Cesarina
21 | 19 | 19 | $39

36 W. 52nd St. (bet. 5th & 6th Aves.), 212-582-6900

■ "Coming into its own", this "classical" Midtown Northern Italian is "perfect for business lunch", preferably on an "expense account"; "fine food", "gracious service" (at least "for regulars") and "elegant" decor are appreciated.

Chantal Café
19 | 16 | 18 | $30

257 W. 55th St. (bet. B'way & 8th Ave.), 212-246-7076

■ A "petite" French bistro that's a "breath of fresh air" in an unlikely West Midtown location; "amiable, quiet and good" with a "pretty" skylit setting, it's "a bargain", especially for pre-B'way dinner.

Chantale's Cajun Kitchen ⇄
_ | _ | _ | I

510 Ninth Ave. (bet. 38th & 39th Sts.), 212-967-2623

"Cheap, good and filling" describes this "delightful down-home" Cajun; it's "not much to look at" but the food's "spicy", the folks are "friendly" and the tab's gentle; there's takeout, too.

CHANTERELLE
27 | 26 | 26 | $67

2 Harrison St. (bet. Hudson & Greenwich Sts.), 212-966-6960

■ Surveyors can't help but be "swept away" by Karen and David Waltuck's "exquisite" TriBeCa French; "everything is ethereal" from the "understated" space warmed by "amazing flowers" to the "absolutely gracious" service and "sublime" food; prices are equally stunning, but the prix fixe lunch helps make this "paradise" more attainable.

Chao Chow S ⇄
▽ 20 | 3 | 9 | $14

111 Mott St. (bet. Canal & Hester Sts.), 212-226-2590

■ Wonderful noodle soups win fans for this Chinatown dive – it sure isn't the dismal decor or service.

Charley O's S
9 | 9 | 10 | $24

*218 W. 45th St. (bet. B'way & 8th Ave.), 212-626-7300 *
761 Seventh Ave. (50th St.), 212-767-8348
☑ "Strictly for convenience" is the consensus on these "dark and dreary", "mock Irish" pubs; they're "not bad as an after-work beer hangout" or for a burger pre–Madison Square Garden, as long as you steer clear of the "steam table from hell."

Charlotte S
19 | 21 | 19 | $40

Hotel Macklowe, 145 W. 44th St. (bet. 6th & B'way), 212-789-7508
■ A "calm, spacious, comfortable" restaurant with "lovely service" and "very good" American food would be welcome anywhere, but it's a "true find" near Times Square; this "classy" room may be "on the expensive side", but the pre-theater special is a "good deal."

Charlton's S
▽ 23 | 21 | 23 | $41

922 Third Ave. (bet. 55th & 56th Sts.), 212-688-4646
■ "High-quality fresh fish", "nice atmosphere" and "good service" highlight this "casual" new Eastsider; steaks also earn favorable mention, as does the wine list.

Chat 'n' Chew S ⊅
17 | 13 | 12 | $18

10 E. 16th St. (bet. 5th Ave. & Union Sq. W.), 212-243-1616
☑ "Whopping portions" of "fattening", "heartland" food ("juicy turkey", "layer cake like Aunt Bea made") are served by a "perky" if "amnesiac" staff in this "rustic" new Union Square American; it's "cheap as hell", which is lucky since some "chat, chew, then spit out."

Chaz & Wilson Grill ● S
14 | 15 | 14 | $27

201 W. 79th St. (Amsterdam Ave.), 212-769-0100
☑ It still sees plenty of "night action", but this former singles mecca has "settled in as a reliable Upper West Side spot for good food and music" in "comfortable" surroundings; the basic American menu "isn't thrilling" but it's "very reasonable."

Chef Ho's S
20 | 12 | $16 | $22

1720 Second Ave. (bet. 89th & 90th Sts.), 212-348-9444
☑ "A cut above" the usual Chinese, serving "fresh, delicious" food in relatively classy, "comfortable" East Side digs; critics say it "ain't what it used to be", but you can still "feed the family on great dumplings for a pittance" and the "lunch menu is cheap and good."

Chelsea Clinton Cafe S
13 | 11 | 13 | $23

184 Eighth Ave. (bet. 19th & 20th Sts.), 212-989-5289
☑ Partisans call this Chelsea bistro a "sweet spot" that's "inexpensive and satisfying", but opponents say if the name's not a coincidence "the President's daughter should sue."

Chelsea Commons, The ● S
13 | 13 | 13 | $19

463 W. 24th St. (10th Ave.), 212-929-9424
■ There's nothing uncommon about the pub food, but this well-worn, "unassuming" Chelsea bar is a "good place for burgers and beer", especially by the fireplace or in the garden.

Chelsea Grill S
16 | 13 | 15 | $23

135 Eighth Ave. (bet. 16th & 17th Sts.), 212-929-9766
☑ "Huge burgers", "outrageous" waffle fries and other "decent" bar food draw big eaters with slim wallets to this Chelsea "neighborhood burger/beer joint"; critics say it's "only a notch above run-of-the-mill."

Chelsea Trattoria
20 16 18 $34
108 Eighth Ave. (bet. 15th & 16th Sts.), 212-924-7786
■ "You can count on this" Chelsea Northern Italian for "solid if unexceptional" food served in a "pleasant" brick-walled setting by a "professional" staff; if a few detractors find it "so-so" and "pricey for the neighborhood", they're far outvoted.

Chez Brigitte ⊭
16 7 15 $14
77 Greenwich Ave. (bet. Bank St. & 7th Ave.), 212-929-6736
■ "A lunch counter the way God intended", this "tiny" 12-stool Village "landmark" dispenses hearty French stews "that taste like they were made by someone's grandmother"; it's "charming" in a "dingy" sort of way and very "affordable."

Chez Jacqueline ⑤
20 17 18 $36
72 MacDougal St. (bet. W. Houston & Bleecker Sts.), 212-505-0727
■ Villagers appreciate this "relaxed", "reliable" bistro for its "solid", country French cooking, "unrushed" service and "comfortable" ambiance; "maybe not worth a detour", but it's sure nice to have around.

Chez Josephine ❶
18 19 18 $37
414 W. 42nd St. (bet. 9th & 10th Aves.), 212-594-1925
■ "The spirit of Josephine Baker lives on" in this "sexy" Theater District bistro, a tribute to the late singer by her son, Jean Claude ("the best host this side of Sirio"); the food's "not bad", but it's upstaged by the jazz piano, "colorful" French poster decor and amusing "side shows"; "Josephine must be smiling."

Chez Ma Tante ❶⑤
19 18 17 $34
189 W. 10th St. (bet. W. 4th & Bleecker Sts.), 212-620-0223
■ "Charming" if "somewhat claustrophobic", this tiny Village bistro has "very dependable" food, "friendly" service and a "genuine French feel"; it "won't break the bank" and the crowding is eased in summer when it opens onto the street for sidewalk dining.

Chez Michallet ⑤
23 21 22 $42
90 Bedford St. (Grove St.), 212-242-8309
■ On a pretty Village corner stands this "cozy" bistro with "delightful" country French food and "charming" service; "you need a shoehorn to get in, but it's worth it"; try the prix fixe for the "value of the century."

Chez Napoleon
18 12 18 $32
365 W. 50th St. (bet. 8th & 9th Aves.), 212-265-6980
■ "Time stands still" at this "homey" Theater District veteran; "your parents probably ate here" and enjoyed the same bistro fare served "sans" frills (or elbow room) at "reasonable" prices; calling the decor "quaint" is a polite way of saying "old."

Chiam ❶⑤
23 21 23 $37
160 E. 48th St. (bet. Lexington & 3rd Aves.), 212-371-2323
■ "A revelation in postmodern Chinese cuisine", this Midtowner wins raves for its "exceptional" food, "elegant" setting and "lovely" staff; with a Wine Spectator certified "excellent wine list" and dim sum that's unrivaled for "freshness and variety", it's a "truly special" experience.

Chicken Chef ❶⑤⊭
∇ 12 4 9 $10
1177 Second Ave. (62nd St.), 212-308-9400
■ "Good for emergency dining", this "cheerful" takeout joint "can't be beat for a quick chicken fix"; it's perfect for the "microwave generation" and costs chicken feed.

Chikubu ▽ 22 | 14 | 19 | $36

12 E. 44th St. (bet. 5th & Madison Aves.), 212-818-0715

■ The "sophisticated" Kyoto-style cuisine at this Grand Central–area Japanese "takes getting used to": it's "nuanced", so ask the staff or a native for advice; lunch is "very popular" (i.e. "rushed"), dinner quieter.

China Fun ◐ [S] 16 | 6 | 11 | $17

1239 Second Ave. (65th St.), 212-752-0810

246 Columbus Ave. (bet. 71st & 72nd Sts.), 212-580-1516

◪ "The name says it all": "big, noisy" East and West Side twins filled with loads of people slurping up "oodles of noodles", "satisfying soups" and other "quick", "fresh", "cheap" Chinese chow; the decor's "fast-foodish" and service minimal.

China Grill [S] 22 | 21 | 18 | $39

CBS Bldg., 52 W. 53rd St. (6th Ave.), 212-333-7788

◪ This International Midtowner may be "a little too '80s" (i.e. "loud", pricey and filled with "cellular phones"), but its "dazzling" food, "smashing decor" and "showy" crowd are "still exciting"; service might improve if the waiters didn't "carry pocket mirrors."

Chin Chin ◐ [S] 24 | 21 | 21 | $39

216 E. 49th St. (bet. 2nd & 3rd Aves.), 212-888-4555

■ Many people's choice for NY's "best Chinese" and understandably so: this "chic" Midtowner combines "inventive, wonderful" food with a "sophisticated", postmodern setting and "stellar" service; it's "first-class" all the way and "expensive, of course."

Chock Full o' Nuts [S] – | – | – | I

422 Madison Ave. (bet. 48th & 49th Sts.), 212-754-1222

1267 Second Ave. (66th St.), 212-794-2600

Back in business, this famous old coffee-and-sandwich shop chain is forging its own path in the current caffeine wave; it has updated its quick-eats-and-coffee formula to fit the '90s and is said to be "full of beans."

Choshi [S] 19 | 13 | 16 | $27

77 Irving Pl. (bet. Park & 3rd Aves.), 212-420-1419

■ "Swimmingly fresh sushi" and "interesting specials" at "moderate prices" make this a "great Gramercy value"; the room's simple but "pleasant" and service is "friendly" – you could almost call it a "Japanese with gemütlichkeit."

Christ Cella 22 | 13 | 17 | $50

160 E. 46th St. (bet. Lexington & 3rd Aves.), 212-697-2479

◪ Opinion on this "old-school" Midtown steakhouse runs the gamut from "tip-top", "no-nonsense", "one of the best" to "boorish", "ugly", "an expensive joke"; most agree that the meat is high quality, but it's the "zilch" masculine decor, "gruff" attitude and high tab that many find hard to swallow.

Christer's 23 | 22 | 20 | $43

145 W. 55th St. (bet. 6th & 7th Aves.), 212-974-7224

■ A "bright new star" in Midtown, this "exciting" Scandinavian is "a delightful surprise" with a menu that's a virtual "dreamscape of salmon" and a "lovely", "witty" lodgelike setting ("L.L. Bean on acid"); service "could be better", but it's one of last year's most "exciting" entries.

Christine's [S] 14 | 5 | 11 | $16

462 Second Ave. (26th St.), 212-779-2220
208 First Ave. (bet. 12th & 13th Sts.), 212-254-2474 🚫

■ You can fill up on soups, blintzes, pierogies, kielbasas and other "rib-sticking" fare at this mini-chain of plain Polish coffee shops and all it will cost is a few dollars and a case of "clogged arteries"; just "don't look at the walls" or expect much service.

Christo's Steak House ◐ [S] 19 | 15 | 18 | $40

Doral Inn, 541 Lexington Ave. (bet. 49th & 50th Sts.), 212-355-2695

◪ Though not a steakhouse major leaguer, this Midtown Eastsider is a "good" pinch-hitter and the only game in town late at night; steaks and service both score well, but it's a "bit downscale for an upscale place."

Chumley's [S] 🚫 – | – | – | M

86 Bedford St. (Barrow St.), 212-675-4449

Opened in 1923 as a speakeasy, this West Village "great old bar" still seems to be hiding out, but its beer and pub grub are no secret to locals.

Churchill's ◐ [S] 10 | 10 | 13 | $25

1277 Third Ave. (73rd St.), 212-650-1618

◪ The food's "not the greatest", but this "warm, neighborly" East Side pub is "relaxed" and "open late", making it a "welcome refuge."

Chutney Mary [S] – | – | – | M

40 E. 20th St. (bet. B'way & Park Ave.), 212-473-8181

Brand-new "organic Indian" in attractive, modern duplex, un-Indianlike quarters; in sum, it's an interesting change of pace.

Ciao Europa ◐ [S] ▽ 21 | 21 | 21 | $39

63 W. 54th St. (bet. 5th & 6th Aves.), 212-247-1200

■ "Pasta at its best" and some of the "best tarts in town" win admirers for this Midtown Italian; it has a "pleasant, relaxed" "European feel" and "attentive" service.

Ciccio & Tony's [S] 16 | 16 | 14 | $26

320 Amsterdam Ave. (75th St.), 212-595-0500

◪ "Everything looks good" at this "airy", mural-filled West Side Tuscan (including the crowd), but whether it tastes good is up for debate; still, most like its "lusty pastas", "lively" ambiance and neighborly prices, even if critics call it a loud, "theme-park Italian."

Cinquanta ◐ [S] 20 | 19 | 20 | $42

50 E. 50th St. (bet. Park & Madison Aves.), 212-759-5050

◪ Most consider this Italian a "solid choice" in Midtown, even if it is "somewhat expensive for very good, but not great food"; "super-friendly service" and attractive quarters help tilt the balance in its favor.

Cité and Cité Grille ◐ [S] 20 | 20 | 19 | $41

120 W. 51st St. (bet. 6th & 7th Aves.), 212-956-7100

◪ "Steadily improving", this "pretty" if rather "slick" Midtowner's strengths include "solid" steaks, "great frites" and "efficient" service, but it really hit on an "inspired idea" with its prix fixe dinners including fine wines (a "best buy"); it's roomy and "handy" for theatergoers, and the adjoining, more casual grill offers much the same quality at lower prices.

City Bakery, The 19 | 13 | 13 | $14

Sony Plaza, 550 Madison Ave. (bet. 55th & 56th Sts.), 212-833-8020
22 E. 17th St. (bet. B'way & 5th Ave.), 212-366-1414

◪ "Fabulous ingredients plus imagination" go into the "knockout" pastries, breads and light lunch fare at this "hip" Union Square–area bakery and its Midtown sibling; most find them "tasty" and "fresh", but critics say high prices and "sterile" decor "dilute the ecstasy."

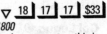

City Crab & Seafood Co. ◐ [S] — 18 | 16 | 15 | $33

235 Park Ave. S. (19th St.), 212-529-3800

In Cafe Iguana's former berth, this fish house "isn't Baltimore" but it's "lively" and "huge" with "great crabs" and other "fresh", affordable seafood; critics crab about "confused" service and "uneven" quality.

City Grill — ▽ 18 | 17 | 17 | $33

23 W. 39th St. (bet. 5th & 6th Aves.), 212-764-1800

"The Garment Center desperately needs good restaurants – this is not the answer" say surveyors of this "unimaginative" new Continental grill; but despite mostly negative comments it gets decent ratings, suggesting that it's worth another look especially as it occupies the handsomely renovated quarters of what was once Lavin's.

Ci Vedeamo ◐ [S] — 20 | 16 | 18 | $23

85 Avenue A (bet. 5th & 6th Sts.), 212-995-5300

Cheap and "cheerful" with "surprisingly good" food, this below-ground East Village Italian recently expanded into a "humongous" St. Marks Square–size new dining room, which should ease "long waits."

Claire ◐ [S] — 17 | 15 | 15 | $30

156 Seventh Ave. (bet. 19th & 20th Sts.), 212-255-1955

"A shot of the tropics" in Chelsea that evokes Key West with "fresh, varied" seafood, "sublime Key lime pie" and "colorful" decor; it's a "big gay date spot but all feel welcome"; if some call it "tired", others say it's "even more appealing" with new lower prices.

Clarke's, P.J. ◐ [S] — 13 | 13 | 11 | $23

915 Third Ave. (55th St.), 212-759-1650

Many NYers have "a soft spot in their hearts" (and their livers) for this "landmark" 1890 saloon; it may be "dingy" with "overpriced little burgers" and "classic surly bartenders", but it's "Midtown's premier spot for an after-work pop" or a late-night prowl.

Cleopatra's Needle ◐ [S] — 13 | 10 | 12 | $21

2485 Broadway (92nd St.), 212-769-6969

"If the food were as good as the live jazz, what a place!"; as it is, this Upper Westsider's Middle Eastern–Continental menu is "different" but "not always successful", though the couscous, falafel and sweets are good bets and cheap.

Cloister Cafe, The ◐ [S] ≠ — 9 | 21 | 9 | $18

238 E. 9th St. (bet. 2nd & 3rd Aves.), 212-777-9128

This East Villager can be summed up in four words: "bad food, beautiful garden"; "stick to coffee" and avoid the rest of the French-Italian menu; service is "inept but friendly."

Coconut Grill ◐ [S] — 15 | 13 | 13 | $25

1481 Second Ave. (77th St.), 212-772-6262

Though some would "leave it to the monkeys", this Eastsider is a popular "local hangout" with "great" summer sidewalk seating and a "good bar" for "twentysomethings"; the American menu is "decent" and reasonable but "nothing stands out", except maybe brunch.

Coco Pazzo ◐ [S] — 22 | 21 | 19 | $49

23 E. 74th St. (Madison Ave.), 212-794-0205

Despite debate over the new chef, this East Side Northern Italian remains a "sizzling", "star-gazing" scene, with "lusty" fare and "lots of energy"; but not everyone's pazzo about it: "snotty", "exorbitant."

| | | | F | D | S | C |

Coffee Shop ◑Ⓢ
14 | 12 | 10 | $24
29 Union Sq. W. (16th St.), 212-243-7969

☑ "Pseudo Brazilian" food is "served by and to" model wanna-bes at this "off-tilt", "very cool" Union Square scene; "flaky service", "massive attitude" and "acoustic trauma" are part of the package; for best results, "bring your shades, sit outside and strike a pose."

Col Legno ◑Ⓢ
18 | 11 | 13 | $28
231 E. 9th St. (bet. 2nd & 3rd Aves.), 212-777-4650

■ "A simple Tuscan pleasure" with "excellent coal-oven pizza", "decent" pastas and grill food; this East Village "sleeper" has a "spare" but "comfortable" setting and modest prices, but some think the alternately "surly" and "doleful" servers "need Prozac."

Coming Or Going
20 | 15 | 18 | $27
38 E. 58th St. (bet. Madison & Park Aves.), 212-980-5858

■ "Coming here feels like you're going elsewhere – Vermont, perhaps" thanks to its "cute-as-a-bug's-ear" decor and "warm" attitude; "very good" American-Mediterranean food is also why this Midtowner is "a godsend" for the area.

Conservatory Ⓢ
12 | 14 | 14 | $31
Mayflower Hotel, 15 Central Park W. (61st St.), 212-265-0060

☑ "Stodgy but convenient", this "old-fashioned" hotel cafe makes up for "pedestrian" Eclectic food with long hours (breakfast through late-night) and a "nice location."

Contrapunto ◑Ⓢ
18 | 13 | 15 | $30
200 E. 60th St. (3rd Ave.), 212-751-8616

☑ It can be a "madhouse", but this "cheerful" mezzanine Italian across from Bloomies revives shoppers and local moviegoers with "terrific" pastas that most feel are worth the "hike upstairs", "tight quarters" and "sneakily expensive" tab.

Cooking With Jazz (Queens) Ⓢ
– | – | – | M
12-01 154th St. (12th Ave.), 718-767-4647

The cooking's jazzy indeed at this Cajun newcomer in Whitestone: "big portions, big flavors, moderate prices" and a "staff aiming to please" make it "worth the trip" even if it is a bit "cramped."

Cooper's Coffee Bar Ⓢ ⇗
– | – | – | I
2151 Broadway (bet. 75th & 76th Sts.), 212-496-0100
159 Columbus Ave. (67th St.), 212-362-0100
2315 Broadway (84th St.), 212-724-0300

Part of the coffee craze "perking up" NYC, these West Side coffee bars are good for a quick snack and socializing only.

Copeland's Ⓢ
▽ 20 | 12 | 17 | $23
547 W. 145th St. (bet. B'way & Amsterdam), 212-234-2357

☑ Soul Food enthusiasts give solid marks to this Harlem kitchen where modest prices and a good jukebox add appeal, and the Southern breakfasts and brunches are sure bets; still, some say there's "not enough down-home flavor."

Cornelia Street Cafe ◑Ⓢ
16 | 15 | 15 | $24
29 Cornelia St. (bet. Bleecker & W. 4th Sts.), 212-989-9319

■ The kind of "West Village hangout" you don't often find these days: "laid-back and cozy" with "simple" American-French food and "friendly service"; it's especially "pleasant" for a "leisurely brunch" or summer sidewalk dining on a "quiet side street."

F	D	S	C

Corner Bistro ◐ [S] ≠ | 18 | 10 | 9 | $14 |

331 W. 4th St. (Jane St.), 212-242-9502
■ The "perfect dive", this "old Village haunt" is renowned for its "awesome" burgers – "huge" and "so messy you need a towel"; good fries, cold beer and a "great jukebox" are further pluses; it's "musty and dark", but "you wouldn't want to see it in bright light."

Corrado ◐ [S] | 21 | 16 | 17 | $34 |

1373 Sixth Ave. (bet. 55th & 56th Sts.), 212-333-3133
1013 Third Ave. (bet. 60th & 61st Sts.), 212-753-5100
■ This "refreshing" Midtown Italian serves "gigantic" portions of "very satisfying" food at "honest" prices; it's a "perfect" pasta pit stop pre–Carnegie Hall or City Center, albeit "noisy" and crowded; there's "great takeout", too and a simpler sibling cafe/espresso bar for quick snacking on Third Avenue.

Cotton Club [S] | – | – | – | M |

656 W. 125th St. (bet. B'way & Riverside Dr.), 212-663-7980
"A legend, what more can we say?" – only that this Harlem institution is "always dependable" for "typical Southern" food and "a hoot for Sunday gospel brunch"; but it "needs more crowds."

Cottonwood Cafe ◐ [S] | 15 | 10 | 13 | $20 |

415 Bleecker St. (bet. W. 11th & Bank Sts.), 212-924-6271
◪ "The food sticks to your ribs and everything else" at this "down-home and deep-fried" West Village Tex-Mex, where the young and "rowdy" line up to enjoy "cheap" "cholesterol highs"; critics shout "lighten the food, lower the music."

Country Club | 11 | 17 | 13 | $34 |

210 E. 86th St. (bet. 2nd & 3rd Aves.), 212-879-8400
◪ "Dance a little harder" and you won't notice that the Italian-American food served at this East Side supper club is "uninspired" and "kind of pricey"; there's "lots of room" for "ballroom dancing followed by late-night disco"; "great for celebrations."

Court of the Three Sisters, The [S] | 18 | 16 | 16 | $37 |

157 E. 55th St. (bet. Lexington & 3rd Aves.), 212-832-5865
◪ Perhaps "not a standout, but nice", this East Side "sleeper" has a "creative, well-thought-out" Italian menu, a "pretty", "low-key" setting and "a piano bar to boot"; still, some find it "uneven" and "overpriced."

Courtyard Cafe [S] | 15 | 19 | 15 | $33 |

Doral Court Hotel, 130 E. 39th St. (Lexington Ave.), 212-779-0739
■ What raises this Murray Hill dining room from "average" to "delightful" is its "lovely" courtyard garden, a "pleasant" setting for "low-key breakfasts" and relaxed business lunches over "not inspired but likable" grill food.

Cowgirl Hall of Fame ◐ [S] **(94)** | 14 | 18 | 14 | $21 |

519 Hudson St. (10th St.), 212-633-1133
◪ West Village Southern and Tex-Mex restaurant–cum–curiosity shop with a cowgirl theme that will never make it to the hall of fame, but knows how "to throw a rowdy party."

C.T. | – | – | – | VE |

111 E. 22nd St. (bet. Park Ave. S. & Lexington Aves.), 212-995-8500
Claude Troisgros, of the renowned Roanne restaurant family, "has arrived" in NY after a 10-year stint in Brazil; although the modern space and open kitchen are a bit hard-edged, Troisgros' Brazilian-accented French food deserves to be tasted by any serious foodie.

C3 S
103 Waverly Pl. (McDougal St.), 212-254-1200
■ A "charming Village" American bistro with an "experimental" bent—some dishes are "very good", some "weird", but it's always "relaxing" and "reasonable" with a simple but "pleasant" below-street-level setting and solicitous service.

Cub Room ◑
131 Sullivan St. (Prince St.), 212-677-4100
Cub Room Cafe
183 Prince St. (Sullivan St.), 212-777-0030 S
Named after the inner sanctum of The Stork Club, this stylish new SoHo bar/cafe/restaurant is entertaining a new generation of young see-and-be-seeners; chef Henry Meer (ex Lutece) is producing New American food that's reported to be very good indeed; there are three separate rooms, a low-key, modestly priced cafe, an elegant, pricier main dining room in back and a barroom that's steaming.

CUCINA (Brooklyn) S   25 | 21 | 21 | $33
256 Fifth Ave. (bet. Garfield Pl. & Carroll St.), 718-230-0711
■ A "boon for Brooklyn", this "impressive" Northern Italian turns out "dazzling" antipasti, "heavenly pasta" and other "A-plus" fare that "would be twice the price in Manhattan"; "classy yet unpretentious", its main fault is that it's "getting too popular."

Cucina & Co.   16 | 12 | 13 | $21
MetLife Bldg., 200 Park Ave. (45th St.), 212-682-2700
☑ Often "more hectic than neighboring Grand Central Station", this "cute" cafe "serves a purpose when you're on the run" with Italian-accented "upscale fast food" at "modest" prices; even those who call it "average" admit you "can't beat the $20 dinner for two."

Cucina della Fontana ◑ S ⇄   15 | 18 | 14 | $20
368 Bleecker St. (Charles St.), 212-242-0636
☑ "Bargain" Village Italian with a "rambling" setting and indoor grotto room; it strikes some as "tasty", "romantic" and "friendly", others as "bland", "tacky" and "apathetic"; one theory holds that "the busier it gets, the worse the food", so go at off-hours.

Cucina di Pesce ◑ S ⇄   18 | 12 | 13 | $21
87 E. 4th St. (bet. 2nd & 3rd Aves.), 212-260-6800
☑ "Eternal waits" (eased by "free mussels") are an obligatory appetizer at this "funky", "overly crowded" East Villager; the lines are due to "low, low prices" for good Italian seafood and pasta, but some feel it's no bargain for a "loud", "rushed" meal.

Cucina Stagionale ◑ S ⇄   17 | 11 | 13 | $19
275 Bleecker St. (bet. 6th & 7th Aves.), 212-924-2707
■ The long line is "good for making new friends", and if you "survive the wait" there's "enjoyable" Tuscan fare that's "cheap as hell" at this BYO West Villager; the room's as "tiny" as the tab.

Cuisine de Saigon S   19 | 12 | 17 | $24
154 W. 13th St. (bet. 6th & 7th Aves.), 212-255-6003
☑ "One of the city's first Vietnamese" is still "one of the best" according to admirers of this West Villager's "varied" cuisine and "very attentive" service; ambiance is "lacking", but it's "tranquil" and "well-priced."

At top right: F | D | S | C

For C3: ▽ 18 | 15 | 16 | $25

For Cub Room: – | – | – | E

Cupcake Cafe ⓈＣ 19 | 6 | 10 | $12
522 Ninth Ave. (39th St.), 212-465-1530
■ "Don't be put off by its appearance" or the "Beirut"-like locale: this "tiny", "dingy" West Side "dive" has good home cooking and, better yet, "out-of-this-world" donuts, pies and cakes that are "too pretty to eat, but too good not to"; both service and prices are "rock-bottom."

Cupping Room Cafe ◑Ⓢ 16 | 15 | 13 | $21
359 W. Broadway (bet. Broome & Grand Sts.), 212-925-2898
☑ There's a "major Sunday brunch crunch" at this "airy", "warm" SoHo American, but it's also well-liked for other meals thanks to the "varied menu", "big portions", "reasonable" prices and "calm" ambiance; on the other hand, critics find it "pedestrian."

Dakota Bar & Grill ◑Ⓢ 14 | 14 | 13 | $26
1576 Third Ave. (bet. 88th & 89th Sts.), 212-427-8889
☑ Very loud, "'80s attitude", Upper East Side, yuppie meet-market bar scene that's "pure fromage" – "all trend, little substance"; it's "nothing special in the food" department, but quite "decent" when the company includes the "most beautiful women in the world."

Dallas BBQ ◑Ⓢ 13 | 7 | 11 | $16
1265 Third Ave. (72rd St.), 212-772-9393
27 W. 72nd St. (bet. CPW & Columbus Ave.), 212-873-2004
21 University Pl. (Washinton Sq. Pk.), 212-674-4450
132 Second Ave. (St. Marks Pl.), 212-777-5574
■ "Cheap" and "greasy", "the Big Apple's answer to Lone Star fare" includes "mass-produced" "hefty portions", "fishbowl margaritas" and "20-oz. Texas-size beer"; a "step above KFC", "perfect for the kids" and "a big bargain", but "anyone who thinks this is real Dallas BBQ probably thinks Spam is Roanoke ham."

Danal Ⓢ 20 | 20 | 17 | $25
90 E. Tenth St. (bet. 3rd & 4th Aves.), 212-982-6930
■ "Great" Village French bistro with "charming" "country atmosphere and country prices", that's like "going to a friend's home for dinner" except for "distracted service"; it's a "romantic" "rainy day place" for a "wonderful" brunch or high tea.

Da Nico Ⓢ ▽ 19 | 14 | 17 | $25
164 Mulberry St. (bet. Broome & Grand Sts.), 212-343-1212
■ A new contender for Little Italy – "upbeat" and "airy" with "fantastic" brick-oven pizza; fans say it has "the best pizza in NY – Italian without red sauce", and there's also a full menu plus rotisserie-cooked meats and fish.

DANIEL (aka Restaurant Daniel) 27 | 25 | 23 | $66

20 E. 76th St. (bet. 5th & Madison Aves.), 212-288-0033
☑ Our reviewers rave that "chef Daniel Boulud is an impressionist painter with food" (some say "Michelangelo with a mixing spoon") who, by general agreement, produces "orgasmic" French fare for his "well-heeled" Upper East Side clientele; however, they also feel that a certain "magic" is missing and that a meal in these "elegant" quarters can be marred by "indifferent service" and "crowding."

Danny's Grand Sea Palace ◑Ⓢ ▽ 15 | 12 | 14 | $37
346-348 W. 48th St. (bet. 8th & 9th Aves.), 212-265-8130
☑ An odd choice for the Theater District; strange multicultural fare – French, Thai and American – in a "skylight room"; it's "consistent" and "fun", but there's a shorter wait for a new nation to get into the U.N.

Darbar ⬛
21 19 19 $35

44 W. 56th St. (bet. 5th & 6th Aves.), 212-432-7227

⬛ "Bombay on the Hudson"; this elegant (some say "stiff") Midtowner serves "fine Indian chow" that's "second only to Dawat", and big eaters "achieve nirvana" over the $13.95 all-you-can-eat buffet lunch; "they get you on the price of drinks", but the sitar calms most critics.

Da Rosina ◐⬛
_ _ _ M

342 W. 46th St. (bet. 8th & 9th Aves.), 212-977-7373

Crowded Theater District place with "canned red sauce" and "pre-heated dinner"; typical comments include "ok" and "my parents loved it"; the waiters are too busy finding inspiration to refill water glasses.

Da Silvano ◐⬛
21 17 19 $41

260 Sixth Ave. (bet. Bleecker & Houston Sts.), 212-982-2343

⬛ Lively, longstanding Village Tuscan favorite that's touted for its game dishes, veal chop and "outside tables for summer"; detractors say it's "never quite as good as one hopes" and you get "second-class" treatment unless you're a regular.

Da Tommaso ◐⬛
20 14 19 $36

903 Eighth Ave. (bet. 53rd & 54th Sts.), 212-265-1890

⬛ A "very old-world" Italian "family restaurant" that's a perfect pre-theater stop with "great pastas" and "portobello mushrooms a must"; both fans and critics say it's "a bit tacky" and has a poor location, but it's "dependable" and a "good value."

DA UMBERTO
25 19 22 $47

107 W. 17th St. (bet. 6th & 7th Aves.), 212-989-0303

⬛ "Inventive" Tuscan that's a "treasure" and an "exuberant" "happening"; admirers rave about the "best antipasti outside Florence" and the "best tiramisu in NYC"; it's a crowded, "noisy" "neighborhood place" with "cheeky, seasoned waiters" that's "family run with family pride"; who needs to go to Italy?

DAWAT ⬛
24 19 20 $36

210 E. 58th St. (bet. 2nd & 3rd Aves.), 212-355-7555

⬛ "Gourmet Indian", "spices you didn't think possible" and, in short, "the finest Indian money can buy"; it's "elegant", "divine" and probably what Columbus was looking for; critics claim it's "overpriced" and "impersonal", but even they admit it's a "hip place."

Dazies (Queens) ⬛
▽ 20 17 19 $29

39-41 Queens Blvd. (40th St.), 718-786-7013

⬛ Recently refurbished, "long-running" Queens Italian where the food is "zippy", "tasty" and the setting "attractive", albeit a "little dark"; it's worth the trip just to meet Lilly, "the hostess with the mostess."

DeGrezia
23 22 23 $44

231 E. 50th St. (bet. 2nd & 3rd Aves.), 212-750-5353

⬛ "Somehow not discovered", this good, "old-fashioned", classy Northern Italian "attracts an older set for business lunch" and for being "fussed over"; it's a joy to listen to the waiters describe the daily specials, at least until they tell you the prices.

Delia's Supper Club ◐
▽ 15 21 15 $32

197 E. Third St. (bet. Avenues A & B), 212-254-9184

⬛ Lower East Side supper club with "red velvet and gold candelabras" all over the "happening" place, most go for the nightlife and "great dancing", and despite modest food ratings regulars report they "have never had a bad meal here."

Demarchelier ◐ §
16 | 16 | 15 | $37
50 E. 86th St. (Madison Ave.), 212-249-6300
■ "Uneven" East Side "neighborhood" French bistro that's handy for "lunch near the Met"; the menu is "NY interpreted", but "just like in Paris the waiters ignore you" and it's "smoky" and "noisy."

Demi §
20 | 18 | 20 | $41
1316 Madison Ave. (93rd St.), 212-534-3475
◪ "A sleeper", this Carnegie Hill Continental yearling in a "pleasant townhouse setting" divides our surveyors: fans call it "understated", "cozy", with "good food"; foes say the kitchen "tries too hard to be gourmet" and service "has gone to hell."

Dish §
16 | 16 | 15 | $28
100 W. 82nd St. (Columbus Ave.), 212-724-8700
◪ With a "great-looking crowd and staff" outshining "not-so-great", "health-conscious" Californian-Mediterranean food and "minimalist industrial decor", this "bit of TriBeCa on the Upper West Side" gets "dissed" as "disorganized" and "bland", but "a few pitchers of sangria make the meal a lot better."

Dish of Salt ◐
20 | 20 | 19 | $35
133 W. 47th St. (bet. 6th & 7th Aves.), 212-921-4242
◪ Most customers agree that this "pre-theater Chinese" boasts "beautiful surroundings" and a "wonderful piano", and some even claim it's the "best in town"; however, critics carp that it's "overpriced", "antiseptic", "corporate" and "about as Chinese as tacos."

Diva ◐ §
▽ 18 | 18 | 14 | $31
341 W. Broadway (bet. Broome & Grand Sts.), 212-941-9024
◪ A "real scene" in SoHo with a "sexy red" setting, "nice pasta dishes" and brunch; fans cite "beautiful" people on both sides of the bar, and insist that, despite "ungodly service", "it's the best of its genre"; critics counter "overrated, overcrowded, over nothing."

Divan Kebab House ◐ §
– | – | – | M
102 MacDougal St. (Bleecker St.), 212-598-9789
"Great lamb" and some reviewers' pick as "best shish kebab in NYC"; it also has a "beautiful breakfast", but it's the finger-dirtying kebab experience that makes the trip, though it leaves the querulous questioning "how does it stay in biz with such marginal quality?"

Divino ◐ §
18 | 14 | 17 | $33
1556 Second Ave. (bet. 80th & 81st Sts.), 212-861-1096
■ "An old favorite" for East Side Italian "neighborhood dining" with a choice of three physically separate storefronts: "fancy", "family" and "funky"; though you can "eat like a king and pay like a pauper", we hear reports it's "declining."

Diwan Grill §
▽ 23 | 20 | 21 | $30
148 E. 48th St. (bet. Lexington & 3rd Aves.), 212-593-5425
■ "Definitely a comer" with a "top-notch" bargain buffet lunch; with comments ranging from "promising" to "divine", you should give this "romantic" Indian "hideaway" a try.

Dix et Sept ◐ §
20 | 17 | 18 | $35
181 W. 10th St. (7th Ave.), 212-645-8023
◪ "Very French", "very gay", "very good" is how admirers sum up this West Village bistro; however, doubters say it has gone "down since being reviewed in *The Times*" and is "not le vrai français."

DOCKS OYSTER BAR 🆂
21 17 17 $36

633 Third Ave. (40th St.), 212-986-8080
2427 Broadway (89th St.), 212-724-5588

☑ "Go fish" – immensely popular, "congenial", "feisty" seafood duo, operating out of Midtown and the Upper West Side; "always fresh" and "amazingly good" can translate into "amazingly loud"; the "catch of the day" may refer to one's success at the bar.

Dojo ●🆂⊄
13 7 11 $13

14 W. 4th St. (bet. B'way & Mercer Sts.), 212-505-8934
24-26 St. Marks Pl. (bet. 2nd & 3rd Aves.), 212-674-9821

■ You "can't beat the prices" for the veggie burgers and "healthy diner fare" at these NYU-area twins; they may be "grungy" and "packed with college students", but for "cheap", fast, "healthy" (e.g. "brown rice and veggies") it does the trick.

Dok Suni 🆂⊄
▽ 18 11 16 $20

119 First Ave. (bet. 7th & 8th Sts.), 212-447-9506

☑ "Don't let the hipsters scare you away" from this "funky East Village joint"; the "tasty", "authentic Korean home cooking" is "inexpensive" and "good for groups to share and cook at the table."

Dolce
18 19 17 $35

60 E. 49th St. (bet. Madison & Park Aves.), 212-692-9292

☑ Midtown Italian boasting "comfortable armchairs" and "beautiful lighting" that's "an 'up' place for pasta" and "a favorite lunch spot"; critics say despite a "great location", both "food and service don't cut it" and overall the place "lacks charm and spark."

Dolcetto 🆂
20 16 18 $32

1378 Third Ave. (bet. 78th & 79th Sts.), 212-472-8300

☑ "Sweet a go-go" in a "zippy neighborhood", this East Side Italian with a "cheap and good early-bird menu" does a "huge pre-theater dinner"; at other hours it's a "great hangout" that "pleases trendoids and old-time locals, no easy task."

Dominick's (Bronx) 🆂⊄
22 7 14 $27

2335 Arthur Ave. (bet. 187th and 188th Sts.), 718-733-2807

■ "Bring 12 friends and an empty stomach" to this Bronx "family-style" Southern Italian; it's a "happy place" with "no menus, no bills, no frills" and "monstrous servings" where amazingly "everything always comes to $42"; "everyone should go at least once a year", but no reserving means "come early or late, or stand and wait."

Donald Sacks 🆂
15 12 12 $22

World Financial Ctr., 220 Vesey St. (West St.), 212-619-4600

☑ "Best for lunch specials" of soups, salads, pastas and "pseudo-clever sandwiches", DS is a "business lunch standby" for the WFC crowd; detractors say it's "an overpriced Burke & Burke."

Don Giovanni ●🆂
– – – I

214 Tenth Ave. (bet. 22nd & 23rd Sts.), 212-242-9054

A range of tasty brick-oven pizzas keynote this busy West Chelsea Italian, which also has pastas and omelets with pizza toppings; ample sidewalk tables give its neighbor, Empire Diner, a run for its trade.

Dosanko 🆂⊄
12 5 10 $13

423 Madison Ave. (bet. 48th & 49th Sts.), 212-688-8575
217 E. 59th St. (bet. 2nd & 3rd Aves.), 212-752-3936

☑ "Filling", "fast" and cheap, these "cafeteria-style", "Japanese McDonald's" are best for a good hot soup, dumplings or "slurping noodles" "on a cold day"; but don't expect a smile with your meal.

Dragon Village (Queens) 🅂
135-20 40th Rd. (bet. Main & Prince Sts.), Flushing, 718-762-1717
Located in Flushing's Chinatown, this attractive modern newcomer
boasts a former top chef from Shun Lee who's specializing in Shanghai
cuisine best enjoyed by a crowd on a budget.

Duane Park Cafe
23 | 18 | 21 | $40
157 Duane St. (bet. W. B'way & Hudson St.), 212-732-5555
■ "TriBeCa's outstanding midpriced restaurant" is "an undiscovered
star" that reaches its zenith with "wonderful wine dinners"; the
kitchen's "clever blend of Asian and French styles" at "sane prices"
sparkles in a "peaceful" understated setting.

Due ◑🅂🗗
19 | 16 | 17 | $32
1396 Third Ave. (bet. 79th & 80th Sts.), 212-772-3331
■ Upper East Side Italian that's "not too jazzed up"; it's an "intimate",
rose-colored place where waiters "actually speak Italian" and there's
"beautiful background music" well-suited to an evening of "pasta,
pasta and more pasta."

Ear Inn ◑🅂
13 | 14 | 13 | $17
326 Spring St. (bet. Washington & Greenwich Sts.), 212-226-9060
☑ Locals love this Holland Tunnel hangout that "could be right out of
The Iceman Cometh" with its "funky, wear-your-bathrobe" ambiance
and "surprisingly good pub food"; they warm up to the "very good
value" and cool off with the "best draft Guinness in town"; dissenters
think "it's time for a change in cobwebs."

East 🅂
18 | 12 | 14 | $24
1420 Third Ave. (bet. 80th & 81st Sts.), 212-472-3975 ◑
251 W. 55th St. (bet. B'way & 8th Ave.), 212-581-2240
210 E. 44th St. (bet. 2nd & 3rd Aves.), 212-687-5075
366 Third Ave. (bet. 26th & 27th Sts.), 212-889-2326
354 E. 66th St. (bet. 1st & 2nd Aves.), 212-734-5270
9 E. 38th St. (bet. 5th & Madison Aves.), 212-685-5205
137 E. 47th St. (bet. 3rd & Lexington Aves.), 212-980-7909
■ Westerners go to these "soooo busy" Japanese chain outposts for
almost "always fresh", "above average" ("depending on location")
sushi at "reasonable rates", not the "unexciting", pseudo settings;
"wear good socks since everyone will see them."

Eastern Seafood Co. 🅂
16 | 18 | 14 | $30
212 W. 79th St. (bet. B'way & Amsterdam Ave.), 212-595-5007
☑ A new West Side fish house with a "luncheonette" ambiance;
some like the "fresh fish" and think it's "like a trip to the Hamptons",
others say "overpriced" and "dingy" with "indifferent service."

East River Cafe
– | – | – | M
1111 First Ave. (61st St.), 212-980-3171
Better than eating at home and possibly less expensive, this low-key,
attractive Far East Side Italo-Continental looks like a good bet for a
pleasant meal in the 'hood; there's jazz Wednesday– Saturday nights.

E.A.T. 🅂
21 | 10 | 12 | $31
1064 Madison Ave. (bet. 80th & 81st Sts.), 212-772-0022
■ "Always crowded" Upper East Side über-deli with super soups,
salads and sandwiches on "the best breads in the world"; it's all, as
they say, "to die for, and you may when you get the bill!"

F | D | S | C

Ecco
`22 | 18 | 19 | $37`
124 Chambers (bet. W. B'way & Church St.), 212-227-7074
■ Wall Streeters throng to this "hearty" Italian Downtown "1900s saloon room" for its "great antipasti", hearty pastas and "friendly service"; come for power lunch, but "bring your expense voucher."

Ecco-La ◐ 🅂 ⇗
`19 | 14 | 14 | $21`
1660 Third Ave. (bet. 92nd & 93rd Sts.), 212-860-5609
■ A "young, noisy" crowd comes for "great pizza" and "cheap, hearty" "pasta prepared about any way you can think of"; if you mind being "cramped", reserve in the more "romantic back room."

Ecco L'Italia ◐ 🅂
▽ `16 | 16 | 16 | $25`
289 Bleecker St. (7th Ave. S.), 212-929-3355
☑ A "Village Italian bargain" with "good pastas" despite a "manager on the street hustling people in" and a "limited wine list"; the food gets mixed reviews, but everyone agrees on the music – "the worst piano I've ever heard!"

Eden Rock 🅂
`– | – | – | I`
2325 Broadway (bet. 84th & 85th Sts.), 212-873-1361
"Bargain" Middle Eastern food across from the West Side movies keeps this "no Eden" luncheonette-style joint rocking.

Edison Cafe 🅂 ⇗
`13 | 7 | 11 | $16`
Hotel Edison, 228 W. 47th St. (bet. B'way & 8th Ave.), 212-840-5000
☑ "Good, quick and cheap", this "run down" Theater District coffee shop is a "real NY experience" filled with a cast from the Shuberts to the chorus line and stage-door Johnnys; the food is "like your Jewish mother-in-law's" – what soup! what blintzes!

Edwardian Room 🅂
`20 | 26 | 22 | $50`
The Plaza Hotel, 768 Fifth Ave. (59th St.), 212-759-3000
☑ A "grand", "elegant" landmark in The Plaza that's a trip to "the old-world – long before Trump"; most find it "very *Belle Epoque*" with fine food and service, but some gripe that the Continental cuisine deserves to be better – if only to equal Donald's hype.

Edward Moran Bar & Grill 🅂
`11 | 13 | 10 | $23`
World Financial Center, 250 Vesey St., 212-945-2255
☑ "Crammed to the rafters with young Wall Streeters" who congregate after work for the "great harbor views" and "pickup scene" at the bar, not the "mediocre food" or "slow service"; it's said to be hottest on Thursday nights.

Eighteenth & Eighth ◐ 🅂
`17 | 11 | 15 | $18`
159 Eighth Ave. (18th St.), 212-242-5000
■ A "fun, hip, little" upscale coffee shop for an "inexpensive lunch and dinner" "with gay boys and girls" enjoying "homey but tasty fare"; even breakfast is "très trendy"; the biggest complaint is crowds.

EJ's Luncheonette 🅂 ⇗
`16 | 11 | 14 | $17`
447 Amsterdam Ave. (bet. 81st & 82nd Sts.), 212-873-3444
1271 Third Ave. (73rd St.), 212-472-0600
☑ Hugely popular, easily affordable, "retro-'50s" "yuppie diners" on the East and West Sides with "the best brunch in town" and portions that go "beyond generous"; our surveyors say it's "hash-brown heaven" and fantasize about the meat loaf, tuna melts and milkshakes, but also warn of "cholesterol" and "long lines."

62

Elaine's ◐ [S] — 11 | 11 | 11 | $35

1703 Second Ave. (bet. 88th & 89th Sts.), 212-534-8103

■ "Overhyped" Upper East Side Italian that's almost as famous for its "terrible food" and "rude waiters" as its celeb clientele – "you'd think notables would be ashamed to be noted here"; this could be the place that originated the term "writer's cramp."

El Charro — 18 | 11 | 17 | $27

4 Charles St. (bet. 7th & Greenwich Aves.), 212-243-5413 ◐ [S]

58 E. 34th St. (bet. Madison & Park Aves.), 212-689-1019

■ A "quaint" Spanish duo with what some claim is "the best paella in NY"; they're "neighborhood favorites" for "good service", "reasonable rates" and simple, authentic fare.

Elephant & Castle ◐ [S] — 15 | 12 | 14 | $19

68 Greenwich Ave. (7th Ave. & 11th St.), 212-243-1400

◪ Lots of Village "bang for the buck in a mellow, friendly atmosphere" that's "great for brunch" with "outrageous omelets" and burgers, but dissenters say that it's "crowded and noisy" with "scatterbrained service."

El Faro ◐ [S] — 19 | 10 | 15 | $28

823 Greenwich St. (Horatio St.), 212-929-8210

◪ A Village joint with "unquestionably the best classic Spanish food in the city and friendly service"; the paella is a garlic lover's dream, though some object to the "dark, almost depressing atmosphere."

Elias Corner (Queens) ◐ [S] ≠ — 24 | 5 | 15 | $26

2401 31st St. (24th Ave.), Astoria, 718-932-1510

■ "One of the best fish restaurants in the city – definitely worth the trip" (across the Triborough Bridge, first left); reviewers rave about the "excellent grilled seafood" and "killer garlic potatoes" and just about anything else at this "not pretty", "family-style Greek"; the only complaints come with popularity – "frazzled" staff and "a wait."

Elio's ◐ [S] — 22 | 16 | 18 | $41

1621 Second Ave. (bet. 84th & 85th Sts.), 212-772-2242

■ "One of the best Italians in NY" with a "very Upper East Side", celeb-centered, "clubby atmosphere" and "pricey", "simple, elegant food with consistently rich ingredients"; some find it "too noisy" and the "rushed" waiters "grumpy", but that comes with the territory; as Yogi Berra once said, "nobody goes there anymore, it's too crowded."

Ellen's Stardust Diner ◐ [S] — 12 | 14 | 11 | $17

1377 Sixth Ave. (56th St.), 212-307-7575

◪ "A total throwback to the '50s", this "good time", "pure camp", "chrome and shtick" "Midtown greasy spoon" has a menu "packed with Eclectic favorites" like "tuna melts" and "malteds"; the "food is just ok" but it's "a great place to take the kids" and "show them how it was – doo wop."

El Parador Cafe [S] — 17 | 14 | 18 | $29

325 E. 34th St. (bet. 1st & 2nd Aves.), 212-679-6812

◪ "Authentic Mexican" old-timer with "fairly elegant" (albeit "a little run-down") decor and "service so friendly it's hard to believe you're in NY", but most diners think it never was the same after the beloved former owner Carlos left years ago.

El Pollo [S] ≠ — 19 | 6 | 12 | $15

1746 First Ave. (bet. 90th & 91st Sts.), 212-996-7810

■ A "cheap and tasty" spot with "marinated", "spicy" Peruvian roasted chicken that "should be in the dictionary under 'succulent'"; bring your own wine or beer to this tiny "Upper East Side treasure" or take out at "bird-food prices."

El Pote Español ▽ 17 | 12 | 15 | $28
718 Second Ave. (bet. 38th & 39th Sts.), 212-889-6680
◪ Enthusiasts come here to "satisfy a basic Spanish urge" in "a neighborhood devoid of good restaurants", enjoying "very good food" and "fair prices"; however, some have a problem because there's "minimal decor", "no non-smoking section" and lackluster service.

El Quijote ◐ [S] 18 | 11 | 15 | $27
226 W. 23rd St. (bet. 7th & 8th Aves.), 212-929-1855
◪ A "cozy", "old-style", "neighborhood place" with a "Spanish lobster festival", "free-flowing" sangria and "great paella" "year-round"; it's "worth fighting a windmill for", just "don't plan on having a quiet conversation"; N.B. "gentlemen must wear shirts."

El Rincon de España [S] 18 | 10 | 16 | $29
226 Thompson St. (bet. Bleecker & W. 3rd Sts.), 212-260-4950
◪ An "old Village standby", as in "old and worn", with "plentiful" "traditional Spanish food" and "guitar players to match"; some surveyors say "it's past its glory days" and "needs new decor."

El Rio Grande [S] – | – | – | M
160 E. 38th St. (3rd Ave.), 212-867-0922
A sprawling, block-long Tex-Mex standby with an entertaining bar scene and outdoor patio; otherwise, it's pretty much par for the course.

El Teddy's ◐ [S] 17 | 18 | 14 | $29
219 W. Broadway (bet. Franklin & White Sts.), 212-941-7070
◪ "A circus" or "a travesty" that people either love for its "wild", "wacky decor", "atomic margaritas" and "inventive Mexican food" or deplore as "too trendy" with "rude" service and an "unappetizing" menu; it's a pickup scene for a "Downtown crowd" that mixes SoHo art types and "slumming Republicans."

Embers (Brooklyn) [S] 21 | 13 | 17 | $29
9519 Third Ave. (bet. 95th & 96th Sts.), 718-745-3700
■ "Where's the beef? – right here and it's good"; "go early to avoid the lines" and crowds at this "no-reserving", "poor man's Peter Luger"; though the "decor could be beefed up", the "excellent porterhouse" and filet mignon "ooze value."

Emily's [S] ▽ 21 | 11 | 15 | $18
1325 Fifth Ave. (111th St.), 212-996-1212
■ "Good, basic Southern cooking" that's a "great value" with "the best ribs and fried chicken" in a "casual" setting with music on weekends; however, service can be "slow and disorganized."

Empire Diner ◐ [S] 14 | 14 | 13 | $20
210 Tenth Ave. (22nd St.), 212-243-2736
◪ What some call "the ultimate diner" has "black-lacquered tables and candles" that can make it "a romantic space"; open 24 hours, it's popular for its late-late (or early-early) Chelsea scene which is at least as good for scoping as for its "upscale diner food."

Empire Szechuan ◐ [S] 14 | 7 | 13 | $18
381 Third Ave. (bet. 27th & 28th Sts.), 212-685-6215
193 Columbus Ave. (bet. 68th & 69th Sts.), 212-496-8778
2574 Broadway (97th St.), 212-663-6005
251 W. 72nd St. (bet. B'way & West End Ave.), 212-496-8460
15 Greenwich Ave. (bet. 6th Ave. & W. 10th St.), 212-691-1535

Empire Szechuan (Cont.)
1194 First Ave. (bet. 64th & 65th Sts.), 212-744-9400
173 Seventh Ave. S. (bet. 11th & Perry Sts.), 212-243-6046
◪ "Neighborhood Chinese dives" with quality that varies according to location from "assembly line" to the "best takeout in NYC"; dim sum is served at all the branches; everyone agrees: "stop with the menus!"

Ennio and Michael [S] 20 | 16 | 21 | $34
539 La Guardia Pl. (bet. Bleecker & W. 3rd Sts.), 212-677-8577
■ A "sentimental favorite" in the Village that has "nostalgic Italian cooking" and a "warm, friendly staff"; the outdoor cafe reminds some "of the streets of Europe."

Erminia ◐ 24 | 23 | 23 | $46
250 E. 83rd St. (bet. 2nd & 3rd Aves.), 212-879-4284
■ "Bring someone you love" to this "truly romantic" little spot with "marvelous country atmosphere" and "excellent", albeit pricey, Italian food; try the "wonderful shrimp dishes", but don't worry, there are no duds on this menu.

Ess-a-Bagel [S] 22 | 5 | 11 | $9
831 Third Ave. (bet. 50th & 51st Sts.), 212-980-1010
359 First Ave. (21st St.), 212-260-2252
■ The "bagels are as big as baseball mitts" and loyalists call them "best in town"; don't forget "great spreads", including "the best whitefish salad", and expect long lines, especially Sunday mornings.

Est! Est!! Est!!! [S] 21 | 17 | 20 | $36
64 Carmine St. (bet. Bedford St. & 7th Ave.), 212-255-6294
■ "The friendliest of the Village Italians", offering solid Tuscan cuisine in a simple, "cozy setting"; but for an abundance of nearby Italian options, this one would be better known.

Estia ◐ ▽ 15 | 14 | 15 | $30
308 E. 86th St. (bet. 1st & 2nd Aves.), 212-628-9100
◪ Reviewers are split between thinking this "noisy" nightspot is "a little, cozy Greek villa" with "good food" and "authentic music", or "slowly declining" and "not worth the trip" – maybe it depends on how much retsina they've had.

Etats-Unis 23 | 15 | 20 | $44
242 E. 81st St. (bet. 2nd & 3rd Aves.), 212-517-8826
◪ "This postage stamp–size family business" serves "meticulously prepared", "innovative" American food, but some find it "cramped" and "overpriced"; still, it's difficult to get a reservation.

Evergreen Cafe ◐ [S] – | – | – | M
1288 First Ave. (bet. 69th & 70th Sts.), 212-744-3266
Promising addition to far East Side dining, this brand new Chinese, from the pros who created Chiam, has handsome, modern "un-Chinese" decor and an open Hong Kong–style kitchen focusing on dim sum and noodle dishes.

Fanelli ◐ [S] ⇏ 13 | 14 | 13 | $18
94 Prince St. (Mercer St.), 212-226-9412
■ "The real McCoy", "one of the city's oldest watering holes (circa 1872)" is "a haven in winter, cool and dark in summer"; it serves "good bar food and beer" and perhaps "the best under $10 burger in town"; on the downside, look for tourists, smoke and noise.

Fantino 🅂 ▽ 23 26 24 $54
Ritz-Carlton, 112 Central Park S. (59th St., bet. 6th & 7th Aves.),
212-664-7700
◪ This new Northern Italian in the Ritz-Carlton boasts a "comfortable", "elegant setting", "light, creative" food and smooth service, yet it may prove too rich for younger tastes and pocketbooks.

Federico's 🅂 14 12 16 $28
1981 Broadway (67th St.), 212-873-4210
◪ "Moderate price, moderate quality" sums up this "quintessential so-so Italian" near Lincoln Center; though "reasonable", it's "strictly for the Joe Franklin audience."

FELIDIA 25 23 22 $52
243 E. 58th St. (bet. 2nd & 3rd Aves.), 212-758-1479
◼ In an "elegant", wood-panelled, flower-filled Midtown brownstone, Lidia Bastianich's "unrepentantly classic ristorante" provides "carefully prepared" Trieste-style cuisine that gives rise to "gastronomical ecstasy"; only service lapses ("pompous") and high prices ("bring a Brinks truck") explain occasional "disappointment."

Felix ●🅂⊅ 18 17 13 $34
340 W. Broadway (Grand St.), 212-431-0021
◼ "The best of the bunch on SoHo's hottest corner", this French bistro has "surprisingly good" food for an "oh-so-trendy" spot which is known "more for people-watching" of the "Armani/Porsche set" than for filling stomachs; "eat outside, kiss on both cheeks and be cool."

Ferdinando's Focacceria 🅂⊅ ▽ 18 8 15 $17
(Brooklyn)
151 Union St. (bet. Hicks & Columbia Sts.), 718-855-1545
◼ "A real gem hidden on the Brooklyn waterfront", this "old Italian" is "just like it was a century ago"; "the home-cooked food" ranges from "excellent to mediocre", but with "everyone talking in friendly Italian/ English" and "maternal waitresses", it's "worth the trip."

Ferrara ●🅂 – – – M
195 Grand St. (bet. Mott & Mulberry Sts.), 212-226-6150
You don't last 100 years, as this 1892 Little Italy landmark has, without doing something right – the "something" here is cappuccino and Italian pastries that attract hordes of tourists.

Ferrier ●🅂 18 15 13 $38
29 E. 65th St. (bet. Madison & Park Aves.), 212-772-9000
◪ While some consider this "cramped" Eastsider "a French bistro par excellence", others "go for the scene, not the food"; the motto here is "be Euro, young and cool"; the best advice is "go early for peace, late for action."

Fez ●🅂 15 22 13 $20
380 Lafayette St. (bet. 3rd & 4th Sts.), 212-533-3000
◼ Eccentric NoHo "faux Middle Eastern" place best for "atmosphere, company and drinks, not the New American food"; "like the inside of a genie's bottle", it can be "romantic" but it may also make you "smell like smoke" and have one wish: "where's the waitress?"

Fiesta Mexicana ●🅂 ▽ 13 13 14 $21
680 Columbus Ave. (93rd St.), 212-662-2212
2823 Broadway (109th St.), 212-662-2535
◼ Upper West Side neighborhood Mexicans that get cool reviews for food ("fair" and "mediocre"), but high marks for "great margaritas", "festive decor" and outdoor seating; critics say "buy a frozen Mexican dinner – save your time, money and taste buds."

Fifty-Seven, Fifty-Seven [S] — 22 | 23 | 22 | $48
Four Seasons Hotel, 57 E. 57th St. (bet. Park & Madison Aves.), 212-758-5757
◪ "Power brunches grow up to power lunches at this New American", one of NYs most promising new hotel dining rooms; although critics say it's "overpriced" and "impersonal", the food is "inventive", service "gracious" and the I.M. Pei decor "stunning"; it may lack electricity, but most say "I'll be back."

Figaro Pizza [S] ≠ — ▽ 18 | 8 | 12 | $8
1469 Second Ave. (bet. 76th & 77th Sts.), 212-472-2220
■ At a low cost, this "hole-in-the-wall" pizzeria serves what may be "the best pizza in Midtown" with "toppings heaped on"; and if you don't mind grease on your desk, they "never fail to deliver."

Fine & Schapiro [S] — 14 | 5 | 10 | $19
138 W. 72nd St. (bet. B'way & Columbus), 212-877-2874
◪ "Not what it once was", but "exactly what a NY deli should be – loud and tacky" with "rude waiters" "dipped in vinegar", and they know how to make a sandwich and "chicken soup like grandma's" – "so what's not to like?"

Finnegan's Wake ◐ [S] ≠ — 12 | 10 | 14 | $18
1361 First Ave. (73rd St.), 212-737-3664
◪ Find "a bit of Ireland" in this "no-frills", "dark wood", "neighborhood pub" where "everybody knows your name"; it's a "cheap" place "for salty food and beer", but some say "you get what you pay for."

Fino — 20 | 18 | 19 | $39
4 E. 36th St. (bet. 5th & Madison Aves.), 212-689-8040
■ This "classy", "pricey" Murray Hill favorite serves "reliable", "tasty Northern Italian" cuisine; though it can be "loud and noisy" at lunch, it's less "stuffy" and less crowded at night.

Fiorello's Roman Cafe ◐ [S] — 19 | 16 | 17 | $33
1900 Broadway (bet. 63rd & 64th Sts.), 212-595-5330
■ Just across from Lincoln Center is "NYC's Tuscan answer to the steak pub"; athough "a madhouse pre-theater" and "a bit overpriced", it has "quick" service, "large portions" and "wonderful" pizza, pasta and antipasti, plus premier people-watching.

Fiorentino (Brooklyn) [S] — 21 | 11 | 15 | $23
311 Avenue U (bet. McDonald & West Sts.), 718-372-1445
◪ A "Brooklyn Italian neighborhood restaurant" characterized by "no reservations, no ambiance, but good food at good prices"; "huge portions" and "pasta to live by" are rivaled only by crowds and noise "like being at a rock concert."

Fiori — 14 | 16 | 13 | $25
4 Park Ave. (33rd St.), 212-686-0226
■ Once "Cornelius Vanderbilt's private train station", this Murray Hill Italian is "cheap and reliable in its inoffensive mediocrity"; it's "best at lunch" or "for a few beers and a burger after work."

Firenze ◐ [S] — 21 | 17 | 19 | $36
1594 Second Ave. (bet. 82nd & 83rd Sts.), 212-861-9368
■ "Stands out in the East 80s Italian genre" thanks to a "cozy", "romantic" storefront setting and kitchen that make you feel "almost like being in Florence"; there's "wonderful, personal service" too.

First ◐[S] — | — | — | M

87 First Ave. (bet. 5th & 6th Sts.), 212-674-3823

This sleek East Village newcomer with an open-view kitchen, exposed-brick walls and comfortable, circular banquettes reportedly serves terrific seasonal New American fare at reasonable prices; late kitchen hours (2 AM weekdays) make it invaluable for the local "in" crowd.

First on 59th ◐[S] ▽ 13 | 12 | 15 | $24

1079 First Ave. (59th St.), 212-888-7884

◪ "Trying very hard", this Midtown bar/restaurant serves "so-so" Continental food that's not bad for a neighborhood joint; it "gets better each time" and "just might make it."

1st Wok ◐[S] 15 | 6 | 13 | $17

1570 Third Ave. (88th St.), 212-410-7747
1374 Third Ave. (78th St.), 212-861-2600

◪ Look for "always predictable, good value" at this "solid Szechuan chain", but also anticipate "no atmosphere" and little service which makes "fast-as-lightning" takeout the only way to go for many.

Fishin Eddie ◐[S] 19 | 16 | 16 | $35

73 W. 71st St. (Columbus Ave.), 212-874-3474

◪ In digs described as "Vermont goes chic", this Westsider's seafood garners reactions ranging from "imaginative" and "amazing" to "nothing special" and "another one-time-only" place.

Fish Restaurant ◐[S] 20 | 12 | 16 | $26

2799 Broadway (108th St.), 212-864-5000

■ A unanimously "welcome addition to the Far Upper West Side", this "fresh" and "friendly" seafooder offers an "excellent relationship between price and quality."

5 & 10 No Exaggeration ◐[S] — | — | — | M

77 Greene St. (bet. Broome & Spring Sts.), 212-925-7414

Though it looks "furnished from a tag sale", this camp, Eclectic SoHo haunt can be lotsa fun, especially if you take it over for a private party.

Five Oaks ◐[S] ▽ 14 | 16 | 17 | $28

49 Grove St. (Bleecker St.), 212-243-8885

◪ At this Village night spot you'll take "a step back to the beat of the '50s" at "the friendliest bar in town" with nice music, where "nostalgia works for the cabaret" more than for the "good", but "forgettable" American-Continental food.

Flight 151 ◐[S] ▽ 11 | 11 | 11 | $16

151 Eighth Ave. (bet. 17th & 18th Sts.), 212-229-1868

■ "Corny but cute", a "WWII flight theme" is the setting for this "no-frills" Chelsea "drinking establishment" that serves "middling bar food" (e.g. burgers or "cheap Sunday brunch") in a background of "good music"; it's basically "a place to have fun with friends."

Florent ◐[S]🚫 17 | 13 | 13 | $25

69 Gansevoort St. (bet. Washington & Greenwich Aves.), 212-989-5779

◪ It ain't what it used to be, but "where else can you get steak au poivre at 3 AM?"; though this 24-hour, "terminally groovy" French bistro/diner in the Meat Packing District is "smoky, noisy and crowded", it's "like a Fellini film" where "limos to skateboards" and "drag queens to truck drivers" come at all hours.

Floridita ◐ [S] — | — | — | M

3451 Broadway (142nd St.), 212-926-0319
3219 Broadway (129th St.), 212-662-0090
"Mojo gone Asian" describes this way Uptown Latin in a "basic Formica" atmosphere that serves "very good food at low prices"; it's a "best buy" in the barrio with "huge portions" and "good service."

Flowers ◐ 17 | 18 | 15 | $36

21 W. 17th St. (bet. 5th & 6th Aves.), 212-691-8888
■ With a "beautiful setting" and "surprisingly good New American food for a flash-in-the-pan scene", this "new and trendy" place is "full of beautiful people" despite "the rudest staff in NY"; as they say, it's the "sceniest of scenes" and "the place to be for the moment."

Flying Burrito Brothers ◐ [S] ≠ — | — | — | I

165 W. Fourth St. (bet. 6th & 7th Aves.), 212-691-FOOD
White trashy in a good way, this cheap late-night West Villager dishes king-sized burritos and other Cal-Mex munchies as a velvet Elvis looks on; there's sidewalk seating if the kitsch inside gets overwhelming.

Follonico [S] 22 | 19 | 20 | $40

6 W. 24th St. (bet. 5th & 6th Aves.), 212-691-6359
■ "Food to light up your taste buds" and a setting that resembles "a warm trattoria in Tuscany" make this Flatiron Italian "a cut above" in anyone's book; with a wood-burning stove and no-smoking policy, one wonders "are we still in NY?"

Food Bar ◐ [S] 14 | 15 | 14 | $22

149 Eighth Ave. (bet. 17th & 18th Sts.), 212-243-2020
■ The "patrons are better looking than the American comfort food" at this busy Chelsea "boy bar"; if you want "men on parade" and a "cheap" meal, you must accept noise, poor service and "plain food."

Fortune Garden [S] — | — | — | M
(fka Taste of Hong Kong)

845 Second Ave. (bet. 45th & 46th Sts.), 212-687-7471
Most agree that "this Midtowner is a "great deal", with a creative "dim sum and noodle lunch"; but some find it "disappointing and ordinary."

44 [S] 21 | 24 | 16 | $43

Royalton Hotel, 44 W. 44th St. (bet. 5th & 6th Aves.), 212-944-8844
■ A "chic", "en vogue dining experience", aka the Condé Nast Cafeteria, that may be a bit "precious", but gets high marks for chef Geoffrey Zakarian's "creative" American food and Philippe Starck's decor and "unusual bathrooms"; come see Tina and Anna, and ignore the pretty waitresses – they're just auditioning.

44 Southwest [S] 17 | 14 | 16 | $25

621 Ninth Ave. (44th St.), 212-315-4582
■ A "bargain" in the Theater District, this small storefront offers "tasteful Continental-Italian entrees" in a "bright, sunny atmosphere" with "accommodating service"; on the other hand, it can get "cramped" at times and has "no real identity."

FOUR SEASONS 27 | 27 | 26 | $60

99 E. 52nd St. (bet. Park & Lexington Aves.), 212-754-9494
■ "A NYC classic" Continental-Eclectic that is close to faultless; the Philip Johnson–designed setting "defines simple elegance" and the crowd defines NYC's power elite (especially at lunch in the Grill Room and at dinner in the Pool Room); although the experience can be "wildly expensive", the $37.50 prix fixe early dinner in the Grill is a great buy; of course there are critics: "cavernous", "stark", "losing its luster", but they are few and far between.

Frankie & Johnnie's ◐ 21 | 12 | 18 | $40
269 W. 45th St. (bet. 7th & 8th Aves.), 212-997-9494
◩ Theater District steakhouse known for its "accordingly priced", "great beef" and "humongous portions"; despite "speakeasy ambiance" and "uneven service", its "solid grilled fare" makes for a "good B'way meal."

Franklin Station Cafe [S] – | – | – | I
222 W. Broadway (Franklin St.), 212-274-8525
There aren't too many Malaysian bistros around town, so this informal TriBeCa cafe is nice to know about; besides soups, curries and noodle dishes, it has a sandwich bar with unusually tasty American sandwiches and salads, all at low prices.

Frank's Restaurant 21 | 11 | 19 | $38
431 W. 14th St. (bet. 9th & 10th Aves.), 212-243-1349
■ A "wonderful Italian family steakhouse in the Meat Packing District", this "film noir" bit of "old NY" specializes in "excellent value" and "special service" in an "authentic" turn-of-the-century bar space; it's an ideal place to go with a group – of 8 to 80; N.B. it's moving to 85 Tenth Avenue (15th Street) in early '95.

Fraunces Tavern 14 | 20 | 16 | $34
54 Pearl St. (Broad St.), 212-269-0144
◩ Most time-travel to this "Wall Street retreat" for its colonial period ambiance (George W. ate here), not for its "pedestrian food"; our surveyors "do breakfast or business lunch" here, even if it's "stuffy", "touristy" and "pricey"; P.S. the "museum upstairs is worth a visit."

Freddie & Pepper's Pizza ◐ [S] 🚫 16 | 3 | 9 | $9
303 Amsterdam Ave. (bet. 74th & 75th Sts.), 212-799-2378
■ West Side "hole-in-the-wall" serving "thick-crust" pizza in "unusual variations" of "garden-fresh toppings"; takeout is recommended since "eating in is like Dante's descent into hell."

French Roast Cafe ◐ [S] 14 | 13 | 10 | $18
456 Sixth Ave. (11th St.), 212-533-2233
◩ A "trendy and crowded French slow boat to Java" describes this studenty "bohemian" West Side version of the Coffee Shop; best for "late brunch or late-night" and as a "place to hang out", it's "otherwise a serviceless ordeal" with undistinguished bistro food.

Fresch ◐ [S] ▽ 16 | 14 | 16 | $26
143 Perry St. (bet. Washington & Greenwich Sts.), 212-243-9287
◩ In a "quiet, out-of-the-way" West Village storefront, "uneven" neo-bistro fare gives rise to contention: "sometimes super, sometimes not"; but the "help tries hard" and with "good desserts" and modest prices it's a nice neighbor.

Fresco 21 | 20 | 19 | $43
34 E. 52nd St. (bet. Park & Madison Aves.), 212-935-3434
■ This "newcomer to the ranks of Midtown Italians" serves "more than ample portions" of "innovative", "pricey" Tuscan dishes, but it's "not quite in the big league of quality" – or service; still, it's well suited for "business lunch" or as an "after-hours meeting place" for "yummy" "grilled pizza at the bar."

Fresco Tortilla Grill [S] 🚫 19 | 2 | 10 | $8
36 Lexington Ave. (bet. 23rd & 24th Sts.), 212-475-7380
253 Eighth Ave. (bet. 22nd & 23rd Sts.), 212-463-8877
126 W. 42nd St. (bet. B'way & 6th Ave.), 212-221-5849
■ "All fast food should be as good" and as "cheap" as at these Mexicans whose "authentic", "freshly rolled tortillas" may be "the best bargain in NY"; you'll want to take out since there's definitely no decor.

Friend of a Farmer S

17 | 17 | 14 | $22

77 Irving Pl. (bet. 18th & 19th Sts.), 212-477-2188

☑ "New Hampshire comes to NYC" at this "reasonably priced" Gramercy Park rustic which wins praise for its brunch ("delicious" baked goods) and American "farmhouse fare", but is knocked for "dull" dishes, "crowded quarters" and a "staff that may be friendly to farmers, but not to patrons."

Frontière S

20 | 18 | 18 | $36

199 Prince St. (bet. Sullivan & MacDougal Sts.), 212-387-0898

■ A "romantic", "candlelit", new SoHo French bistro that's winning support for its "interesting and tasty" country food and "courteous staff"; "SoHo needs more like it."

Frutti di Mare ◐ S ⇆

18 | 13 | 15 | $20

84 E. 4th St. (2nd Ave.), 212-979-2034

■ One of several related and/or "interchangeable Village pastarias" that offer "some of the best values in NY" in "cramped" and "loud" but "festive" digs; despite an "always-long wait", "big portions" for low prices make this "a hot spot for frugal pasta-and-seafood lovers."

Fujiyama Mama ◐ S

21 | 20 | 16 | $31

467 Columbus Ave. (bet. 82nd & 83rd Sts.), 212-769-1144

■ "Disco Sushi Inferno" might be the theme song of this "funky", "techno" West Side Japanese with its own DJ; though it's a little pricey and has "indifferent" service, its "delectable" sushi draws a young crowd that thrives on "smoke" and "din."

Fu's ◐ S

19 | 16 | 18 | $34

972 Second Ave. (bet. 51st & 52nd Sts.), 212-517-9670

☑ "Not the mecca it once was", but this East Side Chinese, relocated to Midtown, still gets above-average marks for its food despite "generic atmosphere" and slightly high prices; the question is "where's Gloria?"

Gabriel's

23 | 18 | 20 | $43

11 W. 60th St. (bet. B'way & Columbus Ave.), 212-956-4600

■ "The best of the West Side", this "culinary symphony" near Lincoln Center serves "inventive" pastas and Tuscan fare at its "blow-the-horn best" in a "minimal yet dramatic" space; some say it's "in danger of self-importance" because of its celebrity-laced clientele (boosted by proximity to Paramount, ABC, CBS and PBS), but not if genial owner Gabriel Aiello is in attendance.

Gage & Tollner (Brooklyn) S

20 | 21 | 20 | $37

372 Fulton St. (bet. Adams & Smith), 718-875-5181

■ For "wonderful" "she-crab soup" and "clam bellies" in "gaslight" that "feels like the 1890s", this "Brooklyn landmark" is "still ticking"; though some say it has been "sinking" since chef Edna Lewis left, it's still "worth a special trip" for "nostalgia galore."

Galil ◐ S

▽ 18 | 8 | 14 | $23

1252 Lexington Ave. (bet. 84th & 85th Sts.), 212-439-9886

☑ Wear your "yarmulke" to this "authentic, sleepy" Kosher–Middle Eastern "godsend"; what this "no-frills" Eastsider lacks in decor it makes up for with "consistently good", easily affordable food.

Gallagher's Steak House ◐ S

20 | 16 | 17 | $43

228 W. 52nd St. (bet. B'way & 8th Ave.), 212-245-5336

■ This Theater District "good ol' boy" steakhouse with stiff drinks, "checked tablecloths", sports art on the walls and a "meat-aging room" is "a beef-lovers' dream"; it almost defines the term "NY Steakhouse."

Gandhi ◐ [S] — 19 | 14 | 16 | $18
345 E. 6th St. (bet. 1st & 2nd Aves.), 212-614-9718
■ "No. 1" on 6th Street's "Indian Row", this "dark and romantic" "best buy" serves "delights" that turn "skeptics into Indian food lovers"; "less greasy" than most of its peers.

Garden Cafe [S] 🚫 — 12 | 16 | 11 | $21
MoMA, 11 W. 53rd St. (bet. 5th & 6th Aves.), 212-708-9719
■ Most agree that the MoMA's "cafeteria-style" soup and salad fare is "overpriced and under-spiced" with service "like airport dining", but it's *so* "convenient" and has a "great garden view"; why go? – "because it's there."

Garden Cafe (Brooklyn) — ▽ 20 | 15 | 19 | $23
620 Vanderbilt Ave. (Prospect Pl.), 718-857-8863
■ A "hideaway" New American with modestly priced, "innovative" fare and a "genius" chef; this "must for Brooklynites" has a shot at becoming a "real NY institution."

Garibaldi ◐ — ▽ 16 | 14 | 15 | $27
7 Washington Pl. (Mercer St.), 212-260-3066
■ NYU-area "neighborhood sleeper" that complements "authentic Italian" pasta and "brick-oven pizza" with a "relaxed" and "friendly" atmosphere in a "great" high-ceilinged room with "French doors."

Gascogne [S] — 22 | 20 | 20 | $39
158 Eighth Ave. (bet. 17th & 18th Sts.), 212-675-6564
■ This "charming" Chelsea bistro is the "cheapest way to go from 8th Avenue to France"; opt for the "garden" in the spring, save the "cozy", "candlelit" room for winter, and leave your diet at home.

Gauguin ◐ — – | – | – | E
The Plaza Hotel, 768 Fifth Ave. (59th St.), 212-319-0404
In the space under the Plaza Hotel that formerly housed Trader Vic's, we now have Trader Vic's Redux, another Polynesian fantasy restaurant with weird island drinks and what purports to be Tahitian food; it's all very colorful and can be lots of fun, but no one is likely to call it a masterpiece, culinary or otherwise.

Genji ◐ [S] — 16 | 10 | 13 | $23
56 Third Ave. (bet. 10th & 11th Sts.), 212-254-1959
◪ If you want to "gorge" on Japanese, this has the "best all-you-can-eat sushi" deal around, though some say that's because they serve "big rice balls"; "newly refurbished", so decor ratings may be out-of-date.

Georgia Diner (Queens) ◐ [S] — 14 | 10 | 12 | $17
86-55 Queens Blvd. (55th Ave.), 718-651-9000
◪ "A diner is a diner" some say, but others call this Queens joint a "paradigm", listing "large portions", "no-nonsense cuisine", "open 24 hours" and cleanliness.

Giambelli ◐ — 20 | 17 | 19 | $45
46 E. 50th St. (bet. Madison & Park Aves.), 212-688-2760
◪ "Expense-accounters" and an "older crowd" remain faithful to this Midtown Northern Italian "classic", but others say it has "gone south."

Gianni's [S] — 17 | 17 | 16 | $36
15 Fulton St. (South St. Seaport), 212-608-7300
■ Go for "Gorgonzola bread" and "people-watching" from window and terrace tables, but only if you're already near the South Street Seaport.

Gianpalu — | — | — | E

277 Church St. (bet. Franklin & White Sts.), 212-219-0677
Named after Christopher Columbus' chef, this unusual newcomer in TriBeCa offers a limited menu based on what its chef finds fresh in the market each day; some of the art on exhibition would make CC feel he had fallen off the edge of the earth.

Gigino S — | — | — | E

323 Greenwich St. (bet. Duane & Reade Sts.), 212-431-1112
Carol Clements, the theatrical designer, has created a "charming" stage set of an Italian country restaurant to showcase chef Luigi Celentano's (ex Positano) affordable Northern Italian menu; mini-pizzas cost under $10 and even shell steak is below $20.

Gingertoon ◐ S 18 | 14 | 15 | $25

417 Bleecker St. (Bank St.), 212-924-6420

Ginger Ty

363 Greenwich St. (bet. Franklin & Harrison Sts.), 212-925-7440
◩ This Downtown duo offers "delicious" and "reasonably priced" Thai cuisine; the TriBeCa spot "looks like Liberace's living room" and "far outshines its Village parent."

Gino of Capri S ≠ 19 | 11 | 16 | $34

780 Lexington Ave. (bet. 60th & 61st Sts.), 212-758-4466
■ "It's a club" and most "like being a member" of this reliable East Side Italian standby; some can't remember why they go, but perhaps it's for the "secret sauce" they put on the "big bowls of pasta", perhaps it's the wacko "zebra wallpaper."

Giovanni ◐ S — | — | — | E

47 W. 55th St. (bet. 5th & 6th Aves.), 212-262-2828
A brand-new "Northeastern Italian" featuring rustic dishes from the Veneto, Friuli and Emilia-Romagna areas, this good-looking newcomer has three distinct dining rooms – the downstairs Pavilion, a bright, garden-style room; the Card Room with a theme of Italian card games; and the Club Room, designed for cigar lovers.

Girafe 22 | 20 | 21 | $46

208 E. 58th St. (bet. 2nd & 3rd Aves.), 212-752-3054
■ This pricey East Side Italian classic in a "pretty townhouse" is a solid bet for "good, basic fare" and "great service"; "good but old" could describe the clientele as well as the restaurant.

Girasole ◐ S 22 | 17 | 19 | $42

151 E. 82nd St. (bet. Lexington & 3rd Aves.), 212-772-6690
■ "Pleasant" and "dependable" Italian in a "romantic townhouse" with "attentive" but "non-hovering" service; it's almost "always crowded", but this being the fancy East Side – "what a crowd."

Golden Unicorn S 20 | 11 | 12 | $22

18 E. Broadway (Catherine St.), 212-941-0911
◩ On the third floor of a Chinatown building many report finding "dim sum heaven", which may explain why there's often an "eternal wait"; come with a group of family or friends and make a party of it; as ratings show, decor and service need help.

Gonzalez y Gonzalez ◐ S — | — | — | M

625 Broadway (bet. Bleecker & Houston Sts.), 212-473-8787
Mega-margaritas and music may make you forgiving towards the second-rate south-of-the-border food and service at this "huge, cheesy Mexican" Villager.

Good Enough to Eat [S] 19 | 15 | 15 | $21

483 Amsterdam Ave. (bet. 83rd & 84th Sts.), 212-496-0163

■ "Cheaper than driving to Vermont"; the "home-cooked" "comfort food", especially brunch, at this "cute" West Side rustic is better than good enough to eat, but with lines "down the street" on weekends the question becomes: is it good enough to wait?

Goody's (Queens) [S] ⊄ ▽ 22 | 5 | 15 | $20

94-03B 63rd Dr. (bet. Booth & Saunders Sts.), 718-896-7159

■ "For once the foodie hype is accurate"; this "superior Chinese" is "worth the trip" to Queens for "fabulous Shanghai specialties" and especially "excellent soupy buns (dumplings)"; attractive Chinese decor is almost an oxymoron.

Googies Italian Diner ◐ [S] ⊄ 15 | 12 | 12 | $19

1491 Second Ave. (78th St.), 212-717-1122

◩ "A scene", this "young", "upbeat", 1950s-style Upper East Side "Italian diner" serves everything from the "best shoestring fries in NYC" to "chocolate-chip pancakes" to "great pastas"; the "pretty", "college-aged crowd" and "indifferent service" can make it seem "more like a bar than a diner."

GOTHAM BAR & GRILL [S] 27 | 25 | 24 | $52

12 E. 12th St. (bet. 5th Ave. & University Pl.), 212-620-4020

■ "A real adventure in NYC dining" that usually "feels like a party"; over 3,000 surveyors voted on this high-ceilinged Village American, with chef Alfred Portale's "skyscraper" creations receiving "soaring" praise from most of them; "always a delight", the restaurant is Bruce Wayne–pricey at night, but even Alfred the butler would find the $19.95 prix fixe lunch a bargain.

Gotham City Diner ◐ [S] 16 | 15 | 14 | $25

1562 Second Ave. (81st St.), 212-570-9334

◩ "If you don't wear black, you may feel out of place" at this "upscale" East Side "diner with attitude"; some love its "Eclectic menu", "excellent salads" and "good buys", others say "the kitchen is still in search of a cuisine" and is capable of screwing up an omelet.

GRAMERCY TAVERN [S] – | – | – | VE

42 E. 20th St. (bet. B'way & Park Ave. S.), 212-477-0777

Despite some recent reviews that have taken this highly visible, Gramercy-area American newcomer to task, most people expect it will live up to its hype thanks to its undeniable assets: handsome, spacious tavern decor, excellent food by chef Tom Colicchio (ex Mondrian) and service supervised by Danny Meyer (Union Square Cafe); dinner is $48 prix fixe, lunch à la carte; there's a three-course meal in the front Tavern Room for under $25 without facing the otherwise difficult task of reserving well in advance.

Gramercy Watering Hole ◐ [S] 13 | 12 | 14 | $20

106 E. 19th St. (bet. Park Ave. & Irving Pl.), 212-674-5783

◩ Gramercy-area bar scene and "grazing ground for animal-watchers"; if desperate for food, try the "Cajun meat loaf" or mashed potatoes.

Grand Ticino 18 | 15 | 18 | $31

228 Thompson St. (bet. W. 3rd & Bleecker Sts.), 212-777-5922

◩ This "cozy", vintage Village Italian sets a "standard" with "simple, reliable" fare, but some say it's just "not as Moonstruck as it used to be."

Grange Hall, The S
20 19 16 $28
50 Commerce St. (Barrow St.), 212-924-5246

A "hip" West Village "farm festival" serving "hearty" (delicious vs. unpredictable) American "comfort food" in a "stylish" "Wisconsin atmosphere"; it can be trendy, "noisy" and "crowded", but that reflects its popularity as "a good date" place.

Grappino (94)
▽ 19 16 17 $33
38 W. 39th St. (bet. 5th & 6th Aves.), 212-398-0350

In the dining desert of the Garment District, this elegant Italian oasis can produce feeding frenzies at lunch with really special specials; like the area as a whole, it's desolate at night.

Gray's Papaya
15 2 10 $6
2090 Broadway (72nd St.), 212-799-0243
402 Sixth Ave. (8th St.), 212-260-3532

"Two Dogs + Drink = $1.95"; these "addictive", "stand-up-and-eat" hot dogs are "a NYC must" and "best in town" according to most; they're great for when you're "dead broke" or on the run; "it may be a dump, but it's our dump"; "a great leveler."

Great American Health Bar S
11 4 8 $14
821 Third Ave (bet. 50th & 51st Sts.), 212-758-0883
35 W. 57th St. (bet. 5th & 6th Aves.), 212-355-5177

"Quasi-healthful", "no ambiance", "tired" remnants of a vegetarian chain that are fine for a "quickie lunch" of soup, yogurt or carrot salad, but most say they just "don't live up to their billing" and "give Health Food a bad name."

Great Jones Cafe
17 12 13 $19
54 Great Jones St. (bet. Bowery & Lafayette Sts.), 212-674-9304

"A dive", yes, but a "very hip", "cramped but spirited" "hole-in-the-wall" where a "young NoHo" crowd says the "music is cool and the food is hot"; try the "Cajun martinis" or brunch.

Great Shanghai S
19 10 13 $20
27 Division St. (Bowery St.), 212-966-7663

For "authentic" Shanghai cuisine, "go with a group" and "don't miss the Peking duck"; though the new decor may be "out of the *Jetsons*", it's still a favorite spot in Chinatown.

Grifone
23 19 23 $44
244 E. 46th St. (bet. 2nd & 3rd Aves.), 212-490-7275

Midtown Italian lunch place that's a "real sleeper", with "excellent quality" food and first-rate service, but it's not unanimous: some say it's "stodgy" and there are "many better" and "cheaper."

Grotta Azzurra S
18 11 15 $31
387 Broome St. (Mulberry St.), 212-925-8775

"Goombah"; after 50 years most still love this crowded Little Italy basement Southern Italian standby that's "like being in Sicily"; others insist that it's strictly for "tourists."

Grove S
20 16 16 $28
314 Bleecker St. (Grove St.), 212-675-9463

The secret is out on this "choice West Village spot" with "reliable American-French food" and a "pretty garden", all for "very reasonable prices"; find out for yourself.

Grove Street Cafe ● S
18 15 17 $29
53 Grove St. (7th Ave. S.), 212-924-8299

A "cute Village nest", this "dark", "romantic" Continental is a "good place to take your honey", especially if you're on "a tight budget"; critics say it's "a shell of its former self."

Gus' Place ◑ [S] 21 | 19 | 20 | $31

149 Waverly Pl. (6th Ave.), 212-645-8511

■ "Charming", low-key Greek-Mediterranean with an "airy room", "ivy-clad walls", a "European" feel and "traditional", "affordable" fare; "share appetizers for an excellent meal"; P.S. "Gus is great."

Hakata [S] ▽ 16 | 11 | 14 | $19

224 W. 47th St. (bet. B'way & 8th Ave.), 212-730-6863

■ Though "a little stark and cold" with service that can be "slow", especially "at lunch", this Theater District Japanese offers "great", "tasty noodles" and "good sushi" for a price that's hard to equal.

Halcyon ◑ [S] 22 | 24 | 22 | $45

Rihga Royal, 151 W. 54th St. (bet. 6th & 7th Aves.), 212-468-8888

◩ The clear majority find "excellent" American food, a "sumptuous" setting and "superb, professional service" at this Midtown hotel, concluding that "it's fast becoming a contender"; dissenters say "something's missing", suggesting that the "beautiful room" is "a little stuffy" and the food "unimaginative."

Hamachi ▽ 22 | 14 | 18 | $30

34 E. 20th St. (bet. B'way & Park Ave. S.), 212-420-8608

■ If you overlook "inconsistent service" and "Spartan decor", this Gramercy-area Japanese has "some of the freshest sushi in NY"; regulars happily note that "the sushi chef knows you when you return."

Hamaya [S] – | – | – | E

152 E. 46th St. (bet. 3rd & Lexington Aves.), 212-972-5979

"Reasonably priced shabu-shabu cuisine" is served in this Japanese that's "popular among Japanese businesspeople"; "if you can afford it, sit at the sushi bar and let the chefs feed you."

Hamburger Harry's [S] 13 | 8 | 11 | $16

145 W. 45th St. (bet. 6th & 7th Aves.), 212-840-2756

157 Chambers St. (bet. Hudson & Greenwich Sts.), 212-267-4446

◩ A real Teflon – despite low ratings and stinging criticism ("tired", "incompetent", "forlorn"), these "grease pits" still get lots of business thanks to producing "a very good burger" at "the right price."

Harbor Seafood (Queens) **◑ [S]** – | – | – | M

84-01 Queens Blvd. (Vanloon St.), 718-803-3833

Although "a little pricey for Queens" (i.e. cheap in Manhattan), this "Chinese seafood restaurant" does a good enough job that "the wait can be a real bummer."

Harbour Lights ◑ [S] 16 | 22 | 15 | $33

South Street Seaport, Pier 17, 3rd fl., 212-227-2800

■ The "beautiful harbor view" and "romantic setting" of this Seaport pier seafood cafe are its real attractions; most clients find its food just "ok", so you may want to go for "drinks only."

Hard Rock Cafe ◑ [S] 12 | 20 | 12 | $22

221 W. 57th St. (bet. B'way & 7th Ave.), 212-459-9320

◩ This "rock 'n' roll museum" attracts an endless crowd with its "great memorabilia" and "good burgers", and has all the charms and repulsions of an "amusement park": "long lines", "tourists", "teenagers", "noise" and "fun"; it seems everyone in America has been at least once and bought a sweatshirt on the way out.

Harley Davidson Cafe ◐ [S] — 12 | 18 | 13 | $23
1370 Ave. of Americas (56th St.), 212-245-6000
◪ "Every bit the tourist trap you'd expect", this new, mega Midtown "theme restaurant" is the Hard Rock "with motorcycles" and "chrome"; some feel its pub "food is surprisingly good" while others "would rather eat tires"; the real draws are "loud music", "kinky decor" and the "roar of ...", you guessed it.

Harpo (Brooklyn) ◐ — ▽ 21 | 18 | 20 | $26
181 West End Ave. (bet. Oriental & Hampton Sts.), 718-743-6900
■ "Off the beaten path" in Manhattan Beach, Brooklyn, this "tiny" Continental has locals raving over its "wonderful salads and pasta", "fabulous service" and "sleek" decor; critics say the superlatives result from lack of competition in the area – "that's why I moved."

Harriet's Kitchen [S] — ▽ 13 | 5 | 12 | $14
502 Amsterdam Ave. (bet. 84th & 85th Sts.), 212-721-0045
◪ A "low-budget haven", this takeout joint offers "great fried chicken", "meat loaf" and other "family cooking"; "hide the bags, they'll think you made it", isn't necessarily a compliment.

Harry Cipriani [S] — 22 | 21 | 21 | $51
Sherry Netherland, 781 Fifth Ave. (bet. 59th & 60th Sts.), 212-753-5566
◪ "As good as its counterpart in Venice", this "glamorous" little East Side Italian is "like a club" for the "bella gente"; admirers swoon over the "classic Italian food", "best Bellinis in town" and "elegant setting"; detractors sniff: "overpriced", "counterfeit Italian", "aspiring snobs."

Harry's at Hanover Square — 15 | 14 | 16 | $33
1 Hanover Sq. (bet. Pearl & Stone Sts.), 212-425-3412
◪ At this "Wall Street classic" (in the basement of India House), "martinis, beef, shots and talk" are the standard fare, and "three-piece suits" standard dress; regulars praise the wine list and steaks; others see it "sinking into the sunset" through the "cigar smoke."

Harry's Burritos ◐ [S] ≠ — 15 | 9 | 11 | $14
241 Columbus Ave. (71st St.), 212-580-9494
91 E. 7th St. (bet. 1st Ave. & Avenue A), 212-477-0773
230 Thompson St. (bet. W. 4th & Bleecker Sts.), 212-260-5588
◪ "Young" West-and-Eastsiders, and some not so young, come for "cheap, tasty, overstuffed burritos" and other low-budget Cal-Mex cooking best enjoyed from "outdoor seating"; critics describe the fare as "glop in a blanket" and the service as "nobody home."

Harvest [S] — ▽ 20 | 20 | 19 | $31
171 W. 4th St. (bet. 6th & 7th Aves.), 212-647-9832
■ "Warm and wonderful", this West Village American yearling has an "imaginative menu", a "pretty" room and a small "backyard garden"; most consider it "a great find" and "a place with potential."

HASAKI ◐ [S] — 25 | 17 | 18 | $29
210 E. 9th St. (bet. 2nd & 3rd Aves.), 212-473-3327
■ East Village Japanese serving "the best-priced", "freshest, tastiest sushi around" plus items "you can't find elsewhere" in "crowded", "postage-stamp quarters"; no reserving means "long lines."

HATSUHANA — 25 | 16 | 19 | $39
17 E. 48th St. (bet. 5th & Madison Aves.), 212-355-3345
237 Park Ave. (46th St.), 212-661-3400
◪ Ever-popular Midtown Japanese famous for "very fresh" and "well-prepared" sushi; loyalists claim it's still "the standard by which to judge all other Japanese restaurants"; Park Avenue is the lesser location.

Haveli ◑ⓢ
21 | 18 | 18 | $23

100 Second Ave. (bet 5th & 6th Sts.), 212-982-0533

■ "A cut above the competition on 6th Street", this Indian East Villager serves "superior food" in a "spacious" interior; although "reasonably priced", it's "a sawbuck above" its neighbors too.

Health Pub ⓢ
▽ 18 | 11 | 14 | $22

371 Second Ave. (21st St.), 212-529-9200

 The "fresh" and "well-prepared" "healthy" fare served here "gives Vegetarian cuisine a good name"; others cite "sterile" quarters and lament "it may be healthy but that's where it ends."

Heidelberg Restaurant ⓢ
– | – | – | M

1648 Second Ave. (bet. 85th & 86th Sts.), 212-650-1385

An old Yorkville German beerhall-cum-restaurant mit all kinds of brats and wursts; it has a homey old-world feel and prices (e.g. a $6.95 lunch) that make a visit almost risk-free.

Henry's End (Brooklyn) ⓢ
23 | 14 | 21 | $32

44 Henry St. (Cranberry St.), 718-834-1776

■ A "vibrant" Brooklyn Heights American "standby" that's heralded for its "knowledgeable", "accommodating waiters", "impressive food" and "great wine selection", but not for its "sardine-can setting."

Hi-Life Bar and Grill ◑ⓢ
14 | 13 | 12 | $23

477 Amsterdam Ave. (83rd St.), 212-787-7199
1340 First Ave. (72nd St.), 212-249-3600

 "More bar than restaurant", these American "hot spots" feature an "eye-catching crowd" and "models as waitresses"; they're a cross between "a Seinfeld episode" and "eating at the Kappa house"; "where the young and beautiful meet – and maybe eat."

Home ⓢ
21 | 17 | 18 | $31

20 Cornelia St. (bet. Bleecker & W. 4th Sts.), 212-243-9579

■ "Imaginative cooking" "better than mom's" is served at this "cozy", "romantic" Villager; although it's narrow and a "bit cramped" it's a "good value" and the back "garden is bliss."

Honeysuckle ◑ⓢ
16 | 14 | 13 | $24

170 Amsterdam Ave. (68th St.), 212-873-4100

 While some rave over "great Soul Food" and "cool cool jazz", others report: "deteriorated since move to Amsterdam" and "a discount coupon pulled me in – it won't work twice."

Hong Fat ◑ⓢ⇗
19 | 4 | 10 | $16

63 Mott St. (bet. Canal & Bayard Sts.), 212-962-9588

 At this "decades-old" Chinatown noodle house, "cheap, excellent Chinese food" is served in "dreary" digs by "mean waiters"; some say "not what it used to be", but "it's been around forever and must be doing something right."

Hong Shoon ⓢ
– | – | – | I

30 Pell St. (bet. Bowery & Mott Sts.), 212-513-0622

"Wonderful dim sum" in "very basic surroundings" at "a great value"; but some think they've "been to better."

Honmura An ⓢ
24 | 23 | 21 | $39

170 Mercer St. (bet. Prince & Houston Sts.), 212-334-5253

■ "Like going to Tokyo" and "almost as expensive", this "charming" SoHo soba shop features "stellar" noodles and soups; fans say "it's as relaxing as a spa" and "very Zen", but it's possible to feel like "an idiot for paying $25 for noodles."

Hop Shing [S] ≠ ▽ 19 | 3 | 8 | $15
9 Chatham Sq. (bet. Bowery & Mott Sts.), 212-267-0220
■ For "great dim sum" and "authentic South Chinese cuisine" this "hectic" Chinatown "total dive" can't be beat; "just close your eyes", ignore the "rude" service and eat.

Hosteria Fiorella ☾ [S] 20 | 18 | 17 | $35
1081 Third Ave. (bet. 63rd & 64th Sts.), 212-838-7570
◪ "Impressive antipasti" and "imaginative" seafood are the specialties of this "spacious" East Side trattoria; with an "upbeat" setting and "fair prices" it's popular, even if cynics say it's "nothing to rave about."

Houlihan's 9 | 9 | 10 | $19
50 Broad St. (Beaver St.), 212-483-8310
1900 Broadway (63rd St.), 212-339-8863 [S]
380 Lexington Ave. (42nd St.), 212-922-5661 [S]
729 Seventh Ave. (49th St.), 212-626-7312 ☾ [S]
7 Hanover Sq. (Water St.), 212-483-8310
677 Lexington Ave. (56th St.), 212-339-8858
350 Fifth Ave. (34th St.), 212-630-0339 [S]
767 Fifth Ave. (bet. 58th & 59th Sts.), 212-339-8850 [S]
196 Broadway (Fulton St.), 212-240-1280 [S]
Penn Station (33rd St., bet 7th & 8th Aves.), 212-630-0348 [S]
◪ "Always reliable if unimaginative", this ubiquitous chain of pseudo-Irish fern bars offers "corporate food" in a "suburban" atmosphere; at best, it's good "for a quick bite that's a step up from McDonald's", at worst, it marks "the decline of democratic culture."

Hourglass Tavern ☾ [S] ≠ 18 | 14 | 17 | $22
373 W. 46th St. (9th Ave.), 212-265-2060
◪ "Get ready, get set, you have one hour" (timed by the hourglass on your table) for pre-theater "honest eats" in this "tiny" triangular Restaurant Row American; some find the hourglass theme "charming", others say "totally obnoxious", but the $12.95 prix fixe dinner makes a visit worth your time.

H.S.F. ☾ [S] 18 | 11 | 14 | $24
46 Bowery St. (Canal St.), 212-374-1319
578 Second Ave. (bet. 31st & 32nd Sts.), 212-689-6969
■ "Delightful" dim sum draws crowds to both locations of this well-known Chinese; although some prefer the "more elegant and cleaner" 32nd Street branch, the Chinatown one is more soulful.

Hudson Grill ▽ 19 | 18 | 17 | $27
350 Hudson St. (King St.), 212-691-9060
◪ Opinions divide over this TriBeCa American "grab-a-bite place": some call the food a "good value", "creative" and "up-and-coming" with a "fantastic" brunch, others simply wonder "what's the big deal?"

HUDSON RIVER CLUB [S] 25 | 27 | 23 | $50
4 World Financial Ctr., 250 Vesey St., 212-786-1500
■ "First-rate" in all respects: starting with chef Waldy Malouf's "elegant" and "delicious" Hudson Valley food, followed by Chris Carey's deft management, a "handsome" wood-panelled setting and an "unbeatable view" of the Hudson and the Harbor; if planning a party Downtown, it's a "spectacular" "place to celebrate."

Hulot's [S] 19 | 17 | 18 | $38
973 Lexington Ave. (bet. 70th & 71st Sts.), 212-794-9800
◪ "Very Uptown" East Side neighborhood bistro offering "pricey but tasty" French food and "French frost for nonregulars"; it's moved down the street to La Petite Ferme's lovely former space and garden.

F | D | S | C

Hunan Balcony ◐ [S] — 16 | 10 | 15 | $18

2596 Broadway (98th St.), 212-865-0400
1417 Second Ave. (74th St.), 212-517-2088

■ "Cheap and reliable" for "fairly standard" to "above-par" Chinese; nobody said either location is attractive, so it may be of interest that takeout is "the fastest ever."

Hunan Fifth Ave. [S] — ▽ 17 | 12 | 16 | $22

323 Fifth Ave. (bet. 32nd & 33rd Sts.), 212-686-3366

◪ "Famous only because of *Seinfeld*" and perhaps because it's "a calm oasis in the Garment District jungle", this misnamed restaurant (it's really Cantonese) is graded from "very good" to just "ok."

Hunan Garden [S] — 16 | 11 | 14 | $17

1 Mott St. (Bowery), 212-732-7270

◪ "Cleaner than most" with food that's "a step up from others" and a "family dinner that's a steal", this Chinatowner may strike some as "a dime a dozen", but it's "fast, cheap and good enough" for others to call it a "reason why people stay in NY."

Hunters [S] — 16 | 15 | 16 | $25

1387 Third Ave. (bet. 78th & 79th Sts.), 212-734-6008

■ "Cozy and friendly" with a "touch of elegance that exceeds the prices", this American Eastsider offers good food in "a non-yuppie atmosphere"; "great for a first date" "by the fireplace" or to "take your parents because it's cheap but will still impress them."

Hurricane Island [S] — 17 | 10 | 13 | $32

1303 Third Ave. (bet. 74th & 75th Sts.), 212-717-6600

◪ "As close as you'll get to Maine in a yellow cab", this East Side storefront seafooder "isn't pretty", but is touted for "fresh, well-prepared fish", especially lobsters; critics yawn "ho hum."

Il Cantinori ◐ [S] — 23 | 22 | 20 | $46

32 E. 10th St. (bet. B'way & University Pl.), 212-673-6044

◪ "Terrific" Tuscan cooking ("inventive pastas", "outstanding game") and a "lovely", "rustic" setting keep this Villager filled with a chic crowd; though critics claim it dispenses "fettuccine alla attitude" and "isn't worth the price", most consider it a top Italian.

Il Corallo Trattoria ◐ [S] ⊘ — ▽ 17 | 11 | 14 | $21

176 Prince St. (bet. Thompson & Sullivan Sts.), 212-941-7119

◪ In contrast to its "small, uninspiring" setting, this SoHo trattoria has "good, cheap pasta" in "more permutations than imaginable", plus pizzas and salads, which is why it's often "crowded."

Il Cortile ◐ [S] — 23 | 22 | 19 | $38

125 Mulberry St. (bet. Canal & Hester Sts.), 212-226-6060

■ A "Mulberry Street standout" that's more "Uptown" in style than most of its Little Italy brethren; with "delicious" Northern Italian food, "delightful" service and a "romantic" courtyard it attracts both tourists and natives, hence it's often "crowded, but worth the wait."

Il Giardinetto (Bronx) [S] — ▽ 18 | 17 | 18 | $30

866 Morris Park Ave., 718-828-9215

■ There's no shortage of "crowds, noise" or garlic at this Bronx Italian; it's "usually very satisfying" and "a real find at these prices", but since it's already been found (by locals) "get there early."

Il Giglio — 25 | 18 | 21 | $48

81 Warren St. (bet. W. B'way & Greenwich), 212-571-5555

■ If "not quite Il Mulino", this TriBeCa Northern Italian has much in common with its illustrious sibling, e.g. "excellent, garlic-infused" food, "formidable" prices and waits, but they're less punishing here.

Il Menestrello 23 | 20 | 22 | $44

14 E. 52nd St. (bet. 5th & Madison Aves.), 212-421-7588

■ "As good as any of this type", i.e. a Midtown "expense-account" Italian that "caters to its regulars" with "first-class" food, "impeccable" service and a "quiet", classy setting; only a few find it "a bit heavy" and "somehow institutional."

Il Monello [S] 22 | 19 | 21 | $47

1460 Second Ave. (bet. 76th & 77th Sts.), 212-535-9310

■ Favored by a tony East Side crowd, this "elegant" yet "relaxed" Northern Italian "classic" provides "delicious" food and "fine service" in an "attractively redone" setting with a pleasant open front; expect to be "greeted warmly and well fed", then handed a fat check.

IL MULINO ◐ 27 | 19 | 23 | $53

86 W. 3rd St. (bet. Thompson & Sullivan Sts.), 212-673-3783

■ "Year after year" surveyors anoint this Villager NY's No. 1 Italian, hailing its "monstrous portions" of gloriously garlicky fare that would satisfy "Caesar" (and his legions); on the minus side, "reservations are a joke" and it's "dark, noisy" and "hopelessly overcrowded", but that's the price you pay for the ultimate Italian "indulgence"; lunch is easier on the nerves.

IL NIDO 25 | 21 | 23 | $50

251 E. 53rd St. (bet. 2nd & 3rd Aves.), 212-753-8450

■ Exemplifying Northern Italian "finesse", this "classy" Eastsider provides "superb" food and "courteous" service in a "quiet", "elegant" setting; though a few dissenters find it "overpriced" and "stuffy", most appreciate its "dependable excellence."

Il Nostro [S] 16 | 13 | 15 | $25

520 Columbus Ave. (85th St.), 212-873-0341

◪ To admirers, this "homey", "high-ceilinged" West Side Italian is a "friendly" neighborhood place with "good pastas", pizzas and risottos at "reasonable prices"; critics say "they try, but just ain't got it."

Il Ponte Vecchio [S] 19 | 15 | 18 | $32

206 Thompson St. (bet. Bleecker & W. 3rd Sts.), 212-228-7701

■ "An old favorite", this Village Italian is a "cut above the average" thanks to its "great variety" of "always well-prepared" food at fair prices; it may be a little "tired looking" but it's still "pleasant."

Il Tinello 24 | 21 | 24 | $48

16 W. 56th St. (bet. 5th & 6th Aves.), 212-245-4388

◪ A touch "of Milano" in Midtown, this "mature" Northern Italian combines "top-notch" food, "just-right" service and an "elegant" setting; however, it's expensive and some find it "too staid."

Il Vagabondo ◐ [S] 15 | 12 | 14 | $28

351 E. 62nd St. (bet. 1st & 2nd Aves.), 212-832-9221

◪ Indoor boccie courts plus "huge portions" of "hearty" red-sauce fare are the hallmarks of this low-cost East Side standby; it's "fun for groups" and "tourists can't believe it", nor can critics who call it a "'50s Italian rec room with blah food and terse service."

Il Vigneto ▽ 18 | 13 | 16 | $26

1068 First Ave. (bet. 58th & 59th Sts.), 212-755-6875

◪ "First Avenue needed something like this": a "very able" Italian with "really tasty pasta" at "low prices"; but it "could use a little ambiance."

Inagiku S
22 | 21 | 21 | $42

Waldorf-Astoria, 111 E. 49th St. (bet. Lexington & Park Aves.), 212-355-0440

■ Some of the "best tempura this side of Tokyo" along with "very fresh sushi and "wonderful specials" make this "corporate" Midtowner an "all-purpose" Japanese "treat" complete with "courteous service" that leaves "guests always impressed."

Indian Cafe ● S
16 | 11 | 15 | $19

201 W. 95th St. (bet. B'way & Amsterdam Ave.), 212-222-1600
2791 Broadway (108th St.), 212-749-9200

▨ West Side Indians with "very decent food and prices"; don't expect decor but do expect "friendly", "prompt" service; naysayers cite "small portions" and "erratic" quality.

Indian Oven S
15 | 10 | 14 | $21

200 W. 84th St. (bet. B'way & Amsterdam Ave.), 212-874-6900

▨ Fans call this Westsider a "good value" for basic Indian fare plus some "unusual dishes"; critics wish they'd "spice up the food", speed up the service and hire a decorator.

India Pavilion S
18 | 11 | 15 | $21

240 W. 56th St. (bet. B'way & 8th Ave.), 212-489-0035
35 W. 13th St. (bet. 5th & 6th Aves.), 212-243-8175

▨ These budget Indians may be "dreary" and "unremarkable", but they offer "good food", convenience and "value", "what else do you want?"

Indochine ● S
19 | 18 | 15 | $36

430 Lafayette St. (bet. 4th St. & Astor Pl.), 212-505-5111

▨ The scene has lost some steam but there's still "good people-watching" plus "creative" Vietnamese cuisine at this "stylish" Village "survivor"; portions are "skimpy" but "what little food there is is good" and the staff looks fetching even if they don't fetch much.

In Padella ● S ⇗
– | – | – | I

145 Second Ave. (9th St.), 212-598-9800

This small, warm East Village newcomer has good antipasti, focaccia, sandwiches and pastas at modest prices; a friendly staff, lively atmosphere and an in-the-know twenty/thirtysomething crowd could make this neighborhood find the next Pisces.

Ipanema S
▽ 20 | 15 | 17 | $30

13 W. 46th St. (bet. 5th & 6th Aves.), 212-730-5848

■ "Tasty" and "quite authentic", this "delightful" Brazilian "sleeper" inspires "dreams of Rio and carnevale" in the heart of Midtown; most praise its "pro service", modest prices and a "fab late-night crowd."

Ipoh Garden Malaysia S ⇗
– | – | – | M

13 Eldridge St., 212-431-3449

"You think you're in Malaysia" at this "hole-in-the-wall" dispensing "well-spiced" food at "low prices"; since it's full of "homesick people from the region", it's probably the real thing.

Iridium ● S
16 | 23 | 15 | $40

44 W. 63rd St. (Columbus Ave.), 212-582-2121

▨ "You'll either love or hate" this new Lincoln Center Eclectic's "Dali discovers Toontown", "Alice in Wonderland on acid", "surreal" decor; the food is "uneven" and service "sloppy"; still, it "must be seen" and there's a "great bar" plus a jazz club downstairs.

Isabella's ◐ [S] 19 | 19 | 16 | $29

359 Columbus Ave. (77th St.), 212-724-2100

◪ This "vibrant" Westsider is often "jammed" with a "chic, young" crowd that likes its "predictably good" Italian food and "people-watching extraordinaire" (best from an outside table); it's "fun" if you "don't take it too seriously."

Island ◐ [S] 16 | 15 | 15 | $34

1305 Madison Ave. (bet. 92nd & 93rd Sts.), 212-996-1200

◪ Though "unremarkable", this "cheerful" Carnegie Hill bistro is a popular preppy pit stop thanks to "good salads" and pastas, a "pretty" setting and sidewalk seating; critics say it's "sliding out to sea."

Island Spice [S] 17 | 12 | 16 | $23

402 W. 44th St. (bet. 9th & 10th Aves.), 212-765-1737
362 W. 23rd St. (bet. 8th & 9th Aves.), 212-807-6411 ◐

■ "Escape to Jamaica" via this "tiny but intensely satisfying" West Side Caribbean duo; it's a "refreshing change" with "excellent jerk chicken" and other "cheap", "flavorful" island fare served in "cheery" settings that, not surprisingly, "get crowded fast."

Iso ◐ 25 | 15 | 16 | $28

175 Second Ave. (11th St.), 212-777-0361

■ "Fantastically fresh, beautifully presented sushi" that many call the "best in NY" explains why there's "always a wait" at this East Village Japanese; it's "small and cramped" but "hip" with Keith Haring art and a nice Downtown crowd; prices are Downtown, too.

Isola [S] 18 | 13 | 15 | $28

485 Columbus Ave. (bet. 83rd & 84th Sts.), 212-362-7400

◪ "Pure Columbus Avenue" with "teeny bistro tables" "stacked tighter than planes at JFK", but a big hit with locals who like its "light, tasty" pastas and pizzas, moderate prices and "lively" atmosphere; how it got into *Gourmet* is anybody's guess.

Istanbul Cuisine [S] ≠ ▽ 19 | 9 | 17 | $23

303 E. 80th St. (bet. 1st & 2nd Aves.), 212-744-6903

■ It "doesn't look like much", but this "hole-in-the-wall" Eastsider is "a find" for "top-notch Turkish" food ("super appetizers", "the best chicken in yogurt") and "warm" service all at low prices.

Itcho [S] ▽ 22 | 10 | 18 | $29

402 E. 78th St. (bet. 1st & York Aves.), 212-517-5340

■ "Above-the-norm" sushi and sashimi, "excellent noodles" and other "always good" Japanese fare make this a "breath of fresh air" on the East Side; it's a "great neighborhood find" that few have found.

I Tre Merli [S] 16 | 17 | 12 | $34

463 W. Broadway (bet. Houston & Prince Sts.), 212-254-8699 ◐
Trump Tower, 725 Fifth Ave. (bet. 56th & 57th Sts.), 212-832-1555

◪ A long-running SoHo Italian "scene" with a new breakfast/lunch Midtown spin-off where the ceiling, prices and attitude are all "high"; for best results, "go late", "wear black", sip drinks and watch the crowd; the pasta's good but it's served by a "spaced-out" staff.

Jackson Heights Diner (Queens) **[S] ≠** 22 | 5 | 14 | $17

37-03 74th St. (bet. 37th & Roosevelt), 718-672-1232

◪ Two rules apply at this Jackson Heights dive: (1) "concentrate on the delicious Indian food" ("amazing samosas", "best masala dosa") and (2) "ignore the surroundings" ("cigarette smoke, dirty mirrors, misbehaving children"); "you'll never go back to 6th Street" after you "stuff yourself with gourmet food for $5 at their lunch buffet."

F | D | S | C

Jackson Hole 🄂   13 | 7 | 11 | $16
232 E. 64th St. (bet. 2nd & 3rd Aves.), 212-371-7187 ☽
517 Columbus Ave. (85th St.), 212-362-5177 ☽
1270 Madison Ave. (91st St.), 212-427-2820
1611 Second Ave. (bet. 83rd & 84th Sts.), 212-737-8788 ☽
521 Third Ave. (35th St.), 212-679-3264 ☽
69-35 Astoria Blvd. (70th St.), Queens, 718-204-7070 ☽
▨ With "big burgers that scream for Rolaids as a garnish", it's easy
to see why many feel that this "hole" chain was "better before the
low-fat craze"; if in the mood for a "cow on a bun", this "NY version
of a roadside diner" "gives the lie to the adage there's never too
much of a good thing"; N.B. "quality varies by location."

Jack's Place 🄂   ▽ 14 | 11 | 14 | $22
320 South End Ave. (bet. Liberty & Albany Sts.), 212-786-5225
■ Downtown "hangout" evolving into a viable "alternative to Edward
Moran's" in a Battery Park–area where there are "few choices"; the
Continental-American "club food" and "happy-hour drink specials"
appeal to "young professionals from the nearby WFC."

Jade Palace (Queens) ☽🄂   ▽ 16 | 9 | 12 | $21
136-14 38th Ave. (Main St.), Flushing, 718-353-3366
■ For "top Cantonese seafood" and dim sum roam no further than
this "non-palace" Flushing spot; it's "frantic" when busy, i.e. often,
but that goes well with the "authentic", "exotic" cuisine.

Jai Ya Thai ☽🄂   22 | 9 | 14 | $23
81-11 Broadway (81st St.), Elmhurst, 718-651-1330
396 Third Ave. (28th St.), 212-889-1330
■ "Spicy and delicious" Thai food that rates as "best in NYC" with
bored Gramercy restaurant-goers despite "tacky" decor and waiters
who "forget you"; adventurous diners should try the original Elmhurst
locale; at either "go with a Thai expert and try what's not on the menu."

Jamaican Hot Pot ☽🄂   – | – | – | M
2260 Seventh Ave. (133rd St.), 212-491-5270
"Excellent Caribbean food" makes up for "snotty service" in a Harlem
"neighborhood bar" setting where "authentic heros bring *the* Jamaican
experience to NYC"; although "worth the trip", delivery is available.

Jane Street Seafood Cafe 🄂   21 | 15 | 18 | $32
31 Eighth Ave. (Jane St.), 212-242-0003
■ "A warm and cozy" fireplace sets the "homey" "plain-Jane" New
England tone ("like you're on Cape Cod") for this "longtime local
rave" which serves "excellent fish" to an upscale Village clientele.

Japonica 🄂   24 | 15 | 18 | $30
100 University Pl. (12th St.), 212-243-7752
■ "As good as Japanese food gets" is the view on this "attractive"
Villager which is also touted for "gigantic fresh sushi", "friendly
staff" and "capable hosts"; "too bad the whole Village knows" sums
up the public's distaste for "long lines."

Jean Claude 🄂 ⌗   21 | 15 | 15 | $33
137 Sullivan St. (bet. Houston & Prince Sts.), 212-475-9232
▨ "Truly Parisian in ways both good and bad"; our SoHo surveyors
laud this "cute, trendy" bistro's "reasonably priced" French cuisine
and "warm environment"; on the downside, they fault "cramped
quarters" and "staff lost in the ozone."

Jean Lafitte ● ⑤ | 18 | 18 | 18 | $39 |
68 W. 58th St. (6th Ave.), 212-751-2323
☑ "Authentic French bistro" where Francophiles gather to enjoy a "great bar scene" post-work; "everything works right but the food", which is "*comme ci, comme ça*", though mostly *comme ci*.

Jekyll & Hyde ● ⑤ | 12 | 22 | 13 | $20 |
91 Seventh Ave. S. (bet. Barrow & Grove Sts.), 212-989-7701
☑ Village "theme restaurant" that's scheduled to open a new, larger Midtown branch; the "gimmicky", "Halloween"-scare setting can be "campy and fun" or "beyond tacky" depending on your threshold for kitsch; you're best off sampling the "extensive beer list" ("Jekyll") and skipping the pub food ("Hyde").

Jerry's ⑤ | 18 | 13 | 14 | $25 |
101 Prince St. (bet. Greene & Mercer Sts.), 212-966-9464
302 Columbus Ave. (bet. 74th & 75th Sts.), 212-501-7500 ●
■ An "artsy SoHo crowd" still gathers to "see and be seen" while eating American "bistro-type food" in a "funky diner" setting; loyalists claim "this is why people live in NY", but even they wish it was legal to "kill a waiter"; the new West Side branch, for better or worse, tries hard to clone Downtown.

Jewel of India ⑤ | 22 | 20 | 20 | $31 |
15 W. 44th St. (bet. 5th & 6th Aves.), 212-869-5544
■ "Every guest feels like a maharaja" at this "Midtown jewel"; the prix fixe lunch minimizes cost while maximizing enjoyment of "elegant, classic Indian food" in a "lovely space" that's "convenient to the theater and Grand Central."

Jezebel ● | 19 | 25 | 18 | $38 |
630 Ninth Ave. (45th St.), 212-582-1045
■ The "sexy" New Orleans "bordello" setting may make you wish you left the kids at home; but kids or not, "wonderful Southern home cooking" makes this Theater District dame good for entertaining out-of-town guests or significant others.

J.G. Melon ● ⑤ ⑰ | – | – | – | ⎮ |
1291 Third Ave. (74th St.), 212-650-1310
East Side "no-nonsense" pub where a congenial crowd thrives on reasonably priced burgers, club sandwiches and cottage fries; it's "one of the few bars where a lady can walk in alone."

Jim McMullen ● ⑤ | 16 | 17 | 17 | $33 |
1341 Third Ave. (bet. 76th & 77th Sts.), 212-861-4700
☑ Many East Side regulars feel this beloved standby's "standards plummeted" since "Jim McMullen sold it"; but old habits die hard and many still enjoy its "well-prepared", "plain" American food and attractive, "clubby", "neighborhood" ambiance, especially at brunch.

Jing Fong ● ⑤ | ▽ 21 | 14 | 13 | $21 |
20 Elizabeth St., 212-964-5256
■ The "typical Chinese tackiness" at this barn-size newcomer takes away from what many feel is the "best dim sum" in town; despite "gaudy Hong Kong–style decor", "banquets here can be superb" and "jam-packed" Chinatown places rarely lie.

Jo-An Japanese Restaurant ⑤ | ▽ 23 | 17 | 22 | $21 |
2707 Broadway (bet. 103rd & 104th Sts.), 212-678-2103
■ A growing number of fans declare this "tiny" Upper West Side Japanese "jewel" a "great addition to the 'hood"; "it's worth the trip to 103rd" to enjoy "extremely interesting" specials like the "huiki rice" and "the best noodles around."

	F	D	S	C

Joe Allen ◐ [S] — 15 | 14 | 15 | $30

326 W. 46th St. (bet. 8th & 9th Aves.), 212-581-6464

◪ Brick-walled, "old-fashioned", "old reliable" American Theater District pub/restaurant that makes a "killer Bloody Mary" and a "perfect burger and fries" and still "gets you to the show on time"; "celebrity-watching" is part of the menu.

Joe's Shanghai (Queens) [S] 🚫 — – | – | – | I

136-21 37th Ave. (bet. Main & 138th Sts.), 718-539-3838

If Chinese diners from around NYC come to this minimally decorated Flushing Cantonese-Shanghai specialist, then why not you?; just about everything from dumplings to main courses is cheap as in "real cheap" and good as in "real good."

John's of 12th Street [S] 🚫 — 19 | 12 | 16 | $22

302 E. 12th St. (2nd Ave.), 212-475-9531

◪ Modest prices, "dripping candles" and "mangia" atmosphere inspire many pizza and pasta fanciers to "head for John's"; others feel that "it used to be great", but no longer rates tops.

John's Pizzeria ◐ [S] 🚫 — 22 | 8 | 12 | $15

408 E. 64th St. (bet. 1st & York Aves.), 212-935-2895
278 Bleecker St. (bet. 6th & 7th Aves.), 212-243-1680
48 W. 65th St. (bet. CPW & Columbus Ave.), 212-721-7001

■ "In a city where pizza is a dime a dozen, John's is a nickel better"; our surveyors rate John's "thin-crust" and "brick-oven" pies "a knockout", many insisting they're the "best in the city"; the original Bleecker Street location is still best, but remember the new 65th Street outlet when you're going to Lincoln Center.

JO JO — 24 | 20 | 20 | $48

160 E. 64th St. (bet. Lexington & 3rd Aves.), 212-223-5656

◪ "Pioneering a lighter preparation of French bistro food", chef Jean-Georges Vongerichten's "elegant" duplex East Side townhouse remains "a best value among NYC's high-priced restaurants"; while it's widely agreed that he produces "great food", some say service, though improving, still has a way to go.

Josephina ◐ [S] — 19 | 16 | 16 | $30

1900 Broadway (bet. 63rd & 64th Sts.), 212-799-1000

■ For "California cuisine without the earthquakes" this Lincoln Center yearling, with lovely muralled walls, stands above its neighbors; it offers the waist-conscious a "healthier way to eat" with enough diversity that "veggieheads and carnivores" praise it equally.

Josie's ◐ [S] — – | – | – | M

300 Amsterdam Ave. (74th St.), 212-769-1212

Beautiful Eastsiders come crosstown to get tables at this attractive new West Side, health-conscious, organic American hot spot; for the unreconstructed, the food is affordable and flavorful and, besides having a juice bar, the main bar mixes a neat martini.

Jour et Nuit [S] — 19 | 18 | 14 | $39

337 W. Broadway (Grand St.), 212-925-5971

◪ This SoHo bistro's "creative menu and exciting ambiance" are "worth the trip"; but it may require fluent French and a companion who's a model to get a prime upstairs table and decent service; "wear black."

J. Sung Dynasty [S] — 20 | 19 | 18 | $32

Hotel Lexington, 511 Lexington Ave. (48th St.), 212-355-1200

■ "One of the best Chinese restaurants in NY", this "attractive" mezzanine Midtowner is an "elegant" place for a business lunch, tête à tête or a party in one of its private rooms.

	F	D	S	C

Juanita's ◑Ⓢ
15 | 11 | 13 | $23

1309 Third Ave. (75th St.), 212-517-3800

▣ An ever-happening "pickup scene" and "killer margaritas", not the "uninspired Mexican" food, distinguish this darkly handsome East Side pub; still, it's "always packed" and costs "less than home."

Jubilee ◑Ⓢ
– | – | – | E

347 E. 54th St. (bet. 1st & 2nd Aves.), 212-888-3569

Something to celebrate, this new Sutton Place–area French bistro has lots of pizzazz thanks to a highly touted menu, an easygoing ambiance and seven-day-a-week convenience; ask for Jean Marc, and don't skip dessert.

JUdson Grill
21 | 21 | 19 | $44

152 W. 52nd St. (bet. 6th & 7th Aves.), 212-582-5252

■ "A jumping brasserie", this newcomer to West Midtown is a "wonderful addition" to an area that could use it; a combination of "classy" American grill food and "sleek", "airy" decor causes most surveyors to predict it will make it big.

Jules ◑Ⓢ⇗
18 | 20 | 15 | $27

65 St. Marks Pl. (bet. 1st & 2nd Aves.), 212-477-5560

■ A "romantic", "authentic" Parisian experience in a "comfy East Village" setting where "a hint of attitude" seasons the "bistro fare"; if you like it "packed and smoky", join the "hip" set on jazz Fridays.

Kabul Cafe Ⓢ
▽ 21 | 14 | 17 | $21

265 W. 54th St. (bet. B'way & 8th Ave.), 212-757-2037

■ Whether "sadly overlooked" or simply "hard to find", this "kozy kebab joint" has "great Afghan food at modest prices"; try it for an affordable, inelegant ethnic experience.

Kaffeehaus Ⓢ⇗
19 | 20 | 17 | $22

131 Eighth Ave. (bet. 16th & 17th Sts.), 212-229-9702

■ "Outside it's Chelsea, but inside it's Vienna" with "terrific, authentic Austrian fare" and "amazing desserts" and coffee at "reasonable prices"; by all accounts this "chic new coffeeteria" is a "wonderful change of pace" – "think Strauss."

Kam Chueh ◑Ⓢ⇗
– | – | – | M

40 Bowery St. (Bayard St.), 212-792-6868

"Walk into the past" where the "seafood is fresh" at this "excellent Chinatown" "exotic"; it's a crowded dive and "Hefty bag tablecloths are comical", "but who cares"; P.S. go with a group.

Kang Suh ◑Ⓢ
▽ 23 | 8 | 13 | $25

1250 Broadway (32nd St.), 212-564-6845

■ Enjoy a "really good and fresh", "authentic Korean barbecue" charcoal-grilled at your table; "bring the gang, everyone else does", and "wear something washable" or "smell like kimchi afterwards."

Kan Pai ◑Ⓢ
18 | 14 | 15 | $24

1482 Second Ave. (bet. 77th & 78th Sts.), 212-772-9560
245 Park Ave. S. (bet. 19th & 20th Sts.), 212-529-2888

▣ Despite blue-neon decor, diners enjoy this "midpriced" Japanese duo's "above-average sushi" and "good tempura" in "semi-chic settings"; the Uptown outlet is "getting to be a scene."

Kaptain Banana
▽ 14 | 16 | 15 | $50

101 Greene St. (bet. Prince & Spring Sts.), 212-343-9000

▣ For "a different evening" this "must-see" transvestite cabaret is "fun once"; the "show is better than the food" which is "pretty generic" French that's "very expensive"; call early – it's "hell to get reservations."

Karyatis (Queens) S   21 | 17 | 18 | $30

35-03 Broadway (bet. 35th & 36th Sts.), 718-204-0666

■ "The best Greek food" makes this a good "reason to drive to Queens"; "classy" decor, "live music" and "pleasant service" at fair prices lead to the inevitable question "why go to Greece?"

Katz's Deli S ⌿   16 | 5 | 8 | $15

205 E. Houston St. (Ludlow St.), 212-254-2246

☑ Huge, cafeteria-style Lower East Side "landmark" deli that many consider "a must" for hot dogs and hefty sandwiches that get heftier if you "tip the carver"; but "grungy" quarters, "in-your-face service" and declining quality cause many to shop elsewhere.

Keens Chophouse S   19 | 20 | 17 | $39

72 W. 36th St. (bet. 5th & 6th Aves.), 212-947-3636

■ A "nostalgic" "gentlemen's place", this "charming" "turn-of-the-century" Clinton chophouse offers "great Scotch", "excellent meats" and "rich desserts"; the upstairs party rooms are really special and ideal for a deal-closing party.

Keewah Yen ◑ S   18 | 16 | 18 | $28

50 W. 56th St. (bet. 5th & 6th Aves.), 212-246-0770

■ "Expensive but worth it", this Chinese Midtowner's "interesting fare" and "attentive" service make for "an above-average business lunch."

Kelley & Ping S   16 | 16 | 12 | $17

127 Greene St. (bet. Prince & Houston Sts.), 212-228-1212

☑ This atmospheric SoHo storefront is like taking "a trip to Shanghai"; it may be "contrived" and "could be better", but the "art crowd" loves it.

Khan Restaurant S   ▽ 19 | 9 | 19 | $21

564 Amsterdam Ave. (bet. 87th & 88th Sts.), 212-721-8700

☑ "A cut above other kebaberies" with "surprising value", this Afghan has "good" food that "tastes like it's been marinated forever" and "friendly service", but "sad ambiance"; at least there's no civil war here.

Khyber Pass ◑ S   18 | 14 | 14 | $21

34 St. Marks Pl. (bet. 2nd & 3rd Aves.), 212-473-0989

☑ "Go with a group so you can taste everything" at this "inexpensive" and "interesting" Afghan; while most surveyors consider it "a fun trip to another time and place", dissenters would settle for almost any other place that had better service.

Kiev ◑ S ⌿   16 | 5 | 11 | $14

117 Second Ave. (7th St.), 212-674-4040

☑ For "a great late-night snack at a great price" this 24-hour Ukrainian coffee shop offers latkes, pierogies, soups and blintzes that are "good and cheaper than eating at home"; still, some say it's just "adequate" and "stuffy" but "at 4 AM who cares."

Kiiroi Hana S   22 | 11 | 17 | $28

23 W. 56th St. (bet. 5th & 6th Aves.), 212-582-7499

■ "More affordable than its neighbors", this "worn-at-the-edges" Midtown Japanese can be summed up as "good, basic, fresh" and "fast" for "superior" sushi and noodles; though "crowded for lunch", "evenings are quieter."

King Crab ◑ S   16 | 12 | 15 | $25

871 Eighth Ave. (52nd St.), 212-765-4393

☑ Diners divide over this storefront seafood house; "dependable", "fresh fish" "cooked to order" and "amiable" staff vs. "King nothing", "mediocre", "tacky" and "cheap", but "you get what you pay for."

King's Carriage House [S] 💳̸ — | — | — | M
251 E. 82nd St. (2nd Ave.), 212-734-5490
Upper East Side Contemporary French townhouse newcomer with lots of charm, and good enough at $29 prix fixe to be worth putting on your list to try.

Kings Plaza Diner (Brooklyn) ◐ [S] 16 | 11 | 14 | $17
4124 Avenue U (bet. Coleman & Hendrickson Sts.), 718-951-6700
■ Aka "the KPD", this is a "serious restaurant" "in a diner-disguise" that "caters to all diets" with everything from "heart-healthy choices" to "humongous desserts" off a "huge menu"; the "owners care about you" and "servers know what to do" ("wanna refill doll?").

Kin Khao ◐ [S] 21 | 19 | 15 | $28
171 Spring St. (bet. W. B'way & Thompson St.), 212-966-3939
◪ "Tongue-tingling" Thai and "tall, tanned" twentysomethings are "a recipe for crowds" and make it "hard to get a table" at this SoHo "scene"; fans say the food's "awesome" and look for "Gere and Crawford"; foes who "don't get it" call it "an overrated joke."

Kinoko ◐ [S] 14 | 8 | 13 | $25
165 W. 72nd St. (bet. B'way & Columbus Ave.), 212-580-5900
■ "All-you-can-eat sushi ($18) is the reason to go" to this Upper West Side "survivor in the land of sushi"; they may go heavy on the rice and seating is "cramped", but Westsiders can't resist "a deal."

Kiss ◐ [S] 13 | 16 | 14 | $23
142 W. 10th St. (bet. 6th & 7th Aves.), 212-242-6444
◪ In a 19th-century Greenwich Village house, this "gay restaurant" serves "offbeat" American food to "beautiful boys" in a "homoerotic" setting; though the price is "decent", "mediocre" meals served by "narcissistic" waiters make some think this space is "cursed."

Kitchen Club [S] 💳̸ ▽ 22 | 18 | 21 | $33
30 Prince St. (Mott St.), 212-274-0025
◪ "Eccentric" or "romantic", this "friendly little place" has "creative" Asian-accented Continental food that "deserves more attention"; dissenters find "too much attitude, too little taste."

KK Restaurant [S] 💳̸ ▽ 15 | 7 | 12 | $13
192-94 First Ave. (bet. 11th & 12th Sts.), 212-777-4430
■ Sit outside in the "back garden" to enjoy the "cheap" "stick-to-your-ribs Polish home cooking" for breakfast, lunch or dinner at this "year-in, year-out old reliable", aka "Cholesterol, Inc."

Kleine Konditorei [S] — | — | — | M
234 E. 86th St. (bet. 2nd & 3rd Aves.), 212-737-7130
One of the last of a dying breed, this fairly priced Yorkville German old-timer offers roast goose, lamb shanks, stuffed cabbage and pastries in quarters that probably haven't seen a decorator since the '50s.

Knickerbocker ◐ [S] 18 | 17 | 17 | $29
33 University Pl. (9th St.), 212-228-8490
■ For "easy jazz", "good pizza" and "eye-opening porterhouse steaks", this "clubby" Village "hangout" is the place to be; it's "hard to beat" for "reliable good food" and "fair prices", but don't expect too much, it's just a step up from a pub; chef Ian de Rouin is now on board.

Kodama ◐ [S] ▽ 18 | 11 | 17 | $24
301 W. 45th St. (bet. 8th & 9th Aves.), 212-582-8065
◪ Nestled in the middle of the Theater District, this "reasonably priced" Japanese boasts "excellent" sushi that's "fresh, delicious and unusual", but we hear that "the hot food strikes out lately" and the decor has always been "tacky."

Kom Tang Soot Bul House ◐ [S] ▽ 20 | 8 | 13 | $23

32 W. 32nd St. (bet. 5th Ave. & B'way), 212-947-8482

◪ "On a cold day, nothing beats Korean BBQ" and this is "one of the best"; give it a try with the weekday lunch special – "a great deal"; otherwise, it's "surprisingly pricey" for a place with pidgin English.

Kum Gang San (Queens) [S] 💳̸ – | – | – | M

138-28 Northern Blvd., 718-461-0909

The most important Korean in NYC, this Flushing palace "does it all"; pricey for Queens, it would be a bargain in Midtown; ya gotta see the waterfall, and there's free parking and a huge banquet hall.

Kurumazushi ▽ 23 | 10 | 17 | $43

18 W. 56th St. (bet. 5th & 6th Aves.), 212-541-9030

◪ Given how "expensive" this Midtown Japanese is, people wonder "why can't they afford decor"; however, for "sushi power lunches" or for an evening meal to linger over, there are few better.

Kwanzaa ◐ [S] ▽ 20 | 19 | 18 | $24

19 Cleveland Pl. (bet. Spring & Lafayette Sts.), 212-941-6095

◪ This "promising newcomer" just north of Little Italy has "downhome", "tasty" Southern/African-American food in "attractive" African-influenced surroundings; "if you hit it right, it's a "happening scene."

La Barca ▽ 20 | 16 | 19 | $40

40 Fletcher St. (bet. Front & South Sts.), 212-514-9704

◪ "One of the better Wall Street finds", this low-profile Italian has what most call "excellent", "no-nonsense" food, "very good service" and an "Uptown feel"; to critics it's "massively overpriced."

La Boheme [S] 17 | 16 | 16 | $32

24 Minetta Ln. (bet. W. 3rd & Bleecker Sts.), 212-473-6447

◪ "Sprightly Provençal" fare, including "addictive" brick-oven pizzas, is served in a "rustic" yet "whimsical" bistro setting at this "Village favorite"; it can be "cramped" when jammed with the pre-curtain crowd from the Minetta Lane Theater next door.

La Boite en Bois [S] 💳̸ 21 | 18 | 20 | $40

75 W. 68th St. (bet. CPW & Columbus Ave.), 212-874-2705

■ "True to its name", this "teeny" Lincoln Center–area bistro is the size of a "box", but it's "warm" and "romantic" with "solid", "satisfying" country French food and "solicitous" service; they should post a sign: "no large patrons allowed."

La Bonne Soupe ◐ [S] – | – | – | M

48 W. 55th St. (bet. 5th & 6th Aves.), 212-586-7650

Good enough for both Midwest tourists and Midtown suits, this "cheap and dependable" soup specialist ladles out decent prix fixe lunch deals and bistro basics; despite "surly" service, it's been bubbling along for over 20 years.

La Bouillabaisse (Brooklyn) [S] 💳̸ 24 | 12 | 20 | $24

145 Atlantic Ave. (bet. Clinton & Henry Sts.), 718-522-8275

■ "So crowded you'd think you were in Manhattan, until you see the prices", this bargain Brooklyn Heights bistro is "a winner" thanks to its "outstanding" namesake dish and other "sunny" French fare; customers "wish it were bigger, so the line would be shorter"; BYO.

La Boulangere [S] 💳̸ 18 | 10 | 10 | $19

49 E. 21st St. (bet. Park Ave. & B'way), 212-475-8582

◪ Man could live by bread alone at this Gramercy bakery/cafe that turns out "amazing" loaves, but that would mean missing out on its pizzas, "fresh salads" and other good, light fare; it's plain-looking but "very French", especially the short-tempered service at lunch.

L'Acajou ◗⧖ 19 | 13 | 18 | $34
53 W. 19th St. (bet. 5th & 6th Aves.), 212-645-1706
■ An "eccentric" Chelsea bistro with a "chemistry" all its own; it fuses "hearty" Alsatian fare, well-priced wines, "friendly" service and "quirky" decor into "different" and, most say, "delightful" dining.

LA CARAVELLE 27 | 26 | 26 | $58
33 W. 55th St. (bet. 5th & 6th Aves.), 212-586-4252
■ "All you dream about" in a classic French restaurant, André and Rita Jammet's "comeback" marvel is again "one of NY's best"; "exquisite haute cuisine with brilliant nouvelle touches", "glorious" decor and "polite, never stuffy" service are all "first class"; so are prices, but the prix fixe menus are a first-class buy.

La Caridad ◗⧖≠ 17 | 3 | 10 | $13
2199 Broadway (78th St.), 212-874-2780
■ It's "a dump", but everyone from cabbies to collegians can be found at this West Side Chino-Latino chowing down on "huge portions" of "belly-stuffing" fare at "bargain-basement" prices; it's "quick" and "satisfying" and there's always a line.

La Chandelle ◗⧖ ▽ 17 | 15 | 19 | $24
2231 Broadway (bet. 79th & 80th Sts.), 212-787-8466
☑ A "sweet setting", "accommodating staff" and "fresh, well-prepared" French-Italian food make this West Side bistro a local fave that's even nicer given its modest prices; dissenters find it just "average."

La Collina ⧖ ▽ 18 | 13 | 18 | $33
1402 Lexington Ave. (92nd St.), 212-860-1218
■ A "worthy stop before or after 92nd Street Y events", this Eastsider provides "interesting pastas" and other "solid" Northern Italian food in a "restful", "warm" setting; still, some think the tab is a bit steep.

La Colombe d'Or ⧖ 22 | 20 | 20 | $44
134 E. 26th St. (bet. Lexington & 3rd Aves.), 212-689-0666
■ If you can't spend "a year in Provence", this is a "charming" option: a "rustic", "romantic" Gramercy bistro with "distinctive" country French cooking that's "on the upswing" again now that Wayne Nish is back; if "not solid gold, it still shines."

LA COTE BASQUE 27 | 27 | 26 | $61
5 E. 55th St. (bet. 5th & Madison Aves.), 212-688-6525
☑ For many NYers this Classic French "masterpiece" is and always has been "the epitome of fine dining", from its "exquisite" haute cuisine to its "impeccable" service and "divine murals" of the Basque coast; dissenters find both the sauces and patrons "too rich" and say unknowns are made to feel like "basquette cases", but for most it's "a joy" that "never changes."

La Dolce Vita ⧖ 19 | 15 | 17 | $27
54 W. 13th St. (bet. 5th & 6th Aves.), 212-807-0580
195 Spring St. (bet. Thompson & Sullivan Sts.), 212-431-1315
■ Dining is indeed a dolce experience at these "unpretentious" Italians; "honest", "well-prepared food" at "fair" prices is served by "friendly" waiters in simple but "pleasant" settings; criticism is sparse and mild: "nothing special", "somewhat slow."

La Focaccia ◗⧖≠ ▽ 18 | 16 | 15 | $28
51 Bank St. (W. 4th St.), 212-675-3754
☑ Concentrate on its assets – "very good breads" from its own brick oven, an "attractive" tile-walled setting – and it's easy to forgive this West Village Italian's faults: an "inconsistent" kitchen and "cramped quarters"; cozy by the fire in winter, it's airy and open in summer.

La Folie ◐ [S] ▽ 20 | 22 | 19 | $38
1422 Third Ave. (bet. 80th & 81st Sts.), 212-744-6327
◩ An East Side French newcomer in a "beautiful" setting that's both "elegant" and "fun"; the "noise grows with the hour" and some find the food "nothing special", but it's a "great neighborhood addition."

La Fondue ◐ [S] 15 | 10 | 12 | $21
43 W. 55th St. (bet. 5th & 6th Aves.), 212-581-0820
◩ You'll leave "10 pounds heavier" and with a "high cholesterol" level, but "when the fondue urge hits" this Theater District Swiss standby lets you "dip your heart out" without denting your wallet; both the service and decor are – dare we say it – "cheesy."

La Fusta (Queens) ◐ [S] ▽ 18 | 7 | 13 | $26
80-32 Baxter Ave. (Broadway), 718-429-8222
■ "Good steaks" at "reasonable prices" in simple surroundings sums up this Elmhurst Argentinean-Italian; maybe it's not the pampas, but it satisfies would-be "neighborhood" gauchos.

La Goulue ◐ [S] 16 | 20 | 15 | $43
746 Madison Ave. (65th St.), 212-988-8169
◩ As "beautiful" as ever, but opinion is split on the cuisine and service at this reincarnated East Side belle monde bistro: "revived", "improved greatly", a "charmer" vs. "never was good, still isn't"; with its looks and location this "could be a prize."

LA GRENOUILLE ◐ 28 | 28 | 27 | $65
3 E. 52nd St. (bet. 5th & Madison Aves.), 212-752-1495
■ "Age cannot wither nor custom stale" the charms of this Classic French grande dame; from its "superb" cuisine to its "spectacular" flowers, it's a "garden of visual and epicurean delights", with "unobtrusive but excellent" service that makes even unknowns among its celebrity clientele "feel pampered"; "somewhat less expensive than a trip to France", it may be "plus magnifique"; P.S. check out the lovely private atelier dining room upstairs.

La Jumelle ◐ [S] 18 | 16 | 14 | $27
55 Grand St. (bet. Wooster & W. B'way), 212-941-9651
◩ "Very French", this SoHo bistro provides "unpretentious, good" food at "relatively cheap prices" plus authentic "Euro atmosphere", right down to the cigarette smoke; people-watchers take note: "late-night" is prime time here; "oh, to be young and single again."

La Lunchonette ◐ [S] 20 | 14 | 17 | $32
130 Tenth Ave. (18th St.), 212-675-0342
■ "The quirks work" at this "off-the-beaten-track find" in a "spooky" Chelsea area; the kitchen turns out "solid" French bistro fare "with flair" and the "junkyard-chic" setting is "dark, cozy" and even "romantic"; it's "offbeat" but on target.

La Maison Japonaise 19 | 18 | 18 | $32
125 E. 39th St. (bet. Park & Lexington Aves.), 212-682-7375
■ A "successful mixed marriage" melding Japanese and French cuisine with "creative", "light" results; even if some dishes are "disappointing", the "smooth" service, modest prices and "lovely", "serene" Murray Hill townhouse setting make it a good option.

La Mangeoire [S] 18 | 18 | 18 | $37
1008 Second Ave. (bet. 53rd & 54th Sts.), 212-759-7086
■ An "old standby that holds up well", this "warm and homey" Midtown bistro is "always satisfying" thanks to "very good, simple, country French cooking", a "charming, cozy" setting and pleasant service; prix fixe menus help keep costs down.

Lamarca ⌿

161 E. 22nd St. (3rd Ave.), 212-674-6363

| 18 | 6 | 12 | $16 |

■ "Excellent homemade pastas and sauces" at "fast-food prices" make this eat-in/take-out spot a "top bargain" in the Gramercy area; both the "cafeteria-like" setting and service are "no-frills", but "at this price" no one's complaining; BYO.

La Méditerranée S

947 Second Ave. (bet. 50th & 51st Sts.), 212-755-4155

| 17 | 15 | 17 | $34 |

■ "Its charm never wears thin" say admirers of this Midtown bistro where the "French peasant food" is "simple" but "solid", the setting "cozy" and service warm; it's a "good value" for the area and the prix fixe menus are a "bargain."

La Mela S

167 Mulberry St. (bet. Grand & Broome Sts.), 212-431-9493

| 20 | 8 | 15 | $30 |

☑ Expect "no menu" but "lots of laughs" at this Little Italy "original", where a "large bottle of house wine" and a steady flow of "good, basic" red-sauce food ensures you "won't leave hungry"; "go with a group" and enjoy the "party", but "bring semaphores to flag the waiter."

La Mère Poulard S

Lombardy Hotel, 109 E. 56th St. (bet. Park & Lexington Aves.), 212-750-2710

| 15 | 18 | 14 | $38 |

☑ The signature omelets are "great", but beyond that this pricey East Side repro of the famed French original from Mont St. Michel isn't all it's cracked up to be.

La Metairie ●S

189 W. 10th St. (W. 4th St.), 212-989-0343

| 23 | 22 | 20 | $41 |

■ "Everything a French bistro should be" ("delicious", "warm", "romantic") and a few things it shouldn't be ("cramped", pricey); still, this West Villager's "rustic" charm and "excellent" cooking, leave satisfied diners asking "are we in France?"

La Mirabelle S

Cambridge Hotel, 333 W. 86th St. (bet. West End Ave. & Riverside Dr.), 212-496-0458

| 20 | 16 | 21 | $37 |

■ "Like dining at your French tante's house", this "quiet" West Side bistro offers "no pretense", just "good, traditional" cooking, a "warm" (if rather "faded") setting and "exceptionally amiable service"; it's a "neighborhood secret" that's "habit-forming."

Landmark Tavern S

626 11th Ave. (46th St.), 212-757-8595

| 16 | 19 | 17 | $27 |

☑ Far West Side "landmark" 19th-century Irish pub with a "woody", "historic" setting, "congenial" service and "hearty" classics such as soda bread, pot pies and fish 'n' chips; even if some find the fare "so-so", the "beer" and "nostalgia" are fine.

Langan's ●S

150 W. 47th St. (bet. 6th & 7th Aves.), 212-869-5482

| 13 | 13 | 15 | $30 |

☑ "Don't let the crowded bar fool you" – beyond lies a "quiet", "comfortable" room where "good, though not gourmet" American food and "gregarious" service makes for decent pre-theater dining.

Lanza Restaurant S

168 First Ave. (bet. 10th & 11th Sts.), 212-674-7014

| 18 | 14 | 16 | $24 |

■ A "born-again bargain", this turn-of-the-century East Village Italian kept its "homey", "old-world" charm but revved up its kitchen, thus attracting a hipper kind of "mob" with its "good homestyle" food and "remarkable" prix fixe deals; a "nice garden" is another asset.

La Petite Auberge §

20 | 16 | 19 | $35

116 Lexington Ave. (bet. 27th & 28th Sts.), 212-689-5003

■ "No surprises" mean "no disappointments" at this "steady old-time" bistro; regulars say you "can't go wrong" with its "honest, hearty" food, "reasonable" prices, and "warm", "comfortable" ambiance; be sure to order the signature chocolate soufflé.

La Portena (Queens) ●§

– | – | – | M

74-25 37th Ave. (bet. 74th & 75th Sts.), 718-458-8111

For typical Argentinean cuisine and gaucho atmosphere, nothing comes close to this modestly priced grill in Jackson Heights; go here and skip the flight to B.A.

La Primavera

18 | 17 | 18 | $36

234 W. 48th St. (bet. B'way & 8th Ave.), 212-586-2797

☑ A "good bet for pre-theater dining", this convenient Northern Italian offers "dependable" food in "elegant" surroundings with solid service; it's "noisy and crowded" pre-curtain, calmer afterwards, but critics find it "routine and unexciting" at any hour.

L'Ardoise ●§⊄

▽ 21 | 11 | 18 | $30

1207 First Ave. (bet. 65th & 66th Sts.), 212-744-4752

■ A "relief from everything chic", this East Side French storefront is a nominee for "find of the year" thanks to "excellent" food at down-to-earth prices; what it lacks in decor it makes up for in "enthusiastic" service led by a "maitre d' straight from central casting."

LA RESERVE

26 | 26 | 25 | $54

4 W. 49th St. (bet. 5th & 6th Aves.), 212-247-2993

■ "Elegant, polished, professional and delicious", this formal French Midtowner "never fails" to impress, whether for a business lunch or "very romantic" dinner; while not a culinary style setter, it's "always special" with "gracious" service, a "lovely" setting and a bargain pre-theater menu; a few critics find it too reserved, but they're far outvoted by those who call it "one of NY's best."

La Ripaille

21 | 19 | 20 | $41

605 Hudson St. (bet. W. 12th & Bethune Sts.), 212-255-4406

■ "Good for lovers", especially of "fine" bistro food and French ambiance, this "cozy" West Villager is "reliable", "cordial" and "romantic": "if you can't make it to Paris, this is the next best thing."

La Rivista ●

17 | 15 | 16 | $39

313 W. 46th St. (bet. 8th & 9th Aves.), 212-245-1707

☑ Most consider this Italian "one of the better Restaurant Row" options, with food that's "not outstanding but good" and service that's always "professional"; however, an opposing faction calls it "ordinary" and in need of a "face-lift"; "parking next door is a plus."

La Scala §

19 | 17 | 20 | $37

60 W. 55th St. (bet. 5th & 6th Aves.), 212-245-1575

■ "Old hat" but "nice", this Italian veteran turns out "traditional", "tasty", food in a "comfy" setting with "very pleasant" service; you don't stay around for 40 years without doing things right.

La Spaghetteria ●§

16 | 14 | 15 | $25

178 Second Ave. (bet. 11th & 12th Sts.), 212-995-0900

☑ "Quite civilized for the nabe", this East Village trattoria has a "classy, comfortable" dining room, a "lovely bar area" and food that's "sometimes tasty, sometimes not" but always reasonably priced; critics shrug "why bother?", but they're probably not locals.

La Strada 2 ◐ [S] ▽ 20 | 15 | 16 | $23
80 E. 4th St. (bet. 2nd & 3rd Aves.), 212-353-8026
◪ Sauces are "heavy" but prices are light at this East Village Southern Italian where the emphasis is on "good food, not exciting atmosphere."

La Taza de Oro ◐ ⊄ ▽ 17 | 4 | 14 | $13
96 Eighth Ave. (bet. 14th & 15th Sts.), 212-243-9946
■ You'll find "no frills" but "lots of characters" at this Cuban-Spanish "truck-stop" that dispenses "wonderful rice and beans" and other "down-to-earth" chow at rock-bottom prices; coffee addicts say the café con leche beats any designer brew in town.

La Tour D'Or ▽ 18 | 19 | 17 | $42
14 Wall St. (bet. B'way & Broad St.), 212-233-2780
■ One of "Wall Street's best-kept secrets", a 31st floor penthouse combining good French food with a "unique setting" in J.P. Morgan's former office apartment; it's a good place to "impress clients", even if the food isn't solid gold and some think it's getting a bit "shabby."

Lattanzi Ristorante 21 | 17 | 19 | $41
361 W. 46th St. (bet. 8th & 9th Aves.), 212-315-0980
■ "Excellent Italian fare" accompanied by "lovely" decor and a garden make this a Restaurant Row "winner"; though "hectic" pre-curtain, at off-hours it has "the warmth and conviviality of a trattoria in Rome", including "unusual" Roman-Jewish dishes.

L'Auberge [S] 19 | 18 | 19 | $31
1191 First Ave. (bet. 64th & 65th Sts.), 212-288-8791
◪ Admirers can't understand why this East Side Lebanese is often "deserted" given its "pleasant" setting and "interesting assortment" of "authentic" fare; surveyors say it "deserves to be discovered."

L'Auberge du Midi ◐ [S] ▽ 20 | 20 | 18 | $36
310 W. 4th St. (bet. Bank & W. 12th Sts.), 212-242-4705
◪ "Cozy" and "romantic", this "charming" West Village bistro "makes you feel like you're in France" with its solid country cooking and "quaint" decor; somewhat high prices may explain why it's often "surprisingly empty", but that's one more reason locals like it.

La Vieille Auberge 20 | 15 | 20 | $36
347 W. 46th St. (bet. 8th & 9th Aves.), 212-247-4284
■ The interior is "vieille" indeed, but this "unheralded" Restaurant Row bistro is an "old favorite" that's "caring, pleasant and just plain good"; the staff has a knack for making diners "feel like family."

La Voce [S] – | – | – | M
274 Third Ave. (bet. 21st & 2nd Sts.), 212-505-2151
"Huge portions of good pasta at a small price" make this Italian a welcome "neighborhood place"; it's not exciting, just pleasant, "friendly" and affordable; "order the veal chop – you won't be sorry."

Le Bar Bat 13 | 19 | 13 | $30
311 W. 57th St. (bet. 8th & 9th Aves.), 212-307-7228
◪ More "theme park" than restaurant, this "wacky" West Side multi-level "bat cave" is a "cool place" to "dance, drink, connect" and simply "hang with friends", but "you'd have to be batty" to dine on the American grill food; it's the place with the line of cabs late at night.

Le Beaujolais ▽ 21 | 17 | 21 | $33
364 W. 46th St. (bet 8th & 9th Aves.), 212-974-7464
■ "Affordable, friendly and reliable" Restaurant Row French bistro with steady cooking, "accommodating" service and a prix fixe menu that makes it a pre-theater "favorite"; the decor timeworn but "sweet."

LE BERNARDIN
| 27 | 27 | 26 | $67 |

Equitable Center, 155 W. 51st St. (bet. 6th & 7th Aves.), 212-489-1515
■ A French "temple of seafood" where surveyors experience oceanic "epiphany" over "the best fish in NY, and maybe the world"; the untimely death of chef/co-owner Gilbert LeCoze came as a shock, however, since then his sister Maguy has almost reinvented the restaurant with a wonderful new menu, and has turned what was a handsome space into a beautiful one; just one thing hasn't changed – you still "pay through the gills" except at the $42 prix fixe lunch.

Le Biarritz
| 17 | 15 | 18 | $35 |

325 W. 57th St. (bet. 8th & 9th Aves.), 212-757-2390
◪ That it's "not fashionable" doesn't bother regulars who consider this West Side French bistro a pleasant "trip down memory lane" with "satisfying" food, a "comfortable" setting and steady service.

Le Bilboquet S
| 18 | 16 | 14 | $39 |

25 E. 63rd St. (bet. Madison & Park Aves.), 212-751-3036
◪ Though a "tad trop French" for some ("attitude", "poodles", "smoke", "cheek kissing"), this "tiny" East Side bistro "is like Paris" with good food, people-watching and an "incredible Euro scene at lunch."

Le Bistrot de Maxim's
▽ | 20 | 22 | 19 | $42 |

680 Madison Ave. (bet. 61st & 62nd Sts.), 212-980-6988
◪ The successor to Omnibus strikes some as a "great rebirth with sensible prices", a "lovely" room and "fine French food", while others find it "overblown" and "too snobby" for a basement.

Le Boeuf a la Mode S
| 20 | 19 | 21 | $39 |

539 E. 81st St. (bet. York & East End Aves.), 212-249-1473
◪ The mode is more "1950s" than '90s, which is what locals like about this Yorkville bistro; it "never changes, but that's ok" given its "reliable" French food, "excellent" service and "stressless" ambiance and prices.

Le Bouchon
| – | – | – | E |

319 W. 51st St. (bet. 8th & 9th Aves.), 212-765-6463
"No-frills" Theater-area bistro that some toast for "good French fare" and warm service, but which others pan as "routine" and costly.

LE CHANTILLY S
| 26 | 25 | 24 | $55 |

106 E. 57th St. (bet. Park & Lexington Aves.), 212-751-2931
■ "Reborn" and "still improving", this "lovely" French Midtowner is again as "delicious" as it is "delightful" to look at thanks to the "first-rate contemporary cuisine" of chef David Ruggerio; "bright", "elegant" and "gracious", it's "special in every way" with a pre-theater menu that's an "exceptional buy."

LE CIRQUE
| 27 | 26 | 24 | $64 |

Mayfair Hotel, 58 E. 65th St. (bet. Madison & Park Aves.), 212-794-9292
■ The "greatest show on earth", Sirio Maccioni's NY "legend" makes dining an "event"; "never mind where you sit", chef Sylvain Portay's French cuisine and pastry chef Jacques Torres' desserts are "fabulous", the room is "elegant" and the crowd "oozes power" and wealth; yes, it's "jam-packed" and Sirio can't cover every table, but that's how it is at the "crossroads" of the social universe; P.S. "the $33.75 prix fixe lunch is a real deal."

L'Ecole
| 22 | 18 | 20 | $35 |

462 Broadway (Grand St.), 212-219-3300
■ A real-life laboratory for students of the French Culinary Institute, but "don't worry, you're not a guinea pig" – the food is "professionally prepared" and "presented with pride", the SoHo setting is "serene" and even given the occasional miss, it's "always fun" and "a bargain."

Le Colonial [S] 22 | 24 | 19 | $42

149 E. 57th St. (bet. Lexington & 3rd Aves.), 212-752-0808

◪ "Hotter than hot" since opening, this "designer Vietnamese" attracts a "sexy", "who's who" crowd with "fresh, light, inventive" French-inspired cuisine and an "exotic", "1950s Saigon" setting; it's "chic" and "happening", but some say it's not worth a war to get a table.

Le Comptoir [S] 19 | 20 | 17 | $42

227 E. 67th St. (bet. 2nd & 3rd Aves.), 212-794-4950

◪ The food "keeps improving" at this stylish East Side bistro but it's still secondary to the "authentic Parisian bistro ambiance" and "pretty" people-watching; the scene's "calmer" now, but there's enough of a "buzz factor" to keep the "Euro-chic crowd" happy.

Lee Mazzilli's Sports Cafe ◐ [S] – | – | – | M

208 W. 70th St. (bet. Amsterdam & West End Aves.), 212-877-6787

Ex-Met, ex-Yankee Lee Mazzilli is trying to become the first person to open a major league sports bar that plays more than one season on the West Side; his burgers, beer, salads and ribs are all hits, and if some entrees are errors, as long as the big TVs are clear, the home team wins.

Le Figaro ◐ [S] ≠ ▽ 14 | 16 | 14 | $15

184 Bleecker St. (MacDougal St.), 212-677-1100

◪ Just what you'd expect from a vintage Village cafe: "excellent cake and coffee", an "unhurried, relaxed atmosphere" and superior sidewalk "people-watching"; "fun for brunch", too.

Le Grenadin ▽ 23 | 18 | 23 | $39

13 E. 37th St. (bet. Madison & 5th Aves.), 212-725-0560

■ "One of NYC's hidden treasures", this "quiet" Murray Hill French has "reliable food", "gracious service" and a "lovingly decorated" setting that make it a local "favorite", expecially for lunch.

Le Madeleine [S] 18 | 17 | 17 | $33

403 W. 43rd St. (bet. 9th & 10th Aves.), 212-246-2993

■ "Satisfying" bistro food, modest prices and a little enclosed garden room make this West Midtown French a "bright spot in a dull area"; it's busiest pre-theater and for brunch, but "pleasurable" anytime.

LE MADRI ◐ [S] 24 | 23 | 21 | $48

168 W. 18th St. (7th Ave.), 212-727-8022

◪ Still "cooking up a storm", this Regional Italian neighbor of Barney's serves "lusty", "imaginative" fare in a "big, glamorous" room filled with an equally glamorous crowd; "stylish" and "show-offy", it's a "delight" to most, but critics think both the attitude and prices could use a shot of '90s humility.

Le Max ◐ [S] 17 | 15 | 17 | $32

147 W. 43rd St. (bet. 6th Ave. & B'way), 212-764-3705

◪ "Often forgotten", but this roomy French-American bistro is worth recalling for a "reasonable and competent" meal near Times Square.

Lenge ◐ [S] 18 | 11 | 14 | $25

1465 Third Ave. (bet. 82nd & 83rd Sts.), 212-535-9661
200 Columbus Ave. (69th St.), 212-799-9188

◪ These crosstown Japanese twins may be "nothing special", but they're "always busy" thanks to "decent, predictable" sushi, soups, teriyaki, etc. at "affordable" prices; neither twin is long on looks.

L'Entrecote 19 | 15 | 20 | $36

1057 First Ave. (bet. 57th & 58th Sts.), 212-755-0080

■ "Possibly the most congenial little bistro in the city", this Eastsider keeps its "regulars" happy with "delicious" steak frites and other "well-prepared French basics", a "cozy" setting and "caring" management.

Leopard, The — 24 | 23 | 25 | $49
253 E. 50th St. (bet. 2nd & 3rd Aves.), 212-759-3735
■ "A great evening can be had" at this "opulent and truly different" East Midtown townhouse; with "fine" French-Continental cuisine, "elegant" decor and "wonderful" service, it's a "sheer delight" and perfect for private parties.

Leo's Famous [S] ≠ — – | – | – | I
100 W. 32nd St. (6th Ave.), 212-695-1099
Dog lovers gladly "walk a mile" for the "crusty" franks served at this Herald Square institution; it's the "place to go for pre-Garden hot dogs or for "fast" fill-ups near Macy's.

Le Pactole [S] — 21 | 24 | 20 | $48
2 World Financial Ctr., 225 Liberty St. (Vesey St.), 212-945-9444
◩ "Gorgeous" views of the Hudson River and a "wonderful" Sunday brunch are the main assets of this "elegant" WFC French; though "well-prepared" and "nicely presented", the food doesn't match the setting and some feel it "should be better" at "pay-their-rent" prices.

LE PERIGORD [S] — 26 | 24 | 25 | $57
405 E. 52nd St. (1st Ave.), 212-755-6244
■ "What a classic French should be": "delectable", "gracious" and "absolutely elegant"; this East Side exemplar of fine dining has been around a long time and is still "maintaining the highest standards" from its "superb" food to its "warm and polished" service; it all adds up to being "a perennial favorite" and "one of the best" in town.

Le Pescadou [S] — 21 | 17 | 18 | $40
18 King St. (6th Ave.), 212-924-3434
◩ A SoHo seafood bistro serving a wide variety of fresh fish "with a French pedigree"; most find it "charming" and "authentic", but it fails to hook critics who say it's "crowded" and has nose-dived.

Le Pistou — 23 | 19 | 21 | $43
134 E. 61st St. (bet. Park & Lexington Aves.), 212-838-7987
■ The Park Avenue Regency set would prefer it if no one else found out about this "fabulous bargain": a La Cote Basque spin-off with "outstanding" French food and very "affordable" prix fixe deals; it's "elegant" but "a little too small" for its myriad devotees.

Le Quercy — 19 | 15 | 19 | $34
52 W. 55th St. (bet. 5th & 6th Aves.), 212-265-8141
◩ "Unexciting" but "worthwhile", this Midtown bistro is "homey and welcoming" with "very competent cooking and service at very fair prices", especially for its prix fixe menus.

Le Refuge [S] — 23 | 22 | 21 | $44
166 E. 82nd St. (bet. Lexington & 3rd Aves.), 212-861-4505
■ "As the name promises", this "tranquil" "hideaway" will transport you "far from the city" with its "lovely", "romantic" French country setting and "flavorful" bistro food; the only thing you can't take refuge from here are East Side prices.

LE REGENCE [S] — 26 | 27 | 26 | $61
Plaza Athenee, 37 E. 64th St. (bet. Madison & Park Aves.), 212-606-4647
◩ "First-class" food, "flawless" service and an "opulent" robin's-egg-blue setting that "would make Marie Antoinette swoon" are the hallmarks of this classic French; it's a "place to be pampered" and perfect "if entertaining royalty", yet some feel it's a little "stuffy" and "only for the ancient"; Sunday brunch, however, is "divine."

F D S C

Le Relais 🄢
18 18 16 $41

712 Madison Ave. (bet. 63rd & 64th Sts.), 212-751-5108

⚫ The bistro food's not bad, but it's the "good scenery", specifically of the Chanel-clad variety, that distinguishes this "very French" Eastsider; it's "pricey" and has no shortage of "attitude", but you "can't beat" a sidewalk seat that affords a fashion show.

Le Rivage
19 16 20 $35

340 W. 46th St. (bet. 8th & 9th Aves.), 212-765-7374

⬛ "A good value", this "old reliable" Theater District bistro provides "heaping portions" of basic "pre-nouvelle" food at "great prices"; "small and cozy" with "no-hassle service", it's "perfect pre-theater" if you can "eat that much and stay awake during the show."

L'Ermitage
– – – M

40 W. 56th St. (bet. 5th & 6th Aves.), 212-581-0777

New Classic French–Russian Midtowner providing unusual elegance and romance at lower prices than its competition; with attentive service and a talented pianist, this pleasant surprise won't remain undiscovered – assuming they cook as good as they look.

LES CELEBRITÉS
27 28 27 $73

Essex House, 155 W. 58th St. (bet. 6th & 7th Aves.), 212-484-5113

⬛ Just a few years old and already a superstar, this Classic French is "simply awe-inspiring" in every regard; chef Christian Delouvrier's "exquisite" cuisine "could not be improved", service is "exemplary" and the "lush", "romantic" setting may be "the poshest in town"; prices are "out of this world" but that's fair because everything else is too; "this is it" for special occasions.

Les Deux Gamins ◑🄢
– – – M

170 Waverly Pl. (Grove St.), 212-807-7047

Like Pierre's, which preceded it in this space, this West Village bistro does a good job of recreating the feel of Paris, if not always the taste, and its tiny outdoor seating area is *très agréable* for people-watching.

Les Friandises 🄢 ⇌
▽ 21 12 12 $16

972 Lexington Ave. (bet. 70th & 71st Sts.), 212-988-1616

⬛ "Ooh la la" is all that some sweet tooths can utter when faced with the "outrageous" pastries at this diet-buster; it's "as close to a French patisserie as you'll find", but "go early for the best selection."

Les Halles ◑🄢
21 15 16 $36

411 Park Ave. S. (bet. 28th & 29th Sts.), 212-679-4111

⚫ "Almost Paris", this "upbeat" bistro/butcher shop makes "meat lovers rejoice" over its "terrific" meats and frites, but it's often as "noisy and crowded" as "le subway"; the "authentic" ambiance includes "uptight waiters" and "secondhand smoke" – call for Philip Morris.

LESPINASSE 🄢
28 28 27 $68

St. Regis Hotel, 2 E. 55th St. (bet. Madison & 5th Aves.), 212-339-6719

⬛ An "ultraluxurious" showcase for "virtuoso" chef Gray Kunz's "incredibly subtle and complex", Asian-accented French cuisine; "every bite brings a new taste sensation" and the dishes are "beautifully presented and splendidly served" in a "lush" Louis XV setting; apart from heart-stopping prices, our surveyors' major complaint is that the "ornate room" is "stuffy" and "pompous."

Les Pyrenees ◑🄢
19 17 19 $37

251 W. 51st St. (bet. B'way & 8th Ave.), 212-246-0044

⚫ Though not a peak experience, this Theater District bistro is a "good buy", especially for its pre-theater prix fixe; it has "dependable" food, "friendly" service and an "unchicness that's appealing."

99

Les Routiers [S] 18 | 16 | 17 | $37
568 Amsterdam Ave. (bet. 87th & 88th Sts.), 212-874-2742
■ Upper Westsiders "need more" places like this "earnest" French truck stop–style bistro that serves "standard" but "satisfying" mid-priced fare in a "rustic", "quaint" setting.

Les Sans Culottes ◐ [S] 15 | 13 | 17 | $30
1085 Second Ave. (bet. 57th & 58th Sts.), 212-838-6660
◪ "Sausages are the centerpiece" at this "cozy" vs. "seedy" East Side bistro where diners whet their appetite on a rack of meats; critics say the rest of the fare is "sans taste", but "filling" and "cheap."

Le Streghe ◐ [S] ▽ 20 | 17 | 17 | $33
331 W. Broadway (Grand St.), 212-343-2080
◪ A "very SoHo" yet "very European" Italian newcomer that pleases most surveyors with its "tasty" food and "nice decor", but which leaves others yawning: "this block doesn't need another bistro."

Le Taxi [S] 18 | 18 | 17 | $41
37 E. 60th St. (bet. Park & Madison Aves.), 212-832-5500
◪ Though hailed by a "chic crowd", this new East Side bistro elicits a checkered reaction: to some it's fast moving with good food and a "very French" feel; to others it's an "expensive" hack.

Letizia ◐ [S] 19 | 17 | 20 | $39
1352 First Ave. (bet. 72nd & 73rd Sts.), 212-517-2244
■ "If you want to be cared for in comfort" with "well-prepared food", try this East Side Northern Italian; "warm, friendly" and "satisfying", it's the kind of "neighborhood" place where "you can linger."

Le Train Bleu 15 | 20 | 17 | $30
Bloomingdale's, 1000 Third Ave., 6th fl., 212-705-2100
◪ "One train you don't want to miss" if worn out by Bloomies: a "delightful" in-store "hideaway" with "lovely" Orient Express decor and good, if not great, International fare; afternoon tea is pleasant.

Levana [S] 20 | 17 | 18 | $45
141 W. 69th St. (bet. B'way & Columbus Ave.), 212-877-8457
■ "Proving kosher need not be boring" ("kosher buffalo and venison isn't chopped liver"), this "elegant", "innovative" Westsider is probably the "best kosher in town", but it's "oy vey" priced.

Le Veau d'Or 18 | 14 | 17 | $41
129 E. 60th St. (bet. Park & Lexington Aves.), 212-838-8133
◪ A "period-piece" bistro with "'50s decor and food", if not prices; to loyalists this Eastsider is "old and excellent" with "classic French food" and an "authentic feel", but to critics it's just old and "tired."

Levee, The ◐ [S] ▽ 16 | 13 | 13 | $20
76 E. First St. (1st Ave.), 212-505-9263
■ "Funky, happening East Village" BBQ-Cajun joint where the crowd is as "colorful" as the divey decor and the food's "filling", "hearty" and "cheap"; "terrific live music" and cold beer can bring a flood of young hirsute customers.

Lexington Avenue Grill ◐ [S] 13 | 12 | 13 | $26
Loews NY Hotel, 569 Lexington Ave. (51st St.), 212-753-1515
◪ "Nothing exceptional", but this East Side hotel grill serves "reliable" Continental fare in a "pleasant", spacious setting at prices that are "reasonable for the area."

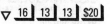

Life Cafe ◐ [S] ▽ 15 | 14 | 14 | $16

343 E. 10th St. (Avenue B), 212-477-8791

■ A "comfortable joint" with a "fresh", "tasty" Vegetarian-Eclectic-Health Food menu that attracts a "grungy" East Village crowd; it's a "good place to take out-of-towners" to observe Downtown life forms.

Lincoln Tavern ◐ [S] – | – | – | M

51 W. 64th St. (bet. Columbus Ave. & CPW), 212-721-8271

Attractive new Lincoln Center pit stop that may be worth trying for a quick American bite and brew.

L'Incontro ▽ 18 | 15 | 18 | $30

75 Fifth Ave. (bet. 15th & 16th Sts.), 212-229-2992

◪ "Very good pasta" and other well-prepared Italian fare served in "big portions" at modest prices makes this a "nice addition" to the Gramercy area; doubters say "unexciting", "something's missing."

Lion's Head ◐ [S] 13 | 16 | 15 | $27

59 Christopher St. (7th Ave. S.), 212-929-0670

■ The food's "decent" but "the bar's the thing" at this "classic" Village pub/restaurant; countless writers have sought inspiration or just intoxication in its "historic" ambiance and "conviviality."

Lipizzana ◐ [S] – | – | – | M

987 Second Ave. (bet. 52nd & 53rd Sts.), 212-753-4858

Though this new mid-priced Viennese Midtowner is not as graceful as its namesake, it does offer a gemütlichkeit not readily available in NYC plus schnitzel, goulash, calf's liver and chicken paprika; if only NYC had a first-rate Viennese!

Lipstick Cafe 18 | 13 | 13 | $20

885 Third Ave. (54th St.), 212-486-8664

◪ "Delicious breakfast pastries" and "tasty, creative" lunch fare make this "airy" lobby cafe a hit with the East Midtown office crowd, but the noontime rush can result in "ditsy service" and "long lines", and some find it a "little pricey" for "soigné fast food."

Little Club – | – | – | E

1394 York Ave. (74th St.), 212-744-2900

Tout East Side; this stylish red, white and black Contemporary American Eastsider is where the smart set stops over between Palm Beach and Newport; it's a younger Mortimer's, but with a better kitchen and much better attitude; check out the private room downstairs.

Little Poland [S] 💳̸ ▽ 17 | 4 | 11 | $12

200 Second Ave. (bet. 12th & 13th Sts.), 212-777-9728

◪ "Diet tomorrow" could be the slogan of this East Village Polish coffee shop; it serves "massive amounts of stick-to-your-ribs food" amidst "Depression-era decor" with prices to match; the "incredibly cheap breakfasts" will keep you stuffed for a week.

Live Bait ◐ [S] 12 | 11 | 10 | $20

14 E. 23rd St. (bet. B'way & Madison Ave.), 212-353-2400

◪ For fine dining "go fish" elsewhere; but if you want to "drink", watch "model wanna-bes" and angle for dates, this Dixie dive's the place; once past the bar scene there are "decent" Southern eats to be had if your waitress isn't "too busy looking good to help."

Lobby Lounge [S] – | – | – | E

Four Seasons Hotel, 57 E. 57th St. (bet. Park & Madison Aves.), 212-758-5700

This "spacious, attractive" cafe overlooking the lobby of the new I.M. Pei–designed Four Seasons Hotel has a "very good" light American menu and smooth service; it's perfect for a civilized tea or cocktails.

F	D	S	C

Lobster Box (Bronx) ◐ [S]

F	D	S	C
16	13	14	$33

34 City Island Ave. (Belden St.), 718-885-1952
◪ Water views are a definite asset at this City Island veteran, which, despite "great lobster" and "decent" seafood, has "barnacles."

Lofland's N.Y. Grill ◐ [S] ▽

F	D	S	C
16	11	14	$23

29 W. 21st St. (bet. 5th & 6th Aves.), 212-924-3264
■ "Good burgers, chicken and beer" plus some of the "best ribs north of Nashville" make this basic bar and grill a Flatiron "find"; it's not much on looks, but it has a "mellow atmosphere."

Lola [S]

F	D	S	C
20	20	18	$37

30 W. 22nd St. (bet. 5th & 6th Aves.), 212-675-6700
◪ "Lively" and "uplifting", this "sassy" Chelsea American-Eclectic makes for a "jazzy night out" with its "hot food, hot crowd" and "pretty", "festive" ambiance; a few agnostics think it has lost its zing, but even they get that good time religion at Sunday gospel brunch.

Lotfi's Moroccan ◐

F	D	S	C
–	–	–	M

358 W. 46th St. (bet. 8th & 9th Aves.), 212-582-5850
After years as a popular Village standby, this simple but attractive, modestly priced Moroccan has moved up to Restaurant Row; for the moment, at least, you won't have any trouble getting in; however, once the public discovers the couscous, tahini, kebabs and b'steeya (all at $12.95 or less), it won't be so easy.

Louie's Westside Cafe ◐ [S]

F	D	S	C
17	14	15	$27

441 Amsterdam Ave. (81st St.), 212-877-1900
◪ "Good vibes" emanate from this "casual, comfortable" West Side cafe thanks to its simple American "homestyle" food, "friendly" service and "fantastic brunch"; still, some find it "ho-hum."

Loui Loui ◐ [S]

F	D	S	C
16	15	14	$31

1311 Third Ave. (75th St.), 212-717-4500
◪ Despite some "imaginative" pastas and "nice decor", that this East Side Italian has "nothing to make it stand out" from the pack, except perhaps "pretentious" service and highish pasta prices.

Louisiana Community Bar & Grill [S]

F	D	S	C
18	17	14	$27

622 Broadway (bet. Bleecker & Houston Sts.), 212-460-9633
■ It's "Mardi Gras every night" at this "sprawling" LoBro Cajun with "heaps" of "spicy" food, "jumping" live bands, "bayou" decor and an "endless bar;" for "tons of fun", "go with a big group" and let "le bon temps rouler"; it's so close to Little Italy that some surveyors think Lou Z. Anna is Italian.

Lucky Cheng's ◐ [S]

F	D	S	C
17	17	17	$26

24 First Ave. (bet. 1st & 2nd Sts.), 212-473-0516
■ "Never a drag", this playfully "decadent" East Village Cal-Asian has "bizarre but delicious combos – that goes for the menu and the transvestite staff"; the food's worth "the crowds, noise and your waitress making four wig changes"; a "must-see at least once"; Barbra Streisand tried, but couldn't get in here.

Lucky's Bar & Grill ◐ [S]

F	D	S	C
–	–	–	M

60 W. 57th St. (6th Ave.), 212-582-4004
A simple Midtown grill that's good for a light, quick, brew-fueled meal.

Lucky Strike ◐ [S]

F	D	S	C
15	14	12	$25

59 Grand St. (bet. Wooster St. & W. B'way), 212-941-0479
◪ If it's "past its prime", no one told the "very Downtown" crowd that still packs this SoHo late-night poserville; the bistro food's "not bad", but it's served by a "too cool" staff amidst "lots of smoke" and noise.

Lucy's Retired Surfers ⦿   10 | 11 | 10 | $19
*503 Columbus Ave. (bet. 84th & 85th Sts.), 212-787-3009*S
79 Pearl St. (Hanover Sq.), 212-809-5592
☑ "The chef must be out surfing", but as long as he whipped up the "Jell-O shots" that's fine with the would-be beach bums and bunnies who jam these surfer-theme bars with Cal-Mex food that's just a chaser.

Ludlow Street Cafe ⦿ S   14 | 10 | 13 | $18
165 Ludlow St. (bet. Houston & Stanton Sts.), 212-353-0536
☑ The Southern-accented food may "vary" in quality, but even so there's something about this "quaint" (some say "dingy") Lower East Side cafe that keeps people "coming back"; it could be "the prices, the crowd", "great brunch" or late-night live music.

L'Udo ⦿ S   – | – | – | M
432 Lafayette St. (Astor Pl.), 212-388-0978
Lovely frescoes have done wonders for this elegant bi-level space across from the Public Theater, now serving country French and Italian dishes from a glassed-in kitchen at modest Village prices; friendly staff and the promise of a large back garden come spring should make this an "in" spot.

Luke's Bar and Grill ⦿ S ≠   14 | 12 | 13 | $21
1394 Third Ave. (bet. 79th & 80th Sts.), 212-249-7070
■ "Perfect for what it is": a "warm" and "easy" East Side local bar/grill serving "good burgers, salads" and other basic "all-American" fare at basic prices to diners from twentysomethings to "retired bikers."

Luma S   23 | 16 | 20 | $36
200 Ninth Ave. (bet. 22nd & 23rd Sts.), 212-633-8033
■ So good "you'll swear it's bad for you" describes the "delicious, innovative" Health Food–American fare at this Chelsea paragon of "organic chic"; with spare but "elegant" decor and good service it even seduces "lifelong meat eaters", but watch for non-PC prices.

Lum Chin (S.I.) ⦿   ▽ 18 | 17 | 18 | $22
1640 Forest Ave. (Willowbrook), 718-442-1707
*1771 Highland Blvd. (Liberty St.), 718-979-6100*S
*4326 Amboy Rd. (bet. Richmond & Armstrong Aves.), 718-984-8044*S
☑ Mixed reactions to this Chinese mini-chain suggest that quality varies, but hit it right and you can find "well-prepared" and even "original" food in space that's more "modern" than the Chinese norm.

Lupe's East L.A. Kitchen S ≠   17 | 8 | 12 | $16
110 Sixth Ave. (Watts St.), 212-966-1326
■ West SoHo meets East LA at this "funky" "dive diner" where the "dirt-cheap" Mexican food is "simple", "quick" and "filling"; the ambiance is "nil" except for the "good-looking" Downtown crowd.

Lusardi's ⦿ S   21 | 18 | 21 | $44
1494 Second Ave. (bet. 77th & 78th Sts.), 212-249-2020
■ "Ticking along like a well-made watch", this East Side Northern Italian is a "minor classic"; "they do everything well" from the "fine" food to the "gracious" service; "in a sea of Italians" this one crests.

LUTÈCE   27 | 24 | 26 | $67
249 E. 50th St. (bet. 2nd & 3rd Aves.), 212-752-2225
☑ For over a generation this haute bistro and its Alsatian chef Andre Soltner defined what a "great French restaurant" should be and, though now overshadowed by younger rivals, it remains "one of the best" and "the standard" by which others are judged; though the restaurant has just been sold, Soltner plans to stay on and has been joined by a new-generation top chef, Eberhard Müller (ex Le Bernardin).

Mackinac Bar & Grill ◐Ⓢ   16 | 18 | 15 | $29
384 Columbus Ave. (bet. 78th & 79th Sts.), 212-799-1750
☒ Located just behind the Natural History Museum, this dark-wood and red would-be Michigan "hunting lodge" and its customers look like they came right out of the "J. Crew catalog"; judging by its "homestyle" American food, they found the chef by catalog as well.

Madison Avenue Cafe Ⓢ   ▽ 16 | 13 | 14 | $24
937 Madison Ave. (74th St.), 212-861-7400
▮ It's "a cafe" or "a coffee shop", depending on how you call it; but given its chic East Side location and clientele it's advisable to "check it out" for a soup, salad or sandwich.

Mad.61 Ⓢ   22 | 20 | 17 | $38
Barney's NY Uptown, 10 E. 61st St. (Madison Ave.), 212-833-2200
▮ It's a mad, mad world ("I sat next to Christie Brinkley!") at Pino Luongo's "sleek" art deco newcomer at Barney's Uptown; besides a charcuterie-style Market menu at lunchtime, there are praiseworthy entrees, plus pizzas, risottos, soups and fresh bread "to dream of"; in short, this may be NYC's best-used basement.

Main Street Ⓢ   16 | 16 | 16 | $25
446 Columbus Ave. (bet. 81st & 82nd Sts.), 212-873-5025
☒ "The portions are huge" at this "family-style American alternative to Carmine's", where the meat loaf and mashed potatoes are "just like mom made", but the "handsome" high-ceilinged space makes you realize "this is eating out"; for best results go with a group.

Malaga Ⓢ   19 | 8 | 16 | $27
406 E. 73rd St. (bet. 1st & York Aves.), 212-737-7659
☒ A "paella lover's dream", this Spanish Eastsider is also "a great garlic bargain"; the decor's "nothing fancy", but "by your second visit you're part of the family"; "try the shrimp" and don't miss the sangria.

Malaysia and Indonesia Ⓢ 𝄫   – | – | – | M
18 Doyers St. (bet. Mott & Pell Sts.), 212-267-0088
The fish and fried chicken with banana leaves are "cheap", "delicious" and "authentic"; but non-English-speaking help seem "frazzled" and the decor is strictly back country.

Mambo Grill ◐Ⓢ   17 | 15 | 17 | $32
174 E. 82nd St. (bet. Lexington & 3rd Aves.), 212-879-5516
☒ "A good change of pace", this "sassy" Venezuelan Eastsider has "spicy" food and clientele; come enjoy the "upbeat" ambiance and dance the night away to live Latin music on Saturday nights.

Mandarin Court ◐Ⓢ   20 | 9 | 12 | $18
61 Mott St. (bet. Canal & Bayard Sts.), 212-608-3838
▮ Some say "item for item, the best dim sum in Chinatown"; expect "attentive" service, "zesty" flavors and huge Chinese crowds on weekends; but there's no denying the decor is "very plain."

Manganaro's Hero-Boy 𝄫   17 | 5 | 10 | $13
492 Ninth Ave. (bet. 37th & 38th Sts.), 212-947-7325
▮ "Delicious six-foot heros" make this inexpensive Ninth Avenue establishment an old favorite with NYers who aren't put off by the "no-frills", "cafeteria-style atmosphere."

Mangia e Bevi ◐Ⓢ   19 | 12 | 15 | $23
800 Ninth Ave. (53rd St.), 212-956-3976
▮ The most colorful trattoria in Hell's Kitchen is "a find that all the locals know about" with "generous" pasta, "super" Caesar salad and affordable wine that make you want to *mangia e bevi*; often "frenetic", it makes "you feel like you're at a party in Italy."

104

Manhattan Bistro ◐ [S] 17 | 16 | 16 | $29
129 Spring St. (bet. Greene & Wooster Sts.), 212-966-3459
◪ Belmondo-style bistro where an "oh-so-cool" crowd does SoHo proud; "polished service" and well-executed bistro fare (from steaks to sweetbreads) are important pluses, but many don't understand what the fuss is about.

Manhattan Brewing Co. [S] 13 | 17 | 13 | $22
42 Thompson St. (bet. W. B'way & Broome St.), 212-925-1515
◪ One "goes to this SoHo brewpub for beer and atmosphere" with food as "an afterthought"; however, "a fabulous array" of beers keeps the young crowd coming.

Manhattan Cafe [S] 22 | 20 | 20 | $42
1161 First Ave. (bet. 63rd & 64th Sts.), 212-888-6556
■ "A dark-wood, fancy" surf 'n' turf, "complete with antiques", that's rated by many "as good as any NY steakhouse" and is compared to "The Palm – with atmosphere"; it's a good value – especially the early dinner, and "deserves more respect."

MANHATTAN OCEAN CLUB ◐ [S] 26 | 24 | 24 | $52
57 W. 58th St. (bet. 5th & 6th Aves.), 212-371-7777
■ "Polished" and "swimmingly wonderful", this Midtowner is "one of the best seafood restaurants in town" and many think it is "*the* best, especially for a business lunch"; come for fish that's "fresh and simple" and plan to "stay for fine wine and desserts."

Manhattan Plaza Cafe [S] (CLOSED) 18 | 18 | 17 | $24
482 W. 43rd St. (bet. 9th & 10th Aves.), 212-695-5808
◪ Hidden away up a flight of stairs in the Manhattan Plaza Health Club, this "diamond in the rough" delights most patrons as an unexpected oasis for inexpensive light American dining with views of the swimming pool in the foreground and Midtown skyline in the background.

Man Ray [S] 16 | 15 | 15 | $28
169 Eighth Ave. (bet. 18th & 19th Sts.), 212-627-4220
◪ "Relaxing" Chelsea hangout with "stark but stylish", "film noir mise en scene" near the Joyce; some say the Contemporary American food is "forgettable", but praise for the calamari and the tarte Tatin rolls in as if they were Proust's madeleines.

Mappamondo ◐ [S] ⇏ 19 | 12 | 15 | $20
11 Abingdon Sq. (8th Ave.), 212-675-3100
581 Hudson St. (Bank St.), 212-675-7474
◪ Two "cute as a button" West Village Italians that attract a "high-spirited" young clientele with "inventive", low-budget pasta and the chance to see their friends.

MARCH 27 | 26 | 26 | $63
405 E. 58th St. (bet. 1st Ave. & Sutton Pl.), 212-754-6272
■ Chef-owner Wayne Nish draws superlatives from most guests for his "first-rate" Contemporary American prix fixe dinners and for the "especially romantic" East Side townhouse dining experience that he and his partner Joe Scalice supply; service is that excellent combo of "friendly" and "professional", and there's a garden too.

Marchi's 19 | 18 | 20 | $39
251 E. 31st St. (bet. 2nd & 3rd Aves.), 212-679-2494
◪ "You have to be an ox" or more sensibly bring your herd to eat the old-fashioned Italian prix fixe dinner served nightly at this "quaint brownstone" from "the 1930s"; "they have a formula that works" some say; for others "once in a rare while is enough."

Marina Cafe (S.I.) � ▽ 19 | 22 | 19 | $34
154 Mansion Ave. (Hillside Terr.), 718-967-3077
☑ Great views of Great Kills harbor and good-looking staff are highlights at this waterfront cafe; the seafood is "good for S.I.", "average for NY."

Marion's Continental 17 | 19 | 16 | $26
Restaurant & Lounge ▣
354 Bowery St. (bet. Great Jones & E. 4th Sts.), 212-475-7621
☑ "Lots of black dresses" fill this "funky" '40s supper-club-style Village "hangout" for Caesar salads and other affordable Continental fare served by "spacey" staff; it's like being "in a Scorsese film."

Mario's (Bronx) ▣ 21 | 14 | 19 | $31
2342 Arthur Ave. (187th St.), 718-584-1188
☑ "One of the best old NY Italian places" where "valet parking is a blessing", this classic "red-sauce" Arthur Avenue eatery is newly decorated and expanded, but be advised, "dress casual", and for the potential wait, well, "bring a chair"; P.S. check out the pizza.

Markham, The ▣ 18 | 16 | 15 | $37
59 Fifth Ave. (bet. 12th & 13th Sts.), 212-647-9391
■ A "nifty" new Greenwich Village "'in' place" where the fashion/ publishing crowd "table-hop and do business at lunch" and serious socializing at dinner; the novel American food with a seasonal twist gets overwhelmingly positive, but a few mixed reviews, which is fortunate because there's not an extra seat available.

MARK'S ▣ 25 | 26 | 24 | $54
The Mark, 25 E. 77th St. (Madison Ave.), 212-879-1864
■ "Prince Charles would feel right at home" in this "elegant" dining room where fine nouvelle French cuisine and relaxed Edwardian ambiance are hallmarks; brunch and tea are a natural in this "oasis"; a few critics find all this chic "boring" and "stuffy."

Marlowe ◗▣ – | – | – | M
328 W. 46th St. (bet. 8th & 9th Aves.), 212-765-3815
Brand-new and attractive Restaurant Row double brownstone American; it has an attractive space, including fireplace and garden, and a Japanese chef (ex Saloon) who is planning an easy-access, fresh American menu – nothing too fancy, nothing too expensive.

Marnie's Noodle Shop ⇄ 16 | 6 | 12 | $14
466 Hudson St. (bet. Barrow & Grove Sts.), 212-741-3214
☑ "Oodles and oodles" of "cheap" and "creative" Asian-accented noodles make this "another West Village staple", but it "needs more space"; critics say it's "one step up from a greasy spoon", but on a cold winter night the crowd is too busy slurping to notice.

Marti Kebab ◗▣ ▽ 19 | 8 | 17 | $20
1269 First Ave. (bet. 68th & 69th Sts.), 212-737-6104
238 E. 24th St. (bet. 2nd & 3rd Aves.), 212-545-0602
■ Beloved for "authentic Turkish kebabs" and other Middle Eastern specialties, these "family establishments" offer "great value"; the First Avenue location is quieter and more spacious than the one at Gramercy Park, which has "only seven tables."

Martini's ◗▣ 18 | 17 | 14 | $35
810 Seventh Ave. (53rd St.), 212-767-1717
☑ "Casual" Theater District newcomer with chef Richard Krause producing a "quick", "clever" Cal-Italian menu of mini-pizzas, grilled dishes, salads and de-lish desserts; the open kitchen adds warmth in winter and house-special icy martinis go down best at sidewalk seats in summer; critics say the experience is like being in *The Flintstones*.

Marumi 🅂
▽ 23 | 15 | 16 | $20
546 LaGuardia Pl. (bet. Bleecker & W. 3rd Sts.), 212-979-7055
■ Despite decor and service that could use some work, "reliable" sushi and Japanese food at "reasonable" prices are touted by NYU neighbors, who would like to "keep it a secret."

Mary Ann's 🅂
17 | 11 | 12 | $20
116 Eighth Ave. (16th St.), 212-633-0877 ⌐
1503 Second Ave. (bet. 78th & 79th Sts.), 212-249-6165
2454 Broadway (91st St.), 212-877-0132
☑ "Crowded", "college"-style hot spots where you wait on line for "cheap", "generic" Mexican food and "great margaritas in plastic containers"; diners "feel welcome" and never leave hungry, but some call the food "Mexa-mush" and service "inept."

Marylou's ◑🅂
18 | 17 | 17 | $34
21 W. Ninth St. (bet. 5th & 6th Aves.), 212-533-0012
☑ Greenwich Village townhouse standby whose "eclectic dining rooms" have housed untold "tête-à-têtes" over "creatively prepared" fresh fish and Continental fare; however, sagging ratings and savage comments suggest an overhaul is overdue.

Mary's Restaurant ◑🅂
▽ 17 | 16 | 17 | $31
42 Bedford St. (bet. Carmine & Leroy Sts.), 212-741-3387
☑ This "charming" Edith Wharton–era West Village "near dive" with a fireplace has loyalists who tout it "for seduction" (especially upstairs), but the light American-Eclectic cuisine doesn't seduce everyone: "used to be better", "not cheap."

Match ◑🅂
– | – | – | E
160 Mercer St. (bet. Houston & Prince Sts.), 212-343-0020
Epitomizing SoHo chic, this crowded artists', models' and wanna-bes' Contemporary American provides a winning combination of good food and better people-watching; go to the Merc Bar across the street before or after to warm-up or cool-down over a drink.

Matthew's 🅂
23 | 22 | 19 | $43
1030 Third Ave. (61st St.), 212-838-4343
■ "Creative and breezy", chef Matthew Kenney's East Side oasis "looks like Rick's Cafe" and has a creative American menu with Mediterranean influences; it's "a real addition to the NY scene", drawing an attractive, sophisticated crowd; "play it again, Sam."

Maurya 🅂
19 | 13 | 16 | $25
129 E. 27th St. (bet. Park & Lexington Aves.), 212-689-7925
131 Duane St. (bet. W. B'way & Church St.), 212-964-8528
■ "Curry Hill" and TriBeCa Indian siblings with "tasty tandoori" dishes at "low prices"; some prefer 27th Street for the service and decor, but both are "consistent" and "a cut above 6th Street"; the $7.95 lunch buffet is "hard to beat."

Mavalli Palace 🅂
▽ 22 | 14 | 19 | $22
46 E. 29th St. (bet. Park & Madison Aves.), 212-679-5535
■ This "unusual" Southern Indian–Vegetarian newcomer is already being called "the nicest place for Indian in town"; it has a "light" interior and "friendly", but "disorganized" staff.

Mayfair ◑🅂
15 | 13 | 18 | $28
964 First Ave. (53rd St.), 212-421-6216
■ A "down-to-earth" "neighborhood standby" where the "hearty" dishes run to pot roast and American comfort food; the service is "warm" and "attentive", which may help account for why it remains "very popular" though "nothing great."

107

Mayrose ◐ [S] 13 | 11 | 10 | $17
920 Broadway (21st St.), 212-533-3663
◪ A "bright" and "cheerful", high-ceilinged "yuppie diner" in the Flatiron District where "they let you come in with rollerblades"; some say its "homestyle menu" "fills a void", but others call it "a real underachiever" that's "tragically hip."

Mazzei [S] 23 | 17 | 20 | $41
1564 Second Ave. (bet. 81st & 82nd Sts.), 212-628-3131
■ "Brick-oven" specialties, "delectable" baby goat and anything with olive oil (i.e. practically everything) stand out at this popular Italian Upper Eastsider where everything is fine except "the noise level."

McSorley's Old Ale House ◐ [S] 🚫 10 | 18 | 12 | $15
15 E. 7th St. (bet. 2nd & 3rd Aves.), 212-473-9148
■ A "must-see" "NYC institution" from 1854, this East Village Irish saloon serves "great ale" and less noteworthy sandwiches and burgers; it's a "prime place to make friends" and so "historic" that "everyone should try it."

Medici 56 [S] 19 | 23 | 19 | $38
25 W. 56th St. (bet. 5th & 6th Aves.), 212-767-1234
■ "Impressive", "too good to be kosher", Kosher-Italian in a soaring modern space with a pianist to boot; "elegant and understated" say all, but some wonder why kosher pasta costs more than the goy variety.

Mediterraneo ◐ [S] 🚫 17 | 13 | 13 | $28
1260 Second Ave. (66th St.), 212-734-7407
■ It's "crowded and noisy" at this "chic and sunny" Italian Eastsider where the "young, attractive clientele" "loves the owners", the "incredible" tomato sauces and "sidewalk"-socializing atmosphere, but not the "cash-only" policy.

Mee Noodle Shop [S] 16 | 4 | 11 | $13
795 Ninth Ave. (53rd St.), 212-765-2929 ◐
922 Second Ave. (49th St.), 212-888-0027
219 First Ave. (13th St.), 212-995-0333
◪ Egalitarian noodle factories where Wall Streeters rub shoulders with FedEx couriers over "generous" bowls of soup, barbecue and Asian spaghetti; arguably "the best bargains in town", the service is so "fast" you won't notice the dive decor.

Memphis ◐ [S] 19 | 18 | 16 | $34
329 Columbus Ave. (bet. 75th & 76th Sts.), 212-496-1840
◪ The '80s are over but no one's singing taps for this Upper West Side Cajun-Southern where a new chef has come with a "more varied" menu, and if you like a lively singles bar scene you won't be disappointed – that is, if you can find the unmarked entrance.

Menchanko-tei 19 | 10 | 14 | $19
39 W. 55th St. (bet. 5th & 6th Aves.), 212-247-1585
131 E. 45th St. (bet. Lexington & Third Aves.), 212-986-6805
5 World Trade Ctr., 212-432-4210
■ "An upscale Dosanko", these modest Midtown and Downtown Japanese "noodle-and-soup shops" have "very healthy food" at very "low prices" that will warm you up all winter.

Merchants N.Y. ◐ [S] 13 | 20 | 15 | $22
112 Seventh Ave. (17th St.), 212-366-7267
◪ Shop at Barney's, wear black, and come to this comfortable wine bar afterward to relax; the "sumptuous velvet" downstairs room with fireplace and "decent, if limited" American menu make for a good buzz.

Merenda ◐ [S] 🚫 — | — | — | M
1538 Second Ave. (80th St.), 212-734-1888
A cross between Due, Luke's and Lusardi's from the pros behind all three, this attractive new Eastsider has won an instant following by truth in advertising (the Italian word "merenda" means a light snack) including everything from pasta to a Cobb salad to turkey club.

Meridiana [S] ▽ 19 | 19 | 16 | $29
2756 Broadway (bet. 105th & 106th Sts.), 212-222-4453
■ "*Carpe diem*" above 96th Street; solid and "needed in the area", this "friendly", neighborhood Italian is designed to "look like the ruins at Pompeii" and is "best in summer when the garden is open."

Meriken ◐ [S] 20 | 15 | 17 | $27
189 Seventh Ave. (21st St.), 212-620-9684
■ "Hip" Chelsea Japanese with lots of art on the walls and arty types in the seats; "when the standard sushi houses bore" come here for an affordable change of pace.

Mesa de España [S] ▽ 15 | 10 | 16 | $29
45 E. 28th St. (bet. Park & Madison Aves.), 212-679-2263
◩ Despite "huge portions" of "well-prepared" paella at a fair price, "tired decor" and "tired food" leave some seeking superior Spanish.

MESA GRILL [S] 25 | 22 | 21 | $41
102 Fifth Ave. (bet. 15th & 16th Sts.), 212-807-7400
■ Chef Bobby Flay's Southwestern grill has a terrific reputation for "standout, original", "palate-tingling" food and a lively, sophisticated mod-industrial ambiance; despite being "trendy" it's good enough to "transcend trend" and become "a perennial favorite."

Mesa Verde ◐ [S] ▽ 18 | 16 | 17 | $29
531 Hudson St. (bet. Charles & W. 10th Sts.), 212-206-7093
◩ This "casual" West Village Southwestern gets mixed reviews: a "clever mixture" of "Mex-Californian" "with flair and personality" vs. "mediocre" and "offbeat to the point of strange."

Metronome ◐ ▽ 22 | 25 | 20 | $36
915 Broadway (21st St.), 212-505-7400
◩ Some see this Gramercy-area newcomer as a "jazzy" art deco place with an "ultrahigh ceiling" and "gorgeously presented" American food; others consider its kitchen and staff offbeat with *Flash Gordon* decor including "plant sculptures from Mars."

Metropolis Cafe ◐ [S] 19 | 21 | 17 | $34
31 Union Sq. W. (16th St.), 212-675-2300
■ Surveyors unanimously praise this old marble-walled Union Square bank, turned restaurant, for its brunch, piano player and "terrace people-watching at sunset"; they divide about the American food, which some say is "overpriced" for "standard" "cafe fare."

Metropolitan Cafe ◐ [S] 17 | 16 | 16 | $28
959 First Ave. (bet. 52nd & 53rd Sts.), 212-759-5600
■ Large, bustling Sutton Place–area cafe to bring the kids or a friend; despite rather "ordinary", "medium-priced" Continental food it's "reliable" and healthy"; the outdoor garden is "lovely and relaxed."

Mezzaluna ◐ [S] 🚫 19 | 14 | 15 | $31
1295 Third Ave. (bet. 74th & 75th Sts.), 212-535-9600
◩ "Always crowded and cramped" thanks to "top-notch" pasta and pizza in "tiny" but "cute" East Side quarters decorated with a collection of half-moon (i.e. *mezzaluna*) paintings; service can wane.

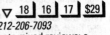

	F	D	S	C

Mezzanine Restaurant ◐ [S] ▽ | 19 | 22 | 16 | $32
Paramount Hotel, 235 W. 46th St. (bet. 8th Ave. & B'way), 212-764-5500
■ Distinctive, modern Philippe Starck mezzanine dining scene overlooking the Paramount Hotel's fishbowl lobby where schools of young Euros and bi-coastals flit about; service is by "existential snails", but the light American menu is "surprisingly" sophisticated.

Mezzogiorno ◐ [S] 🚫 | 20 | 16 | 15 | $33
195 Spring St. (Sullivan St.), 212-334-2112
◩ The SoHo cousin of Mezzaluna has salad, "pasta and pizza with character" to fuel a day of gallery grazing; drawbacks are "small portions", "uncomfortable chairs", frosty waiters and no credit cards.

Michael's | 22 | 22 | 20 | $45
24 W. 55th St. (bet. 5th & 6th Aves.), 212-767-0555
■ A bit of Santa Monica in NYC, this "pricey" Californian's modern grill cuisine, fresh produce and attractive, art-filled setting are popular with chic Midtowners; there's solarium seating in the back, but no brunch.

Mickey Mantle's ◐ [S] | 13 | 17 | 14 | $28
42 Central Park S. (bet. 5th & 6th Aves.), 212-688-7777
■ "Fun for nostalgia lovers, sports fans and baseball-crazy kids", this ultimate memorabilia-and-TV-filled bar/restaurant is a "refreshing alternative"; it's an "informal, relaxed" "place to watch a game" and spot sports stars over "middling food" that isn't the point.

Mi Cocina [S] | 22 | 13 | 16 | $29
57 Jane St. (Hudson St.), 212-627-8273
■ With its "novel" dishes this "cozy" brick-walled Villager gives diners a "glimpse of a different and better" Mexican cuisine; however, its highly appreciated kitchen is "so small, there can be quite a wait."

Mike's Bar & Grill ◐ [S] | 16 | 12 | 14 | $24
650 Tenth Ave. (bet. 45th & 46th Sts.), 212-246-4115
◩ A Far West Side "hole-in-the-wall" with "zany", "campy" quarterly themes that's "hip without attitude"; the "spicy American-Eclectic food" is "better than you'd expect for the modest price", but conservative diners simply "don't get" this "suspicious-looking" dive.

Milano (Brooklyn) [S] ▽ | 22 | 17 | 19 | $35
7514 18th Ave. (bet. Bayridge Pkwy. & 76th St.), 718-259-4300
■ "Top-notch" Bensonhurst "family spot" that's "always a mob scene"; dine and be treated well Italian-style in "Brooklynese" "neighborhood comfort"; P.S. "don't miss dessert."

Minetta Tavern ◐ [S] | 16 | 15 | 17 | $31
113 MacDougal St. (bet. W. 3rd & Bleecker Sts.), 212-475-3850
■ A "fair to middling" Italian with "charming" service, this "classic Village tavern" serves "ample" food at an "historic" site; even if it's "heavy-handed" it's "loaded with atmosphere" and "priced right."

Mingala Burmese [S] | 18 | 10 | 15 | $20
21-23 E. 7th St. (bet. 2nd & 3rd Aves.), 212-529-3656
325 Amsterdam Ave. (bet. 75th & 76th Sts.), 212-873-0787
◩ These Burmese bargain joints have a "1,000-layer pancake soaked in butter that's a dream" and other "original dishes"; "go as a group to try more things", but "don't ask what's in the soup."

Miracle Grill ◐ [S] | 21 | 17 | 17 | $27
112 First Ave. (bet. 6th & 7th Sts.), 212-254-2353
■ If "you can't afford the Mesa Grill and don't feel like seeing suits", this "relaxed", "affordable" East Village "mega" grill serves "now" Southwestern "specialties" and has a beautiful garden to boot; brunch and outdoor dining are "best bets."

Mission Grill [S] (CLOSED) 18 | 14 | 16 | $26
48 MacDougal St. (bet. Houston & Prince Sts.), 212-598-0387
◩ SoHo spot serving San Francisco–style Southwestern fare made with "fresh ingredients"; despite "minimalist decor" there's "lots of activity" and it's "easy to linger" here.

Mitali East/West ◐ [S] 20 | 14 | 17 | $23
336 E. 6th St. (bet. 1st & 2nd Aves.), 212-533-2508
296 Bleecker St. (7th Ave. S.), 212-989-1367
■ Two "mouth-watering", "classic Indians at still affordable prices"; both are "consistently excellent", but the West Village location has "better decor", while Mitali East has "opium-den" ambiance but merits the lines outside; the all-inclusive Sunday buffet (at $10.95) may be "the best value in town."

Mitsukoshi 24 | 20 | 22 | $43
461 Park Ave. (57th St.), 212-935-6444
■ "Elegant" and "gracious" "businesspeople's Japanese" that affords a "quiet" escape from the surrounding Midtown hubbub; it's "expensive", but "very authentic"; check out their bento box lunches.

Mme. Romaine de Lyon [S] 17 | 16 | 16 | $29
29 E. 61st St. (bet. Madison & Park Aves.), 212-758-2422
◩ If your cholesterol level is under control go try one of the "12 zillion omelet combinations" at this French standby; as Marie Antoinette should have said, "let them eat eggs – in the garden."

Mo' Better 14 | 10 | 11 | $24
570 Amsterdam Ave. (bet. 87th & 88th Sts.), 212-580-7755
◩ Westsider where you "wear jeans" and "expect no ambiance", but "good vibes" and "large portions" of some of the "best Southern cooking up North"; dissenters say it "used to be much mo' better."

Mocca Hungarian [S] 💳̸ 16 | 7 | 13 | $21
1588 Second Ave. (bet. 82nd & 83rd Sts.), 212-734-6470
■ "Budapest in Yorkville"; "one of a dying breed" that "still delivers the real goods": "honest" Hungarian food including authentic cherry soup, chicken paprika, veal goulash and cucumber salad at "bedrock prices" in an "old country dining room"; they serve "the best $6 lunch in town."

Monkey Bar [S] – | – | – | E
Hotel Elysée, 60 E. 54th St. (bet. Park & Madison Aves.), 212-838-2600
An all-star team headed by Peter and Penny Glazier (Bridgewaters, Symphony Cafe), chef John Schenk (Mad. 61, W. B'way, Gotham), designer David Rockwell (Vong, Christer's, Nobu) and maitre d' Tony Fortuna (Lespinasse, Lutèce, Lafayette) has created one of the most attractive and appreciated new American restaurants to open in years – the only problem is getting by the young crowd at the bar.

Montebello 23 | 20 | 23 | $39
120 E. 56th St. (bet. Park & Lexington Aves.), 212-753-1447
◩ A Midtown Italian for "dependable" lunch or "leisurely dinner" with an "attractive, dressed-up" crowd; besides "an extensive menu" they'll make almost anything you ask for; dissenters say it's "dated", "overcooked" and "ordinary."

MONTRACHET 26 | 21 | 24 | $54
239 W. Broadway (bet. Walker & White Sts.), 212-219-2777
■ Despite chef Deborah Ponzek's departure this "superior" TriBeCa nouvelle bistro is "still the most comfortable", fancy "French restaurant around"; some find the decor "drab", others say "understated", but almost everyone agrees that this is "still tops" for a "wonderful dinner" with "impressive wines."

Moonrock Diner ◗🅂   13 | 11 | 13 | $15
313 W. 57th St. (bet. 8th & 9th Aves.), 212-397-3131
☑ "A favorite" for budget-watchers, this Midtowner is more "inventive" and "appetizing" than most diners even if "not fit for interplanetary travel."

Moran's ◗🅂   15 | 16 | 15 | $27
146 Tenth Ave. (19th St.), 212-627-3030
■ "6 PM Friday still no date?" try this "intimate" Irishz West Chelsea "neighborhood pub"; even if you don't meet a "master of the universe", "fresh fish" by the fire and service by "attentive, smiling" "colleens" makes this "a place you can bring mom and dad."

Moreno 🅂   21 | 19 | 20 | $40
65 Irving Pl. (bet. Park Ave. S. & 3rd Ave.), 212-673-3939
■ Not everyone reports that they "liked the Northern Italian food and host-owner Moreno so much" that they "were married here", but there's "never a bad meal" and the sidewalk seating is "sensational" at this Gramercy "winner."

Morgan Cafe 🅂   – | – | – | M
Pierpont-Morgan Library, Madison Ave. & 36th St., 212-685-0008, ext. 401
Providing "a lovely interlude in a fascinating museum", the Morgan Library cafe is itself a study in "leafy" solarium lunch; think of it as "déjeuner sur l'herbe", but it's "a bit pricey for snippets."

Moroccan Star (Brooklyn) 🅂   17 | 8 | 15 | $20
205 Atlantic Ave. (bet. Court & Clinton Sts.), 718-643-0800
☑ Can't make it to Marrakesh? then settle for "one of the best Brooklyn oldies" with "excellent" pastilla and lamb that are "quick", "cheap" and "comforting"; sure it's a "dump", but "BYOW and feast."

Mortimer's ◗🅂   13 | 12 | 13 | $39
1057 Lexington Ave. (75th St.), 212-517-6400
☑ Tom Wolfe's "social X-rays" make the "lunch scene" at this clubby Upper East Side "in-crowd" hangout where "air kisses abound if you are somebody, otherwise you'll sit offsides" and eat lots of attitude.

Morton's of Chicago ◗🅂   24 | 21 | 21 | $52
551 Fifth Ave. (45th St.), 212-972-3315
☑ The big noise from Winnetka – and on the "steak scene" coast to coast – is this "plush" new Grand Central–area "men's club" which has locals wondering "how a chain can be this good"; critics cite the "hokey Saran wrap (raw meat) display", "cigar-smoking bond traders" and "yabba-dabba-doo" testosterone spirit.

Mo's Caribbean Bar & Grille ◗🅂   13 | 11 | 12 | $21
1454 Second Ave. (76th St.), 212-650-0561
☑ A "go for mo'", "twentysomething", party-hearty crowd considers this Eastsider "a fun place to hang out", down "potent" frozen "tropical drinks" and try out "island-style food" that "reminds you of your vacation"; critics say "the Caribbean should sue for libel."

Moscow on the Hudson ◗🅂   ▽ 14 | 14 | 15 | $34
1803 Second Ave. (93rd St.), 212-534-4866
☑ A recent Upper East Side arrival where a troika of Russian food, paintings and a gypsy show and live band "packs people in on weekends"; though it has "potential" it still needs to "get it together."

Moustache ◗🅂⇄   ▽ 20 | 10 | 17 | $14
90 Bedford St. (bet. Grove & Barrow Sts.), 212-229-2220
■ A "wonderful, family-run" Village Middle Eastern with cozy brick-and-copper ambiance, trademark brick-oven "pizza", i.e. pita pizza, and "exquisite" hummus; it wins fans' favor for "fast, fresh food for fair fares."

F | D | S | C

Mr. Chow ◐ [S] — 22 | 23 | 19 | $47

324 E. 57th St. (bet. 1st & 2nd Aves.), 212-751-9030

◪ "As elegant as a three-star French restaurant", this East Side Chinese evokes varied reactions: "glamorous", "almost perfect", "best Peking duck", "good for parties" vs. "all hype", "intimidating", "overpriced"; ratings show the ayes, and the eyes, have it.

Mr. Souvlaki (Brooklyn) ◐ [S] ≠ — ▽ 15 | 6 | 12 | $14

147 Montague St. (bet. Clinton & Henry Sts.), 718-858-8997

■ For "great" gyros, moussaka and salad that are "good for the money" try this "neighborhood Greek" in Brooklyn Heights; "reliable" and "friendly", it's also "crowded and not air-conditioned", so it's better to sit back in the garden in summer.

Mr. Tang's (Brooklyn) [S] — 17 | 15 | 17 | $22

1884 86th St. (19th Ave.), 718-256-2100 ◐
7523 Third Ave. (76th St.), 718-748-0400
2650 Coney Island Ave. (Ave. X), 718-769-9444

◪ A Brooklyn Chinese mini-monopoly that draws both yeas and nays: "better than average", "best of Brooklyn options", "always nice" vs. "something's missing", "a has-been", "run of the mill."

Mueng Thai [S] — ▽ 21 | 10 | 18 | $16

23 Pell St. (bet. Mott & Bowery Sts.), 212-406-4259

■ If you can find this Chinatown "dive", "let the owners order for you" because "they know what they're doing"; the food is "subtle", "spicy", "incredible" and no one complains about the bill, either.

Mughlai ◐ [S] — 17 | 12 | 15 | $26

320 Columbus Ave. (75th St.), 212-724-6363

◪ "Location, location, location" is the key to the success of this "busy" Indian; with little local competition its tandoori dishes look especially "good"; but what's "clean", "courteous", "bright and fresh" to fans is just "decent", "cheap and rightly so" to foes.

Mulholland Drive Cafe ◐ [S] — 15 | 14 | 14 | $30

1059 Third Ave. (bet. 62nd & 63rd Sts.), 212-319-7740

◪ "A ladies' lunch place" and "great brunch value" during the day, Patrick Swayze's pastel East Side "hangout" turns into a "swinging" "pickup scene" at night with debatable light Californian cuisine; "good for something quick" doesn't necessarily refer to the food.

Museum Cafe ◐ [S] — 15 | 13 | 14 | $24

366 Columbus Ave. (77th St.), 212-799-0150

◪ An Upper West Side coffee shop "classic" by the Museum of Natural History; it's "great for Sunday brunch" or for "resting your feet", but as for the food: soups, burgers and salads are "safe bets."

Mustang Grill ◐ [S] — 17 | 15 | 15 | $28

1633 Second Ave. (85th St.), 212-744-9194

◪ East 80s Southwestern newcomer "with a spicy kick" and cactus-decorated tables; admirers, "impressed by the menu" and "casual setting", say this is "what the East Side needed"; critics say it's too much like being "back in college" and "mediocre on all counts."

Nadine's ◐ [S] — 17 | 17 | 18 | $26

99 Bank St. (Greenwich St.), 212-924-3165

◪ "Just what you need to escape the real world", this "campy", "cozy", "comforting", "casual" and "caring" West Villager has food and bordello decor that are "Eclectic even by Village standards"; the brunch stands out.

Nanni Il Valletto   22 | 19 | 20 | $48
133 E. 61st St. (bet. Park & Lexington Aves.), 212-838-3939
☑ "Comfortable" and "sedate" Northern Italian for a well-heeled,
"older crowd" that likes its "old-world charm"; the pasta's homemade"
and "exceptional"; owner Nanni "knows all his customers" – it's
somewhat "like eating in a private club" where, if you're not a member,
you may "feel like you're from Mars."

Nanni's   23 | 16 | 21 | $44
146 E. 46th St. (bet. Lexington & 3rd Aves.), 212-697-4161
☑ Serving "some of the best veal and pasta" at "corporate prices",
this Northern Italian Grand Central neighbor is always "noisy and
crowded" for lunch, but much quieter at night; some say it's getting
"old and tired", but most surveyors say it's "old reliable."

Natalino   19 | 12 | 18 | $30
243 E. 78th St. (bet. 2nd & 3rd Aves.), 212-737-3771
71 W. 71st St. (bet. Columbus Ave. & CPW), 212-875-1078Ⓢ
☑ Two "family-run", "hole-in-the-wall" trattorias in the "home-cooked"
mode; maybe it's worth loosening your belt to enjoy their veal chops,
but you only need one notch – these places are "tiny."

National (Brooklyn) ❶Ⓢ   ▽ 12 | 12 | 12 | $42
273 Brighton Beach Ave. (2nd St.), 718-646-1225
☑ Travel to "Russia without passport" for an evening of drinking and
dancing best likened to a "bar mitzvah, birthday and New Year's Eve
all in one"; the vodka is more memorable than the food, but it can be
"a ton of fun" "with the right crowd" and "designated driver."

Neary's ❶Ⓢ   16 | 12 | 19 | $31
358 E. 57th St. (bet. 1st & 2nd Aves.), 212-751-1434
■ "The quintessential Irish pub serving good hearty fare at reasonable
prices" to East Side pundits, politicians, prelates, plutocrats and the
pulchritudinous, including regulars such as Frank and Kathy Lee; host
Jimmy Neary is NYC's favorite leprechaun.

Nello ❶Ⓢ   ▽ 19 | 15 | 15 | $37
696 Madison Ave. (bet. 62nd & 63rd Sts.), 212-980-9099
☑ A "hip Euro" Madison Italian "hangout" that's "one of NYC's coolest"
spots for "sidewalk people-watching"; though the food is "good",
"Mercedes and Porsches driving up get more attention than dinner."

New City Cafe (Brooklyn) Ⓢ   ▽ 25 | 19 | 20 | $28
246 DeKalb Ave. (Vanderbilt Ave.), 718-622-5607
■ This "splendid" newcomer near BAM is "just what Fort Greene (or
for that matter any neighborhood) needs": a "great" Contemporary
American at "ridiculously low" prices; it's "charming" and "delicious"
(with a slight French accent) and has a garden of fresh flowers.

New Deal Ⓢ   20 | 17 | 18 | $33
133 W. 13th St. (bet. 6th & 7th Aves.), 212-741-3663
☑ If you're into wild game (venison, quail, buffalo, etc.) "this West
Villager is your place"; there's a "lovely garden" in season; inside,
however, "it's a bit dreary" and "cute, but no big deal."

New Hong Kong City ❶Ⓢ   ▽ 23 | 6 | 11 | $26
11 Division St., 212-431-1040
■ Could be "best in Chinatown", with "terrific seafood" and the
"sweetest steamed shrimp" at low prices; though there's "not much
English" spoken, ask your waiter for guidance and try to "ignore the
smell at the entrance."

New Prospect Cafe (Bklyn.) [S] — 19 | 9 | 18 | $23
393 Flatbush Ave. (8th Ave.), 718-638-2148
■ "Park Slope's very own" is a "homey", "healthy", little SW-accented New American that "even nonvegetarians like"; the decor may be "funky" and the help "spaced-out", but the P.C. food is sure good.

News Bar [S] — – | – | – | I
2 W. 19th St. (5th Ave.), 212-255-3996
969 Third Ave. (bet. 57th & 58th Sts.), 212-319-0830
366 W. Broadway (Broome St.), 212-343-0053
Attracting both brewhounds and newshounds, this slick new group of coffeehouse/newspaper-magazine shops are hip places to catch up on the headlines over coffee, fresh juices, sandwiches and sweets.

New Viet Huong [S] — ▽ 21 | 5 | 12 | $17
77 Mulberry St. (bet. Canal & Bayard Sts.), 212-233-8988
■ For the price "you can't get better Vietnamese food" in NYC; the menu is "pages and pages of delicious choices" including BBQ beef in grape leaves and "fresh, fresh" fish entrees; "a real find" (though not for its looks), it's "worth the trip" to Chinatown.

New World Grill ◐ [S] — 18 | 16 | 15 | $27
329 W. 49th St. (bet. 8th & 9th Aves.), 212-957-4745
◩ "Pleasant", new, "mid-priced" Eclectic grill that's said to have "good food" with "potential"; however, apart from outside, the New World is "not too comfortable" and "some things shouldn't be grilled."

Nha Trang [S] 🚫 — ▽ 20 | 6 | 15 | $17
87 Baxter St. (bet. Centre & Mulberry Sts.), 212-233-5948
◩ Don't be fooled by "the lack of decor": this "cheap", "no-frills" Chinatown Vietnamese is "genuinely friendly" and offers "delicious, unusual flavors" with beef satay, spring rolls and pho all highly praised; "it almost makes jury duty a treat."

Nice Restaurant, The [S] — 19 | 10 | 11 | $22
35 E. Broadway (bet. Catherine & Market Sts.), 212-406-9510
◩ Dim sum from 8 AM to 4PM is "the only reason to come" to this "cheap" and "crowded" Chinatown Cantonese; plan "to share a large table" and face decor and service that are "not so nice."

Nick & Eddie ◐ [S] — 21 | 17 | 17 | $32
203 Spring St. (Sullivan St.), 212-219-9090
■ A rare combination – "always good" food, "always friendly" service and "fair prices" in a "trendy" restaurant – as a result, this SoHo American is usually "packed"; it's "a little dark", but that helps make it a "great date place."

Nicola Paone — 18 | 17 | 19 | $44
207 E. 34th St. (bet 2nd & 3rd Aves.), 212-889-3239
◩ All together now: *"fettuccine, scaloppine, braccioletta, cotoletta..."*; those radio ads suggest a wonderful Murray Hill Italian "classic" that's "back on track" with "satisfying" food, service and wines; dissenters reply "stuffy", "fake", for "lotto winners."

Nicola's ◐ [S] — 20 | 15 | 18 | $41
146 E. 84th St. (bet. Lexington & 3rd Aves.), 212-249-9850
◩ An East Side Italian "neighborhood staple" that's "clubby" and favors "regulars", but is a "reliable" choice for just about anyone with the bucks; "you can get whatever you want and it will be good."

9 ◑ 🅂 ▽ 20 | 19 | 14 | $15
110 St. Marks Pl. (bet. 1st Ave. & Avenue A), 212-982-7129
■ "Typical" East Village coffeehouse with "neat tables", "rotating artwork" and "health-conscious" fare capped by "great brunch"; it attracts a young "hip crowd", which in this area may mean "funky."

9 Jones Street 22 | 17 | 19 | $35
9 Jones St. (bet. Bleecker & W. 4th Sts.), 212-989-1220
■ An "undiscovered" Village French-accented American with an "inspired" menu; most find it "well-run", "charming" and even "the year's discovery", but some say "this sleeper has yet to make its mark."

Nino's 🅂 20 | 17 | 20 | $36
1354 First Ave. (bet. 72nd & 73rd Sts.), 212-988-0002
■ Upper East Side locals report that this attractive new Italian with a singer/pianist is "a terrific addition to the neighborhood" and they particularly like host-owner Nino.

Nippon 23 | 18 | 20 | $42
155 E. 52nd St. (bet. Lexington & 3rd Aves.), 212-758-0226
119 E. 59th St. (bet. Lexington & Park Aves.), 212-751-7690
■ "One can count on freshness" and "quality" at these Midtown Japanese "standbys" "where the power brokers meet to eat sushi", tempura and other classic fare; a few critics say "fading" and pricey, but it's a bargain to "feel you're in Japan."

Nirvana ◑ 🅂 18 | 26 | 20 | $35
30 Central Park S. (bet. 5th & 6th Aves.), 212-486-5700
■ "Spectacular views" of Central Park and decor out of *The Arabian Nights* make this a "paradise to the eye", while prix fixe menus – lunch at $13.95 and dinner at $22.95 – are "good values"; if the food "doesn't measure up to the view", well "so what?"

NOBU – | – | – | VE
105 Hudson St. (Franklin St.), 212-219-0500
Nobu Matsuhisa is the LA chef who, for five years running, has come in No. 1 or No. 2 in our *Los Angeles Restaurant Survey*; his new TriBeCa restaurant is to Japanese cuisine what Bouley is to French, and as a result it's already packed with foodies and bi-coastals; the splashy David Rockwell space (Christer's, Vong) is the most dramatic of any NYC Japanese restaurant, and with Drew Nieporent at the controls the operation is particularly well-managed.

NoHo Star ◑ 🅂 17 | 15 | 15 | $23
330 Lafayette St. (Bleecker St.), 212-925-0070
■ "A perennial favorite", NoHo Eclectic "stepped-up coffee shop" where the menu is a "fun mix" of everything from burgers to Chinese draws an interesting mix of people, too: "just hang around and watch them write their glow-in-the-dark postcards."

Nosmo King 🅂 20 | 19 | 19 | $34
54 Varick St. (Canal St.), 212-966-1239
■ TriBeCa organic brings "new age" flair to "tantalizing" vegetarian dishes, and nonveggies as well; it's "worth the trip" just to see its "wild" and "wacky, garage-sale" decor; the truly addicted "can smoke on the couch outside" without surcharge.

Ñ 33 Crosby Bar ◑ 🅂 ≠ ▽ 14 | 19 | 13 | $21
33 Crosby St. (bet. Grand & Broome Sts.), 212-219-8856
■ A "cool" spot for tapas and sangria is also a good place "to talk and hang out"; still, some react negatively to this "desolate block."

Nusantara — 19 | 21 | 18 | $32
219 E. 44th St. (bet. 2nd & 3rd Aves.), 212-983-1919
◪ For "introductory Indonesian" "try the rijsttafel" along with a Bintang beer at this attractive UN-area place; it's cheap for an experience that "transports you away" from the anxieties of NY.

N.Y. Delicatessen, The ◐ [S] — 13 | 10 | 11 | $19
104 W. 57th St. (6th Ave.), 212-541-8320
■ "Shellacked" bread in the window points out the fact that this Midtown former automat isn't the real McCoy deli; however, it's "ok if you're really in a hurry and the Carnegie's too crowded."

Oak Room and Bar, The ◐ [S] — 19 | 25 | 21 | $46
The Plaza Hotel, 768 Fifth Ave. (59th St.), 212-546-5330
◪ "A NY classic", this "wood-panelled baronial" dining room and adjoining bar is "the perfect place to pass the Grey Poupon"; it has the "formal English" feel that "makes even a 30-year-old American sip port, smoke a cigar and discuss fine shotguns and Maggie Thatcher."

O'Casey's [S] — ▽ 24 | 14 | 20 | $23
22 E. 41st St. (bet. 5th & Madison Aves.), 212-685-6807
■ "A gem of an Irish saloon" in Midtown that's "a real surprise"; regulars "love to eat at the bar" and report "the new chef is turning out amazing French-accented American food."

OCEANA — 26 | 25 | 24 | $52
55 E. 54th St. (bet. Madison & Park Aves.), 212-759-5941
■ In the running for the "best fish in NYC", this remodelled modern Midtown townhouse restaurant resembles the first-class dining room on a cruise ship and offers "a serene dining experience" with "meticulous" service and "exquisite and delicate" seafood by chef Rick Moonen (ex Water Club); more and more surveyors seem to agree: "destined to be great."

Odeon, The ◐ [S] — 19 | 18 | 16 | $34
145 W. Broadway (Thomas St.), 212-233-0507
◪ This "hip" TriBeCa coffee shop "where DeNiro really eats" is a "classic for late-night people-watching" and "reliable" American "bistro food"; it may be "noisy" and "the worse for wear", but the staff is "gorgeous" and "the price is right."

Odessa ◐ [S] ⊘ — 15 | 7 | 13 | $19
117-119 Ave. A (bet. 7th St. & St. Marks Pl.), 212-473-8916
■ A Lower East Side Ukrainian-Polish coffee shop and "neighborhood standby" that offers lots of "old-world" "home cooking" including "awesome challah bread" and the "best pierogies in NY" at "bargain" prices – the "heartburn is free."

Old Bermuda Inn (S.I.) [S] — ▽ 20 | 24 | 18 | $36
2512 Arthur Kill Rd. (Bloomingdale Rd. & Rosville Ave.), 718-948-7600
◪ An historic mansion on Staten Island that's a lovely place for a party; however, the consensus is that the Continental food, though good, doesn't match the setting anymore – "they sure know how to overcook everything"; P.S. check on the "ghosts" with the bartenders.

Old Homestead [S] — 21 | 14 | 17 | $44
56 Ninth Ave. (bet. 14th & 15th Sts.), 212-242-9040
◪ Loyalists say this NYC institution serves the "best piece of meat in the city" in "gargantuan proportions"; detractors complain that the place is "dreary" and wonder "why isn't the food better?"

Old Roma (Queens) 🇸 🚫
– | – | – | M

135-11 40th Rd. (Main St.), 718-359-9453

You don't last in one location since 1918 without doing it right – the "it" in this case is hearty red-sauce Italian food at modest prices served on oilcloth-covered tables with good cheer and no nonsense.

Old Town Bar 🇸
13 | 17 | 13 | $17

45 E. 18th St. (bet. B'way & Park Ave. S.), 212-529-6732

■ "A real slice of old NY", this 1890s vintage tavern near Union Square has a "setting that rivals *Cheers*" and "good" "standard" pub grub; it's "low-key" and a "good place to relax" unless a big game is on or David Letterman's mother shows up – then it gets "rowdy."

Olive Garden, The 🇸
– | – | – | M

201 W. 47th St. (bet. 7th Ave. & B'way), 212-246-4517

At the top of Times Square, this national chain has attempted an upscale, but price-sensitive Italian-American bistro in a block-long duplex space with wraparound windows; it still has an '80s Midwestern mall feel and cross-river clientele.

Ollie's ⦿🇸
17 | 7 | 11 | $17

2957 Broadway (116th St.), 212-932-3300
2315 Broadway (84th St.), 212-362-3712
200B W. 44th St. (bet. B'way & 8th Ave.), 212-921-5988

☑ "Always noisy, always crowded" with diners who report "good", "cheap, reliable Chinese eats" in the soup, dumpling and noodle categories; unm-ollie-fied critics call the chain "a zoo, pure and simple."

Omen 🇸
22 | 17 | 18 | $35

113 Thompson St. (bet. Prince & Spring Sts.), 212-925-8923

■ "It's a good omen" to eat the "artful but traditional Kyoto dishes" at this warm, brick-and-wood SoHo "oasis"; it's "not Americanized" and is "sensual from the menu calligraphy to the handmade serving plates."

O'Neals' ⦿🇸
14 | 14 | 15 | $29

49 W. 64th St. (bet. B'way & CPW), 212-787-4663

☑ "A good bet for Lincoln Center", "The Ginger Man reincarnated" has "charming turn-of-the-century" ambiance and "decent" American food that's best at its simplest – burgers, salads, etc.; it should not be confused with the former O'Neal's Balloon.

ONE IF BY LAND, TIBS ⦿🇸
25 | 27 | 24 | $51

17 Barrow St. (bet. 7th Ave. S. & W. 4th St.), 212-228-0822

☑ "It's Valentine's Day every day at this Village love nest"; lilting piano music, flowers, candlelight and flickering fireplaces all help make Aaron Burr's old home and garden "NYC's most romantic restaurant"; if you like beef Wellington, and most of our surveyors do, the food's "the best ever"; otherwise it's "like eating in Middle America – in 1975."

101 (Brooklyn) ⦿🇸
19 | 15 | 16 | $26

10018 Fourth Ave. (101st St.), 718-833-1313

101 Seafood (Brooklyn) 🇸
8203 Third Ave. (82nd St.), 718-833-6666

■ These Bay Ridge siblings are respectively praised for "excellent pizza and pasta" and "great seafood"; they're "casual", inexpensive spots where "Brooklyn's beautiful people unite", often noisily.

103 NYC ⦿🇸
19 | 15 | 15 | $29

103 Second Ave. (6th St.), 212-777-4120

☑ Most surveyors enjoy the "wide-ranging American menu with something for everyone" at this "never-too-crowded" East Villager where you can "sit by the window and watch the sights"; however, "minimalist decor" and "benign-neglect" service aren't so popular.

107 West ◐Ⓢ
17 13 14 $25

2787 Broadway (bet. 107th & 108th Sts.), 212-864-1555

■ An Upper West Side Southwestern "haven in a culinary wasteland" serving "decent food" in an "appealing" setting at low prices; it may have "slipped a bit", but "when it's good, it's really good" and noisy.

Opus II ◐
▽ 20 16 21 $40

242 E. 58th St. (bet. 2nd & 3rd Aves.), 212-753-2200

■ Perhaps not the best steakhouse, but for many it's a "better value" – a full three-course fixed-price menu at $29.95 for sirloin or filet mignon and $39.95 for lobster or T-bone and they don't go short on portions; unlike most steakhouses, it's bright, modern and attractive to women.

Orbit ◐Ⓢ
▽ 16 16 15 $25

46 Bedford St. (Leroy St.), 212-463-8717

☒ While some say it's "more of a gay club than a serious eatery" and that it gets "too loud to hold a conversation", other reviewers find this West Village hangout lots of "fun" and enjoy the burgers, "upscale pizza" and other bar food amidst the "lively atmosphere."

Oriental Garden ◐Ⓢ
▽ 23 8 10 $23

(fka Oriental Town Seafood)
14 Elizabeth St. (Canal St.), 212-619-0085

☒ "Consistently fabulous seafood" at "good prices" is the draw at this Chinatown Cantonese; it's so popular with locals that it's "annoyingly difficult to get into" despite the perception that there's "better ambiance on a slave ship" and you don't have to tip the whipper.

Oriental Pearl Ⓢ
19 7 10 $20

103 Mott St. (bet. Hester & Canal Sts.), 212-219-8388

■ How can you argue with "big", "noisy" and "terrific dim sum"?; go with a group for a "hectic, wonderful Chinatown experience"; it's always crowded on weekends "but worth the chaos"; "if you're lucky you'll see a wedding reception or two."

Original California Taqueria Ⓢ⊅
 19 5 11 $11

8 Bergen St. (Court St.), Brooklyn, 718-624-7498
72 Seventh Ave. (bet. Lincoln & Berkeley Sts.), Brooklyn, 718-398-4300
341 Seventh Ave. (bet. 9th & 10th Sts.), Brooklyn, 718-965-0006
355 Sixth Ave. (bet. Washington & W. 4th Sts.), 212-229-0999

■ A nabe fave and for good reason, this inexpensive, mostly takeout Cal-Mex mini-chain makes heavyweight burritos, nachos and fresh guacamole that "are meals unto themselves"; "not too original, not too California, but not too bad" – it sure beats McDonald's.

Orleans Ⓢ
18 15 15 $25

1438 Third Ave. (bet. 81st & 82nd Sts.), 212-794-1509

☒ "Yuppified Cajun" with "fair prices" and "friendly service"; it might be "unimpressive" on the bayou, but it's a great way "to spice up your life" on the Italian Upper East Side and is plenty busy as a result.

Orologio ◐Ⓢ⊅
▽ 20 17 16 $20

162 Avenue A (bet. 10th & 11th Sts.), 212-228-6900

■ East Village relative of Mappamondo with the same young crowd, "good pasta and prices" and "clocks everywhere" yet "time to relax."

Orso ◐Ⓢ
23 19 20 $39

322 W. 46th St. (bet. 8th & 9th Aves.), 212-489-7212

■ Again and again this rustic Contemporary Italian "celebrity haunt" is called "the best in the Theater District" by surveyors who love its "delicious little pizzas", risotto and "professional, unobtrusive" service; sure it's "hard to get reservations" pre-theater, but once in, there's "great people-watching and eavesdropping"; "go after 8 to relax."

Orson's ◐ [S] ▽ 17 | 11 | 11 | $24
175 Second Ave. (bet. 11th & 12th Sts.), 212-475-1530
◪ A "perfect, dark and tiny" East Village dive that serves "creative martinis" and "fine bar food" until 2 AM; don't miss "the train over the bathroom"; as ratings show, decor and service aren't so swift.

Oscar's ◐ [S] 17 | 14 | 16 | $29
Waldorf-Astoria, 301 Park Ave. (50th St.), 212-872-4920
◪ No surprise, "it's the same as when I was there in 1973", the Waldorf's "upscale coffee shop" is "filled with people of all ages, tourists and NYers alike" who come for serviceable food served by "middle-aged waitresses" whom "your mother would like."

Osso Buco [S] 17 | 14 | 16 | $26
88 University Pl. (bet. 11th & 12th Sts.), 212-645-4525
◪ "Best of the Carmine clones", so expect "tremendous portions" and "Italian family-style fun" at this Villager; go with a group to share dishes, but don't be surprised if the experience is "slapdash."

Osteria al Doge ◐ [S] ▽ 20 | 18 | 18 | $33
142 W. 44th St. (bet. 6th & 7th Aves.), 212-944-3643
■ "Welcome to the Theater District", this Northern Italian has "fab grilled vegetables", "wonderful pastas" and "inventive pizzas"; fans say it's "Venice without the canals" and "Euro but not trashy."

Ottomanelli's Cafe 11 | 7 | 11 | $18
237 Park Ave. (45th St.), 212-986-6886
1626 York Ave. (bet. 85th & 86th Sts.), 212-772-7722 [S]
439 E. 82nd St. (bet. York & 1st Aves.), 212-737-1888 [S]
1518 First Ave. (79th St.), 212-249-5656 [S]
1370 York Ave. (73rd St.), 212-794-9696 [S]
1199 First Ave. (65th St.), 212-249-7878 [S]
951 First Ave. (bet. 52nd & 53rd Sts.), 212-758-3725 [S]
337 Third Ave. (25th St.), 212-532-2929 [S]
119 E. 18th St. (bet. Irving Pl. & Park Ave.), 212-979-1200 [S]
62 Reade St. (bet. B'way & Church St.), 212-349-3430
◪ Loyalists like the "dependable" burgers, pastas and chicken at "affordable prices" at this "solid, unpretentious" chain that's "a step above a diner"; critics say "exceedingly mediocre" with "no ambiance"; neutrals note it's "functional" because "ubiquitous."

Our Place [S] 20 | 15 | 20 | $29
1444 Third Ave. (82nd St.), 212-288-4888
■ "They almost love you to death" at this modern Upper East Side "gourmet" Chinese that's "a cut above" the competition; the fixed price menus are an "excellent value."

OYSTER BAR 23 | 15 | 16 | $37
Grand Central Station, lower level (bet. Vanderbilt & Lexington Aves.), 212-490-6650
■ "A fabulous turn-of-the-century seafood restaurant in the belly of Grand Central Station" famed for the "best assortment of fresh fish and shellfish in NYC"; the cooking may be "simple", but it's "consistently fine" and the choice of white wines is sensational; of course, it's often "noisy" and "crowded", but what else would you expect of such "a true NY institution."

Palio 23 | 26 | 23 | $55
151 W. 51st St. (bet. 6th & 7th Aves.), 212-245-4850
■ This "high-end Northern Italian" in Midtown offers "superb" but "pricey" cuisine in an "elegant" duplex space that's "excellent for impressing business friends"; the "spectacular" downstairs bar with a marvelous Sandro Chia four-wall mural "transports you to Sienna."

	F	**D**	**S**	**C**

PALM ◑
	25	14	18	$50

837 Second Ave. (bet. 44th & 45th Sts.), 212-687-2953

Palm Too S
840 Second Ave. (bet. 44th & 45th Sts.), 212-697-5198

■ "A classic for *Moby Dick* lobsters" and "solid, succulent slabs of beef"; this macho "old NY steakhouse" in Midtown with its "locker-room atmosphere", "sawdust floors" and "surly service" is a "sentimental favorite" for "when you're in the mood to overdo it"; splitting makes economic, and possibly medical, sense.

Palm Court, The ◑ S
	19	25	19	$41

The Plaza Hotel, 768 Fifth Ave. (59th St.), 212-546-5350

■ "No civilized person who can afford it should miss afternoon tea" or Sunday brunch at this "lovely", old-world, "European-style oasis" in The Plaza; "strolling musicians" and a "divine", appropriately named setting make this an ideal place to take visiting great-aunts.

Pamir S
	20	16	18	$28

1437 Second Ave. (bet. 74th & 75th Sts.), 212-734-3791
1065 First Ave. (58th St.), 212-644-9258

■ "Exotic Afghani fare" "served in a sheik's tent" is "a great value" at either of two East Side locations; "more than kebabs", the food is downright "perky", service "personable" and portions "ample."

Panchitos ◑ S
	▽ 15	13	13	$19

105 MacDougal St. (bet. Bleecker St. & Minetta Ln.), 212-473-5239

☑ "A Village tradition", this "cavelike" Tex-Mex boasts a wide range of frozen drinks; the food is "nothing special", but if you'd like "the feeling of being a student again" this "hangout" may do the trick.

Pandit S
	▽ 20	11	17	$20

566 Amsterdam Ave. (bet. 87th & 88th Sts.), 212-724-1217

☑ A "find" for Indian-starved Upper Westsiders who "don't need giant menus and prices" or fancy decor.

Paola's S
	23	19	21	$42

347 E. 85th St. (bet. 1st & 2nd Aves.), 212-794-1890

■ "Cozy, romantic" Upper East Side side-street Italian serving "lovely" "home-cooked country" fare in a "charming but cramped" narrow storefront setting; with Paola present "you're always treated like family."

Paolucci's S
	16	10	15	$26

149 Mulberry St. (Grand St.), 212-226-9653

■ Touted by "Canal Street jewelry dealers", this "long-running Little Italy favorite" is "an old faithful" for "decent", modestly priced Southern Italian food; however, some "liked it better before renovations."

Papa Bear S
	16	4	11	$15

210 E. 23rd St. (bet. 2nd & 3rd Aves.), 212-685-0727

■ For "pierogies from heaven" in Gramercy, this low-to-no-frills greasy spoon is "the eighth Polish wonder of the world", serving "papa bear portions" of mama bear "home cooking" at baby bear prices.

Papaya King ◑ S
	18	3	9	$6

179 E. 86th St. (3rd Ave.), 212-369-0648

■ Many claim "the best hot dog in NYC" is to be had "on the run" at this feisty, fast-food frank and fruit drink stand; it's an ideal bargain "snack at 3 AM" or at any hour, and don't miss the fruit drinks.

121

F | D | S | C

Paper Moon Milano 19 | 16 | 16 | $37
39 E. 58th St. (bet. Madison & Park Aves.), 212-758-8600
■ An "upscale vehicle for pizza/pasta", this Midtown Milanese trattoria offers "sleek eating in fashiony decor" to "lots of white shirts", but it's "a little overrated" for basically "good Italian food."

Pappardella ◐ [S] 17 | 15 | 16 | $29
316 Columbus Ave. (75th St.), 212-595-7996
◪ "Wonderful people-watching" from the outdoor tables enhances the "inconsistent" Tuscan food at this Columbus Avenue Italian; while some find the pastas "innovative" and sauces "fabulous", others claim the cuisine is "typical" and "totally forgettable."

Paradis Barcelona [S] 20 | 21 | 20 | $39
145 E. 50th St. (bet. Lexington & 3rd Aves.), 212-754-3333
◪ Despite a "great flamenco show" and "terrific tapas" this Midtown Barcelonan simply hasn't caught on; it's "best on a warm evening when you can sit outside and pretend the food is better than it is" and the prices are lower than they are.

Paradise (Brooklyn) – | – | – | E
8017 Fifth Ave. (bet. 80th & 81st Sts.), 718-921-0266
"You'll feel married to the mob" at this "funsky" "old Russian standby" in Brooklyn; funky and "très romantique with great food and great decor", it's been a "constant for 20 years."

PARIOLI ROMANISSIMO 25 | 25 | 22 | $64
24 E. 81st St. (bet. 5th & Madison Aves.), 212-288-2391
◪ "Exorbitantly priced", "fine" Northern Italian in an "elegant" East Side townhouse setting" – admirers consider it "classy, "comfortable" and "charming"; critics call it a "stiff", "stuffy", "old" "elephant."

Paris Cafe ◐ [S] – | – | – | I
119 South St. (Peck Slip), 212-608-2600
It sure ain't Paris, but this Seaport-area bar/restaurant (with the accent on bar) draws throngs of after-work Wall Streeters who come more for its good beer and cheer than for its basic American fare.

Paris Commune ◐ [S] 18 | 17 | 16 | $27
411 Bleecker St. (bet. W. 11th & Bank Sts.), 212-929-0509
■ "Perfect for that snowy winter night when you need a fireplace and hearty country French food", this "cozy" semi-bohemian West Village bistro is usually "good", but can be "inconsistent"; it's so popular for brunch that it "can be a very long wait."

Park Avalon ◐ [S] 20 | 20 | 17 | $32
225 Park Ave. S. (bet. 18th & 19th Sts.), 212-533-2500
■ There's both "style and substance" at this large, "lively, loud" postmodern Italo-Mediterranean "new favorite"; our surveyors say it's "here to stay" thanks to "surprisingly good" food and prices; it's "jammed with beautiful people" in baseball caps.

PARK AVENUE CAFE [S] 25 | 23 | 23 | $51
100 E. 63rd St. (Park Ave.), 212-644-1900
■ "A class act in every way"; chef "David Burke's mastery in the kitchen rivals the beautiful interior" of this "sophisticated" yet "fun" filly; his "novel" American fare is of "Faulknerian complexity", but "superb" according to the "do-I-know-you?, haute East Side crowd"; for something "special" have a party in the kitchen.

Park Avenue Country Club S
11 14 12 $26
381 Park Ave. S. (27th St.), 212-685-3636

☑ Whimsical country-club decor, simulated golf, pool tables, lots of TVs and a large bar highlight this "spacious" sports bar, but note: "it's packed on big-event nights, "the hamburger-type food" is "average to hopeless" and "if you're over 30, forget it."

Park Bistro S
23 16 18 $42
414 Park Ave. S. (bet. 28th & 29th Sts.), 212-689-1360

■ "If you can't get to Paris" try the "gold standard of NY bistros" with Parisian "crowds, noise and attitude"; "close quarters are overcome" by consistently "great value in food and spirit"; it's "where the cultured, working rich go" for "a warm place on a cold day."

Park Side (Queens) ◑ S
23 18 20 $35
107-01 Corona Ave. (108th St. & 51st Ave.), 718-271-9274

■ An "immensely popular", "landmark", "old-fashioned family-type" Corona-area Italian that's "one of the better rewards of living in Queens"; it's "a pinky ring paradise", but the "food is tremendous" and valet parking makes driving over no problem.

Parma ◑ S
20 12 18 $38
1404 Third Ave. (bet. 79th & 80th Sts.), 212-535-3520

☑ Opinion divides on this Upper East Side "neighborhood Italian": admirers say that "though decor is bare, the food is unbeatable", like a "personal kitchen"; however, critics complain that it's a "has-been" where "regulars get the best tables and service."

Pasqua Coffee Bar

100 Church St. (Barclay St.), 212-513-1006
450 Lexington Ave. (bet. 44th & 45th Sts.), 212-661-5459
1345 Sixth Ave. (bet. 54th & 55th Sts.), 212-265-8610
1290 Sixth Ave. (bet. 51st & 52nd Sts.), 212-977-4861
WFC, 250 Vesey St., AmEx Tower Concourse, 212-587-9512 S
55 E. 53rd St. (bet. Park & Madison Aves.), 212-750-7140
2 Broadway (Bond St.), 212-509-9159
Citicorp Courtyard, 153 E. 53rd St. (Lexington Ave.), 212-421-4229
Liberty Plaza, 165 B'way (Liberty St.), 212-608-6481
Bank of America Bldg., 335 Madison Ave. (43rd St.), 212-370-3510

"Great big salads" outshine the array of coffees, bagels, pastries and ice cream at this new coffee bar chain; unusual for the genre, it also offers outdoor dining and table service for its reasonable prices.

Passage to India ◑ S
18 14 16 $19
308 E. 6th St. (bet. 1st & 2nd Aves.), 212-529-5770

■ Fans call this "authentic" North Indian tandoori specialist "the shining star of 6th Street's Curry Row" due to "gracious service", "restful atmosphere", "superb food" and "great prices"; but based on recent meals, some think "the chef went down the street."

Passport ◑ S
▽ **16 19 16 $19**
79 St. Marks Pl. (bet. 1st & 2nd Aves.), 212-979-2680

☑ For "decent Mexican food" this duplex East Villager offers "nice dining on a budget"; the "low-key atmosphere could use a spark, but the owners truly care about the food and customers."

Pasta Lovers S
15 12 14 $22
158 W. 58th St. (bet. 6th & 7th Aves.), 212-582-1355

☑ A "pasta-porium" for "bargain mass-market Italian"; "the portions and prices are more enticing than the atmosphere" or "pedestrian" pasta, but it's a "good quick bite" in Midtown.

Pasta Presto [S] — 13 | 10 | 12 | $19

959 Second Ave. (51st St.), 212-754-4880
613 Second Ave. (34th St.), 212-889-4131
93 MacDougal St. (bet. Bleecker & W. 3rd Sts.), 212-260-5679

◪ The "McDonald's of pasta", these "generic pasta factories" are a "functional" choice for "pasta in a hurry" with "big selections" and "early-bird specials"; critics say "stay home and boil your own water."

Pasticcio ▽ 20 | 16 | 19 | $31

447 Third Ave. (bet. 30th & 31st Sts.), 212-679-2551

■ "Happy meals" can be had at this "great neighborhood" Italian that's "personally run"; it has "fine homemade pasta" and a bargain lunch.

Pastrami King (Queens) [S] — 18 | 5 | 11 | $17

124-24 Queens Blvd. (82nd Ave.), 718-263-1717

◪ Diehards say it's "worth the trip to Queens" for "the best corned beef and pastrami in the Tri-State" area with "a distinctive smoky quality"; otherwise this "greasy old-style" deli offers little.

Patría — 23 | 21 | 20 | $44

250 Park Ave. South (20th St.), 212-777-6211

◪ "A welcome newcomer" to the hot Gramercy dining scene, this handsome, multilevel "high-tech" Nuevo Latino has introduced NY to the "creative" Contemporary South American cooking of chef Doug Rodriguez (ex Coral Gables' Yuca); most find the food "fascinating", even "thrilling", especially the desserts, but traditionalists simply "can't understand the hype."

Patrissy's [S] — 22 | 13 | 19 | $33

98 Kenmare St. (bet. Mulberry & Centre Sts.), 212-226-2888

■ "A 40-year favorite", this "sedate" ("no flashing lights") "traditional Southern Italian" is "hidden in Little Italy"; you should try the spiedini a la Romana or simply "let the 'neolithic' waiters order for you."

Patsy's [S] — 19 | 14 | 18 | $39

236 W. 56th St. (bet B'way & 8th Ave.), 212-247-3491

◪ This "tacky", "old-world classic" Italian in Midtown was out of tune 20 years ago but its "robusto" Neapolitan cuisine still has plenty of celebrity devotees: "go late and see stars dine."

Patsy's Pizza ◐ [S] ⊄ ▽ 23 | 6 | 11 | $16

2287-91 First Ave. (bet. 117th & 118th Sts.), 212-534-9783

◪ For "cheesy", "greasy", "awesome" pizza it's hard to beat this East Harlem specialist, but those put off by the 'hood or the "vernacular decor" suggest you "call in an order and have the cab wait."

PATSY'S PIZZA (Bklyn) [S] ⊄ — 25 | 10 | 15 | $16

19 Old Fulton St. (bet. Water & Front Sts.), 718-858-4300

■ Our surveyors exclaim "drive, walk or crawl to this pizza heaven" "on a deserted street" "right under the Brooklyn Bridge"; they say "it's to the competition as Peter Luger is to Tads"; "Patsy himself circulates majestically" through this authentic "brick-oven" charmer as Sinatra croons from the "best jukebox to learn Italian by."

Patzo ◐ [S] — 13 | 14 | 13 | $21

2330 Broadway (85th St.), 212-496-9240

■ Large, airy, brick-oven Italian that's "one of the better choices when you find yourself on upper B'way"; the "staff is inefficient", but the food's "decent" and "dependable" for the price; "have the antipasti."

Paul & Jimmy's 🄂
18 | 14 | 18 | $35

123 E. 18th St. (Irving Pl. & Park Ave. S.), 212-475-9540

■ "A rock-solid" Gramercy bistro for "reliable" "Italian the way it was years ago"; the "consistent" food, "comfortable ambiance" and "friendly service" make it "a neighborhood favorite."

Peacock Alley 🄂
21 | 24 | 22 | $45

Waldorf-Astoria, 301 Park Ave. (bet. 49th & 50th Sts.), 212-872-4895

■ "Vastly improved"; "more NYers should rediscover" the "sleek elegance" and "classy atmosphere" that make this French dining room a "great place for a power breakfast" or "a special evening" complete with piano music; it "still has that Cole Porter feel."

Pearson's Stick To Your Ribs BBQ
22 | 4 | 10 | $17

(Queens) 🥢

5-16 51st Ave. (west of Vernon Blvd.), 718-937-3030

■ "The closest thing to real Texas BBQ NY has to offer" will be even closer with the upcoming opening of a new West Side branch; soon Manhattanites can enjoy "melt-in-your-mouth", "stick-to-your-hips" ribs and brisket without making the trek to the Queens original.

Pedro Paramo 🄂
▽ 20 | 12 | 20 | $23

430 E. 14th St. (bet. 1st Ave. & Ave. A), 212-475-4581

☑ "They really care" at this "authentic Mexican" "mom and pop" in the East Village; the "intense flavors" are "much more rich and true than typical NY Tex-Mex"; however, critics claim it's a "dump."

Peking Park 🄂
▽ 16 | 14 | 16 | $29

100 Park Ave. (40th St.), 212-725-5570

☑ "Best for banquets", this sprawling Chinese just south of Grand Central "can be wonderful, but usually isn't"; "decent" food is "overpriced", but the atmosphere is "quiet" and "businesslike."

Pellegrino's 🄂
▽ 19 | 13 | 19 | $31

138 Mulberry St. (bet. Hester & Grand Sts.), 212-226-3177

■ "Little Italy in true form" – "good food, fair price"; "summertime is great here with pink tablecloths" out on the terrace; the "service is slow" but this is one of those easygoing, "old-fashioned" places where most people couldn't care less.

Pen & Pencil Restaurant 🄂
19 | 17 | 19 | $42

205 E. 45th St. (bet. 2nd & 3rd Aves.), 212-682-8660

☑ "A NY perennial"; most surveyors consider this "clubby" Midtown steakhouse's "cedar-scented steaks" and accompanying wines a "solid tradition", but others find the restaurant "a little worn" and say they'll "go with mom and dad, but prefer more action."

PERIYALI
25 | 21 | 23 | $43

35 W. 20th St. (bet. 5th & 6th Aves.), 212-463-7890

■ "The gods have smiled upon" this "truly exceptional", "upscale" "gourmet Greek" in the Flatiron District; enormously popular, it provides "a level of elegance not normally associated with Greek restaurants"; sure, the prices make the Astoria Greeks envious, but they're modest for "a short vacation to the Greek Islands."

Perks Fine Cuisine
– | – | – | M

553 Manhattan Ave. (123rd St.), 212-666-8500

Upscale Harlem American is a bargain for "chicken and gravy and biscuits on Sunday morning" or "good music at night"; it's best enjoyed "with a crowd", and at these prices anyone can afford to host.

Perretti Italian Cafe ◐ 🅂
13 | 12 | 13 | $23

270 Columbus Ave. (bet. 72nd & 73rd Sts.), 212-362-3939

☑ The word is "they never should have revamped" this "basic Italian"; though some prefer the "more upscale decor" and "better new menu", others call it "pedestrian."

Persepolis 🅂
▽ 17 | 13 | 17 | $26

1423 Second Ave. (bet. 74th & 75th Sts.), 212-535-1100

■ "When in the mood for something different" come here for pleasingly priced "Persian cuisine that would make even an ayatollah smile"; the decor is "modest", but "they have a way with seasonings" and "the rice alone is worth the visit."

Peruvian Restaurant 🅂 ⊄
▽ 18 | 9 | 13 | $20

688 Tenth Ave. (bet. 48th & 49th Sts.), 212-581-5814

☑ The food is "good, cheap and different" at this Hell's Kitchen Peruvian, home of the "you-point-they-bring-it" menu, but some find the "permanent Christmas decor" "depressing."

Pescatore 🅂
19 | 16 | 16 | $32

955 Second Ave. (bet. 50th & 51st Sts.), 212-752-7151

■ "Well on its way to becoming an institution", this "busy Italian" Midtowner offers "excellent fish and pasta", "friendly service" and sidewalk dining at a "great value" for the area.

Petaluma ◐ 🅂
20 | 17 | 18 | $35

1356 First Ave. (73rd St.), 212-772-8800

☑ This "airy" Eastsider has "good to excellent", "basic" Northern Italian cuisine "in a pleasant atmosphere"; surviving its original trendy period, it has become "a neighborhood standby" for normal folks seeking a good simple meal of pizza, pasta or grilled items.

PETER LUGER STEAK HOUSE (Brooklyn) 🅂 ⊄
27 | 16 | 20 | $49

178 Broadway (Driggs Ave.), 718-387-7400

■ Again easily leading the herd as "NYC's No. 1 steakhouse", this century-old Brooklynite is our surveyors' idea of "red-meat nirvana"; super enthusiastic diners insist that Luger porterhouse steaks, chops and side dishes are "better than sex"; despite a "German brauhaus" setting, "gruff waiters" and high prices, it's "a required course in any NY culinary education."

Petes' Place ◐ 🅂
▽ 13 | 11 | 12 | $18

256 Third Ave. (21st St.), 212-260-2900

☑ "Fuel up like an old farmhand" on "whopping portions" at this "homey", "grungy" but "upscale" Gramercy coffee shop with a "tin ceiling, panelled walls" and "low prices" for a wide range of dishes.

Pete's Tavern ◐ 🅂
13 | 15 | 14 | $24

129 E. 18th St. (Irving Pl.), 212-473-7676

☑ This Gramercy "landmark" is a "NYC staple"; the pub food is "nothing special" and TV distracts, but it's "like eating in a history book"; "try the booth where O. Henry wrote *The Gift of the Magi.*"

PETROSSIAN ◐ 🅂
25 | 25 | 23 | $56

182 W. 58th St. (7th Ave.), 212-245-2214

■ A "caviar lover's heaven", and for foie gras and smoked salmon lovers too, this "enchanting", modern Russian-Continental near Carnegie Hall offers "lavish dining" in "art deco elegance"; however, you can also eat affordably via the prix fixe menus.

Phoebe's S
15 | 16 | 15 | $24

380 Columbus Ave. (78th St.), 212-724-5145

◪ "Homey", brick-walled "West Side hangout" that "fills a need" with its "cozy fireplace" and "comfort food"; critics cite "long waits" and "marginal" quality, but locals could live on the mashed potatoes alone.

Phoenix Garden
22 | 9 | 12 | $23

242 E. 40th St. (bet. 2nd & 3rd Aves.), 212-983-6666

◪ A "Chinatown standard rejuvenated on East 40th Street", this "creative" Cantonese has "the best salt-and-pepper shrimp dish in NY"; though the decor is minimal and the "staff needs smiling lessons", most people are happy to see this old favorite back in business.

Pho Pasteur Vietnam S ⌷
19 | 3 | 11 | $14

85 Baxter St. (bet. Centre & Mulberry Sts.), 212-608-3656

■ "Who would have thought a hole-in-the-wall in the shadow of the Tombs would have such good food?" ask the many devotees of this "excellent", "unbelievably cheap", "lively", "no-frills" Vietnamese.

Piccola Venezia (Queens) S
24 | 15 | 21 | $40

42-01 28th Ave. (Steinway St.), 718-721-8470

■ "Molto bene" – you're treated like family" at this "raucous", "old-fashioned" Queens Italian where dinner is "a scene right out of *The Godfather*"; "huge portions" of "excellent food" and a "superb wine list" make it "well worth cruising for a parking space."

Piccolo Angolo S
▽ 22 | 14 | 22 | $26

621 Hudson St. (Jane St.), 212-229-9177

■ A little-known, "un-Manhattan" "jewel", this "family-run West Village Italian" with "really good food" is "like going to your grandparents' for dinner" and not that much more expensive; the "friendly" owner is, if anything, "overdetermined" to make you "feel at home."

Piccolo Pomodoro S
17 | 12 | 15 | $24

1742 Second Ave. (bet. 90th & 91st Sts.), 212-831-8167

Pomodori S ⌷
1425 Second Ave. (bet. 74th & 75th Sts.), 212-472-5225

Tre Pomodori S ⌷
210 E. 34th St. (bet. 2nd & 3rd Aves.), 212-545-7266

◪ "Inexpensive pasta joints" with "a vast following"; this mini-chain serves "huge portions" of "zesty pasta" and good salads in "relaxed" settings; critics of "cookie-cutter" fare would "rather do it" at home.

Picholine ☺
23 | 20 | 20 | $45

35 W. 64th St. (bet. B'way & CPW), 212-724-8585

◪ The "best new addition to the Lincoln Center scene"; chef Terry Brennan is producing "innovative" Mediterranean "gourmet" fare in a warmly "attractive", "calming setting"; the pre-theater "service needs brushing up", but otherwise it has few flaws and more and more neighbors are treating it as their dining room.

Pierre au Tunnel
20 | 16 | 20 | $36

250 W. 47th St. (bet. B'way & 8th Ave.), 212-575-1220

■ "The whole is greater than the sum of the parts" at this "busy" but "reliable", "classic" French bistro in the Theater District; the "pre-theater prix fixe is worthwhile" and service is "polished and low-key."

Pier 25A (Queens)
16 | 13 | 15 | $29

215-16 Northern Blvd. (bet. 215th & 216th Sts.), Bayside, 718-423-6395

◪ You and your family will get "massive portions" of "wonderful fresh fish" at this quintessential seafood restaurant in Queens; those who are unaffected by the casual "old-world charm" insist that it's "overpriced" because "a diner is a diner is a diner."

Pie, The S
19 | 12 | 16 | $24

340 E. 86th St. (bet. 1st & 2nd Aves.), 212-517-8717

■ "Everything from the tablecloth" to the zany hostess says "welcome to this tiny slice of Russia"; it's "eccentric" but "authentic", "dark" but "friendly", "filling" but "cheap."

Pietro & Vanessa S
19 | 14 | 16 | $26

23 Cleveland Pl. (bet. Lafayette & Spring Sts.), 212-941-0286

☑ "Like a night out in Milan", "the back garden is a great place to enjoy a leisurely plate" of "no-frills pasta", but the interior is "sort of tacky" at this Little Italy "hideaway"; anyway it's a "bargain."

Pietro's
22 | 13 | 19 | $46

232 E. 43rd St. (bet. 2nd & 3rd Aves.), 212-682-9760

☑ Despite "very good" steak, Caesar salad and "lots of dishes to share", "bland" decor and "uneven" performance hold this old-time Midtown Italian steakhouse back in facing the tough local competition.

Pigalle S
21 | 18 | 18 | $38

111 E. 29th St. (bet. Lexington & Park Aves.), 212-779-7830

■ "French through and through", this "intimate" Gramercy bistro "transplants you to the Left Bank" with its "charming", "very fine fare" and "typical French aloof staff"; standout dishes such as the rack of lamb, fries and crème brûlée keep it "packed."

Pig Heaven ◑ S
16 | 11 | 14 | $26

1540 Second Ave. (bet. 80th & 81st Sts.), 212-744-4333

☑ Serving "pig a thousand ways", this Upper East Side Chinese retains a robust family-with-children clientele thanks to its "heavenly" pork ribs, spring rolls and dumplings and "cute pig-theme decor"; however, its kitchen has "slipped" and the place is starting to "look like a sty."

Pink Tea Cup ◑ S⌿
17 | 11 | 15 | $17

42 Grove St. (bet. Bleecker & Bedford Sts.), 212-807-6755

■ "Authentic Southern food" (including "the best fried chicken in town") in a tiny, homey West Village kitchen with a "hearty" anytime breakfast that's "hell on arteries" but "easy on pocketbooks"; this place "defines finger-lickin' good; say, there's Whoopi.

Pinocchio S
19 | 17 | 19 | $38

170 E. 81st St. (bet. Lexington & 3rd Aves.), 212-650-1513

☑ The majority reports "you'll check all your cares and stress" at the door of this "romantic and intimate" East Side Italian where "mother's in the kitchen, son's on the floor"; dissenters find the food "uninspired" and a bit "pricey", and the interior "gloomy."

Pipeline S
– | – | – | M

2 World Financial Ctr., 225 Liberty St. (South End Ave.), 212-945-2755

Don't expect culinary riches from this low-budget WFC American's pipeline; inside is like a Con Ed power station, but sitting outside and watching a Hudson sunset can feel like you've just struck a gusher.

Pisces ◑ S
21 | 17 | 17 | $28

95 Avenue A (6th St.), 212-260-6660

■ "There should be more seafood restaurants like this" "interesting, inexpensive" "oasis in the East Village"; "innovative preparations", "open-air" summer dining and "amiable" staff keep this "hip" yearling "packed" with "trendy" Downtowners.

Pizzapiazza S
14 | 10 | 12 | $18

785 Broadway (10th St.), 212-505-0977

☑ Offering a "variety of well-made, deep-dish" pizzas and salads in "light and airy", "mall-decor" digs, this Village joint is a "good value" for family dining; "go for the pizza-movie special."

Pzzeria Uno
13 10 11 $16

432 Columbus Ave. (81st St.), 212-595-4700
55 Third Ave. (bet. 10th & 11th Sts.), 212-995-9668
391 Sixth Ave. (bet. 8th St. & Waverly Pl.), 212-242-5230
220 E. 86th St. (bet. 2nd & 3rd Aves.), 212-472-5656
South St. Seaport, 89 South St. (Pier 17), 212-791-7999

☑ "A factory for deep-dish pizza – but hey, sometimes you're in the mood" for "a greasy, doughy meal" at this "predictable" Chicago chain; "only in a food court would it stand out", but it's "open late", "the bathrooms are clean" and "kids love it."

Planet Hollywood
13 22 14 $23

140 W. 57th St. (bet. 6th & 7th Aves.), 212-333-7827

☑ Keith Barish and Robert Earl's "glitzy" shrine to Hollywood is a "perfect place to take people you don't want to talk to so you can watch movies play on the wall" and gawk at genuinely amazing "movie memorabilia" while wolfing down a wide range of American fare that's "surprisingly good" and "reasonable"; it's "a 'must do' for tourists" and "sure to dazzle kids", especially if you stop at the shop on the way out.

Plaza Oyster Bar, The
20 21 18 $39

The Plaza Hotel, 768 Fifth Ave. (Central Park S.), 212-546-5340

☑ "Uniquely old NY", this "classic" oyster-bar saloon in The Plaza Hotel is mostly touted as "great for talk", "drinks and seafood", but some diners find it "musty" and "overrated."

Pó
21 17 19 $32

31 Cornelia St. (bet. Bleecker & W. 4th Sts.), 212-645-2189

■ Village Northern Italian serving "original" creations in an "intimate" ("cramped") bistro setting; if some say recent "hype" has hurt this popular newcomer, others only notice that it's "hard to get in" here.

Poiret (CLOSED)
20 17 18 $37

474 Columbus Ave. (bet. 82nd & 83rd Sts.), 212-724-6880

☑ Though opinion is sharply divided on the effect of recent menu and decor "upgrades" at this "classy" bistro, most agree that it's "the best French food on the Upper West Side" with "great big portions" "presented beautifully" in a "pretty" but "noisy" setting.

Polo, The
22 23 23 $51

Westbury Hotel, 840 Madison Ave. (69th St.), 212-439-4835

☑ "Even lunching with a former President in the room didn't distract from the food" at this "very English", "upper-crust" East Side hotel room; "elegant" ambiance plus "good service and presentation" contribute to a "superior Continental dining experience."

Pomaire
− − − M

371 W. 46 St. (bet. 8th & 9th Aves.), 212-956-3055

Finding Chilean food in NYC is like finding a needle in a haystack; this exemplar on Restaurant Row provides a pleasant, low-key, ethnic evening.

Pongsri Thai Restaurant
21 12 17 $23

244 W. 48th St. (bet. B'way & 8th Ave.), 212-582-3392

■ "A great find for the economy-minded", this Theater District Thai is "consistently excellent" and "affordable"; even native Thais tout it as "simple and delicious."

Ponticello (Queens)
▽ 24 16 22 $33

46-11 Broadway (bet. 46th & 47th Sts.), 718-278-4514

■ "A diamond in the rough", "Queens can be proud of this "cheerful but dignified", "outstanding", Italian where "delicious food" can be had "at less-than-Manhattan prices."

F | D | S | C

Popover Cafe 🅂
18 | 15 | 15 | $21
551 Amsterdam Ave. (bet. 86th & 87th Sts.), 212-595-8555
☑ Despite "torturous waits" for Sunday brunch, Westsiders can't resist this "cutesy", "cushy breakfast-type place"; lunch and dinner are "fresh, wholesome and well-prepared", but it's the "divine" popovers that keep the crowds coming back.

Portico ❶🅂
21 | 17 | 20 | $33
1431 Second Ave. (bet. 74th & 75th Sts.), 212-794-1032
☑ "Innovative" "homemade pastas with delicious sauces" and "winning service" make this Northern Italian "a cut above the string of 2nd Avenue" places; some say it's "uneven" and "expensive."

POST HOUSE 🅂
24 | 21 | 22 | $52
Lowell Hotel, 28 E. 63rd St. (bet. Madison & Park Aves.), 212-935-2888
■ "Among NYC's top steakhouses", this "handsome" "Americana-decorated" Eastsider is a "safe bet" and "not just for steak" – its seafood, desserts and wines are all first-rate; though some call it a "chauvinist monument to meat and martinis", this is one of the few steakhouses where women feel welcome.

Presto's ❶🅂
15 | 13 | 15 | $23
2770 Broadway (bet. 106th & 107th Sts.), 212-222-1760
434 Amsterdam Ave. (81st St.), 212-721-9141
■ Though "nothing to get excited about", for "decent pasta in a minute" this "healthy and cheap" Upper West Side "neighborhood" Italian duo is certainly "acceptable" and has home-baked bread.

PRIMAVERA ❶🅂
25 | 22 | 23 | $55
1578 First Ave. (82nd St.), 212-861-8608
■ "First-rate on all counts", this pricey, "clubby" Upper East Side Northern Italian classic has "outstanding food" "exquisitely served" in a "beautiful, wood-panelled room" that exudes "old-world charm"; hand-kissing owner-host Nicola Civetta "coddles" his boardroom-style, "sophisticated" clients who reciprocate by chanting "class, class, class"; of course, it's impossible to please everybody.

Prime Burger ⊟
▽ 17 | 9 | 16 | $13
5 E. 51st St. (bet. Madison & 5th Aves.), 212-759-4729
■ For "hamburgers that are real fresh" and "excellent pies and cakes", this Midtown burger joint is an "institution"; devotees "love the old-time waiters", "1950s atmosphere" and "classic" cheeseburger decor.

Primola ❶🅂
22 | 16 | 19 | $43
1226 Second Ave. (bet. 64th & 65th Sts.), 212-758-1775
■ "The Northern Italian food is "always good" and often "superb" at this "trendy" Eastsider which is always bustling with "bigwigs" and "high rollers" who look totally at home.

Privé 🅂
▽ 19 | 19 | 17 | $41
24 E. 80th St. (bet. Madison & 5th Aves.), 212-772-1541
☑ To admirers, this "romantic, elegant newcomer" is "a hidden piece of NY" offering "wonderful" French-American cuisine "in a nice, quiet townhouse" to a "jet-set" crowd; the less-impressed call this former club "pricey" and "pretentious" and ask "who are they kidding?"

Provence ❶🅂
23 | 22 | 19 | $41
38 MacDougal St. (bet. Prince & Houston Sts.), 212-475-7500
■ Like "a brief trip to the south of France", the "authentic ambiance" extends from the "excellent" "country fare" to the wood panelling and long bar at this "popular", "crowded" SoHo bistro; the "garden in back is a dream"; owners Michel and Patricia Jean are real pros.

Pudgie's [S] — 12 | 3 | 8 | $10

411 Amsterdam Ave. (bet. 79th & 80th Sts.), 212-799-9999
344 Ninth Ave. (30th St.), 212-563-3500
156 Chambers St. (bet. W. Broad & Greenwich Sts.), 212-374-9100

◩ "Better than the Colonel" and they deliver; "skinless fried chicken" is an "interesting approach" at these "cheap", "fast-food" joints; "convenient on a no-cook night", but they're "no Boston Chicken."

Puket ◐ [S] — 15 | 12 | 15 | $27

945 Second Ave. (bet. 50th & 51st Sts.), 212-759-6339

◩ "Middle-of-the-pack Thai in Midtown"; despite "great lunch deals" and generally "good food", critics of the "depressing decor" and "small portions" tend to be harsh.

Quartiere (Queens) ◐ [S] — 15 | 16 | 13 | $28

107-02 Queens Blvd. (70th Ave.), 718-520-8037

◩ "Convenient" for variety-starved Queensites, this "popular" "Upper East Side Italian in Forest Hills" is best for pizza; the "Euro-style outdoor cafe is neat in warm weather."

Quatorze Bis ◐ [S] — 21 | 18 | 19 | $41

323 E. 79th St. (bet. 1st & 2nd Aves.), 212-535-1414

■ "Attractive and lively", this "great neighborhood bistro" is "a wonderful oasis" on the Upper East Side for "consistently very good" French fare, especially the grilled chicken or steak frites.

Queen (Brooklyn) [S] ⇏ — 21 | 12 | 20 | $29

84 Court St. (bet. Livingston & Schermerhorn Sts.), 718-596-5955

■ "A favorite of judges, lawyers and court employees", this "homey", "gracious" "old NY Italian" serves up "fabulous homemade pastas" that are "plentiful and cheap" enough to compensate for jury duty.

Quisisana ◐ [S] — 19 | 17 | 18 | $36

1319 Third Ave. (bet. 75th & 76th Sts.), 212-879-5000

◩ "Another Italian on Third Avenue", but this "attractive" "newcomer" is "trying hard to please"; "relaxing" atmosphere and "well-presented food" put it "a cut above" the competition.

Rachel's [S] — 21 | 16 | 18 | $28

608 Ninth Ave. (bet. 43rd & 44th Sts.), 212-957-9050

■ "You'll feel welcome" in this "friendly" Hell's Kitchen American bistro; a "fresh and delicious" pre-theater stop with "pot pie" and the "best rolls in NY", it's a "cozy", "affordable" surprise.

Raffaele [S] — – | – | – | M

1055 First Ave. (57th St.), 212-750-3232

Newly opened Sutton Place Southern Italian that has quickly become a neighborhood favorite; good food, simple warm decor and friendly proprietor Raffaele have won a celebrity following among neighbors such as Bill Blass and Bobby Short; open seven days.

RAINBOW ROOM ◐ [S] — 21 | 28 | 23 | $58

GE Bldg., 30 Rockefeller Plaza, 65th floor (bet. 49th & 50th Sts.), 212-632-5100

■ Years ago you'd say it's the "only place in NY to take your best girl dancing"; today, this "quintessential NYC" art deco, Contemporary Continental, skyscraper-top, dine-and-dance "landmark" has been recreated by restaurant impresario Joe Baum and is still "magical" – like "being in an elegant 1930s movie" where "troubles and money melt like lemon drops"; N.B. this is really a two-story complex with extensive party facilities, an elegant cabaret (Rainbow & Stars), and an informal cafe (Promenade) for affordable, low-key dining and sunset/skyline-scoping.

Rancho Mexican Cafe ●⧗ ▽ 19 15 17 $29
466 Amsterdam Ave. (bet. 82nd & 83rd Sts.), 212-362-1514
☑ "Tijuana atmosphere" plus the "best frozen margaritas in NYC" and "great fajitas"; critics think it's just another "noisy" Mexican "for entertaining cousins from Pittsburgh."

RAO'S ⌿ 25 13 20 $46
455 E. 114th St. (Pleasant Ave.), 212-722-6709
■ It'll be real tough to get into this "East Harlem landmark" if you don't know Frankie personally, but "the legend lives up to its reputation"; "they tell you what you want" and then they make it "in God's own kitchen" – "homestyle Italian at its best"; the place looks like a Cagney movie set and, if you get in – a big "if" – you're likely to sit between the Godfather and the governor.

Raoul's ●⧗ 22 20 18 $41

180 Prince St. (bet. Sullivan & Thompson Sts.), 212-966-3518
■ A "SoHo haven" that "after all the years" is still "full of energy" and has first-rate French bistro fare including "the best steak au poivre in town"; add a "garden that's a world unto its own", "a beautiful young crowd" and cool bartenders and you've got "fab French fun."

RAPHAEL 25 24 24 $50
33 W. 54th St. (bet. 5th & 6th Aves.), 212-582-8993
■ This "elegant spot for top-of-the-line French cooking" is "exquisite in every way": there's chef Jean Michel Bergougnoux's fine hand in the kitchen, the gracious reception of owners Raphael and Mira Edery and a charming Midtown townhouse space.

Rascals ●⧗ ▽ 11 11 11 $21

12 E. 22nd St. (bet. B'way & Park Ave. S.), 212-420-1777
☑ Flatiron "watering hole" that's "fun for burgers" and "onion rolls"; it can be good for an "easygoing Saturday night", but watch out for the "invasion of hair spray" that makes it seem like a "Jersey bar."

Rasputin (Brooklyn) ●⧗ ▽ 19 18 16 $46
2670 Coney Island Ave. (Ave. X), 718-332-8333
☑ "Eat, dance and celebrate"; this noisy restaurant-cum-nonstop-party is "the best of the Brooklyn Russians"; it's "a must-see" and "must-drink" place that nowadays is "even more like being in Russia than being in Russia."

Red Lion ●⧗⌿ ▽ 12 12 13 $19
151 Bleecker St. (Thompson St.), 212-473-9560
☑ "You can't talk over the music" in this "loud rugby pub"; it's a Village hangout that's "good for burgers, beer and a little folk music", but the food "tastes like it was made by Brits."

Red Tulip ⧗ 16 17 17 $31
439 E. 75th St. (bet. 1st & York Aves.), 212-734-4893
■ "Authentic" Hungarian with "boisterous, infectious charm" and "real character"; expect "heavy, tasty food" in a "colorful" setting that "looks like it should be run by gnomes"; "strolling musicians" help create an Eastern European "change of pace."

Regency (aka 540 Park) ●⧗ 21 23 21 $46

The Regency Hotel, 540 Park Ave. (61st St.), 212-759-4100
■ "Civilized" American dining that's "always an enjoyable, relaxing meal" and the "best pre-theater buy in town"; "home of the power breakfast", originated by Bob Tisch a generation ago, it's where the city does business before going to the office.

Regional Thai Taste [S] — ▽ 18 | 13 | 15 | $21
208 Seventh Ave. (22nd St.), 212-807-9872
◪ "Imaginative" Thai with "unique blends of sweet and spice", and where the "waiters are cute too"; critics say it's "nothing special" and has "noxious green walls."

Reidy's — 13 | 13 | 15 | $27
22 E. 54th St. (bet. Madison & 5th Aves.), 212-753-2419
◪ An "old reliable" Midtown Irish pub with a "plain meat-and-potatoes menu"; regulars love the "best cheap sit-down meal in Midtown", but critics cite boarding school fare from "the '50s."

REMI ◐ [S] — 24 | 24 | 21 | $46
145 W. 53rd St. (bet. 6th & 7th Aves.), 212-581-4242
■ "It all works" at Adam Tihany's "classy" Midtown Italian "souvenir of Venice"; a "gorgeous mural" of the Grand Canal and "soaring ceilings" are the setting for chef Francesco Antonucci's "sleek, sophisticated pasta sophistry", i.e. "the perfect marriage of wine and food"; translated into NYese, "Remi means wow."

René Pujol — 22 | 20 | 21 | $41
321 W. 51st St. (bet. 8th & 9th Aves.), 212-246-3023
■ Some say this French bistro is the "best of the B'way French standards"; don't miss the lobster bisque and chocolate soufflé in a "lovely townhouse" which is ideal "for a romantic tête-à-tête."

Restaurant Two Two Two [S] — 24 | 21 | 21 | $49
222 W. 79th St. (bet. B'way & Amsterdam Ave.), 212-799-0400
■ "Haute cuisine on the Upper West Side" is hard even to imagine so it should come as no surprise that Frank Valenza's "elegant" townhouse exemplar is "tops in the neighborhood" with fine "wine service" and "unsurpassed dishes"; all agree the American food's "top-notch", the only regret is that, by local standards, the price is too.

Revolution ◐ [S] — ▽ 16 | 16 | 15 | $24
611 Ninth Ave. (bet. 43rd & 44th Sts.), 212-489-8451
■ "VH-1 monitors", "a live DJ", "trendy clientele" and "decent", affordable food create a "bit of SoHo in Hell's Kitchen"; it's "not your typical Theater District restaurant", but it's a "hopping spot" for "the young and young at heart."

Rib'n & Blues — – | – | – | M
390 Eighth Ave. (bet. 29th & 30th Sts.), 212-971-9037
Advertised as "the best BBQ in a building that hasn't been condemned" catches the spirit of this cheap, funky MSG neighbor; on Wednesday–Friday nights you get rhythm & blues along with your pork.

Rice and Beans ⊭ — – | – | – | M
744 Ninth Ave. (bet. 50th & 51st Sts.), 212-265-4444
A "find", this "homey, authentic Cuban–Latin American" serves "food like only Havana mothers make"; it's "one of those great, cheap ethnics that make NY special" and a "bargain for lunch."

Right Bank ◐ [S] — 14 | 12 | 15 | $28
822 Madison Ave. (69th St.), 212-737-2811
■ "Very French in a casual sort of way", this Madison Avenue "fixture" is a "hidden favorite" that's a "good place to stop" for a wine and burger after the Met, especially in the "lovely" garden.

Rio Mar ◐ [S] — 18 | 9 | 15 | $25
7 Ninth Ave. (W. 12th St.), 212-243-9015
■ For garlic lovers this "glorious dump" in the Meat Packing District produces "intense flavors" that "linger" not just in memory; the locale is "out of *Blade Runner*", but the Spanish food's "worth the trip."

RIVER CAFE (Brooklyn) ◐ S
26 | 28 | 24 | $57
1 Water St. (East River), 718-522-5200
■ Buzzy O'Keefe's floating "jewel box" offers an extraordinary American menu and the "best view of the Big Apple"; its myriad admirers say the food competes with the best and "if I was rich I'd eat here everyday"; sure there's an occasional disappointment that's felt acutely at these prices, but the consensus is "words fail" to express NYers' "love for this place" – "it doesn't get more romantic."

Riverrun ◐ S
– | – | – | M
176 Franklin St. (bet. Greenwich & Hudson Sts.), 212-966-3894
Casual TriBeCa fixture, providing decent pub food and drink without fanfare; on the block between the trendy TriBeCa Grill and supertrendy Nobu, it feels like Lexington, Kentucky.

Road to Mandalay S
▽ 20 | 9 | 15 | $23
380 Broome St. (bet. Mott & Mulberry Sts.), 212-226-4218
☑ Very good Burmese in "lackluster" Chinatown digs with "fantastic soups" and "coconut rice" that "simply sing"; critics feel it can be "off-key" and "has no Hope" – nor Crosby for that matter.

Rocco S
▽ 19 | 11 | 17 | $28
181 Thompson St. (bet. Houston & Bleecker Sts.), 212-677-0590
☑ A Village Italian with "nice pasta", but not-so-nice decor; locals love the cannoli – "they put the filling in when you order it" which gives it that "old-world feel", but critics say it has slipped recently and is "more show than food."

Rocking Horse Mexican Cafe ◐ S
17 | 12 | 16 | $21
182 Eighth Ave. (bet. 19th & 20th Sts.), 212-463-9511
☑ "Better-than-average Tex-Mex" place that can really rock when the locals are horsing around, but it's "a bit too much like Taco Bell" to cross the border for; they give you crayons at the table and enough margaritas to turn just about anyone into a Jackson Pollock.

Roebling's S
13 | 14 | 13 | $26
South St. Seaport, 11 Fulton St. (South St.), 212-608-3980
☑ Seaport American "stalwart" named after the engineer who built the nearby Brooklyn Bridge; it's "good for a quick lunch or an after-work drink" and to "watch the scene", but he "made a better bridge."

Roettelle A.G.
21 | 17 | 18 | $31
126 E. 7th St. (bet. 1st Ave. & Avenue A), 212-674-4140
■ A tiny East Village storefront "find" that gets three "hoorays for German, Austrian and Swiss cuisines" that include cheese fondue; some say it's a little pricey, but the "warm and cozy", "homespun feeling" is worth it, "especially in the garden."

Rolf's S
18 | 18 | 15 | $29
281 Third Ave. (22nd St.), 212-477-4750
☑ It's tough to find "good German food" including "velvety sauerbraten" in NYC, much less in a "Black Forest setting" that feels like Christmas year-round; this Gramercy mainstay would be a "wunderland" – if only its service was better.

Rosa Mexicano ◐ S
22 | 18 | 19 | $37
1063 First Ave. (58th St.), 212-753-7407
■ Besides its signature, made-tableside guacamole ("a must", "best on planet"), Josephine Howard's East Side "upscale Mexican" is a perennial favorite among our surveyors; it's one of NYC's only "adult" Mexicans with "authentic" food and a "soothing" setting.

	F	D	S	C

Rose Cafe
24 Fifth Ave. (9th St.), 212-260-4118

18 | 18 | 17 | $31

■ "Tasty California-inspired menu" in a "glassed-in sidewalk cafe" on Lower Fifth; fans tout it for "satisfying", "nuts-and-bolts" food, especially brunch, "people-watching from window tables" and "lovely service"; detractors say it's "sometimes good", "sometimes clueless."

Rosemarie's
145 Duane St. (bet. W. B'way & Church St.), 212-285-2610

24 | 20 | 22 | $42

■ "Well worth the trip Downtown" to TriBeCa, this "relaxed", "cozy dining room" with "intimate" lighting produces "flawless" Italian food; it's a "wonderful place to go *after* you decide you like her a lot."

Rose of India
308 E. 6th St. (bet. 1st & 2nd Aves.), 212-533-5011

18 | 15 | 18 | $16

■ "6th Street's tastiest and most lively" Indian serves "cheap", "monstrous portions" and "looks like a subway car decorated for Christmas"; for a "change of pace" that will have you "clapping your hands", "just tell them it's your birthday."

Rosie O'Grady's
800 Seventh Ave. (52nd St.), 212-582-2975

15 | 14 | 16 | $27

■ A "good place" for a "relaxing business lunch" of American-Irish fare; it's one of those rare "drinking holes" that is also a safe spot "to meet your parents" or go "before theater" – except on St. Patrick's Day.

Rosolio
11 Barrow St. (bet. 7th Ave. S. & W. 4th St.), 212-645-9224

▽ 19 | 15 | 17 | $38

■ "Warm", "serene", modern Village Italian that reminds some of a "Roman evening"; "once truly exceptional", it "has been uneven", but insiders "have high hopes for its returned chef."

Roumeli Taverna (Queens)
33-04 Broadway (33rd St.), 718-278-7533

17 | 10 | 14 | $24

■ One of the few places for "BBQ octopus that's mmm", this "open-kitchen", "down-home Greek" in Astoria carries a "great wine list" and "honest food" at a "family price"; critics say "the spark is gone", but anywhere in Manhattan this would be a bonfire.

Royal Canadian Pancake
1004 Second Ave. (53rd St.), 212-980-4131
2286 Broadway (bet. 82nd & 83rd Sts.), 212-873-6052
180 Third Ave. (17th St.), 212-777-9288

13 | 6 | 9 | $16

■ The only question about these "mutant" ("pizza", "manhole cover", *"Starship Enterprise"*–size) pancakes is "how much bigger could they be?"; fans find them "flat out firm" and tout the rest of the breakfast too; critics, citing "unreal" lines and syrup, "plaster-of-paris batter" and "early gray" decor, conclude it's a good argument against NAFTA.

Royal Siam
240 Eighth Ave. (bet. 22nd & 23rd Sts.), 212-741-1732

– | – | – | M

Formerly Singha, this Chelsea Thai is a "charming" and "inexpensive" "oasis of calm"; it's "one of those nice surprises."

Ruby's River Road
1754 Second Ave. (bet. 91st & 92nd Sts.), 212-987-8179

▽ 13 | 10 | 12 | $20

■ "Good dives", especially Cajuns, aren't supposed to be any fancier than this "grungy" watering hole where "Jell-O shots" in front and po' boys, jambalaya and gumbo in back have young diners saying "very cool" and their elders saying "don't bother"; N.B. nka Ruby's Tap House, with a new beer-oriented menu (not reflected in ratings).

Rumpelmayer's ◑⒮   – | – | – | M
St. Moritz Hotel, 50 Central Park S. (6th Ave.), 212-755-5800
Just overhauled, this longtime favorite for rich desserts and stuffed toy animals has lost its former tacky charm and is now little more than a sterile coffee shop with unusually somnolent service; about all that's left is the dessert menu and that's not enough.

Ruppert's ◑⒮   13 | 11 | 13 | $18
269 Columbus Ave. (bet. 72nd & 73rd Sts.), 212-873-9400
1662 Third Ave. (93rd St.), 212-831-1900
☑ "Basic, but at '70s prices", hardly anyone is complaining about this crosstown duo of "neighborhood" pubs where burgers, brunches and brew go well with bar socializing; dissenters call this "eating not dining" and recommend it "only in a snowstorm."

Russell's American Grill ⒮   ▽ 16 | 18 | 16 | $39
Sheraton Park Ave., 45 Park Ave. (37th St.), 212-685-7676
■ "The formula works" for this "comfortable" Murray Hill "oasis" which, more than anything, resembles the best hotel dining room in, say, Paducah; it's "cheap, fast and fresh" and always "full of regulars."

Russian Samovar ◑⒮   18 | 15 | 18 | $35
256 W. 52nd St. (bet. B'way & 8th Ave.), 212-757-0168
■ "Much subtler than the Tea Room" at a much lower price, and with "real Russian food" and music; it may be "slightly seedy", but expatriates swear that after a few of Roman Kaplan's vodkas they feel like they're back home.

RUSSIAN TEA ROOM ◑⒮   19 | 24 | 19 | $47
150 W. 57th St. (bet. 6th & 7th Aves.), 212-265-0947
☑ While a few say it's "touristy" and "on a sleigh-ride downhill", this celeb-centered NY "landmark" next to Carnegie Hall is absolutely "one of those things you have to do" for "perfect" "blinis and Champagne", "caviar and vodka" and enough "glitz and kitsch" to make you feel it's "Christmas all year-round."

Rusty Staub's on Fifth   18 | 16 | 17 | $34
575 Fifth Ave. (47th St.), 212-682-1000
☑ A "great original" for "manly" portions, sports memorabilia and good wine, this Midtowner is a hit, especially "if Rusty is around"; opponents say "just like the Mets this place has gone south."

Ruth's Chris Steak House ◑⒮   22 | 20 | 20 | $46
148 W. 51st St. (bet. 6th & 7th Aves.), 212-245-9600
☑ Parochial NYC beef-eaters hate to admit it, but this New Orleans–based Midtown steakhouse chain produces "big, buttery, juicy steaks" that are right "up there" and at least worth a personal taste test; the one nagging criticism, besides "reservations mean nothing", is that "the damn name makes no sense."

Sahara East ◑⒮⟱   – | – | – | M
184 First Ave. (bet. 11th & 12th Sts.), 212-353-9000
Despite the "no-frills" setting and "confused service" this East Villager offers "good" Middle Eastern food at prices even a nomad could afford; some say poor climate control can make it "feel like the desert."

Saigon House and Bar ⒮   ▽ 19 | 10 | 15 | $23
8941 Bayard St. (Mulberry St.), 212-732-8988
■ A "popular lunch spot for attorneys" and a "pleasant switch from Chinese while on jury duty", this Vietnamese has "excellent food" and "friendly service", but "no atmosphere" to speak of; a few dissenters say "not as good as it used to be."

Sakura of Japan ◐ [S] 15 | 11 | 14 | $23

2298 Broadway (83rd St.), 212-769-1003
581 Third Ave. (38th St.), 212-972-8540

◩ "Average" but "affordable" Japanese crosstown twins that are "nothing special", but popular for "decent sushi" and "good early-bird specials"; the B'way branch is convenient to the Sony sixplex.

Salaam Bombay [S] – | – | – | I

317-319 Greenwich St. (bet. Duane & Reade Sts.), 212-226-9400

A spacious, comfortable new North Indian a few blocks from the WTC that should be an interesting option for an all-you-can-eat buffet lunch at $8.95 (why doesn't the city hire these guys to feed the homeless?) or for a quiet, more formal tandoori dinner.

Sal Anthony's [S] 18 | 16 | 18 | $33

55 Irving Pl. (bet. 17th & 18th Sts.), 212-982-9030

■ Devotees of this "classy Italian" Gramercy Park "mainstay" love its "consistent" food, "very attentive service" and the "excellent value" of its prix fixe menus; but a few quibblers say "old faithful" is "tired" and "heading into a slide."

Sala Thai ◐ [S] 20 | 13 | 17 | $25

1718 Second Ave. (bet. 89th & 90th Sts.), 212-410-5557

■ "Innovative combos" of "tasty Thai" food that's "authentic, flavorful" and "hot, hot, hot" plus a staff that "aims to please" make this a popular (read "crowded") East Side "neighborhood haunt."

Saloon, The ◐ [S] 14 | 12 | 12 | $25

1920 Broadway (64th St.), 212-874-1500

◩ Cynics call it a "jack of all foods, master of none", but this often "frenetic", "cavernous" West Side standby with an Eclectic menu as long as *War and Peace* has plenty of customers for its fair prices, "great sidewalk sight-seeing" and "Lincoln Center convenience."

Samalita's Tortilla Factory [S] ≠$ ▽ 18 | 13 | 14 | $15

1429 Third Ave. (81st St.), 212-737-5070

◩ "If June Cleaver were Mexican" she might cook the kind of "fresh", "healthy" food served at this "cheery" Eastsider, though we hear complaints of "cramped quarters" and uncaring service.

Sambuca [S] 19 | 14 | 17 | $25

20 W. 72nd St. (bet. CPW & Columbus Ave.), 212-787-5656

◩ "A close second to Carmine's", but "much easier to get into", this family-style Italian Westsider wins praise for its "congenial" staff, "tasty" fare, "large portions" and prices that "won't break the bank"; not everyone sees it that way – "a college cafeteria on Italian night."

Sammy's Roumanian [S] 17 | 7 | 14 | $40

157 Chrystie St. (Delancey St.), 212-673-0330

◩ The place for "unhealthy food the way your grandma made it", this "loud", "crowded" Lower East Side Jewish-Roumanian "loony bin" serves up a "bellyful of chicken fat and laughs" amidst "the tackiest decor in NYC"; "you'll need a gastroenterologist" afterwards, but it's worth it ("once every five years").

Sam's Rest./Pizzeria (Bklyn) [S] ≠$ ▽ 18 | 12 | 16 | $21

38 Court St. (bet. Baltic & Kenneth Sts.), 718-596-3458

■ A "comfortable" "neighborhood joint" where the "cranky staff" serves "fine pizza" and other "standard Italian cuisine"; while the pizza gets a unanimous thumbs up, the rest of the menu is "only ok."

F | D | S | C

SAN DOMENICO [S] — 25 | 24 | 23 | $55

240 Central Park S. (bet. B'way & 7th Ave.), 212-265-5959

■ "A gem", Tony May's "refined" Italian wins consistent praise for its "impeccable service" and "calm", "luxurious setting" as well as for chef Theo Schoenegger's "exquisite haute" Bolognese cuisine; yes, it can be pricey, but most customers don't mind given the quality, and there are always "fabulous value" prix fixe menus.

San Giusto — 21 | 19 | 21 | $45

935 Second Ave. (bet. 49th & 50th Sts.), 212-319-0900

◩ It strikes some as a little stuffy and "overpriced", but this East Midtown Italian pleases most with its "tasty" cooking, "gracious" service and "relaxed" feel; if "not exciting", it's "dependable" and fine for business dining.

San Martin's ◐ [S] — 19 | 15 | 19 | $35

143 E. 49th St. (bet. 3rd & Lexington Aves.), 212-832-0888

■ "Excellent paella" is a good bet among the Spanish-Mediterranean choices at this "intimate", friendly Midtowner; most find it "solid" all around, but a few doubters think it "needs an identity."

San Pietro — 23 | 19 | 20 | $46

18 E. 54th St. (bet. 5th & Madison Aves.), 212-753-9015

◩ Critics charge that it "has no soul", but for most this Sistina sibling is one of "the best" Midtown Italians with "sparkling" food, a "lovely" setting and fine service; a "see-and-be-seen" spot, it can be "crowded, noisy" and "like a club at lunch."

Santa Fe [S] — 19 | 19 | 17 | $34

72 W. 69th St. (bet. CPW & Columbus Ave.), 212-724-0822

◩ A "classy" Santa Fe–style standby serving "intriguing" Tex-Mex food and "lethal margaritas" in a "soft and soothing" pastel setting near Lincoln Center; to a few, it's "pretty, but not worth the high price."

Sant Ambroeus [S] — 20 | 17 | 17 | $39

1000 Madison Ave. (bet. 77th & 78th Sts.), 212-570-2211

◩ Since "outstanding gelato" is a forte, maybe it's only fitting that this "elegant" East Side Milanese can seem as "cold as ice"; "scrumptious" tea sandwiches and pastas notwithstanding, the food's "pricey", service "haughty" and the decor "coffinlike."

Sapporo East ◐ [S] — 20 | 11 | 15 | $20

245 E. 10th St. (1st Ave.), 212-260-1330

◩ The ambiance may recall "Nedick's", but this "overloaded", "noisy" Japanese is "popular because it's good", "fast" and "unbelievably cheap"; the crowd offers a "primer on the East Village."

Sarabeth's [S] — 20 | 17 | 17 | $28

Hotel Wales, 1295 Madison Ave. (bet. 92nd & 93rd Sts.), 212-410-7335
423 Amsterdam Ave. (bet. 80th & 81st Sts.), 212-496-6280
Whitney Museum, 945 Madison Ave. (75th St.), 212-570-3670

◩ "Brilliant" for brunch and "just as good" (but less "mobbed") for dinner, these all-Americans serve "delicious baked goods", "splendid omelets" and other "wholesome" fare; it's "like brunch at a country inn, only you wait two hours instead of driving two hours."

Saranac [S] — 14 | 16 | 15 | $27

1350 Madison Ave. (bet. 94th & 95th Sts.), 212-289-9600

◩ The American food can be "as bland as mom's mashed potatoes", but East Side yuppies say this "Adirondack escape" is "cozy", "cute" and a "perfect place for the kids"; the staff is "friendly" if "untrained."

Sardi's ◐ 13 | 18 | 15 | $37
234 W. 44th St. (bet. B'way & 8th Ave.), 212-221-8444
◪ "Improved" since Vincent Sardi regained control, but not what it was in its heyday, this Continental Theater District "legend" has become a lightning rod for criticism; with a great location opposite Shubert Alley, familiar B'way folks in the seats and their caricatures on the walls, it still attracts tourists and loyal locals, and at long last, insiders say a new chef is making progress in the kitchen.

Sasso [S] – | – | – | E
1315 Second Ave. (bet. 69th & 70th Sts.), 212-472-6688
Brand-new East Side Tuscan with a serious menu from a chef who has come to NYC from a career in Pisa; accommodations are bright and comfortable; the wine list invites trying.

Savoy [S] 22 | 19 | 20 | $38
70 Prince St. (Crosby St.), 212-219-8570
■ A "SoHo find" with a "creative" American-Mediterranean menu, "wonderful desserts" and an "affordable wine list"; it's "crowded" but "cozy" by the fire in winter and "savory" on all counts.

Sawadee Thai Cuisine ◐ [S] 14 | 9 | 13 | $20
888 Eighth Ave. (52nd St.), 212-977-3002
225 Columbus Ave. (bet. 70th & 71st Sts.), 212-787-3002
◪ "The McDonald's of Thai food" is how detractors view this duo, but supporters say they're "decent", "affordable" and "good for a quick" Thai fix, even if service and decor both "need work."

Sazerac House [S] 16 | 13 | 15 | $26
533 Hudson St. (bet. W. 10th & Charles Sts.), 212-989-0313
◪ A neighborly bit of the bayou in the West Village with "itsy-bitsy booths", a "friendly, honky-tonk crowd" and "tasty" Cajun-style food that makes up for the "tired decor" and smoke; Sunday jazz brunch is a good time to "hang loose."

Scaletta [S] (94) 20 | 19 | 21 | $38
50 W. 77th St. (bet. CPW & Columbus Ave.), 212-769-9191
◪ This "sedate", one-flight-down West Side Italian puzzles drop-ins; "well-spaced tables" mean "you can talk" and the food, while "a bit pricey", is "satisfying"; but there are always empty tables.

Scalinatella ◐ [S] 24 | 18 | 21 | $45
201 E. 61st St. (bet. 2nd & 3rd Aves.), 212-207-8280
■ Though in the basement, this Eastsider is a "top" Italian in terms of quality; its food is "heavenly", the stone-wall setting "very pretty" and the waiters well-versed; ask for prices on specials to avoid a "surprise."

Seafood Palace ◐ [S] ▽ 19 | 13 | 18 | $27
50 Mott St. (Bayard St.), 212-223-8898
◪ "The name says it all" claim admirers, though they surely aren't referring to the "tacky" decor, but rather to the "fresh and good" seafood at this little-known Chinatown fish specialist.

SeaGrill 23 | 25 | 21 | $47
19 W. 49th St. (Rockefeller Skating Rink), 212-246-9201
■ A grand Rockefeller Center setting (with a view of the skating rink in winter and outdoor summer dining) enhances the "wonderful seafood" at this NY "treasure" (now with chef Ed Brown, ex Tropica, at the helm); "great wines", "elegant" art deco decor and smart service are extra reasons why most people leave happy.

Seattle Bean Co. S
18 | 14 | 15 | $9
1573 Second Ave. (bet. 81st & 82nd Sts.), 212-794-4233
☑ Coffee cravers say this East Side bean brewer is a "cut above the rest", dispensing some of the "best coffee" variations east of Seattle, but those looking for something other than caffeine may find the muffin-based menu lacking in "real food"; "service is friendly, seating isn't."

SECOND AVENUE DELI ◑S
21 | 7 | 12 | $19
156 Second Ave. (10th St.), 212-677-0606
■ NY's "best deli", this East Village "institution" has "primo pastrami" plus all the other "good, greasy Jewish deli specials you'd expect" served by "appropriately rude" waiters amidst "less-than-zero" decor; you get "almost too much for your money" so "bring your Tums", pass the pickles and "enjoy."

Seeda Thai S
18 | 12 | 16 | $23
309 W. 50th St. (bet. 8th & 9th Aves.), 212-586-4040
☑ It's not much on ambiance, but this "modest" Thai on a "seedy block" near the Theater District is a "good value" for "fresh, spicy, interesting" food; service is "attentive" if somewhat "slow."

Sel et Poivre S
17 | 16 | 17 | $35
853 Lexington Ave. (bet. 64th & 65th Sts.), 212-517-5780
☑ "A pretty, well-done French bistro" in "Bloomie country"; most find it "cozy and reliable" with "good" if "undistinguished" food.

Sequoia S
16 | 19 | 13 | $27
Pier 17, 89 Fulton St. (South Street Seaport), 212-732-9090
☑ "Great" East River views and "big portions" compensate for the "average" American seafood at this airy Seaport hot spot; it's "nice for a date" or drinks, and even cynics who call it a "tourist trap" admit it's "one of the better ones."

Serendipity 3 ◑S
17 | 20 | 15 | $22
225 E. 60th St. (bet. 2nd & 3rd Aves.), 212-838-3531
■ An "old-fashioned ice cream parlor" (and more) crossed with a "toy museum", "you never outgrow" this amusing Eclectic and its foot-long hot dogs, juicy burgers, sandwiches and *"Jurassic*-sized desserts" such as the signature frozen hot chocolate.

SERYNA
25 | 23 | 23 | $52
11 E. 53rd St. (bet. 5th & Madison Aves.), 212-980-9393
☑ Kobe beef "seared on hot stones" yields "melt-in-your-mouth" steaks at this Midtown Japanese where both decor and prices are "stunning"; "miniscule portions" aside, it has superb sushi, smooth service and is "perfect for business entertaining."

Sette Mezzo ◑S⊄
22 | 16 | 17 | $41
969 Lexington Ave. (bet. 70th & 71st Sts.), 212-472-0400
☑ As crowded as a "subway", but "delicious" Italian food and "celeb-spotting" "make up for the discomfort" at this "clubby" Eastsider; expect "haphazard" service unless you're a regular, as most are.

Sette MoMA ◑S
15 | 18 | 14 | $37
Museum of Modern Art, 11 W. 53rd St. (bet. 5th & 6th Aves.), 212-708-9710
☑ As controversial as any modern artwork, this Nuovo Italiano is called a "lovely diversion" by some, but blasted by critics for "pricey, disappointingly bland" food and poor service.

F **D** **S** **C**

7th Regiment Mess
| 9 | 14 | 13 | $25 |

The Armory, 643 Park Ave. (bet. 66th & 67th Sts.), 212-744-4107
☑ A "wonderful cross section of society" files into this "anomaly" set upstairs in a real armory; serving "cheap, simple American food" in a "time-warp" 19th-century setting, it's "kinda fun", especially on live music nights, but to critics "mess" says it all.

Sevilla ⬤ S
| 20 | 12 | 16 | $26 |

62 Charles St. (W. 4th St.), 212-929-3189
■ You're advised to "arrive hungry and eat everything in sight" at this often-crowded "Village classic" serving "hearty", garlic-heavy Spanish food plus sangria "that makes you want to run with the bulls."

Sfuzzi S
| 17 | 18 | 16 | $35 |

58 W. 65th St. (bet. CPW & Columbus Ave.), 212-873-3700
2 World Financial Ctr., Winter Gdn. (Liberty St.), 212-385-8080
☑ The "designer" pizzas and pastas take some sflak ("unusual for Cleveland, ordinary for NY"), but these "Euro-slick" Italians still pack 'em in thanks to "good energy", "sleek" neo-Pompeiian decor, "terrific Sunday brunch" and brain-draining Bellinis.

Shaan
| – | – | – | E |

57 W. 48th St. (bet. 5th & 6th Aves.), 212-977-8400
A spacious Rockefeller Center newcomer, this elegant Indian is lively at lunch, but quiet at night.

Shabu Tatsu S
| 21 | 14 | 17 | $28 |

216 E. 10th St. (bet. 1st & 2nd Aves.), 212-477-2972 ⬤
1414 York Ave. (75th St.), 212-472-3322
☑ "Participatory food prep" is the concept at these first-rate Japanese BBQ/soup specialists; "helpful staff" makes it "an event" so "go with a group" and don't mind "the wait"; the new Uptown outlet is as handsome as the original 10th Street locale is tacky.

Shaliga Thai Cuisine S
| 19 | 13 | 17 | $28 |

834 Second Ave. (bet. 44th & 45th Sts.), 212-573-5526
☑ Admirers think this "spicy" Midtowner is Thai-rrific citing "tasty" food and "gracious" service; critics, in turn, point to "small portions" at not-so-small prices.

Shanghai Manor S
| ▽ 21 | 16 | 20 | $26 |

141 E. 55th St. (bet. Lexington & 3rd Aves.), 212-753-3900
☑ "Solid neighborhood Chinese" that's "consistent", "comfortable" and "not too expensive"; "it says something that they flourish just a few doors from Shun Lee Palace" and have done so for years.

Shanghai 1933 S
| – | – | – | E |

209 E. 49th St., 2nd Fl. (bet. 2nd & 3rd Aves.), 212-486-1800
Despite beautifully decorated mezzanine space on a prime Midtown block, this Shanghai specialist seems rudderless and is often empty.

Shark Bar ⬤ S
| 18 | 13 | 14 | $27 |

307 Amsterdam Ave. (bet. 74th & 75th Sts.), 212-874-8500
■ "Down-home Soul Food" served with "metropolitan flair" draws a sports-star-studded crowd to this "hip, happening" Westsider; the "funky appetizers", blackened catfish, candied yams and other "fattening" treats are "worth every calorie" as is the jazz brunch.

Shelby S
| 16 | 15 | 15 | $35 |

967 Lexington Ave. (bet. 70th & 71st Sts.), 212-988-4624
☑ You'll find "fine burgers" and other "decent" food at this very East Side American; the menu may not be very interesting but the "preppy" "pickup" "scene" at the bar usually is.

141

Shinbashi-an [S] ▽ 22 | 19 | 20 | $40

141 E. 48th St. (bet. 3rd & Lexington Aves.), 212-752-0505

■ Shabu-shabu enthusiasts and other lovers of "quality" Japanese food extol this Midtowner's "scrumptious" flavors, "good service" and "spacious" modern setting for gracious, if pricey, dining.

Shin's [S] ▽ 14 | 19 | 14 | $44

Le Parker Meridien, 109 W. 56th St. (bet. 6th & 7th Aves.), 212-708-7444

◪ A "beautiful setting" for "East-West fusion cuisine" which, as ratings show, hasn't fused so well; most say this "high-priced" yearling is "a big disappointment."

Shinwa ▽ 21 | 19 | 18 | $36

Olympic Tower, 645 Fifth Ave. (51st St.), 212-644-7400

■ Japanophiles savor this "serene", "sophisticated" "hidden gem" in Olympic Tower; a "lunchtime oasis for noodles" and "heavenly sushi and sashimi", it's so tasty "you almost forget the price."

Shopsin's General Store ⊘ ▽ 21 | 14 | 13 | $21

63 Bedford St. (Morton St.), 212-924-5160

◪ This "disheveled" Village grocery serves "a million items" and they're "all good", but don't be surprised if you "get yelled at" by the owner.

Shun Lee Cafe ◐ [S] 21 | 16 | 17 | $30

43 W. 65th St. (bet. CPW & Columbus Ave.), 212-769-3888

◪ The "prerequisite pre–Lincoln Center pit stop" is lauded for its "wonderful dim sum" and stylish black-and-white decor that's better-looking than the Chinatown competition; detractors bemoan "robot" waiters and "small portions" that add up.

SHUN LEE PALACE ◐ [S] 24 | 21 | 22 | $40

155 E. 55th St. (bet. Lexington & 3rd Aves.), 212-371-8844

■ Surveyors agree: it's "worth the high prices" for "NY's best Chinese food"; Michael Tong's handsomely redecorated, Midtown "champion" is on "a higher plane" with "exquisite" food and fine service: "put yourself in (your captain's) hands, you won't be disappointed."

Shun Lee West ◐ [S] 23 | 22 | 21 | $38

43 W. 65th St. (bet. CPW & Columbus Ave.), 212-595-8895

■ "Nearly as good" as its East Side sibling, this "upscale" Lincoln Center Chinese serves a "wide array of authentic" dishes amidst "dramatic" ("dig that dragon") decor; the staff "copes well with the pre-concert crowds."

Siam Cuisine ◐ [S] ▽ 19 | 14 | 16 | $25

1411 Second Ave. (bet. 73rd & 74th Sts.), 212-988-5348

◪ "Tasty lemon grass" and "spicy chilies" spark the "authentic" Thai cooking at this "interesting, inexpensive" Eastsider; since the drinks "pack a wallop" maybe you won't notice "slow" service or simple decor.

Siam Inn ◐ [S] 20 | 13 | 17 | $24

916 Eighth Ave. (bet. 54th & 55th Sts.), 212-489-5237

854 Eighth Ave. (bet. 51st & 52nd Sts.), 212-757-4006

■ Candidates for "best Thai" on a stretch of Eighth Avenue that could be called "Bangkok Row"; though lacking in decor, they're strong on "authentic, pungent" flavors and "warm, friendly" service; prix fixe dinner is a "great value."

Sichuan Palace [S] ▽ 21 | 15 | 19 | $28

310 E. 44th St. (bet. 1st & 2nd Aves.), 212-972-7377

■ With a "diverse menu" of "very good" Chinese food plus "excellent" service, this Midtowner is considered "worth the tab"; "UN types lend a touch of class" to the clientele.

SIGN OF THE DOVE [S] 24 | 27 | 23 | $52

1110 Third Ave. (65th St.), 212-861-8080

■ Perennially "one of NY's prettiest" and lately one of its best, with fine French-American fare and "solicitous service"; the "exquisite", flower-filled rooms "radiate romance" and they do terrific private parties; there's also an informal, less expensive and more crowded upfront cafe, but by all means "sign on: the place has class."

Silk Restaurant [S] ▽ 22 | 18 | 19 | $35

378 Third Ave. (bet. 27th & 28th Sts.), 212-532-4500

■ "A nice newcomer that deserves a following" for its "different and delicious" French-Asian fusion cuisine, "lovely" decor and "smooth-as-silk" service; it "shines in an area devoid of good restaurants."

Silk Road Palace [S] ⇏ 20 | 7 | 16 | $17

447B Amsterdam Ave. (bet. 81st & 82nd Sts.), 212-580-6294

■ "Sprightly, fresh" Chinese food, "smiling service" and "free wine" explain the line outside this "atmosphereless" Westsider; you can't get "drunk and stuffed" for much less, and delivery is super fast.

Sirabella's [S] ⇏ 21 | 13 | 19 | $30

72 East End Ave. (bet. 82nd & 83rd Sts.), 212-988-6557

■ Upper East Side Italian "hideaway" that's loved for its "consistency", "delicious specials", "attentive service" and "caring owner"; a recent expansion answers complaints about "cramped" quarters.

Sistina ◐ 23 | 18 | 20 | $46

1555 Second Ave. (bet. 80th & 81st Sts.), 212-861-7660

◩ There's "quality" Italian food at this tiny, "attractive" wood-panelled Eastsider, but it's "expensive", especially for "high-end specials."

Sloppy Louie's [S] 17 | 9 | 12 | $29

92 South St. (bet. Fulton & John Sts.), 212-509-9694

◩ "The last old Fulton Fish Market seafooder", this "landmark" lost its charm after its Seaport spiff-up, but still has "fresh", "nothing-fancy" fish served amidst "sparse" decor by perfunctory staff.

Small Cafe, The ◐ [S] 17 | 17 | 18 | $36

Sutton Hotel, 330 E. 56th St. (bet. 1st & 2nd Aves.), 212-753-2233

◩ Nostalgists miss the "intimacy of the old space", but most say this "not-so-small-anymore" Sutton Place Continental cafe is a "comfy" "retreat" that's pleasant for a "moderately priced", light meal and "enchanting in the garden."

SMITH & WOLLENSKY ◐ [S] 24 | 17 | 19 | $48

201 E. 49th St. (3rd Ave.), 212-753-1530

■ "A real man's place", this noisy "NYC institution" is a "rock solid" steakhouse that "makes you want to light up a cigar" and enjoy "super", "brontosaurus-sized" steaks and "great wine" served by "old-time waiters" amid a "sea of suits"; you get "no surprises", except possibly seeing the large number of your fellow citizens prepared to join in this coronary trauma.

Snaps 21 | 20 | 19 | $41

Helmsley Building, 230 Park Ave. (46th St.), 212-949-7878

◩ "Soaring", "serene" and, most say, scrumptious, this Scandinavian Midtown Aquavit sibling has flavors that make you "snap to attention" and a staff that does the same; however, critics say it's already slightly seedy and "doesn't live up to its prices."

Sofia's ◐ [S] 15 | 14 | 16 | $30

221 W. 46th St. (bet. B'way & Eighth Ave.), 212-719-5799

◩ With a "friendly staff" and "pleasant piano", this Times Square Italian serves "big portions" of decent food, but its "main plus" is convenience.

SoHo Kitchen and Bar
16 | 17 | 14 | $25

103 Greene St. (bet. Prince & Spring Sts.), 212-925-1866

☑ The American fare is "unexciting", but this brick-walled SoHo fixture's wine flights attract a crew of "under-30" frequent flyers; keep the food "simple" and "enjoy the ride."

Soleil
19 | 16 | 16 | $36

1160 Third Ave. (bet. 67th & 68th Sts.), 212-717-1177

☑ California meets Provence at this "exceptionally cheerful" Eastsider where the yellow-and-blue decor is "sunny" and the food "bold" and "creative", if not always successful; locals find it "uneven", possibly due to chef changes.

Solera
23 | 22 | 22 | $45

216 E. 53rd St. (bet. 2nd & 3rd Aves.), 212-644-1166

■ In a town "mysteriously lacking" in fine Spanish restaurants, this "charming" Midtowner fills the gap with "different" and "delicious" food, "beautifully prepared and served" in a "pretty", "romantic" room; its tapas are highly touted.

SONIA ROSE S
25 | 23 | 24 | $44

132 Lexington Ave. (bet. 28th & 29th Sts.), 212-545-1777

■ Behind a plain Gramercy storefront lies this "hidden treasure" offering "superb" Eclectic-French food and "first-rate" service in a "most romantic" setting; "understated" and "intimate", it's "NY's best-kept secret" ("don't print this review").

Sorelle S
▽ 14 | 11 | 15 | $28

994 First Ave. (bet. 54th & 55th Sts.), 212-753-0520

☑ Some call this Sutton Place Italian a "lively newcomer" with "reasonable" food, "delightful" staff and an "upbeat, homey" feel; others say "what a disappointment", "bring back Stephanie's."

Souen S
16 | 12 | 14 | $19

210 Sixth Ave. (Prince St.), 212-807-7421
28 E. 13th St. (bet. 5th Ave. & University Pl.), 212-627-7150

☑ The "Birkenstock crowd" likes these Downtown Vegetarians for their "feel-good" food and "very Zen" ambiance, but dissenters, citing "bland" food, say "if this is healthy I'd rather be sick."

Soul Fixins' ⊅
– | – | – | I

371 W. 34th St. (9th Ave.), 212-736-1345

A "Midtown Sylvia's" with "convincing" Soul Food at low prices; no-frills decor makes it best for takeout or a quick bite "before a Knicks or Rangers game"; don't miss the sweet potato pie.

Soup Burg S ⊅
10 | 5 | 10 | $13

922 Madison Ave. (73rd St.), 212-734-6964
1026 First Ave. (56th St.), 212-421-9184
1150 Lexington Ave. (bet. 79th & 80th Sts.), 212-737-0095 ●
1347 Second Ave. (71st St.), 212-879-4814

☑ "Honest, clean and filling" as well as "quick" and "cheap", this chain serves a purpose for breakfast and soup, burgers and cottage fries "in a pinch", but you "can get better food and decor at a diner."

SPARKS STEAK HOUSE
26 | 19 | 21 | $52

210 E. 46th St. (bet. 2nd & 3rd Aves.), 212-687-4855

■ Arguably "the best steakhouse" in NY, where "no one even thinks of cholesterol" when faced with "huge, succulent steaks and lobsters"; a "knockout wine list", "long waits" and a "big bill" are also part of this "masculine" Midtown experience; the usual "suits" crowd is replaced on weekends by "big hair, red sculpted nails and men with as much gold jewelry as the women."

Spartina ◐
_ _ _ M

355 Greenwich St. (Harrison St.), 212-274-9310

An inexpensive, casual pan-Mediterranean TriBeCa cafe that draws from France, Greece, Morocco, Spain and Turkey as well as Italy; though too new to survey, early reports are positive.

S.P.Q.R. ◐ S
20 20 19 $35

133 Mulberry St. (bet. Hester & Grand Sts.), 212-925-3120

☑ "They put on quite a show" at this "elegant" Little Italy Genovese; most like its "excellent" food and "handsome", wood-and-frosted-glass decor, but to some it's "pretentious."

Spring Street Natural ◐ S
18 15 15 $22

62 Spring St. (Lafayette St.), 212-966-0290

☑ "Not just for hard-core" health-a-holics, "even meat eaters" like the "fresh", "wholesome" choices at this "creative" SoHo Vegetarian-Eclectic; service is "slow", so relax and enjoy the "earthy" atmosphere; the unconverted yawn "everything tastes the same."

Spring St. Restaurant ◐ S
17 15 16 $27

162 Spring St. (W. B'way), 212-219-0157

☑ A "reasonable" SoHo option for Contemporary American food served in a "comfortable, relaxing" setting; critics say "nothing stands out" except maybe Sunday brunch.

Stage Deli ◐ S
17 9 11 $20

834 Seventh Ave. (bet. 53rd & 54th Sts.), 212-245-7850

☑ The "overstuffed sandwiches" aren't chopped liver and overstuffed waiters give tourists a taste of real NY "attitude", but picky pickle eaters say this chaotic Midtown deli is best when "the line at the Carnegie is too long."

Starbucks S

_ _ _ I

1117-1123 Lexington Ave. (78th St.), 212-517-8476
2379 Broadway (87th St.), 212-875-8470
1128 Third Ave. (66th St.), 212-472-6535
400 E. 54th St. (1st Ave.), 212-688-0700
1445 First Ave. (75th St.), 212-472-7784
1559 Second Ave. (81st St.), 212-472-7972

The nation's leading espresso purveyor has finally flowed into NYC in an effort to prove that Manhattan can support as many espresso bars as Italy and Seattle.

Steak Frites ◐ S
18 15 15 $34

9 E. 16th St. (bet. 5th Ave. & Union Sq. W.), 212-463-7101

☑ "Stick to the namesake" and you're likely to find this "funky" Union Square French bistro a "tasty, reasonable" steakhouse alternative; it's something of "a scene" so "wear black", bring earplugs and don't mind the "unemployed actors" playing waiter.

Steamers Landing S
13 19 13 $29

On the Esplanade (bet. Liberty & Albany Sts.), 212-432-1451

☑ It's "best to be a fair-weather friend" of this waterfront cafe, since the "uninspired seafood" isn't memorable but the "sunset views" across the Hudson are; "sit outside and you forget you're in NY."

Stella del Mare
22 20 21 $45

346 Lexington Ave. (bet. 39th & 40th Sts.), 212-687-4425

■ A "very well-kept Midtown secret", this Italian seafood specialist provides "sublime" meals in an "intimate" setting with "super service"; only "sticker shock" mars this picture.

Stellina 🅂 ▽ 17 | 12 | 16 | $26
220 W. 49th St. (bet. B'way & 8th Ave.), 212-541-6601
◪ Though no showstopper, this "tasty, well-priced" Theater District Italian lets you make the curtain "on time" and reasonably well-fed; just don't expect ovation-worthy decor.

Stingy Lulu's ◗🅂⊅ 13 | 16 | 13 | $15
129 St. Marks Place (bet. Avenue A & 1st Ave.), 212-674-3545
◪ "For what it is, it couldn't be better"; this "damn cool" East Village "retro diner" is hardly gourmet ("even mom cooks better") and service can be "slow", but there's "entertaining 3 AM people- watching" and at these prices there's nothing stingy about it.

Stromboli Pizza ◗🅂⊅ – | – | – | I
83 St. Marks Pl. (1st Ave.), 212-673-3691
An East Village dough palace serving great pies at low prices for 15 years; those in the know take it and go, as there's only limited counter space and even that's not too attractive.

Sugar Reef ◗🅂 15 | 14 | 12 | $22
93 Second Ave. (bet. 5th & 6th Sts.), 212-477-8427
◼ "Yah mon, feelin' funky? c'mon down to Jamaica" via this East Village "island shack" with "wacky waiters", "tropical neon decor", "loud reggae", "knock-you-off-your-seat" drinks and choice Caribbean fare; it's "almost as fun as the real thing and a lot cheaper."

Sukhothai West 🅂 ▽ 18 | 18 | 18 | $25
411 W. 42nd St. (bet. 9th & 10th Aves.), 212-947-1930
◪ A Thai to try in the Theater District; most surveyors praise its "wonderful flavors" and even those who say "too mild" applaud its "beautiful" decor, "tranquil" ambiance and "pleasant" service.

Sumptuary, The ◗🅂 18 | 20 | 18 | $31
400 Third Ave. (bet. 28th & 29th Sts.), 212-889-6056
◪ The rococo, "funky", "country-inn atmosphere" complete with fireplace and "wonderful hideaway garden" may outshine the food, but most think this "unheralded" Continental is "very pleasant" and a "good value"; it's easy to "succumb to passions of the heart" here.

Sun Cafe ◗🅂 – | – | – | M
214 E. 9th St. (bet. 2nd & 3rd Aves.), 212-598-4308
With sunny decor this midpriced East Village Mediterranean cafe/ juice bar serves warm-weather dishes, e.g. mango salad with mint, poached salmon and tapas, all fresh from the Greenmarket.

Sunny East ▽ 20 | 16 | 18 | $31
21 W. 39th St. (bet. 5th & 6th Aves.), 212-764-3232
◼ "Chinatown" quality in the Garment District is "rare", which is why this "creative, tasty" Szechuan is packed at lunch; it's "friendly" and attractive too, but quibblers still think "prices are too high."

Supper Club 15 | 20 | 16 | $42
240 W. 47th St. (bet. B'way & 8th Ave.), 212-921-1940
◪ Everyone loves the live music and "wonderful" decor at this Midtown throwback to a "classic 1920s nightclub", but the American food and service are out of step; Fridays and Saturdays only.

Supreme Macaroni Co. ⊅ 15 | 11 | 14 | $24
511 Ninth Ave. (bet. 38th & 39th Sts.), 212-564-8074
◪ A "nice mom-and-pop feel" pervades this Hell's Kitchen Southern Italian; though savants say it's "not so supreme", most like its "tangy" sauces, "bargain prices" and "old-world dive" decor.

Sushiden 23 | 16 | 19 | $36

19 E. 49th St. (bet. 5th & Madison Aves.), 212-758-2700

◪ Sushi "so fresh it swims to your table" and "personalized service" are the draws at this "classy" Midtowner; it's "warm, busy" and often "filled with Japanese", but some patrons say portions could be bigger and prices smaller.

Sushihatsu ◐ [S] ▽ 25 | 10 | 14 | $41

1143 First Ave. (bet. 62nd & 63rd Sts.), 212-371-0238

◪ This Eastsider may be "dumpy", "tired" and "no bargain", but it's well worth sampling its "excellent selection" of "superb" sushi and sashimi; N.B. non-Japanese speakers may find it "non-user-friendly."

SUSHISAY 27 | 19 | 21 | $41

38 E. 51st St. (bet. Madison & Park Aves.), 212-755-1780

■ "Sushi nirvana", this fresh-fish lover's "paradise" is acclaimed as NY's "best Japanese"; "sleek" and "calming" with "lovely service", it induces "gastronomic orgasm" with its "pristine" flavors; reserving can be tough and critics cite "micro-sushi at macro prices"; unusual for a Japanese restaurant, they have a female manager.

Sushi Zen 24 | 17 | 19 | $35

57 W. 46th St. (bet. 5th & 6th Aves.), 212-302-0707

■ "Innovative sushi that melts in your mouth", "gorgeous presentation" and "tranquil, Zenlike" decor make this Midtown Japanese a lunchtime favorite and a "balm for the spirit"; only highish prices and service lapses draw complaints.

Swiss Inn 17 | 13 | 17 | $30

311 W. 48th St. (bet. 8th & 9th Aves.), 212-459-9280

◪ This Theater District standby may be "uncreative" and flat with "hokey Swiss posters and cobwebs", but it peaks with hearty "comfort food", "modest prices" and "amiable" service.

Sylvia's Restaurant [S] 19 | 11 | 16 | $23

328 Lenox Ave. (bet. 126th & 127th Sts.), 212-996-0660

■ "The heart and soul" of Harlem, Sylvia Wood's "institution" is famed for "great" greens, ribs, chicken and other "fattening" but "fabulous" down-home delights (don't miss the cakes); it's "touristy" and "greasy", but it's a "NY must" and "worth the trek."

Symphony Cafe [S] 20 | 18 | 18 | $36

238 W. 56th St. (8th Ave.), 212-397-9595

◪ "On the upswing" thanks to "super" new chefs and owners, this "handsome" Contemporary American near Carnegie Hall wins applause for its "ambitious" cuisine and "artistic" desserts; even if service misses a few beats, the overall impression is "melodic" and they have major party capacity.

Symposium ◐ ▽ 13 | 12 | 15 | $21

544 W. 113th St. (bet. B'way & Amsterdam Ave.), 212-865-1011

◪ A "reliable", modestly priced neighborhood Greek-Vegetarian; it's no world-beater but that doesn't bother the late-night Columbia crowds drawn by its "cute" decor, garden and sangria.

Szechuan Hunan Cottage ◐ [S] 20 | 8 | 15 | $16

1588 York Ave. (bet. 83rd & 84th Sts.), 212-535-5223
1433 Second Ave. (bet. 74th & 75th Sts.), 212-535-1471

■ "Good, quick" Chinese food, "bargain" prices and "bottomless" glasses of free wine explain the lines outside these Eastsiders; "friendly" service makes the "shoebox" settings bearable and the "fastest delivery in NY" is also an option.

Szechuan Kitchen 🅢 ⌿
22 | 6 | 14 | $17

1460 First Ave. (76th St.), 212-249-4615

☑ Though a "hole-in-the-wall", it's an East Side favorite for "great" (if "greasy") Chinese food at "ridiculously low prices"; it's "cramped" and "super rushed", so takeout may be better.

Table d'Hôte 🅢
22 | 19 | 22 | $40

44 E. 92nd St. (bet. Madison & Park Aves.), 212-348-8125

☑ You'll feel like you're "in a friend's dining room" at this "intimate", "postage stamp"–size Carnegie Hill French bistro; the French-American cuisine is "creative" and "nicely served", mais "cher."

Taci International ◗🅢⌿
▽ 11 | 16 | 11 | $18

2841 Broadway (110th St.), 212-678-5345

☑ Columbia-area diners claim this "mutt" of a restaurant "can't make up its mind", pointing to its "too-ambitious International menu" and "wild" eclectic decor; "value" is a plus, service a minus.

Tacomadre 🅢 ⌿
12 | 7 | 9 | $11

2345 Broadway (bet. 85th & 86th Sts.), 212-873-0600
1991 Broadway (bet. 67th & 68th Sts.), 212-874-0556

☑ "Mexico City it ain't", but these "inexpensive", "very basic" West Side taquerias make for a "tasty, on-the-run" bite; there's "no decor" so "takeout is the way to go."

Taco Taco 🅢 ⌿
▽ 15 | 6 | 14 | $15

1726 Second Ave. (bet. 89th & 90th Sts.), 212-289-8226

■ Despite minimal seating and decor this simple Eastsider does have "real Mexican tacos" and other good eats plus "warm, friendly service", all "for a pittance."

Tai Hong Lau ◗🅢
▽ 22 | 8 | 10 | $23

70 Mott St. (bet. Canal & Bayard Sts.), 212-219-1431

☑ "Big portions" of "terrific" Szechuan and Cantonese plus "dim sum made to order" score well with those who know "authentic" Chinese; but plan to "beg for service" in these "typical Chinatown" digs.

Takahachi ◗🅢
▽ 24 | 14 | 19 | $25

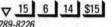

85 Avenue A (bet. 5th & 6th Sts.), 212-505-6524

■ "Delicious" soups, noodles and "top-of-the-line sushi" at modest prices are served at this family-friendly East Village Japanese; despite the locale, it's "not funky at all."

Take-Sushi
21 | 13 | 16 | $35

71 Vanderbilt Ave. (bet. 45th & 46th Sts.), 212-867-5120

☑ For "fresh" sushi and other "excellent" fare this Grand Central Japanese is "right up there"; not so is the "ungracious" service and decor that's "utterly without character."

Taliesin 🅢
22 | 22 | 20 | $44

Hotel Millenium, 55 Church St. (bet. Fulton & Dey Sts.), 212-312-2000

■ "Class food, class room, class service" sums up this "elegant" Contemporary American with a Frank Lloyd Wright look; "dignified", "discreet" and "delicious", it's ideal for Downtown "deal-making."

Tan Go
▽ 20 | 12 | 16 | $35

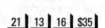

43 W. 54th St. (bet. 5th & 6th Aves.), 212-765-4683

■ The few surveyors who know this "serene" Midtown Japanese call it a "hidden treasure" with "first-rate sushi" and other "consistent", "genuine" fare; it's a "good lunch" option.

Tang Pavilion [S] 21 | 16 | 17 | $30
65 W. 55th St. (bet. 5th & 6th Aves.), 212-956-6888
■ A "wide selection" of "unusual", "great-tasting" Shanghai dishes served in a "clean", "attractive setting" makes this one of the "best Midtown Chinese"; better yet, it's reasonably priced for the area.

Tang Tang [S] 16 | 7 | 12 | $18
236 E. 53rd St. (bet. 2nd & 3rd Aves.), 212-355-5096
1700 Second Ave. (88th St.), 212-360-7252
1328 Third Ave. (76th St.), 212-249-2102
◪ East Side "noodle shops" offering "better-than-average" Chinese chow "for cheap"; cold sesame noodles win raves, and service is so speedy "the food arrives almost before you order."

Tanti Baci Cafe [S] ▽ 21 | 14 | 18 | $20
163 W. 10th St. (bet. Waverly Pl. & 7th Ave.), 212-647-9651
■ A "great addition to the Village" for "delicious" and "affordable", "low-key" Italian dining, this newcomer is "a little cramped but well worth the squeeze"; BYO.

Taormina ◐ [S] 20 | 17 | 19 | $35
147 Mulberry St. (bet. Grand & Hester Sts.), 212-219-1007
■ "One of Little Italy's best"; "superb" Sicilian cuisine, "gracious" service and "pretty" decor explain why surveyors report it can be "too crowded" and "very noisy."

Taqueria de Mexico [S] ≠ ▽ 19 | 7 | 12 | $11
93 Greenwich Ave. (bet. Bank & W. 12th Sts.), 212-255-5212
◪ You may "feel like you're tasting tacos and tamales for the first time" at this "happy", "authentic" West Village Mexican newcomer; the setting's "simple" and prices "cheap", but big eaters fault small portions.

Tartine [S] ≠ – | – | – | I
253 W. 11th St. (W. 4th St.), 212-229-2611
This Village BYO French bistro is often packed with its sidewalk tables especially hard to come by; the food is fine, it's the waitresses who seem to be AWOL.

Tasca do Porto ◐ [S] ≠ – | – | – | M
525 Broome St. (bet. Thompson & Sullivan Sts.), 212-343-2321
Manhattan's only Portuguese tapas bar suffers from an out-of-the-way basement location in SoHo, and the tab for the teeny tidbits, though good, can climb if you're not careful.

Taste of Tokyo ◐ [S] ▽ 19 | 11 | 17 | $25
54 W. 13th St. (bet. 5th & 6th Aves.), 212-691-8666
◪ A "secret Village value", this "cramped" "cubbyhole" provides "dependable" Japanese "home cooking" at modest prices; "decor is minimal", but to devotees it's "a little piece of Zen."

Tatany [S] 23 | 14 | 18 | $27
380 Third Ave. (bet. 27th & 28th Sts.), 212-686-1871
Tatany 52 ◐ [S]
250 E. 52nd St. (bet. 2nd & 3rd Aves.), 212-593-0203
■ "A sparkling winner"; this Gramercy Japanese and its new Uptown "late-night sake" sibling are among the "best sushi values in NYC", serving "lush, large portions" of fish "so fresh it wiggles"; expect lines but it's "worth waiting for" what they serve.

Tatou 20 | 22 | 18 | $40

151 E. 50th St. (bet. Lexington & 3rd Aves.), 212-753-1144

■ A "restaurant-cum-nightclub that works", this Midtowner combines "elegant" decor, "great jazz" and "surprisingly very good" New American food; the mood varies from "romantic" (with a "harpist at lunch") to "jumping" when a flashy "Euro"-and-Boro crowd pours in to dance; "don't miss" the bargain prix fixe.

TAVERN ON THE GREEN ◐ [S] 15 | 26 | 18 | $44

Central Park West & 67th St., 212-873-3200

◩ Gothamites have long had a love-hate relationship with this "glitzy NY landmark"; all adore its "enchanting" Central Park setting and "glittering", "kitschy", "flower-filled", chandelier-and-mirrored decor, but not necessarily its American food; still, it's a "top choice for private parties" or to "dazzle your country cousin" with that "magical Manhattan feeling" or just to treat oneself to a special sunny-day outdoor lunch or a snowy-day Crystal Room dinner.

Tavola ◐ [S] 21 | 17 | 19 | $36

1481 York Ave. (bet. 78th & 79th Sts.), 212-570-9810

■ A new Yorkville "favorite", this "creative" country Italian "tastes and feels like Florence"; with "fabulous" antipasti, "charming" service and a "beautiful" garden, it's "a winner."

Tea Box, The ▽ 21 | 22 | 19 | $36

Takashimaya Dept. Store, 693 Fifth Ave. (bet. 54th & 55th Sts.), 212-350-0100

■ A "tranquil oasis amidst the frenzy of Fifth Avenue" serving "dainty and delectable" Japanese-Eclectic cuisine and an "exotic choice of teas" in a "jewel-box" space; "very special" sums it up.

Teachers Too ◐ [S] 15 | 10 | 14 | $23

2271 Broadway (bet. 81st & 82nd Sts.), 212-362-4900

◩ Making the grade as a "simple" "neighborhood staple", this "dark" and "comfy" West Side American comes with a "varied" menu and "decent prices"; service can be so poor "they should tip you."

Tea Den ◐ [S] ▽ 20 | 12 | 15 | $17

940 Eighth Ave. (bet. 55th & 56th Sts.), 212-265-8880

■ Bright white Formica Midtown West Chinese with super soups, "lip-smacking ribs and chicken" and service that's "more accommodating than most of its kind."

Telephone Bar & Grill ◐ [S] 14 | 15 | 13 | $21

149 Second Ave. (bet. 9th & 10th Sts.), 212-529-5000

◩ England meets the East Village at this "lively", "British pub" hangout; Anglophiles say "nothing beats it for a snakebite (beer and cider) and shepherd's pie", but some say it proves "the English can't cook."

Telly's Taverna (Queens) ◐ [S] ≠ ▽ 21 | 9 | 17 | $24

28-13 23rd Ave. (bet. 28th & 29th Sts.), Astoria, 718-728-9056

■ It's just across the bridge in Queens, but dig into some "excellent grilled seafood on the outdoor patio and you think you're in Greece"; the decor "is nothing much", but the food is "simply prepared, incredibly fresh" and "inexpensive."

Temple Bar ◐ [S] 15 | 26 | 16 | $26

332 Lafayette St. (bet. Bleecker & Houston Sts.), 212-925-4242

■ A "sophisticated", "slightly racy" and "glamorous" Village "inner sanctum" that "brings out the seducer and seducee in all of us"; it's "NY's sexiest bar" so "who cares about the American food?"; just "wear black", sip pricey martinis and be "cool."

Tempo
24 | 18 | 23 | $40

30 E. 29th St. (bet. Madison & Park Aves.), 212-532-8125

■ "A secret no more", this "homey, well-run" Gramercy Italian serves flavorful food, including "incredible, fresh pasta" to a "businesslike crowd"; recent converts wish they'd "known sooner."

Ten Kai 🅢
▽ 22 | 14 | 18 | $34

20 W. 56th St. (bet. 5th & 6th Aves.), 212-956-0127

■ "As the 95 percent Japanese clientele attests", this Midtowner is as authentic as it gets with sushi "so fresh it's scary"; aside from the "giant" fish tank, the decor consists of "a room with walls – that's it."

Tennessee Mountain 🅢
16 | 10 | 12 | $23

143 Spring St. (Wooster St.), 212-431-3993

☑ BBQ buffs feud over this "smoky" SoHo take on a "hillbilly" "rib shack": rooters call it "NY's best BBQ", while bone-pickers insist it's "not the real thing"; still, crowds come for "lots of food", brew and "fixin's" at Appalachian prices.

Tequila Sunrise
10 | 9 | 10 | $19

(fka Tequila Willie's)

99 Park Ave. (39th St.), 212-922-5680
729 Seventh Ave. (49th St.), 212-626-7313 🅢
12-14 Vanderbilt Ave. (42nd St.), 212-922-5664
64 W. 52nd St. (bet. 5th & 6th Aves.), 212-767-8338
498 Seventh Ave. (37th St.), 212-630-0330

☑ "Bright, colorful", "fast-food Mexicans" that are "good for chips, margaritas" and unwinding "after work", but not much else given "standard cardboard" fare and "assembly-line" service.

Teresa's 🅢
17 | 7 | 13 | $16

103 First Ave. (bet. 6th & 7th Sts.), 212-228-0604 ◖⊄
80 Montague St. (bet. Hicks St. & Montague Terrace), Brooklyn, 718-797-3996 ⊄
70-34 Austin St., Queens, 718-520-2910

■ You can "fill up cheap" on "fantastic" pierogies, blintzes and other "hearty" Polish "comfort food" at these "unpretentious" Polish pit stops; service and decor are minimal, but so are the prices.

TERRACE
26 | 27 | 25 | $54

400 W. 119th St. (bet. Amsterdam & Morningside Aves.), 212-666-9490

■ Perched on a Morningside Heights rooftop, this "gracious and elegant" French restaurant is a "wonderful" exception to the 'great view/bad food' rule; with "fabulous" cuisine and service to complement its "spectacular cityscape" vista it's a perfect "special-occasion" place; "proposals are likely to be accepted here."

Terramare Café 🅢 ⊄
– | – | – | M

22 E. 65th St. (bet. Madison & 5th Aves.), 212-717-5020

Eastsiders cite this tiny cafe/gourmet store for "inventive sandwiches"; true, they're pricey, but ingredients like these don't come cheap.

Tevere 84 🅢
19 | 17 | 18 | $41

155 E. 84th St. (bet. Lexington & 3rd Aves.), 212-744-0210

■ "If you have to eat kosher" (or even if you don't) put this "cozy" "high-performing" East Side Kosher-Italian on your list; all agree it's a "premier" of its type.

T.G.I. Friday's
10 | 10 | 10 | $20

1680 Broadway (53rd St.), 212-767-8326 ◖🅢
21 W. 51st St. (bet. 5th & 6th Aves.), 212-767-8352 🅢
661 Broadway (Bond St.), 212-982-6000 🅢
430 Lexington Ave. (bet. 42nd & 43rd Sts.), 212-922-5667

T.G.I. Friday's (Cont.)
47 E. 42nd St. (bet. Madison & Vanderbilt Aves.), 212-922-5671 S
47 Broadway (Trinity Place), 212-483-8322
1450 Broadway (41st St.), 212-626-7399
484 Eighth Ave. (34th St.), 212-630-0309 S
☑ "What do you expect from a chain named after a cliche?"; about what you get from these "glorified" fast-fooders: a big menu of "run-of-the-mill pub grub", "inept" service and "look ma, I'm in a mall" ambiance; still, they're ok for "quick" eats with the kids.

Thai Chef ● S
∇ | 18 | 13 | 17 | $25
1466 First Ave. (bet. 76th & 77th Sts.), 212-734-2539
☑ Though this French-accented East Side Thai has "light, tasty, original" cooking, "pleasant" decor and "decent prices", it hasn't lived up to its early promise and is often "empty"; critics attribute its problem to being "careless" and "commercial."

Thai House Cafe S
20 | 8 | 17 | $21
151 Hudson St. (Hubert St.), 212-334-1085
■ Ignore the drab setting and "Holland Tunnel locale", "the key" to this "cheap, cheerful" TriBeCa house is to let Eddie, the owner, order for you – you'll be rewarded by "dependable", "spicy" Thai fare.

Thailand Restaurant ● S
23 | 7 | 14 | $19
106 Bayard St. (Baxter St.), 212-349-3132
■ This Chinatown Thai is a favorite thanks to "delicious" food; despite "third-world" decor and "careless" service, "it's the real thing at pushcart prices" and handy for jurors.

Thai Orchid S
∇ | 16 | 11 | 16 | $24
936 First Ave. (bet. 51st & 52nd Sts.), 212-308-2111
☑ The "owner takes a personal interest" and the staff is so "sweet" it's "surreal" at this "tasty Thai"; though the interior is "modest", brunch in the garden is "gorgeous" and the "lunch buffet is a deal."

Thai Taste (Brooklyn) S
∇ | 16 | 12 | 15 | $23
125 Seventh Ave. (Carroll St.), 718-622-9376
☑ Reactions to this "fiery and cheap" Brooklyn Thai run the gamut from "excellent" to "no excuse" and "yecch"; one possible explanation – "every time it differs."

3rd Avenue Delicatessen S
∇ | 17 | 8 | 14 | $20
276 Third Ave. (bet. 21st & 22nd Sts.), 212-228-8484
☑ It's "not the Carnegie", but this "old-fashioned" deli has a "huge menu" of "standard", "well-prepared" fare, and the fact that it's the only deli nearby doesn't hurt.

Thomas Scott's on Bedford S
∇ | 21 | 22 | 22 | $34
72-74 Bedford St. (Commerce St.), 212-627-4011
■ "Dignified and imaginative", this "romantic" West Village newcomer is an ideal "date place" with fine New American cuisine, "solicitous" service" and an attractive, "quiet" setting.

Three Degrees North ● S
— | — | — | M
(fka Cafe)
210 Spring St. (6th Ave.), 212-274-0505
Richard Widmaier-Picasso and friends, including a Malaysian princess, have just converted his SoHo Cafe into Manhattan's first style-setting Malaysian restaurant.

	F	D	S	C

Three Guys [S] — 12 | 6 | 14 | $16
49 E. 96th St. (Madison Ave.), 212-348-3800
960 Madison Ave. (bet. 75th & 76th Sts.), 212-628-8108
◪ "Quintessential Greek diners" providing Eastsiders with "typical" but tasty food in "busy" no-frills settings complete with "crashing dishes"; their best assets are "location, location, location."

Three of Cups ◐ [S] — 17 | 13 | 14 | $20
83 First Ave. (5th St.), 212-388-0059
◪ "Old hippie meets new hippie" and both enjoy the pastas and pizza from a wood-burning oven at this "funky" and "cheap" East Village Italian; dissenters find the decor "weird" and the service somnolent.

Tibetan Kitchen ⊄ — 17 | 8 | 15 | $19
444 Third Ave. (31st St.), 212-679-6286
◪ "Far-out Tibetan home cooking" served in a "sparse" Murray Hill "matchbox" makes for "authentic, inexpensive cultural" dining; "slow service allows time to reflect" on the "Dalai Lama's picture."

Tibetan Restaurant [S] — ▽ 16 | 9 | 15 | $18
96 Second Ave. (bet. 5th & 6th Sts.), 212-979-9202
◪ It resembles a "storage closet" and service can be "slow", but fans call this low-budget East Village Tibetan a "tasty change from Chinese"; foes say "after an endless wait you get watery gruel."

Tibet Shambala [S] — ▽ 15 | 10 | 18 | $16
488 Amsterdam Ave. (bet. 83rd & 84th Sts.), 212-721-1270
◪ Westsiders now have a Tibetan to call their own in this "friendly, family-run" yearling; it's "a bargain" for "wonderful dumplings, vegetables and noodle dishes", but "be prepared for a long meal."

Tien Fu [S] — ▽ 14 | 13 | 14 | $20
180 Third Ave. (bet. 16th & 17th Sts.), 212-505-2000
◪ Even if the menu is "uneven", locals like this "solid neighborhood Chinese" for its "soothing" setting with "tiny lights and sounds of water"; service is "quick" for both sit-down and delivery.

Time Cafe ◐ [S] — 18 | 17 | 14 | $26
380 Lafayette St. (bet. Great Jones & E. 4th Sts.), 212-533-7000
◪ "Organic chic", "cool" NoHo cafe that's an "overly popular", "beautiful-people hangout" serving "wholesome", "P.C." fare in an "airy" setting; but the staff, like time itself, "waits on no man"; outdoor seating and Fez, the downstairs lounge, are bonuses.

Tina's ◐ [S] — 16 | 12 | 14 | $23
249 Park Ave. S. (20th St.), 212-477-1761
◪ While critics insist "there's no difference between this upscale Chinese and your average take-out joint", others find it "a little less greasy", "a little more pricey" and a little better looking.

Tirami Su ◐ [S] ⊄ — 18 | 14 | 14 | $28
1410 Third Ave. (80th St.), 212-988-9780
◪ "Another Upper East Side Italian", this one with "pretty good" brick-oven pizzas, pastas and, of course, tiramisu; it's "crowded, noisy" and "surprisingly cheap."

Tiziano Trattoria ◐ [S] — 19 | 15 | 16 | $32
165 Eighth Ave. (bet. 18th & 19th Sts.), 212-989-2330
◪ A "tasty neighbor to the Joyce Theater", this "charming, old-world" Chelsea trattoria has fresh pastas and wood-oven pizzas prepared and served "with care"; it's "not inspired" but "pleasant."

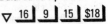

Toast ⬤ S
428 Lafayette St. (bet. Astor Pl. & E. 4th St.), 212-473-1698
Across from the Public Theater, this happening International wins
fans with good food (curried-lamb wontons, mussels in wine broth,
yellowfin tuna on sesame-soba-noodle salad) and a serious bar; it's
pricey, but the mood is toasty.

Tommaso's (Brooklyn) S
21 | 17 | 20 | $35
1464 86th St. (bet. 14th & 15th Sts.), 718-236-9883
☑ The "pride of Bensonhurst", this "archetype" Italian is "louder and
larger than life" from its "lusty", "authentic" cooking to its "genial"
owner who "serenades you with opera"; P.S. the reserve wine list
holds "treasures at rock-bottom prices."

Tony Roma's S
13 | 9 | 12 | $22
1600 Broadway (48th St.), 212-956-7427 ⬤
565 Third Ave. (bet. 37th & 38th Sts.), 212-661-7406
☑ To some, these "loud", "family-style" joints have "surprisingly
decent" ribs, chicken and onion loaves, but are "underestimated
because they're a chain"; others say "grease pits", "in decline."

Tony's Di Napoli S
15 | 12 | 14 | $24
1606 Second Ave. (bet. 83rd & 84th Sts.), 212-861-8686
☑ Upper East Side "Carmine's wanna-be" with "no gourmet ambitions",
just "copious portions" of "filling", family-style Italian fare; "if you have
to take the in-laws and other tag-alongs, you'll get off cheap."

Top of the Sixes
17 | 23 | 19 | $38
666 Fifth Ave., 39th fl. (bet. 52nd & 53rd Sts.), 212-757-6662
■ There's "no better view for the price", but the same can't be said
of the "dependable" but "uninspiring" American food at this "staid"
rooftop Midtown "old-timer"; it's best "for frugal aunts and uncles."

Tortilla Flats ⬤ S
15 | 14 | 14 | $20
767 Washington St. (W. 12th St.), 212-243-1053
☑ With "Bingo nights", an "Ernest Borgnine shrine" and "Elvis all
over" this "funky" West Village Mexican is "the ultimate in kitsch"
and a favorite of "rowdy" hipsters "with a taste for fun" and tequila:
"who remembers the food" anyway?

Toscana S
∇ 19 | 16 | 16 | $37
843 Lexington Ave. (bet. 64th & 65th Sts.), 212-517-2288
☑ The East Side has no shortage of Italians, but this "friendly" recycled
place has a flair for food that should help it do well; "quality" cooking
and "crisp" decor bode well for its future.

Totonno Pizzeria Napolitano
∇ 24 | 4 | 8 | $14
(Brooklyn) S ⇆
1524 Neptune Ave. (W. 16th St.), 718-372-8606
■ Congressman Chuck Schumer first put us onto this "old favorite"
Coney Island pizzeria whose "paper-thin crust", "charcoal-oven"
pies have no equal; "lousy decor" and staff needing "sensitivity
training" are simply part of its charm.

Toukie's ⬤
_ | _ | _ | M
220 W. Houston St. (Varick St.), 212-255-1411
Toukie Smith, ex-model and sister of the late designer Willi Smith,
runs this sassy TriBeCa American that leans towards Southern dishes;
the stationary decor includes red leather banquettes, a mural of Ms.
Smith and red rose petals scattered on the tables; the moving decor
is more interesting and comes late.

Tout Va Bien ◗S
19 | 14 | 18 | $33

311 W. 51st St. (bet. 8th & 9th Aves.), 212-265-0190

◪ A "classic" Theater District bistro serving "retro" French food in a "never-changing setting"; some say it "treads a fine line between authentic and shabby", but most call it a "warm", "likable" good buy.

Townhouse, The S
14 | 16 | 16 | $32

206 E. 58th St. (bet. 2nd & 3rd Aves.), 212-826-6241

■ "Gentlemen of distinction" enjoy this "elegant" East Side Continental that caters to a "very refined, upscale" gay clientele; the food is "nothing special", but the waiters are, and "everyone is welcome."

Trastevere 83
21 | 17 | 20 | $42

309 E. 83rd St. (bet. 1st & 2nd Aves.), 212-734-6343

■ We got some nonkosher egg on our face after calling this East Side Roman-style Italian kosher last year; we're doing it again – because it's become glatt kosher; either way, fans call it "best of the breed" and say it "recalls Roma" with a "dark, romantic" feel and "friendly" service.

Trattoria Alba S
19 | 16 | 19 | $31

233 E. 34th St. (bet. 2nd & 3rd Aves.), 212-689-3200

■ The word's out that this "secret" Murray Hill Italian is a "fine neighborhood" place with a "comfortable" setting, "accommodating" service and modest prices; "will go back again" says it all.

TRATTORIA DELL'ARTE ◗S
23 | 22 | 19 | $39

900 Seventh Ave. (bet. 56th & 57th Sts.), 212-245-9800

■ Milton Glaser's "whimsical", body-part decor ("the nose knows") sets the tone at this "bustling" trattoria near Carnegie Hall, but "artistry" is also evident in the "sensual" Italian food and "fabulous antipasti bar"; it's a "high-energy", "beautiful-people" scene which translates as "noise", "crowds" and "people-watching."

Trattoria Pesce Pasta ◗S
▽ 20 | 15 | 18 | $25

262 Bleecker St. (bet. 6th & 7th Aves.), 212-645-2993

■ Some prefer the pesce, others the pasta, but most agree that this "homey" trattoria makes "Bleecker less bleak" for lovers of "fresh, cheap" Italian fare; it can be "crowded" with "waits during prime time."

Trattoria Siciliana S
▽ 20 | 14 | 20 | $30

517 Second Ave. (bet. 28th & 29th Sts.), 212-684-9861

◪ "Every neighborhood should have a place" like this simple Kips Bay trattoria that's been around "for years" serving "familiar" Sicilian fare at modest prices; a few surveyors say its best days are behind it.

Trattoria Trecolori S
▽ 19 | 17 | 20 | $27

316 E. 53rd St. (bet. 1st & 2nd Aves.), 212-355-5360
133 W. 45th St. (bet. 6th & 7th Aves.), 212-997-4540

■ There's "no stinting on garlic" at this Theater District Italian (and its new East Side sibling); with "good, cheap" food, an "attractive" setting and "great service" it's "a real sleeper."

Triangolo ◗S⊅
21 | 16 | 18 | $29

345 E. 83rd St. (bet. 1st & 2nd Aves.), 212-472-4488

■ This "inviting" storefront pasta place charms locals with its "fine" Northern Italian food, "reasonable prices" and "pretty, peachy" decor; "it's a little short on space", but not on flavor or friendliness.

TriBeCa Grill S
22 | 20 | 19 | $42

375 Greenwich St. (Franklin St.), 212-941-3900

■ Owned by DeNiro and pals, this "spacious", brick-walled, chic TriBeCa American grill is "improving" as it "concentrates on food", "not celebs"; though the "waiters will drop you in a minute for Bill Murray", all in all it's a "solid performer" with a probable long run.

Trilogy Bar & Grill ◐ [S] | 13 | 12 | 12 | $24

1403 Second Ave. (73rd St.), 212-794-1870

◪ The food's "not so hot", but the scene is at this "trendy" Eastsider where "everyone knows everyone" and "you need earplugs after 10 PM"; it may have only "15 minutes of fame", but for now it's "cheap", lively and a "good place to hang out"; try Sunday jazz brunch.

Trionfo ◐ | 21 | 17 | 21 | $40

224 W. 51st St. (bet. B'way & 8th Ave.), 212-262-6660

■ "No staff tries harder" than the team at this "elegant and satisfying" Theater District Italian, and the effort pays off: with its "very good food", "pretty setting", "warm" feel and "reasonable prices", most consider it a low-key "triumph."

Triple Eight Palace ◐ [S] | 19 | 11 | 11 | $22

78 E. Broadway (bet. Division & Market Sts.), 212-941-8886

◪ "Dim sum madness" reigns at this huge Chinatown eatery, where lunch resembles "rush hour" in "Hong Kong" as crowds endure "waits" and "decibels" to savor "an unlimited variety" of dim sum; if your Chinese is rusty "just point and enjoy"; P.S. dinner is deadly.

Triplets Roumanian [S] | 16 | 13 | 18 | $38

11-17 Grand St. (6th Ave.), 212-925-9303

■ "Like a Yiddish theme park", this "rowdy" SoHo Roumanian with "waiters who put on a show" is "a fun place to get indigestion" via "enormous quantities" of garlic and cholesterol-laden food sure to scare "vampires" and cardiologists; "bring grandma and Alka Seltzer, stuff yourself and have a ball."

Tripoli (Brooklyn) [S] | 17 | 13 | 14 | $22

156 Atlantic Ave. (Clinton St.), 718-596-5800

◪ "Still one of the better places for Middle Eastern", this Atlantic Avenue Lebanese standby wins praise for its "succulent shish kebab" and "enjoyable appetizers", but the decor's "getting frayed" and service can be "out to lunch."

Trois Jean [S] | 20 | 18 | 19 | $41

154 E. 79th St. (bet. Lexington & 3rd Aves.), 212-988-4858

■ "Sophisticated and chic", this East Side duplex bistro offers "elegant French dining without the snobbery"; most give it "trois bravos" for "superlative" food, "stylish" decor and "caring" service.

Trompe l'Oeil ◐ [S] | – | – | – | E

55 Carmine St. (bet. 6th & 7th Aves.), 212-647-1840

The few who've tried this Village International send back mostly good reports: "innovative" menu, "very good pasta", "beautiful decor", "friendly service"; "they're trying hard" and it shows.

Tropica | 23 | 20 | 19 | $43

200 Park Ave. (bet. 45th St. & Vanderbilt Ave.), 212-867-6767

■ "A godsend near Grand Central", this attractive Key West–style seafooder is like a mini Caribbean "vacation"; it's making waves with "fabulous" fresh fish featuring "unique spices", but it's most restful after the business lunch throngs and commuters leave.

Truffles | – | – | – | M

227 E. 50th St. (bet. 2nd & 3rd Aves.), 212-750-5315

This rosy-hued East Midtown French-Italian hasn't caught on with our surveyors, but the few we hear from have good things to say: "satisfying food", "huge portions", "calm and timeless"; service is its weak link.

T Salon ◐ [S] ▽ 19 | 24 | 14 | $23

142 Mercer St. (Prince St.), 212-925-3700

■ As in "*tea*house" and boutique under the SoHo Guggenheim; it's a "tranquil oasis" with "charming" decor, "a great selection of teas" and "inventive" cafe fare including "vegetarian sushi"; but a few sippers are teed-off at "terrible", "petulant" service.

TSE YANG [S] 24 | 25 | 23 | $47

34 E. 51st St. (bet. Madison & Park Aves.), 212-688-5447

■ Everything about this "haute Chinese" is on a "royal level" including its "superb" Shanghai-style cuisine, "lushly decorated" setting, fine service and, alas, its "nosebleed prices."

T.S. Ma [S] 16 | 13 | 16 | $23

5 Penn Plaza (33rd St. & 8th Ave.), 212-971-0050

◪ "Convenience to MSG" is the best thing about this "boring but reliable" Midtown Chinese; the food's "nothing spectacular", but it's "decent" and "you won't be late for the game."

Turkish Cuisine [S] ▽ 19 | 12 | 17 | $24

631 Ninth Ave. (bet. 44th & 45th Sts.), 212-397-9650

◪ "Exotic" Theater District newcomer with "unusual", "tasty" Turkish food, "reasonable" prices and an "owner who couldn't be nicer"; it's the real thing, right down to the "rugs on the walls."

Turkish Kitchen [S] 21 | 17 | 18 | $30

386 Third Ave. (bet. 27th & 28th Sts.), 212-679-1810

■ A "Turkish delight", this "authentic", "family-run" Gramercy ethnic is like "Istanbul" with "delectable" flavors, "gracious" staff and a "striking red" setting; to save money "make a meal" of the appetizers.

Tuscany Grill (Brooklyn) [S] ▽ 24 | 16 | 20 | $34

8620 Third Ave. (bet. 86th & 87th Sts.), 718-921-5633

■ A "Tuscan oasis" in Bay Ridge, this "cross between a local joint and a special-event restaurant" offers "wonderful" Italian food, a pleasant setting and "attentive" service; it's "a find" and the "price is right", too.

Tutta Pasta ◐ [S] 16 | 10 | 13 | $19

504 La Guardia Pl. (bet. Bleecker & Houston Sts.), 212-420-0652

26 Carmine St. (bet. Bleecker & Bedford Sts.), 212-463-9653

◪ To some they're "tutta average" with "no decor", but most like these Village twins for their "wide variety" of "competent", "filling" pastas, "bargain" prices and congenial democratic crowds.

20 Mott Street ◐ [S] 20 | 8 | 11 | $21

20 Mott St. (bet. Bowery & Pell Sts.), 212-964-0380

■ Some of "NY's most authentic" dim sum is found at this no-frills, three-floor Chinatown Cantonese, but you may face "long waits", a "language barrier" and "prison-camp" service; it's "crazy Sunday mornings, but worth it."

"21" CLUB, THE 21 | 23 | 21 | $52

21 W. 52nd St. (bet. 5th & 6th Aves.), 212-582-7200

■ A "NY landmark" that "oozes power", attracting "CEOs", celebs and other "big spenders" who enjoy its renowned downstairs bar and attractive upstairs party rooms, "fine service" and "solid" American food that's "better than ever" under chef Michael Lomonaco; for an easy intro, try the prix fixe deals.

Twigs ◐ [S] 16 | 12 | 16 | $24

196 Eighth Ave. (20th St.), 212-633-6735

■ "Unremarkable but pleasant" Chelsea "neighborhood hangout" for "simple", "satisfying" Italian food at "budget-minded" prices; locals "hate to call attention" to it, since it's "already very popular."

Two Boots S
18 | 12 | 14 | $17
37 Avenue A (bet. 2nd & 3rd Sts.), 212-505-2276 ●
514 Second St. (bet. 7th & 8th Aves.), Brooklyn, 718-499-3253
■ "Cajun meets Italian" and "hey, it works" at these "cool pizza joints";
they're known for "zippy", "original" toppings, "lively, funky" ambiance
and "great jukeboxes" plus "welcoming rug rats", i.e. "shrieking kids."

Two Eleven ●S
19 | 19 | 19 | $34
211 W. Broadway (Franklin St.), 212-925-7202
■ A TriBeCa American bistro offering "creative" food in an "airy",
"upscale" loft setting with a "happening bar scene" and "wonderful"
patio; it's a "hangout for City Hall lawyers" and the occasional celeb.

Uncle Nick's S
19 | 6 | 14 | $23
747 Ninth Ave. (bet. 50th & 51st Sts.), 212-315-1726
■ Now in new digs just a few doors down from its previous locale (not
reflected in decor rating), this Westsider has admirers hyperventilating
over its "fresh", "authentic", "cheap" Greek taverna fare; it's the next
best thing to a trip to Astoria or Athens; P.S. "wear jeans."

Uncle Vanya Cafe S
▽ 20 | 17 | 17 | $26
315 W. 54th (bet. 8th & 9th Aves.), 212-262-0542
■ "Campy" in an "old country-Russian way", this Westsider's kitchen
turns out "good blinis and lox", fresh-baked breads and other modestly
priced Russian food; occasional singers and poetry readings "spice
up" the otherwise bland ambiance.

UNION SQUARE CAFE S
27 | 24 | 25 | $47
21 E. 16th St. (bet. 5th Ave. & Union Sq. W.), 212-243-4020
■ "Superlative from start to finish", Danny Meyer's "sensational"
Contemporary American that almost guarantees a "modern classic"
a "perfect" time; chef Michael Romano's "creative" cooking "sparkles"
and is served in a space featuring several separate, attractive sections,
including an unusually pleasant bar for dining; add the fact that no place
in NY has a friendlier, more knowledgeable staff and it's no wonder
that USC ranks No. 3 overall among our surveyors' favorite restaurants.

Universal Grill ●S
17 | 15 | 16 | $25
44 Bedford St. (Leroy St.), 212-989-5621
■ This "kitschy" Villager may be the "gayest restaurant" in town; it
isn't the "decent" American fried food that draws mobs, but rather the
"hilarious", nonstop "party" scene, complete with the staff "dancing
to Abba" and birthday celebrations to the "theme from *Maude*."

Urban Grill S
16 | 8 | 13 | $18
1613 Second Ave. (bet. 83rd & 84th Sts.), 212-744-2122
330 W. 58th St. (bet. 8th & 9th Aves.), 212-586-3300
☑ "They do the basics well" ("good pastas", "fantastic burgers",
"healthy chicken") which is why these simple standbys are judged
"solid values"; both service and decor are better at the more formal
West Side branch, but you can get good "takeout" from either.

Uskudar ●S
19 | 9 | 17 | $27
1405 Second Ave. (bet. 73rd & 74th Sts.), 212-988-2641
■ "Tiny" but "terrific" Turkish lodged in a "sliver" of an East Side
storefront; "genuine" "home cooking" at low prices and a staff that
"remembers you" make it "worth the wait" and "cramped" quarters.

Va Bene S
22 | 18 | 19 | $38
1589 Second Ave. (bet. 82nd & 83rd Sts.), 212-517-4448
■ Admirers can't believe that this "upscale pasta house with old-
world Italian flavors" is also a "top-quality" Kosher; happily, a "pretty"
East Side setting and "good service" complement the food.

Veniero's ◐Ⓢ
22 | 12 | 12 | $12

342 E. 11th St. (bet. 1st & 2nd Aves.), 212-674-7264

■ "The grandfather" of all bakery/coffeehouses, this century-old East Villager "blows away the trendy new places" with "the best Italian pastries", gelati, espresso and cappuccino served in an over-"bright" setting; but "don't expect to be coddled."

Verbena Ⓢ
— | — | — | M

54 Irving Pl. (bet. 17th & 18th Sts.), 212-260-5454

Using fresh, seasonal ingredients, this New American is too new to rate but appears to have unusual promise; it also has low-key, modern light-wood decor and a large courtyard for summer.

Vernon's Jerk Paradise
16 | 11 | 14 | $21

252 W. 29th St. (bet. 7th & 8th Aves.), 212-268-7020

◪ Paradise it's not, but this "cheap" Chelsea Jamaican has "spicy jerk chicken", "terrific drinks" and "delightful" (if "slow") service; dissenters say "you're the jerk" if you think this is the real thing.

Veselka ◐Ⓢ
17 | 6 | 10 | $13

144 Second Ave. (9th St.), 212-228-9682

◪ When you're starving and broke this "less-than-pristine" 24-hour East Village Polish-Ukrainian coffee shop comes to the rescue with "heavy duty" "comfort food" at "ultracheap" prices; aka the "gulag" and "salt mine", it's "best for hardened NYers."

Vespa ◐Ⓢ
▽ 20 | 15 | 19 | $32

1625 Second Ave. (84th St.), 212-472-2050

■ "Small" Upper East Side Northern Italian storefront that "has it all" (except for space): "wonderful" food, modest prices and "gracious service"; it's "little-known, but shouldn't be."

Viand Ⓢ
16 | 5 | 14 | $15

300 E. 86th St. (2nd Ave.), 212-879-9425
1011 Madison Ave. (bet. 78th & 79th Sts.), 212-249-8250
673 Madison Ave. (bet. 61st & 62nd Sts.), 212-751-6622 ⌐

■ "Diner food the way it ought to be" ("killer turkey sandwiches") attracts a "cross section of NY" to these "classic" East Side Greek coffee shops; service is usually "swift and courteous", but you can't check your furs and must beware the "evil eye if you linger too long."

Via Oreto Ⓢ ⌐
23 | 16 | 21 | $33

1121 First Ave. (bet. 61st & 62nd Sts.), 212-308-0828

■ For best results "let mama take care of you" at this mother-and-son East Side Italian; it's "a real charmer" with "unusually good" food and service plus a "warm", family feel.

Viceroy, The ◐Ⓢ
— | — | — | M

160 Eighth Ave. (18th St.), 212-633-8484

A bustling new Chelsea scene offering affordable American fare to an obviously appreciative audience; the huge wooden bar has to be seen to be believed; at times it resembles boys' night out.

Vico ◐Ⓢ⌐
20 | 14 | 17 | $40

1302 Madison Ave. (92nd St.), 212-876-2222

◪ This "clubby" Carnegie Hill Italian "takes standard fare and makes it tasty", which in turn means it's often "crowded" and "noisy"; dissenters cite "testy service", "pricey pasta" and the no-plastic policy.

Victor's Cafe 52 ◐Ⓢ
18 | 16 | 17 | $34

236 W. 52nd St. (bet. B'way & 8th Ave.), 212-586-7714

■ An "upscale", "airy" Theater District Cuban that fans say "feels and tastes" like "Havana" with roast suckling pig, black-bean soup, "great sangria" and other "savory" standards.

View, The 🅂   18 | 26 | 20 | $44
Marriott Marquis Hotel, 1535 B'way (bet. 45th & 46th Sts.), 212-704-8900
☑ One of B'way's best shows: a revolving rooftop with "dazzling" "360-degree" views, "better-than-expected" Continental food and "good service"; a "must-see" with brunch and pre-theater dinner as best bets.

Villa Berulia   ▽ 20 | 17 | 21 | $37
107 E. 34th St. (bet. Park & Lexington Aves.), 212-689-1970
■ "A sleeper on 34th Street", this "jacket-and-tie" Northern Italian can be counted on for "satisfying" fare, but it's the "caring" service that makes it special – "go a few times" and you feel like an old friend.

Village Atelier   22 | 22 | 21 | $38
436 Hudson St. (Morton St.), 212-989-1363
■ "Charming" is the word most often used to describe this West Village country French; with "delightful" food, "intuitive" service and a "romantic, flowery" setting, "a first date here guarantees a second."

Village Crown 🅂   ▽ 19 | 11 | 18 | $21
96 Third Ave. (bet. 12th & 13th Sts.), 212-674-2061
■ "The place to go for hummus" and other "above-average" Kosher fare that ranges from the Mideast to the Mediterranean; despite simple decor, a "lovely" garden and "eager-to-please" service make this East Villager "feel like Tel Aviv."

Villa Mosconi   19 | 13 | 18 | $32
69 MacDougal St. (bet. Bleecker & Houston Sts.), 212-673-0390
■ Regulars "never tire" of this "classic", family-owned Village Italian that serves food "like mama made" in a comfy "old-world", (as in old), setting; it has a "low profile but is always busy" and rarely disappoints.

Vince and Eddie's ◑🅂   20 | 17 | 18 | $38
70 W. 68th St. (bet. Columbus Ave. & CPW), 212-721-0068
■ "Loaded with charm", this "cozy" (aka "cramped") American near Lincoln Center looks like a "country inn" and tastes even better thanks to chef Scott Campbell's cooking; its main faults: "too many people like it" and both Vince and Eddie have left.

Vincent's ◑🅂   ▽ 19 | 11 | 14 | $24
119 Mott St. (Hester St.), 212-226-8133
☑ "It's all in the sauce" (so "hot" it "burns") at this low-budget Little Italy old-timer that's famed for its spicy seafood-pasta combos, but certainly not for either its decor or service.

Vinnie's Pizza ◑🅂⇄   20 | 3 | 11 | $9
285 Amsterdam Ave. (73rd St.), 212-874-4382
☑ Pizza partisans who prefer "thick, doughy crusts" and lots of cheese say this "cheap" Westsider's slices "put John's to shame"; on the other hand Formica decor and counter service leave some saying "even if he were my cousin Vinnie, I wouldn't go."

Vinsanto 🅂   17 | 16 | 16 | $29
1619 Second Ave. (84th St.), 212-772-3375
☑ Though the Northern Italian food doesn't wow everyone ("typical", "decent"), this Eastsider's "soothing" ambiance, warm service and prix fixe "steal" make it a "good neighborhood place."

Violeta's   ▽ 15 | 9 | 13 | $22
Mexican Restaurant ◑⇄
220 W. 13th St. (bet. 7th & Greenwich Aves.), 212-255-1710
☑ "Like dropping in on the Mexican in-laws", this West Village "hole-in-the-wall" has a "real family-run" feel, and food that varies from "sublime" to "uninspired", as if they weren't expecting you.

Virgil's BBQ ◐Ⓢ

19 | 16 | 18 | $25

152 W. 44th St. (bet. 6th & 7th Aves.), 212-921-9494

■ "Hooray! real BBQ at last" cheer boosters of this "big, noisy", "pseudo-homey" Times Square entry that covers a wide range of regional BBQ styles; "badly needed", "the spice is right", "fabulous pig-out" is the majority view, and even dissenters who say "mass-produced" admit it's a "great B'way-area value."

Vittorio Cucina Ⓢ

▽ 19 | 20 | 20 | $36

308 Bleecker St. (bet. 7th Ave. S. & Grove St.), 212-463-0730

☑ Despite its "good concept" (monthly changing Regional menus), "caring" staff and "romantic rear garden", this brick-walled Village Italian remains suprisingly "underpatronized"; some blame "small portions" and "high prices."

Vivolo ◐

20 | 20 | 19 | $37

140 E. 74th St. (bet. Park & Lexington Aves.), 212-737-3533

■ "Upstairs or down", this "romantic" East Side townhouse offers a "warm", "clubby" setting for its "always dependable" Italian fare; if some find it "staid", it's well-liked by a "smart", older crowd that appreciates steadiness and prix fixe values.

Volare

▽ 21 | 17 | 23 | $33

147 W. 4th St. (bet. 6th Ave. & Wash. Sq. Park), 212-777-2849

■ "If looking for hearty Italian this is it": an old Village standby offering "really fine" food, "excellent" service and "old speakeasy" charm; popularity-produced "noise" seems to be its worst fault.

VONG Ⓢ

23 | 24 | 20 | $48

200 E. 54th St. (3rd Ave.), 212-486-9592

☑ "Exotic" and "showy" in both taste and looks, Jean-Georges Vongerichten's "Thai-French fantasy" brings Pacific New Wave dining into the "21st century" with its "explosive" flavors and "stunning", "movie-set" decor; "dishy, daring and delicious" it's "so good you forgive it" for also being "deafening" and a bit disdainful.

Voulez-Vous ◐Ⓢ

20 | 14 | 19 | $37

1462 First Ave. (76th St.), 212-249-1776

■ "Civilized and delicious" East Side bistro where the soufflés, cassoulets and crème brûlée all win praise as does the "gracious" staff; neighbors say it "always feels like you're coming home" and you "can't beat its Sunday brunch."

Vucciria Ⓢ

19 | 19 | 17 | $35

422 W. Broadway (bet. Prince & Spring Sts.), 212-941-5811

■ With a "romantic" trompe l'oeil Palermo setting for its "awesome artichokes", "pungent" pastas and other "authentic" Italian food this SoHo Sicilian is a "pleasure for a very good, casual meal."

Walker's ◐Ⓢ

15 | 13 | 14 | $21

16 N. Moore St. (Varick St.), 212-941-0142

■ "On everyone's best bar list", this "prototypical NY tavern" is a revered TriBeCa "hangout" with "cheap", "respectable" pub grub and lots of old-time ambiance; it's a "favorite" for anything from "business-buddy" lunches to "late-night" carousing to Sunday brunch.

Wally's and Joseph's ◐

20 | 15 | 19 | $42

249 W. 49th St. (bet. B'way & 8th Ave.), 212-582-0460

■ When "in the mood for meat, potatoes and a cigar" this "nostalgic" Theater District steakhouse fills the bill – just overlook the Houlihan's-style decor and don't give your arteries a thought.

Water Club, The ◐ⓢ

22 | 26 | 22 | $48

500 E. 30th St. (on East River), 212-683-3333

■ Given its "dream setting" and "sensational" views, this East River barge doesn't need much else to stay afloat, but "surprise" – the American food is "always good", brunch is "terrific" and service "classy"; yes it's "touristy", but it always feels "special", does great parties and "even makes Queens look good."

Water's Edge (Queens)

22 | 26 | 22 | $49

44th Drive & East River, Long Island City, 718-482-0033

■ Moonstruck NYers wonder "how many engagement rings have been presented" at this "romantic" riverside oasis in Queens; it's not just the "awe-inspiring" Midtown view that makes it seductive, but also the "elegant" decor and "wonderful" American cuisine; the free water taxi makes "getting there and back half the fun."

Well's ◐ⓢ

– | – | – | M

2247-49 Seventh Ave. (bet. 132nd & 133rd Sts.), 212-234-0700

The critic who claims this Harlem American isn't as good as "when it first opened" has a long memory since it's been around since 1938; but others say that for the "best chicken and waffles" plus "nostalgia" all's well that ends Well's.

West Bank Cafe ◐ⓢ

– | – | – | M

Manhattan Plaza, 407 W. 42nd St. (9th Ave.), 212-695-6909

Congenial Theater District pub/restaurant that's handy for an easygoing, low-key, no-frills American meal; it's nothing to get excited about, but plenty convenient and plenty potable.

Westside Brewing Company ⓢ

11 | 12 | 11 | $18

340 Amsterdam Ave. (76th St.), 212-721-2161

☑ "The beer's the thing" at this "happening" West Side microbrewery that attracts a "lively" local crowd with its "interesting" fresh brews; the "mediocre" food is only "an afterthought."

Westside Cafe ⓢ

▽ 17 | 10 | 14 | $19

892 Ninth Ave. (bet. 57th & 58th Sts.), 212-245-8822

■ "Quick, cheap Chinese" with "more spice and less grease" than some, plus steamed dishes "for the health-conscious"; "speedy delivery" spares you the "nonexistent" decor and "sloppy service."

Westside Cottage ⓢ

17 | 9 | 15 | $17

689 Ninth Ave. (bet. 47th & 48th Sts.), 212-245-0800
788 Ninth Ave. (bet. 52nd & 53rd Sts.), 212-957-8088

☑ "Fresh, tasty", "nongreasy" Chinese food and "quick, courteous service" are reason enough to like these Midtown standbys, but they also have "free wine" and "you won't believe how cheap the bill is."

West 63rd Street Steakhouse ⓢ

– | – | – | E

44 W. 63rd St. (B'way), 212-246-6363

Just opened and too new to call, but this roomy mezzanine steakhouse couldn't be more comfortable or more convenient for Lincoln Center.

Westway Diner ◐ⓢ

▽ 9 | 4 | 10 | $13

614 Ninth Ave. (bet. 43rd & 44th Sts.), 212-582-7661

☑ A "New Jersey–style" diner that appeals to NYers with "solid" food, low prices and round-the-clock service; both locals and theatergoers like it for "quick, hearty" bites, but it's definitely not for the effete.

White Horse Tavern ◐ⓢ⇥

11 | 14 | 12 | $18

567 Hudson St. (11th St.), 212-243-9260

☑ It's "fun to drink with Dylan Thomas' ghost" at this "landmark" West Village pub, but eat here and "you have to wonder what really killed him" – the booze, the food or the waiters.

Whole Wheat 'n Wild Berrys [S] — 17 | 11 | 16 | $18

57 W. 10th St. (bet. 5th & 6th Aves.), 212-677-3410

◪ "Granola eaters" tout the "joys of tahini" and other "wholesome, tasty" Health Food at this Village "vegetarian delight"; with a "friendly staff" and "organically casual" ambiance it's "good for purists", but others may crave a little more meat and decor.

Wilkinson's Seafood Cafe [S] — 24 | 18 | 20 | $46

1573 York Ave. (bet. 83rd & 84th Sts.), 212-535-5454

■ A "calm", "classy" Eastsider that satiates seafood lovers with the "freshest fish around" served by a "gracious" staff in a "quiet" setting; it's "expensive" for a neighborhood place, but "worth it."

Windows on India ◐ [S] — ▽ 17 | 16 | 15 | $17

344 E. 6th St. (1st Ave.), 212-477-5956

◪ One of "the most attractive" of the 6th Street Indians with "airy", "pretty" decor and an "above-average" kitchen (Indonesian dishes spice up the menu); to say it has the "atmosphere of a restaurant twice its price" is overstating, but not by much.

WINDOWS ON THE WORLD — – | – | – | E

1 World Trade Ctr., 107th fl., West St., 212-938-1111

Closed for renovations.

Wing Wong [S] 🚫 — ▽ 21 | 4 | 14 | $12

119 Lafayette St. (bet. Canal & Howard Sts.), 212-274-0690
102 Mott St. (bet. Canal & Hester Sts.), 212-274-0696

■ "Unpretentious" Downtown noodle shops that dish up "big servings" of "great soups, congee" and other Cantonese-Mandarin fare; prices are modest and so is decor, but they're "the real thing."

Wolf's 6th Avenue Delicatessen ◐ [S] — 15 | 7 | 11 | $20

101 W. 57th St. (6th Ave.), 212-586-1110

◪ "Bustling" Midtown old-timer with "skyscraper sandwiches" and other "adequate-to-good" deli food plus the traditional "rude service" and "Formica decor"; it's handy "in a pinch", despite critics who say "Little Red Riding Hood was right."

Wollensky's Grill ◐ [S] — 22 | 15 | 17 | $36

205 E. 49th St. (3rd Ave.), 212-753-0444

■ "Smith & Wollensky lite"; this "solid" grill is "just as good, cozier and cheaper" and hence, some say, "better than its big brother" next door; service is "friendly" even to those "not dressed like masters of the universe"; open til 2 AM, it's a "wee-hours savior."

Wong Kee [S] 🚫 — 22 | 4 | 9 | $15

113 Mott St. (bet. Canal & Hester Sts.), 212-966-1160

■ "The ambiance is as bad as the food is good" at this "tacky" but "top-notch" Chinatown Chinese, and you sure "can't go wong at these prices"; it's "crowded and crazy" so "bring earplugs and wear sunglasses" to block out the decor.

Woo Chon ◐ [S] — 21 | 14 | 15 | $26

8-10 W. 36th St. (bet. 5th & 6th Aves.), 212-695-0676

■ "Illustrated English menus" help make this 24-hour Midtowner a "good place to start" on Korean cuisine; "friendly" and "reasonably priced", it serves "delicious" BBQ, kimchi and other "authentic" dishes in a "pleasant" if "smoky" setting.

Woo Lae Oak of Seoul 🅂
20 | 13 | 14 | $28
77 W. 46th St. (bet. 5th & 6th Aves.), 212-869-9958
☑ "Bring a group" and "make merry around a grill" at this "do-it-yourself" Midtown Korean BBQ; it's "tasty" and "fun" but also "smoky" and "greasy", so have your "dry cleaner" on standby; detractors cite "Ho Jo decor" and "D.M.V. service."

World Cafe ◐🅂
17 | 16 | 14 | $27
201 Columbus Ave. (69th St.), 212-799-8090
☑ "Uneven but sometimes inspired", this "affordable" West Side newcomer with a menu that "spans the globe" draws a "noisy" crowd willing to give it "time to mature"; but critics say it's "proof that if you try to do everything, you do nothing well."

World Yacht 🅂
13 | 24 | 16 | $53
Pier 81, W. 41st St. (Hudson River), 212-630-8100
☑ The Continental cuisine leaves some wishing they could "brown-bag it", but when you're "nearly on the Statue of Liberty's lap" even "rubber chicken" tastes fine; this dinner cruise is "a must" for "magical" views, "romance" and wowing out-of-towners.

Wylie's Ribs ◐🅂
15 | 8 | 12 | $24
891 First Ave. (50th St.), 212-751-0700
■ You still get "lots of food for little money" at this "rather seedy" East Side rib shack, but while some think it's "as tasty as ever" others say "gone way downhill": "even Eve would give these back."

Yaffa Tea Room ◐🅂
– | – | – | M
353 Greenwich St. (Harrison St.), 212-274-9403
19 Harrison St. (Greenwich St.), 212-274-9403
Two side-by-side TriBeCa spaces – one a funky corner bar with tables outside, the other a slightly bohemian tearoom with music; neither costs very much for its Eclectic home cooking and hip local people-watching.

Yamaguchi 🅂
19 | 14 | 17 | $30
35 W. 45th St. (bet. 5th & 6th Aves.), 212-840-8185
☑ The "sushi lunch box is a great value", but beyond that this Midtown Japanese produces debate: "excellent", "good variety" vs. "soggy rice", "overpriced"; most agree the "decor leaves much to be desired."

Yankee Clipper, The 🅂
18 | 17 | 18 | $33
170 John St. (South St.), 212-344-5959
■ The "Wall Street crowd" likes this Seaport fish specialist for "power lunches" in an "attractive, quiet" setting, and word is that a new chef is "working wonders" at "very reasonable prices"; service is shipshape, too.

Yellowfingers ◐🅂
16 | 13 | 14 | $26
200 E. 60th St. (3rd Ave.), 212-751-8615
☑ "Upbeat", "all-purpose" East Sider where everyone from "beautiful people" to B&Ters munch on salads, sandwiches and pizza before Bloomies or the movies; it's "convenient", "not too pricey" and the window tables offer "perfect people-watching."

Ye Waverly Inn 🅂
15 | 21 | 16 | $26
16 Bank St. (Greenwich Ave.), 212-929-4377
☑ On a "cold winter's night" it's "lovely" to sit by the fire at this "charming" West Village "colonial haunt" where the "Americana" decor and fare seem equally "authentic", which suggests to some that "there were no gourmets back then."

Yuka [S] 19 | 10 | 15 | $24
1557 Second Ave. (bet. 80th & 81st Sts.), 212-772-9675
■ The "eat-til-you-pop" sushi special ($18) is a "fresh", "high-quality" deal, which is why this "publike" Japanese Eastsider is often "crowded" with big eaters who don't care that there's little decor besides "origami butterflies."

Yura [S] 20 | 13 | 16 | $24
1645 Third Ave. (92nd St.), 212-860-8060
■ "Adventurous" Eclectic food served in the sit-down section of a food market makes this "spacious, pleasant" Eastsider a welcome "neighborhood resource"; brunch and takeout both get thumbs up, but the "friendly" staff can "get lost when busy."

Zacki's Carolina Pit BBQ ◐ [S] ▽ 18 | 8 | 13 | $17
1752 Second Ave. (bet. 91st & 92nd Sts.), 212-987-1424
■ This pit "is legit" say BBQ buffs who swear there's "no better pork till North Carolina"; the decor may be basic, but this mostly take-out East Side yearling's "tasty" ribs, greens and banana pudding will fill you up without emptying your wallet.

ZARELA 23 | 16 | 17 | $35
953 Second Ave. (bet. 50th & 51st Sts.), 212-644-6740
◪ Zarela is the "queen of Mexican food" and her cooking "comes from the heart", which is why this "lively" East Midtowner is No. 1 in its class; with a menu full of "explosive flavors", decor "like the inside of a piñata" and "knockout" margaritas, it often "feels like a fiesta"; for some peace sit upstairs.

Zen Palate [S] – | – | – | M
663 Ninth Ave. (46th St.), 212-582-1669
34 Union Square East (16th St.), 212-614-9345
It's a miracle what they can do with tofu at these extraordinary Chinese Vegetarians, respectively located in the Theater District and on Union Square; it's even more impressive to see Tony Chi's handsome modern decor at both, but especially the newer Zen-like Downtown location.

Zephyr Grill [S] 17 | 16 | 16 | $33
Beekman Tower Hotel, 3 Mitchell Pl. (bet. 1st Ave. & 49th St.), 212-223-4200
◪ Though some say its menu and prices tend to shift with the winds, this "restful hotel hideaway" near the UN is "good for a casual", midpriced American meal in a "'30s-style" setting.

Zinno [S] 19 | 18 | 19 | $32
126 W. 13th St. (bet. 6th & 7th Aves.), 212-924-5182
■ A winner all around, this "soothing" Village Northern Italian is good enough that "you'd frequent it even if they got rid of the jazz piano", but don't worry, the music plays on at this "harmonious" standby.

Zip City Brewing Co. [S] 15 | 17 | 13 | $23
3 W. 18th St. (bet. 5th & 6th Aves.), 212-366-6333
◪ "Great brew, decent food" sums up this microbrewery with "gleaming" beer-vat decor; it's "loud" and "crowded" with a big "Generation X" bar scene and "not-so-zippy" service.

Zitella ◐ [S] ▽ 24 | 24 | 23 | $33
131 Avenue A (bet. St. Marks Pl. & 9th St.), 212-777-5642
◪ "Not well-known but should be", this "happening" East Village "notable newcomer" has a pleasant, open-to-the-street setting and a changing menu of "flavorful", "well-priced" Italian fare; dissenters warn that it's "hit-or-miss."

Zoë 🅂
90 Prince St. (bet. B'way & Mercer Sts.), 212-966-6722

24 | 21 | 20 | $40

■ The "cutting-edge" cuisine "keeps getting better" at this "exciting" SoHo American with "all the right ingredients": "incredible" food, an "amazing wine list", "chic" crowd and "artsy", open-kitchen space; if the "ambiance is like LA", the "energy" and "din" are pure NY.

Zucchero 🅂 🍴
1464 Second Ave. (bet. 76th & 77th Sts.), 212-517-2541

18 | 13 | 16 | $25

☑ One of the "best of the pasta clones" according to admirers of this "tasty and cheap" East Side Italian; it's "crowded" but "cute" with prices that make its "expensive neighbors look ridiculous."

Zucchini 🅂
1336 First Ave. (bet. 71st & 72nd Sts.), 212-249-0559

15 | 12 | 14 | $22

☑ An East Side "utilitarian Vegetarian" that some commend for "fresh, well-prepared" food, but which others squash for "making 'healthy' and 'bland' synonymous"; modest prices work in its favor.

Zula ◑🅂
1260 Amsterdam Ave. (122nd St.), 212-663-1670

▽ 21 | 10 | 15 | $16

■ "Don't let the decor deter you": this Upper Westsider is a "seriously authentic" Ethiopian with "tasty food that you scoop up with spongy bread" and wash down with "honey wine"; we can't vouch that it's "better than Addis Ababa", but it's "very cheap."

Zuni ◑🅂
598 Ninth Ave. (43rd St.), 212-765-7626

– | – | – | M

For an attractive, informal Southwestern meal in the Theater District you should consider giving this cheerful newcomer a try; there's not much to lose since its menu is a cut above typical border fare and prices are a cut below.

Zutto ◑🅂
77 Hudson St. (bet. Jay & Harrison Sts.), 212-233-3287

19 | 16 | 15 | $28

☑ "Food and art collide" at this TriBeCa Japanese with an attractive setting and what most call "fresh", "well-prepared" sushi; it's "low-key and relaxing", but mixed comments suggest that "some days are better than others"; "outside seating is a plus."

INDEXES TO
RESTAURANTS

SPECIAL FEATURES
AND APPEALS

TYPES OF CUISINE*

Afghan
Afghan Kebab Hse.
Bamiyan
Kabul Cafe
Khan Restaurant
Khyber Pass
Pamir

American (New)
Abby
Adrienne
Alley's End
Alva
American Festival
Amer. Renaissance
Amsterdam's
An American Place
Annie Beneau
Arcadia
Assembly
Aureole
Beer Bar
Between the Bread
Big Sur
Bistro 790
Boathouse Cafe
Bridge Cafe
B. Smith's
Busby's
Cafe Botanica
Cafe de la Paix
Cafe Europa
Cafe Lalo
Cafe Nicholson
Cafe S.F.A.
Cafe Tabac
Café Word of Mouth
Cake Bar & Cafe
Cal's
Carnegie Hill
Cascabel
Century Cafe
Chaz & Wilson
Chelsea Clinton
Chock Full o' Nuts
Cité
City Bakery
City Crab
Coconut Grill
Coming Or Going
Cooper's Coffee
Cornelia St. Cafe
Country Club
Courtyard Cafe
C3
Cub Room
Dakota Bar/Grill
Dojo
Donald Sacks

Duane Park Cafe
Etats-Unis
Fez
57, 57
First
Five Oaks
Flowers
44
Garden Cafe (Bklyn)
Gotham Bar/Grill
Gramercy Tavern
Grove
Halcyon
Harvest
Henry's End
Hourglass Tavern
Hudson Grill
Hudson River Club
Island
Jerry's
Josephina
Josie's
JUdson Grill
King's Carriage
Kiss
La Boulangere
Le Bar Bat
Le Max
Levana
Lipstick Cafe
Little Club
Lobby Lounge
Lola
Lucky Strike
Luma
Mad.61
Manhattan Ocean
Manhattan Plaza
Man Ray
March
Marlowe
Mary's
Match
Matthew's
Merchants N.Y.
Metronome
Metropolis Cafe
Mezzanine
Michael's
Miracle Grill
Monkey Bar
Museum Cafe
Nadine's
New City Cafe
New Deal
New Prospect Cafe
New World Grill
Nick & Eddie

---

* "Coffeehouses," "Health/Spa Menus," and "Pubs" are listed under Special Features and Appeals, p. 196.

9 Jones Street
NoHo Star
Nosmo King
Odeon, The
Olive Garden
103 NYC
Orbit
Orson's
Park Ave. Cafe
Pipeline
Planet Hollywood
Privé
Rachel's
Restaurant 222
Revolution
River Cafe
Rose Cafe
Russell's
Sarabeth's
Savoy
SeaGrill
Sequoia
Sign of the Dove
SoHo Kitchen
Spring St. Rest.
Symphony Cafe
Table d'Hôte
Taliesin
Tatou
Tavern on Green
Teachers Too
Temple Bar
Thomas Scott's
Time Cafe
Toukie's
TriBeCa Grill
Trilogy Bar/Grill
Tropica
Truffles
T Salon
Two Eleven
Union Square Cafe
Universal Grill
Verbena
Viceroy
Water's Edge
Zip City Brewing
Zoë

American (Traditional)
Acme Bar & Grill
Aggie's
America
Anglers & Writers
Area Code Cafe
Atomic Wings
Barking Dog
Beach Cafe
Bill's Gay 90's
Book-Friends Cafe
Boston Chicken
Boulevard
Boxers
Bridge Cafe
Brighton Grill

Broadway Diner
Broome Street Bar
Bubby's
Bull & Bear
Burger Heaven
Busby's
Cafe Beulah
Charley O's
Chat 'n' Chew
Chelsea Commons
Chelsea Grill
Chock Full o' Nuts
Chumley's
Churchill's
Claire
Clarke's, P.J.
Cotton Club
Cupping Room Cafe
Dallas BBQ
Danny's Grand
Ear Inn
E.A.T.
Edward Moran
EJ's Luncheonette
Elephant & Castle
Fanelli
Finnegan's Wake
Fiori
Fish Restaurant
Flight 151
Food Bar
Fraunces Tavern
Friend of Farmer
Gage & Tollner
Georgia Diner
Good Enough to Eat
Gramercy Watering
Grange Hall
Great Jones Cafe
Hard Rock Cafe
Harley Davidson
Harriet's Kitchen
Hi-Life Bar/Grill
Home
Houlihan's
Hunters
Jackson Hole
Jack's Place
J.G. Melon
Jim McMullen
Joe Allen
Knickerbocker
La Chandelle
Landmark Tavern
Langan's
Lee Mazzilli's
Lincoln Tavern
Lion's Head
Lofland's N.Y.
Louie's Westside
Lucky's Bar/Grill
Luke's Bar/Grill
Mackinac
Main Street
Manhattan Plaza
Markham

Mayfair
Mayrose
McSorley's
Mickey Mantle's
Mike's Bar/Grill
Moran's
Mortimer's
Mulholland Drive
Oak Room & Bar
O'Casey's
Old Town Bar
O'Neals'
One If By Land
Oscar's
Ottomanelli's
Paris Cafe
Park Ave. Country
Perks
Pete's Tavern
Phoebe's
Pizzapiazza
Post House
Pudgie's
Rascals
Regency
Reidy's
Riverrun
Roebling's
Rosie O'Grady's
Royal Canadian
Ruppert's
Rusty Staub's
Saloon
Sarabeth's
Saranac
7th Regiment Mess
Shelby
Smith & Wollensky
Steamers Landing
Stingy Lulu's
Supper Club
Tennessee Mtn.
T.G.I. Friday's
Top of the Sixes
"21" Club
Urban Grill
Vince & Eddie's
Walker's
Water Club
Well's
West Bank Cafe
Westside Brewing
Westway Diner
Wollensky's Grill
W. 63rd St. Stkhse.
Wylie's Ribs
Yankee Clipper
Ye Waverly Inn
Zephyr Grill

Argentinean
Argentine Pavilion
La Fusta
La Portena

Asian
Asia
Bright Food Shop
Gauguin
Kelley & Ping
Kitchen Club
Lucky Cheng's
Marnie's Noodle

Austrian
Kaffeehaus
Roettelle A.G.

Bar-B-Q
Boulevard
Brother Jimmy's
Brothers BBQ
Chicken Chef
Dallas BBQ
Levee
Lofland's N.Y.
Pearson's BBQ
Rib'n & Blues
Rusty Staub's
Tennessee Mtn.
Tony Roma's
Virgil's BBQ
Wylie's Ribs
Zacki's PBQ

Belgian
Cafe de Bruxelles

Brazilian
Cabana Carioca
Coffee Shop
C.T.
Ipanema

Burmese
Bali Burma
Mingala Burmese
Road to Mandalay

Burritos/Tacos
Arriba Arriba
Benny's Burritos
Bertha's Burritos
Burritoville
Calif. Burrito Co.
Flying Burrito
Harry's Burritos
Orig. Cal. Taqueria

Cajun/Creole
Acadia Parish
Acme Bar & Grill
Baby Jake's
Cajun
Chantale's Cajun
Cooking With Jazz
Great Jones Cafe
Levee
Louisiana Commun.
Ludlow St. Cafe
Memphis
Mo' Better
107 West
Orleans

Ruby's River
Sazerac House
Two Boots

Californian
Calif. Burrito Co.
California Pizza
Dish
Flying Burrito
Harry's Burritos
Josephina
Lucky Cheng's
Lucy's Surfers
Martini's
Mesa Verde
Michael's
Mission Grill
Mulholland Drive
103 NYC
Orig. Cal. Taqueria
Planet Hollywood
Rose Cafe
Samalita's
Yellowfingers

Caribbean
Caribe
Island Spice
Jamaican Hot Pot
Kwanzaa
Mo's Caribbean
Sugar Reef
Tropica
Vernon's Jerk

Caviar
Caviarteria
Petrossian
Russian Tea Room

Chinese
Asia
Au Mandarin
Bayamo
Beijing Duck Hse.
Big Wong
Bill Hong's
Bo Ky
BOS
Bruce Ho's
Canton
Chao Chow
Chef Ho's
Chiam
China Fun
Chin Chin
Dish of Salt
Dragon Village
Empire Szechuan
Evergreen Cafe
1st Wok
Fortune
Fu's
Golden Unicorn
Goody's
Great Shanghai
Harbor Seafood

Hong Fat
Hong Shoon
Hop Shing
H.S.F.
Hunan Balcony
Hunan Fifth Ave.
Hunan Garden
Jade Palace
Jing Fong
Joe's Shanghai
J. Sung Dynasty
Kam Chueh
Keewah Yen
La Caridad
Lum Chin
Mandarin Court
Mee Noodle Shop
Mr. Chow
Mr. Tang
New Hong Kong City
Nice Restaurant
Ollie's
Oriental Garden
Oriental Pearl
Our Place
Peking Park
Phoenix Garden
Pig Heaven
Seafood Palace
Shanghai Manor
Shanghai 1933
Shun Lee Cafe
Shun Lee Palace
Shun Lee West
Sichuan Palace
Silk Road Palace
Sunny East
Szechuan Hunan
Szechuan Kitchen
Tang Pavilion
Tang Tang
Tea Den
Tien Fu
Tina's
Triple Eight
Tse Yang
T.S. Ma
20 Mott Street
Westside Cafe
Westside Cottage
Wing Wong
Wong Kee
Zen Palate

Coffee Shops/Diners
Aggie's
Angelika Film Ctr.
Bendix Diner
Broadway Diner
Burger Heaven
Chock Full o' Nuts
Christine's
Cupcake Cafe
Edison Cafe
Eighteenth & 8th

EJ's Luncheonette
Ellen's Stardust
Empire Diner
Florent
Georgia Diner
Googie.
Gotham City Diner
Gray's Papaya
Jackson Hole
Kiev
Kings Pl. Diner
Madison Ave. Cafe
Mayrose
Moonrock Diner
Museum Cafe
Odeon, The
Odessa
Palm Court
Petes' Place
Rumpelmayer's
Soup Burg
Stingy Lulu's
Symphony Cafe
Ter.amare Café
Three Guys
Viand
Veselka
Westway Diner

Continental
Algonquin Hotel
Ambassador Grill
Au Cafe
Back Porch
Box Tree
Cafe Melville
Cafe Nicholson
Caffe Lure
Caffe Rafaella
Chez Josephine
City Grill
Cleopatra's
Demi
East River Cafe
Edwardian Room
First on 59th
Five Oaks
44 Southwest
Four Seasons
Gianpalu
Grove St. Cafe
Harpo
Island
Jack's Place
Kitchen Club
Leopard, The
Lexington Grill
Marion's Cont.
Mark's
Marylou's
Metropolitan Cafe
Old Bermuda Inn
O'Neals'
One If By Land
Petrossian

Polo
Rainbow Room
Restaurant 222
Sardi's
Sign of the Dove
Small Cafe
Sumptuary
Tavern on Green
Townhouse
Wally's & Joseph's
World Yacht
View

Cuban
Bayamo
Cafe Con Leche
La Caridad
La Taza de Oro
Patría
Rice & Beans
Victor's Cafe

Delis
Bloom's Deli
Carnegie Deli
E.A.T.
Ess-a-Bagel
Fine & Schapiro
Katz's Deli
N.Y. Deli
Pastrami King
Second Ave. Deli
Stage Deli
3rd Ave. Deli
Wolf's Deli

Dim Sum
Asia
China Fun
Empire Szechuan
Evergreen Cafe
Fortune
Fu's
Hong Shoon
Hop Shing
H.S.F.
Jade Palace
Mandarin Court
Mr. Tang
Nice Restaurant
Oriental Pearl
Phoenix Garden
Shun Lee Cafe
Tai Hong Lau
Tang Tang
Triple Eight
20 Mott Street

Eclectic
Adoré
Anarchy Cafe
Aunt Sonia's
Bar and Books
Barnes & Noble
Bell Caffe
Bendix Diner
Bimini Twist

Blue Ribbon
Blu Restaurant
Boom
Bright Food Shop
Broadway Grill
Bubby's
Cafe du Pont
Carnegie Hill
Claire
Conservatory
Donald Sacks
Eighteenth & 8th
Ellen's Stardust
5 & 10
Four Seasons
Gotham City Diner
Hourglass Tavern
Iridium
Jekyll & Hyde
Life Cafe
Lola
Mary's
Merenda
Mike's Bar/Grill
Nadine's
New Deal
New World Grill
9
NoHo Star
Popover Cafe
Revolution
Rose Cafe
Saloon
Seattle Bean Co.
Serendipity 3
Shopsin's
Sonia Rose
Spring St. Natural
Starbucks
Trilogy Bar/Grill
Tropica
T Salon
Universal Grill
Wilkinson's
Yaffa Tea Room
Yura
Zip City Brewing
Zucchini

Ethiopian
Zula

Frankfurters
Gray's Papaya
Leo's Famous
Papaya King

French
Au Troquet
Box Tree
Brasserie
Danny's Grand
La Caravelle
La Colombe d'Or
La Cote Basque
La Folie
La Fondue

La Grenouille
La Mère Poulard
La Tour D'Or
Le Cirque
Le Grenadin
Le Pactole
Le Perigord
Le Pistou
Le Refuge
L'Ermitage
Les Celebrités
Les Friandises
L'Udo
Lutèce
Mme. Romaine
Peacock Alley
Right Bank
Trois Jean
Truffles
Village Atelier

French-Asian
Can
Indochine
La Maison Japon.
Lespinasse
Silk Restaurant

French Bistro
Alison
Au Bon Coin
Bar Six
Bienvenue
Bistro 36
Bistro du Nord
Black Sheep
Cafe Centro
Cafe de Paris
Cafe des Artistes
Cafe des Sports
Cafe Loup
Cafe Luxembourg
Cafe St. John
Cafe Un Deux Trois
Capsouto Frères
Casanis
Chantal Café
Chez Brigitte
Chez Jacqueline
Chez Josephine
Chez Ma Tante
Chez Michallet
Chez Napoleon
Danal
Demarchelier
Dix et Sept
Felix
Ferrier
Florent
French Roast Cafe
Frontière
Gascogne
Hulot's
Jean Claude
Jean Lafitte
Jo Jo

Jour et Nuit
Jules
La Boheme
La Boite en Bois
La Bonne Soupe
La Bouillabaisse
L'Acajou
La Chandelle
La Goulue
La Jumelle
La Lunchonette
La Mangeoire
La Mediterranée
La Metairie
La Mirabelle
La Petite Auberge
L'Ardoise
La Ripaille
L'Auberge du Midi
La Vieille Auberge
Le Beaujolais
Le Biarritz
Le Bilboquet
Le Bistrot
Le Boeuf ala Mode
Le Bouchon
L'Ecole
Le Comptoir
Le Madeleine
Le Max
L'Entrecote
Le Pescadou
Le Quercy
Le Relais
Le Rivage
Les Deux Gamins
Les Halles
Les Pyrenees
Les Routiers
Les Sans Culottes
Le Taxi
Le Veau d'Or
Lucky Strike
Manhattan Bistro
Montrachet
Morgan Cafe
Paris Commune
Park Bistro
Pierre au Tunnel
Pigalle
Poiret
Provence
Quatorze Bis
Raoul's
Raphael
René Pujol
Sel et Poivre
Steak Frites
Table d'Hôte
Tartine
Tout Va Bien
Voulez-Vous

French (New)
Alison
Annabelle

Bouley
Cafe Botanica
Cafe Metairie
Cafe Pierre
Can
Carlyle
Chanterelle
Chez Brigitte
Cité
Cloister Cafe
C.T.
Daniel
Grove
Kaptain Banana
King's Carriage
La Boulangere
La Caravelle
La Reserve
Le Bernardin
Le Chantilly
Leopard, The
Le Regence
Lespinasse
Mark's
Privé
Sign of the Dove
Sonia Rose
Table d'Hôte
Terrace
Vong

German
Heidelberg
Kleine Konditorei
Mayfair
Roettelle A.G.
Rolf's

Greek
Ambrosia Tavern
Elias Corner
Estia
Gus' Place
Karyatis
Mr. Souvlaki
Periyali
Roumeli Taverna
Symposium
Telly's Taverna
Three Guys
Uncle Nick's
Viand

Grills
Ambassador Grill
Brighton Grill
Broadway Grill
Century Cafe
Chaz & Wilson
Chelsea Grill
Coconut Grill
Col Legno
Courtyard Cafe
Edward Moran
Elias Corner
Four Seasons

Frankie & Johnnie's
Fresco
Gotham Bar/Grill
Hard Rock Cafe
Harley Davidson
Hi-Life Bar/Grill
JUdson Grill
Lexington Grill
Lofland's N.Y.
Loui Loui
Luke's Bar/Grill
Mackinac
Martini's
Mesa Grill
Michael's
Petaluma
Quatorze Bis
TriBeCa Grill
Urban Grill
Wollensky's Grill
Zephyr Grill

Hamburgers & Beer
Broadway Diner
Burger Heaven
Charley O's
Chelsea Commons
Chelsea Grill
Chumley's
Churchill's
Clarke's, P.J.
Corner Bistro
Fanelli
Flight 151
Hamburger Harry's
Hard Rock Cafe
H-arley Davidson
Hi-Life Bar/Grill
Jackson Hole
Jekyll & Hyde
J.G. Melon
Joe Allen
Lee Mazzilli's
Leo's Famous
Lincoln Tavern
Lion's Head
Lofland's N.Y.
Lucky's Bar/Grill
Luke's Bar/Grill
Manhattan Brewing
McSorley's
Mickey Mantle's
O'Neals'
Orbit
Park Ave. Country
Planet Hollywood
Prime Burger
Red Lion
Ruppert's
Shelby
Urban Grill
Walker's
White Horse Tavern

Health Food
Angelica Kitchen
Apple Restaurant

Bachué Café
Bell Caffe
City Bakery
Dojo
Great Am. Health
Health Pub
Josie's
La Boulangere
Life Cafe
Luma
Nosmo King
Souen
Spring St. Natural
Whole Wheat
Zen Palate
Zucchini

Hungarian
Caterina's
Mocca Hungarian
Red Tulip

Indian
Akbar
Baluchi's
Bombay Palace
Chutney Mary
Darbar
Dawat
Diwan Grill
Gandhi
Haveli
Indian Cafe
Indian Oven
India Pavilion
Jackson Hts. Diner
Jewel of India
Maurya
Mavalli Palace
Mitali East/West
Mughlai
Nirvana
Pandit
Passage to India
Rose of India
Salaam Bombay
Shaan
Windows on India

Indonesian
Bali Burma
Malaysia/Indonesia
Nusantara

International
Boom
China Grill
Delia's
Le Train Bleu
Madison Ave. Cafe
Passport
Soleil
Taci Int'l
Toast
Trompe l'Oeil
World Cafe

Irish
Landmark Tavern
McSorley's
Moran's
Neary's
O'Casey's
Reidy's
Rosie O'Grady's

Italian
(N = Northern;
S = Southern;
N&S = Includes both)
Acappella (N)
Ahnell (N&S)
Allegria (N)
Amarcord (N)
Amici Miei (N&S)
Anche Vivolo (N)
Angelo's (N&S)
Angel's (N&S)
Antico Caffee (N&S)
Aperitivo (N)
Appetito (N)
Arcimboldo (N)
Aria (N)
Arlecchino (N&S)
Arqua (N)
Artepasta (N)
Arturo's Pizzeria (N&S)
Avanti (N&S)
Azzurro (S)
Baci (S)
Ballato's (N&S)
Baraonda (N)
Barbetta (N)
Barocco (N)
Barolo (N)
Bar Pitti (N)
Basco (N&S)
Basta Pasta (N&S)
Becco (N&S)
Bella Donna (N)
Bella Luna (N)
Bello (N)
Benito I (N&S)
Benito II (N&S)
Benvenuti (N)
Bice (N)
Biricchino (N)
Bistro Cafe (N&S)
Black Sheep (N)
Bora (N)
Borsalino (N)
Brio (N&S)
Briscola (S)
Brunetta's (N&S)
Bruno Ristorante (N)
Cafe Baci (N&S)
Cafe Cento Sette (N&S)
Cafe Nosidam (N&S)
Cafe Trevi (N)
Caffe Biondo (S)
Caffe Bondí (S)
Caffe Buon Gusto (N&S)

Caffé Carciofo (N&S)
Caffe Cielo (N)
Caffe di Nonni (N)
Caffe Grazie (N&S)
Caffe Rosso (N)
Caffe Vivaldi (N&S)
Campagna (N&S)
Campagnola (N&S)
Canastel's (N)
Capriccio (N)
Carino (S)
Carmine's (S)
Casa Di Pre (N)
Casalone (N)
Castellano (N&S)
Cent'Anni (N)
Cesarina (N)
Chelsea Trattoria (N)
Ciao Europa (N&S)
Ciccio & Tony's (S)
Cinquanta (N)
Ci Vedeamo (N)
Cloister Cafe (N&S)
Coco Pazzo (N)
Col Legno (N&S)
Contrapunto (N)
Corrado (N)
Country Club (N&S)
Court of 3 Sisters (N&S)
Cucina (N)
Cucina & Co. (N&S)
Cucina De Fontana (N&S)
Cucina di Pesce (N&S)
Cucina Stagionale (N)
Da Nico (N&S)
Da Rosina (N)
Da Silvano (N)
Da Tommaso (N)
Da Umberto (N)
Dazies (N&S)
DeGrezia (N)
Diva (N)
Divino (N)
Dolce (N)
Dolcetto (N&S)
Dominick's (S)
Don Giovanni (N&S)
Due (N)
East River Cafe (N&S)
Ecco (N&S)
Ecco-La (N&S)
Ecco L'Italia (N&S)
Elaine's (N&S)
Elio's (N&S)
Ennio & Michael (N&S)
Erminia (N&S)
Est! Est! Est! (N)
Fantino (N)
Federico's (N)
Felidia (N)
Ferdinando's (S)
Fino (N)
Fiorello's Roman (N)
Fiorentino (S)

Fiori (N&S)
Firenze (N)
Fishin Eddie (N&S)
Follonico (N&S)
44 Southwest (N&S)
Frank's (N)
Fresch (N&S)
Fresco (N)
Frutti di Mare (N)
Gabriel's (N)
Garibaldi (N&S)
Giambelli (N)
Gianni's (N)
Gigino (N)
Gino (S)
Giovanni (N)
Girafe (N)
Girasole (N&S)
Googies (N&S)
Grand Ticino (N)
Grappino (N&S)
Grifone (N)
Grotta Azzurra (S)
Harry Cipriani (N)
Hosteria Fiorella (N&S)
Il Cantinori (N)
Il Corallo (N&S)
Il Cortile (N)
Il Giardinetto (N&S)
Il Giglio (N)
Il Menestrello (N)
Il Monello (N)
Il Mulino (N)
Il Nido (N)
Il Nostro (N)
Il Ponte Vecchio (N)
Il Tinello (N)
Il Vagabondo (N)
Il Vigneto (N&S)
In Padella (N)
Isabella's (S)
Isola (S)
I Tre Merli (N)
John's of 12th (N&S)
La Barca (S)
La Chandelle (N&S)
La Collina (N)
La Dolce Vita (N&S)
La Focaccia (N)
La Fusta (N&S)
Lamarca (S)
La Mela (N&S)
Lanza (N&S)
La Primavera (N)
La Rivista (N&S)
La Scala (N&S)
La Spaghetteria (N&S)
La Strada 2 (S)
Lattanzi (N)
La Voce (N&S)
Le Figaro (N&S)
Le Madri (N&S)
Le Streghe (N)
Letizia (N)

L'Incontro (N&S)
Lipizzana (N)
Loui Loui (N&S)
L'Udo (N&S)
Lusardi's (N)
Mad.61 (N)
Manganaro's (N&S)
Mangia e Bevi (N&S)
Mappamondo (N)
Marchi's (N)
Marina Cafe (N&S)
Mario's (S)
Martini's (N&S)
Mazzei (S)
Medici 56 (N&S)
Mediterraneo (N&S)
Merenda (N&S)
Meridiana (N&S)
Mezzaluna (N)
Mezzogiorno (N&S)
Milano (N&S)
Minetta Tavern (N&S)
Montebello (N)
Moreno (N)
Nanni Il Valletto (N)
Nanni's (N)
Natalino (N&S)
Nello (N)
Nicola Paone (N&S)
Nicola's (N)
Nino's (N)
Old Roma (S)
Olive Garden (N&S)
101 (N&S)
101 Seafood (N&S)
Orologio (N)
Orso (N)
Osso Buco (N&S)
Osteria al Doge (N)
Ottomanelli's (N&S)
Palio (N)
Palm (N&S)
Palm Too (N&S)
Paola's (N&S)
Paolucci's (S)
Paper Moon Milano (N&S)
Pappardella (N)
Parioli Romanis. (N)
Park Avalon (N&S)
Park Side (N&S)
Parma (N)
Pasta Lovers (N&S)
Pasta Presto (N&S)
Pasticcio (N)
Patrissy's (S)
Patsy's (S)
Patzo (N&S)
Paul & Jimmy's (N&S)
Pellegrino (N)
Perretti Italian (N)
Pescatore (N&S)
Petaluma (N&S)
Piccola Venezia (N)
Piccolo Angolo (N)

Piccolo Pomodoro (N&S)
Pietro & Vanessa (N&S)
Pietro's (N&S)
Pinocchio (N&S)
Pisces (N&S)
Pizzeria Uno (N&S)
Pó (N&S)
Pomodori (N&S)
Ponticello (N)
Portico (N)
Presto's (N&S)
Primavera (N)
Primola (N)
Quartiere (N&S)
Queen (N&S)
Quisisana (S)
Raffaele (S)
Rao's (S)
Remi (N)
Rocco (S)
Rosemarie's (N)
Rosolio (N)
Sal Anthony's (N&S)
Sambuca (N&S)
Sam's Rest./Pizza (N&S)
San Domenico (N)
San Giusto (N)
San Pietro (S)
Sant Ambroeus (N)
Sasso (N)
Scaletta (N)
Scalinatella (N&S)
Sette Mezzo (N)
Sette MoMA (N&S)
Sfuzzi (N)
Sirabella's (N)
Sistina (N&S)
Sofia's (N)
Sorelle (S)
S.P.Q.R. (N&S)
Stella del Mare (N)
Stellina (N)
Supreme Macaroni (S)
Tanti Baci Cafe (S)
Taormina (N&S)
Tavola (N&S)
Tempo (S)
Terramare Café (N&S)
Tevere 84 (N&S)
Three of Cups (S)
Tirami Su (N)
Tiziano Trattoria (N&S)
Tommaso's (N&S)
Tony's Di Napoli (S)
Toscana (N)
Trastevere 83 (N&S)
Trattoria Alba (N&S)
Trattoria dell'Arte (N&S)
Trattoria Pesce (N&S)
Trattoria Siciliana (S)
Trattoria Trecolori (N&S)
Tre Pomodori (N&S)
Triangolo (N)
Trionfo (N&S)

Truffles (N&S)
Tuscany Grill (N)
Tutta Pasta (N&S)
Twigs (S)
Two Boots (N&S)
Urban Grill (N&S)
Va Bene (N&S)
Veniero's(N&S)
Vespa (N)
Via Oreto (S)
Vico (N&S)
Villa Berulia (N)
Villa Mosconi (N)
Vincent's (N&S)
Vinsanto (N)
Vittorio Cucina (N&S)
Vivolo (N&S)
Volare (N)
Vucciria (S)
Yellowfingers (N)
Zinno (N)
Zitella (N&S)
Zucchero (N&S)

Japanese
Ah Umakatta
Avenue A
Awoki
Benihana
Chikubu
Choshi
Dojo
Dosanko
East
Fujiyama Mama
Genji
Hakata
Hamachi
Hamaya
Hasaki
Hatsuhana
Honmura An
Inagiku
Iso
Itcho
Japonica
Jo-An Japanese
Kan Pai
Kiiroi Hana
Kinoko
Kodama
Kurumazushi
Lenge
Marumi
Menchanko-tei
Meriken
Mitsukoshi
Nippon
Nobu
Omen
Sakura of Japan
Sapporo East
Seryna
Shabu Tatsu
Shinbashi-an

Shin's
Shinwa
Sushiden
Sushihatsu
Sushisay
Sushi Zen
Takahachi
Take-Sushi
Tan Go
Taste of Tokyo
Tatany
Tea Box
Ten Kai
Yamaguchi
Yuka
Zutto

Jewish
Barney Greengrass
Cafe Andrusha
Ess-a-Bagel*
Fine & Schapiro*
Galil*
Katz's Deli
Levana*
Medici 56*
N.Y. Deli
Pastrami King*
Rasputin
Sammy's
Second Ave. Deli*
Stage Deli
Tevere 84*
3rd Ave. Deli
Trastevere 83*
Triplets
Va Bene*
Village Crown*
(*Kosher)

Korean
Dok Suni
Kang Suh
Kom Tang Soot Bul
Kum Gang San
Woo Chon
Woo Lae Oak

Lebanese
Al Bustan
Baalbek
Byblos
Cedars Lebanon
L'Auberge
Tripoli

Malaysian
Ipoh Garden Malay.
Franklin Station
Malaysia/Indonesia
Three Degrees N.

Mediterranean
Arté
Cafe Centro
Cafe Crocodile
Cafe Greco

Casa La Femme
Coming Or Going
Dish
Gus' Place
Martini's
Matthew's
Paradis Barcelona
Park Avalon
Picholine
Pó
Provence
Quisisana
San Martin's
Savoy
Soleil
Spartina
Sun Cafe
Twigs
Village Crown

Mexican/Tex-Mex
Aggie's
Armadillo Club
Arriba Arriba
Automatic Slim's
Benny's Burritos
Bertha's Burritos
Blue Moon Mexican
Bright Food Shop
Burritoville
Calif. Burrito Co.
Cantina
Cottonwood Cafe
Cowgirl Hall
El Parador Cafe
El Rio Grande
El Teddy's
Fiesta Mexicana
Flying Burrito
Fresco Tortilla
Gonzalez Y Gonz.
Harry's Burritos
Juanita's
Lucy's Surfers
Lupe's East L.A.
Mary Ann's
Mesa Verde
Mi Cocina
Orig. Cal. Taqueria
Panchitos
Passport
Pedro Paramo
Rancho Mexican
Rocking Horse
Rosa Mexicano
Samalita's
Santa Fe
Tacomadre
Taco Taco
Taq. de Mexico
Tequila Sunrise
Tortilla Flats
Violeta's Mexican
Zarela

Middle Eastern
Al Bustan
Amir's Falafel
Baalbek
Beit Eddine
Byblos
Cedars Lebanon
Cleopatra's
Divan Kebab Hse.
Eden Rock
Galil
Khan Restaurant
L'Auberge
Marti Kebab
Moustache
Persepolis
Sahara East
Tripoli
Village Crown

Moroccan
Andalousia
Lotfi's Moroccan
Moroccan Star

Omelets
Brasserie
Elephant & Castle
Gotham City Diner
La Mère Poulard
Mme. Romaine
Sarabeth's

Pancakes
Bubby's
Googies Italian
Royal Canadian Pancake

Pastries
Au Cafe
Cafe Lalo
Caffe Biondo
Caffe Vivaldi
City Bakery
Cooper's Coffee
Ferrara
Kleine Konditorei
Les Friandises
Lipstick Cafe
Lobby Lounge
Palm Court
Pasqua Coffee
Sant Ambroeus
Veniero's

Peruvian
El Pollo
Peruvian Rest.

Pizza
Arturo's Pizzeria
Caffe Lure
California Pizza
Da Nico
Ecco-La
Figaro Pizza
Freddie & Pepper's's
Garibaldi
John's of 12th
John's Pizzeria
Mad.61
Mario's
Mezzogiorno
Paper Moon Milano
Patsy's
Patsy's Pizza/Bklyn
Patsy's Pizza/NY
Pizzapiazza
Pizzeria Uno
Sam's Rest./Pizza
Sfuzzi
Stromboli Pizza
Totonno Pizzeria
Two Boots
Vinnie's Pizza

Polish
Christine's
KK Restaurant
Little Poland
Odessa
Papa Bear
Teresa's
Veselka

Polynesian
Gauguin

Portuguese
Tasca do Porto

Roumanian
Sammy's
Triplets

Russian
Cafe Andrusha
L'Ermitage
Moscow on Hudson
National
Paradise
Petrossian
Pie, The
Rasputin
Russian Samovar
Russian Tea Room
Uncle Vanya

Sandwiches
Adoré
Between the Bread
Big Cup
Bimmy's
Caffe Reggio
Cake Bar & Cafe
Franklin Station
Garden Cafe
Hard Rock Cafe
Manganaro's
News Bar
Pasqua Coffee
Rumpelmayer's
Terramare Café

Scandinavian
Aquavit
Christer's
Snaps

Seafood
Billy's
Blue Ribbon
Brighton Grill
Brothers BBQ
Caffe Lure
Captain's Table
Charlton's
City Crab
Claire
Cucina di Pesce
Danny's Grand
Docks Oyster Bar
Eastern Seafood
Elias Corner
Fish Restaurant
Fishin Eddie
Frutti di Mare
Gage & Tollner
Harbor Seafood
Harbour Lights
Harry's Hanover Sq.
Hosteria Fiorella
Hurricane Island
Jade Palace
Jane St. Seafood
King Crab
La Bouillabaisse
Le Bernardin
Le Pescadou
Lobster Box
Malaga
Manhattan Ocean
Marina Cafe
Moran's
Oceana
101 Seafood
Oriental Pearl
Oyster Bar
Paris Cafe
Pier 25A
Pisces
Plaza Oyster Bar
Roebling's
Seafood Palace
SeaGrill
Sequoia
Sloppy Louie's
Snaps
Steamers Landing
Stella del Mare
Trattoria Pesce
Tropica
Water Club
Wilkinson's
Yankee Clipper

South American
Argentine Pavilion
Boca Chica
Floridita
La Caridad
Mambo Grill
Patría
Pomaire

Southern/Soul
Acme Bar & Grill
Brothers BBQ
B. Smith's
Cafe Beulah
Copeland's
Cotton Club
Cottonwood Cafe
Emily's
Great Jones Cafe
Honeysuckle
Jamaican Hot Pot
Jezebel
Kwanzaa
Live Bait
Ludlow St. Cafe
Memphis
Mo' Better
Perks
Pink Tea Cup
Ruby's River
Shark Bar
Soul Fixins'
Sylvia's
Tennessee Mtn.
Toukie's
Virgil's BBQ

Southwestern
Albuq. Eats
Arizona 206
Automatic Slim's
Canyon Road
Charlotte
Cottonwood Cafe
Cowgirl Hall
Mesa Grill
Mesa Verde
Miracle Grill
Mission Grill
Mustang Grill
Santa Fe
Zuni
Bright Food Shop

Spanish
Ballroom
Bolo
Cafe Español
Castillo de Jagua
El Charro
El Faro
El Pote Español
El Quijote
El Rincon España
La Taza de Oro
Malaga
Mesa de España
Ñ 33 Crosby Bar
Paradis Barcelona
Rio Mar
San Martin's
Sevilla
Solera

Steakhouses
Assembly
Ben Benson's
Billy's
Charlton's
Christ Cella
Christo's Stkhse.
Cité
Embers
Frankie & Johnnie's
Frank's
Gallagher's
Harry's Hanover Sq.
Keens Chophse.
Knickerbocker
Les Halles
Manhattan Plaza
Morton's Chicago
Oak Room & Bar
Old Homestead
Opus II
Palm
Palm Too
Pen & Pencil
Peter Luger
Pietro's
Post House
Ruth's Chris
Smith & Wollensky
Sparks
Steak Frites
Wally's & Joseph's
Wollensky's Grill
W. 63rd St. Stkhse.

Swiss
La Fondue
Roettelle A.G.
Swiss Inn

Tapas
Ballroom
Ñ 33 Crosby Bar
Solera
Sun Cafe
Tasca do Porto

Thai
Bangkok Cuisine
Bangkok House
Boonthai
Danny's Grand
Gingertoon
Ginger Ty
Jai Ya Thai
Kin Khao
Mueng Thai
Pongsri Thai

Puket
Regional Thai
Royal Siam
Sala Thai
Sawadee Thai
Seeda Thai
Shaliga Thai
Siam Cuisine
Siam Inn
Sukhothai West
Thai Chef
Thai House Cafe
Thailand Rest.
Thai Orchid
Thai Taste
Vong

Tibetan
Tibetan Kitchen
Tibetan Rest.
Tibet Shambala

Turkish
Istanbul Cuisine
Marti Kebab
Turkish Cuisine
Turkish Kitchen
Uskudar

Ukrainian
Kiev
Odessa
Veselka

Vegetarian
(Most Chinese, Indian
and Thai restaurants)
Angelica Kitchen
Apple Restaurant
Bachué Café
Great Am. Health
Health Pub
Life Cafe
Nosmo King
Souen
Spring St. Natural
Symposium
Whole Wheat
Zen Palate
Zucchini

Vietnamese
Cuisine de Saigon
Le Colonial
New Viet Huong
Nha Trang
Pho Pasteur
Saigon House

NEIGHBORHOOD LOCATIONS

East 80s & Up
(East of Fifth Avenue)
Atomic Wings
Azzurro
Barking Dog
Bella Donna
Big Sur
Bistro du Nord
Burritoville
Busby's
Cafe Andrusha
Cafe Metairie
Cafe Trevi
Caffe Grazie
Calif. Burrito Co.
Carino
Carnegie Hill Cafe
Casalone
Chef Ho's
Country Club
Dakota Bar/Grill
Demarchelier
Demi
Divino
East
E.A.T.
Ecco-La
Elaine's
Elio's
El Pollo
Emily's
Erminia
Estia
Etats-Unis
Firenze
1st Wok
Galil
Girasole
Gotham City Diner
Heidelberg
Island
Istanbul Cuisine
Jackson Hole
King's Carriage
Kleine Konditorei
La Collina
La Folie
Le Boeuf ala Mode
Lenge
Le Refuge
Mambo Grill
Mazzei
Merenda
Mocca Hungarian
Moscow on Hudson
Mustang Grill
Nicola's
Orleans
Ottomanelli's
Our Place
Paola's
Papaya King

Parioli Romanis.
Patsy's Pizza/NY
Perks
Piccolo Pomodoro
Pie, The
Pig Heaven
Pinocchio
Pizzeria Uno
Primavera
Privé
Rao's
Ruby's River
Ruppert's
Sala Thai
Samalita's
Sarabeth's
Saranac
Seattle Bean Co.
Sirabella's
Sistina
Starbucks
Szechuan Hunan
Table d'Hôte
Taco Taco
Tang Tang
Tevere 84
Three Guys
Tirami Su
Tony's Di Napoli
Trastevere 83
Triangolo
Urban Grill
Va Bene
Vespa
Viand
Vico
Vinsanto
Wilkinson's
Yuka
Yura
Zacki's PBQ

East 70s
(East of Fifth Avenue)
Afghan Kebab Hse.
Annie Beneau
Antico Caffee
Atomic Wings
Baalbek
Bangkok House
Bar and Books
Baraonda
Basco
Beach Cafe
Bella Donna
Blue Moon Mexican
Boathouse Cafe
Boonthai
Brighton Grill
Brother Jimmy's
Burritoville
Cafe Crocodile
Cafe Greco

Café Word of Mouth
Caffe Buon Gusto
Calif. Burrito Co.
Campagnola
Canyon Road
Carlyle
Churchill's
Coconut Grill
Coco Pazzo
Dallas BBQ
Daniel
Dolcetto
Due
EJ's Luncheonette
Figaro Pizza
Finnegan's Wake
1st Wok
Googies
Hi-Life Bar/Grill
Hulot's
Hunan Balcony
Hunters
Hurricane Island
Il Monello
Itcho
J.G. Melon
Jim McMullen
Juanita's
Kan Pai
Les Friandises
Letizia
Little Club
Loui Loui
Luke's Bar/Grill
Lusardi's
Madison Ave. Cafe
Malaga
Mark's
Mary Ann's
Mezzaluna
Mortimer's
Mo's Caribbean
Natalino
Nino's
Ottomanelli's
Pamir
Parma
Persepolis
Petaluma
Pomodori
Portico
Quatorze Bis
Quisisana
Red Tulip
Sant Ambroeus
Sarabeth's
Sette Mezzo
Shabu Tatsu
Shelby
Siam Cuisine
Soup Burg
Starbucks
Szechuan Hunan
Szechuan Kitchen

Tang Tang
Tavola
Thai Chef
Three Guys
Trilogy Bar/Grill
Trois Jean
Uskudar
Viand
Vivolo
Voulez-Vous
Zucchero
Zucchini

East 60s
(East of Fifth Avenue)
Angel's
Arcadia
Arizona 206
Asia
Aureole
Brio
Burger Heaven
Cafe Nosidam
Cafe Pierre
Capriccio
Chicken Chef
China Fun
Chock Full o' Nuts
Contrapunto
Corrado
East
East River Cafe
Empire Szechuan
Evergreen Cafe
Ferrier
Gino
Hosteria Fiorella
Il Vagabondo
Jackson Hole
John's Pizzeria
Jo Jo
La Goulue
L'Ardoise
L'Auberge
Le Bilboquet
Le Bistrot
Le Cirque
Le Comptoir
Le Pistou
Le Regence
Le Relais
Le Taxi
Le Veau d'Or
Mad.61
Manhattan Plaza
Marti Kebab
Matthew's
Mediterraneo
Mme. Romaine
Mulholland Drive
Nanni Il Valletto
Nello
Ottomanelli's
Park Ave. Cafe
Polo

Post House
Primola
Regency
Right Bank
Sasso
Scalinatella
Sel et Poivre
Serendipity 3
7th Regiment Mess
Sign of the Dove
Soleil
Starbucks
Sushihatsu
Terramare Café
T.G.I. Friday's
Toscana
Viand
Via Oreto
Yellowfingers

East 50s
(East of Fifth Avenue)
Adrienne
Akbar
Al Bustan
Amarcord
Anche Vivolo
Aria
Bar and Books
Beijing Duck Hse.
Benihana
Between the Bread
Bice
Bill Hong's
Bill's Gay 90's
Billy's
Brasserie
Broadway Diner
Bruce Ho's
Bruno Ristorante
Burger Heaven
Cafe du Pont
Cafe Nicholson
Cafe S.F.A.
Caviarteria
Charlton's
Cinquanta
City Bakery
Clarke's, P.J.
Coming Or Going
Court of 3 Sisters
Dawat
DeGrezia
Dosanko
Ess-a-Bagel
Felidia
57, 57
First on 59th
Four Seasons
Fresco
Fu's
Gauguin
Giambelli
Girafe
Great Am. Health

Harry Cipriani
Houlihan's
Il Menestrello
Il Nido
Il Vigneto
I Tre Merli
La Cote Basque
La Grenouille
La Mangeoire
La Mediterranée
La Mère Poulard
Le Chantilly
Le Colonial
L'Entrecote
Leopard
Le Perigord
Lespinasse
Les Sans Culottes
Le Train Bleu
Lexington Grill
Lipizzana
Lipstick Cafe
Lobby Lounge
Lutèce
March
Mayfair
Metropolitan Cafe
Mitsukoshi
Monkey Bar
Montebello
Mr. Chow
Neary's
News Bar
Nippon
Oceana
Opus II
Oscar's
Ottomanelli's
Pamir
Paper Moon Milano
Paradis Barcelona
Pasqua Coffee
Pasta Presto
Pescatore
Prime Burger
Puket
Raffaele
Reidy's
Rosa Mexicano
Royal Canadian
San Pietro
Seryna
Shanghai Manor
Shinwa
Shun Lee Palace
Small Cafe
Solera
Sorelle
Soup Burg
Starbucks
Sushisay
Tang Tang
Tatou
Tea Box

T.G.I. Friday's
Thai Orchid
Tatany
Top of the Sixes
Townhouse
Trattoria Trecolori
Tse Yang
Truffles
Vong
Wylie's Ribs
Zarela

East 40s
(East of Fifth Avenue)
Ambassador Grill
Annabelle
Arcimboldo
Awoki
Beer Bar
Beit Eddine
Bloom's Deli
Box Tree
Bull & Bear
Burger Heaven
Cafe Centro
Cafe de Paris
Captain's Table
Chiam
Chikubu
Chin Chin
Chock Full o' Nuts
Christ Cella
Christo's Stkhse.
Cucina & Co.
Diwan Grill
Docks Oyster Bar
Dolce
Dosanko
East
Fortune
Grifone
Hamaya
Hatsuhana
Houlihan's
Inagiku
J. Sung Dynasty
Mee Noodle Shop
Menchanko-tei
Morton's Chicago
Nanni's
Nusantara
O'Casey's
Ottomanelli's
Oyster Bar
Palm
Palm Too
Pasqua Coffee
Peacock Alley
Peking Park
Pen & Pencil
Phoenix Garden
Pietro's
Rusty Staub's
San Giusto
San Martin's

Shaliga Thai
Shanghai 1933
Shinbashi-an
Sichuan Palace
Smith & Wollensky
Snaps
Sparks
Sushiden
Take-Sushi
Tequila Sunrise
T.G.I. Friday's
Tropica
Wollensky's Grill
Zephyr Grill

West 80s & Up
(West of Fifth Avenue)
Amir's Falafel
Amsterdam's
Armadillo Club
Arriba Arriba
Barnes & Noble
Barney Greengrass
Bella Luna
Birdland
Boulevard
Burritoville
Cafe Con Leche
Cafe Lalo
Cafe St. John
Carmine's
Cleopatra's
Cooper's Coffee
Copeland's
Cotton Club
Dish
Docks Oyster Bar
Eden Rock
EJ's Luncheonette
Empire Szechuan
Fiesta Mexicana
Fish Restaurant
Floridita
Fujiyama Mama
Good Enough to Eat
Harriet's Kitchen
Hi-Life Bar/Grill
Hunan Balcony
Il Nostro
Indian Cafe
Indian Oven
Isola
Jackson Hole
Jamaican Hot Pot
Jo-An Japanese
107 West
Khan Restaurant
La Mirabelle
Les Routiers
Louie's Westside
Lucy's Surfers
Main Street
Mary Ann's
Meridiana
Mo' Better

Ollie's
Pandit
Patzo
Pizzeria Uno
Poiret
Popover Cafe
Presto's
Rancho Mexican
Royal Canadian
Sakura of Japan
Sarabeth's
Silk Road Palace
Starbucks
Sylvia's
Symposium
Taci Int'l
Tacomadre
Teachers Too
Terrace
Tibet Shambala
Well's
Zula

West 70s
(West of Fifth Avenue)
Atomic Wings
Baci
Bertha's Burritos
Bimini Twist
Brothers BBQ
Cafe Luxembourg
Cantina
Chaz & Wilson
China Fun
Ciccio & Tony's
Cooper's Coffee
Dallas BBQ
Eastern Seafood
Empire Szechuan
Fine & Schapiro
Fishin Eddie
Freddie & Pepper's's
Gray's Papaya
Harry's Burritos
Isabella's
Jerry's
Josie's
Kinoko
La Caridad
La Chandelle
Lee Mazzilli's
Mackinac
Memphis
Mingala Burmese
Mughlai
Museum Cafe
Natalino
Pappardella
Perretti Indian
Phoebe's
Pudgie's
Restaurant 222
Ruppert's
Sambuca
Sawadee Thai

Scaletta
Shark Bar
Westside Brewing
Vinnie's Pizza

West 60s
(West of Fifth Avenue)
Cafe des Artistes
Conservatory
Cooper's Coffee
Empire Szechuan
Federico's
Fiorello's Roman
Gabriel's
Honeysuckle
Houlihan's
Iridium
John's Pizzeria
Josephina
La Boite en Bois
Lenge
Levana
Lincoln Tavern
O'Neals'
Picholine
Saloon
Santa Fe
Sfuzzi
Shun Lee Cafe
Shun Lee West
Tacomadre
Tavern on Green
Vince & Eddie's
World Cafe
W. 63rd St. Stkhse.

West 50s
(West of Fifth Avenue)
Afghan Kebab Hse.
Allegria
American Festival
Aperitivo
Aquavit
Arriba Arriba
Assembly
Au Cafe
Bangkok Cuisine
Bello
Ben Benson's
Benihana
Bistro 790
Bombay Palace
Borsalino
BOS
Broadway Diner
Cafe Botanica
Cafe de la Paix
Cafe des Sports
Cafe Europa
Caffe Cielo
Calif. Burrito Co.
Carnegie Deli
Castellano
Cesarina
Chantal Café
Charley O's

Chez Napoleon
China Grill
Christer's
Ciao Europa
Cité
Cité Grille
Corrado
Darbar
Da Tommaso
East
Edwardian Room
Ellen's Stardust
Fantino
Gallagher's
Garden Cafe
Giovanni
Great Am. Health
Halcyon
Hard Rock Cafe
Harley Davidson
Houlihan's
Il Tinello
India Pavilion
Jean Lafitte
JUdson Grill
Kabul Cafe
Keewah Yen
Kiiroi Hana
King Crab
Kurumazushi
La Bonne Soupe
La Caravelle
La Fondue
Le Bar Bat
Le Bernardin
Le Biarritz
Le Bouchon
Le Quercy
L'Ermitage
La Scala
Les Celebrités
Les Pyrenees
Lucky's Bar/Grill
Mangia e Bevi
Manhattan Ocean
Martini's
Medici 56
Mee Noodle Shop
Menchanko-tei
Michael's
Mickey Mantle's
Moonrock Diner
Nirvana
N.Y. Deli
Oak Room/Bar
Palio
Palm Court
Pasqua Coffee
Pasta Lovers
Patsy's
Petrossian
Planet Hollywood
Plaza Oyster Bar
Raphael

Remi
René Pujol
Rice & Beans
Rosie O'Grady's
Rumpelmayer's
Russian Samovar
Russian Tea Room
Ruth's Chris
San Domenico
Sawadee Thai
Seeda Thai
Sette MoMA
Shin's
Siam Inn
Stage Deli
Symphony Cafe
Tan Go
Tang Pavilion
Tea Den
Ten Kai
Tequila Sunrise
T.G.I. Friday's
Tout Va Bien
Trattoria dell'Arte
"21" Club
Trionfo
Uncle Vanya
Uncle Nick's
Urban Grill
Victor's Cafe
Westside Cafe
Westside Cottage
Wolf's Deli

West 40s
(West of Fifth Avenue,
including Theater District)
Afghan Kebab Hse.
Algonquin Hotel
Argentine Pavilion
Avanti
Bali Burma
Barbetta
Becco
Broadway Grill
B. Smith's
Cabana Carioca
Cafe Europa
Cafe Un Deux Trois
Carmine's
Century Cafe
Charley O's
Charlotte
Chez Josephine
Da Rosina
Danny's Grand
Dish of Salt
Edison Cafe
44
44 Southwest
Frankie & Johnnie's
Fresco Tortilla
Hakata
Hamburger Harry's's
Houlihan's

Hourglass Tavern
Ipanema
Island Spice
Jewel of India
Jezebel
Joe Allen
Kodama
Lotfi's Moroccan
Landmark Tavern
Langan's
La Primavera
La Reserve
La Rivista
Lattanzi
La Vieille Auberge
Le Beaujolais
Le Madeleine
Le Max
Le Rivage
New World Grill
Manhattan Plaza
Marlowe
Mezzanine
Mike's Bar/Grill
Pomaire
Olive Garden
Ollie's
Orso
Osteria al Doge
Peruvian Rest.
Pierre au Tunnel
Revolution
Pongsri Thai
Rachel's
Rainbow Room
Shaan
Sardi's
SeaGrill
Sofia's
Stellina
Sukhothai West
Supper Club
Sushi Zen
Swiss Inn
Tequila Sunrise
Tony Roma's
Trattoria Trecolori
Turkish Cuisine
Virgil's BBQ
View
Wally's & Joseph's
West Bank Cafe
Westside Cottage
Westway Diner
Woo Lae Oak
World Yacht
Yamaguchi
Zen Palate
Zuni

Murray Hill
(40th to 30th Sts.,
East of Fifth Ave.)
Back Porch
Bienvenue

Bistro Cafe
Bora
Byblos
Calif. Burrito Co.
Caterina's
Cedars Lebanon
Courtyard Cafe
East
El Charro
El Parador Cafe
El Pote Español
El Rio Grande
Fino
Fiori
Fresco Tortilla
H.S.F.
Houlihan's
Jackson Hole
La Maison Japon.
Le Grenadin
Marchi's
Morgan Cafe
Nicola Paone
Pasta Presto
Pasticcio
Russell's
Sakura of Japan
Stella del Mare
Tequila Sunrise
Tibetan Kitchen
Tony Roma's
Trattoria Alba
Villa Berulia
Water Club

Gramercy Park
(30th to 14th Sts.,
East of Fifth Ave.)
Abby
Albuq. Eats
Alva
America
An American Place
Bamiyan
Bolo
Cafe Beulah
Canastel's
Campagna
Chat 'n' Chew
Choshi
Christine's
Chutney Mary
City Bakery
City Crab
Coffee Shop
C.T.
East
Empire Szechuan
Ess-a-Bagel
Friend of Farmer
Gramercy Tavern
Gramercy Watering
Hamachi
Health Pub
Jai Ya Thai

Kan Pai
La Boulangere
La Colombe d'Or
Lamarca
La Petite Auberge
La Voce
Les Halles
L'Incontro
Live Bait
Marti Kebab
Mayrose
Maurya
Mavalli Palace
Mesa de España
Mesa Grill
Metronome
Metropolis Cafe
Moreno
Old Town Bar
Ottomanelli's
Park Avalon
Papa Bear
Park Ave. Country
Park Bistro
Paul & Jimmy's
Petes' Place
Pete's Tavern
Pigalle
Rascals
Rolf's
Royal Canadian
Sal Anthony's
Silk Restaurant
Steak Frites
Patría
Sonia Rose
Sumptuary
Tatany
Tempo
3rd Ave. Deli
Tien Fu
Tina's
Trattoria Siciliana
Tre Pomodori
Turkish Kitchen
Union Square Cafe
Verbena
Zen Palate

Garment District – Chelsea
(40th to 14th Sts.,
West of Fifth Ave.)
Alley's End
Amir's Falafel
Appetito
Bachué Café
Ballroom
Barnes & Noble
Basta Pasta
Bendix Diner
Benvenuti
Big Cup
Biricchino
Blu Restaurant
Blue Moon Mexican

Book-Friends Cafe
Bright Food Shop
Cafe Baci
Caffe Bondí
Cajun
Calif. Burrito Co.
Cal's
Chantale's Cajun
Chelsea Clinton
Chelsea Commons
Chelsea Grill
Chelsea Trattoria
City Grill
Claire
Cupcake Cafe
Don Giovanni
Flight 151
Flowers
Da Umberto
Eighteenth & 8th
El Quijote
Empire Diner
Follonico
Food Bar
Fresco Tortilla
Gascogne
Grappino
Houlihan's
Hunan Fifth Ave.
Island Spice
Kaffeehaus
Kang Suh
Keens
Kom Tang Soot Bul
L'Acajou
La Lunchonette
La Taza de Oro
Le Madri
Leo's Famous
Lofland's N.Y.
Lola
Luma
Manganaro's
Man Ray
Mary Ann's
Merchants N.Y.
Meriken
Moran's
News Bar
Rib'n & Blues
Old Homestead
Periyali
Pudgie's
Regional Thai
Rocking Horse
Royal Siam
Soul Fixins'
Sunny East
Supreme Macaroni
Tequila Sunrise
T.G.I. Friday's
Tiziano Trattoria
T.S. Ma
Twigs

Vernon's Jerk
Viceroy
Woo Chon
Zip City

Greenwich Village
(14th to Houston Sts.,
West of 5th Ave.)
Andalousia
Anglers & Writers
Apple Restaurant
Area Code Cafe
Arlecchino
Artepasta
Atomic Wings
Au Bon Coin
Automatic Slim's
Au Troquet
Bar and Books
Bar Pitti
Bar Six
Benny's Burritos
Black Sheep
Boxers
Burritoville
Cafe de Bruxelles
Cafe Español
Cafe Loup
Cafe Melville
Caffe Rafaella
Caffe Reggio
Caffe Rosso
Calif. Burrito Co.
Caribe
Casa Di Pre
Cent'Anni
Chez Brigitte
Chez Jacqueline
Chez Ma Tante
Chez Michallet
Chumley's
Cornelia St. Cafe
Corner Bistro
Cottonwood Cafe
Cowgirl Hall
C3
Cucina De Fontana
Cucina Stagionale
Cuisine de Saigon
Da Silvano
Divan Kebab Hse.
Dix et Sept
Dojo
Ecco L'Italia
El Charro
Elephant & Castle
El Faro
Empire Szechuan
Est! Est! Est!
Five Oaks
Florent
Flying Burrito
Frank's
French Roast Cafe
Fresch

Garibaldi
Gingertoon
Grand Ticino
Grange Hall
Gray's Papaya
Grove
Grove St. Cafe
Gus' Place
Harry's Burritos
Harvest
Home
Il Mulino
Il Ponte Vecchio
India Pavilion
Jane St. Seafood
Jekyll & Hyde
John's Pizzeria
Kiss
La Boheme
La Dolce Vita
La Focaccia
La Metairie
La Ripaille
L'Auberge du Midi
Le Figaro
Les Deux Gamins
Lion's Head
Mappamondo
Markham
Marnie's Noodle
Marylou's
Mary's
Mesa Verde
Mi Cocina
Minetta Tavern
Mitali East/West
Moustache
Nadine's
New Deal
One If By Land
Orbit
Orig. Cal. Taqueria
Ottomanelli's
Panchitos
Paris Commune
Pasta Presto
Piccolo Angolo
Pink Tea Cup
Pizzeria Uno
Pó
Red Lion
Rio Mar
Rocco
Rosolio
Sazerac House
Sevilla
Shopsin's
Tanti Baci Cafe
Taq. de Mexico
Tartine
Taste of Tokyo
Thomas Scott's
Tortilla Flats
Trattoria Pesce

Trompe l'Oeil
Tutta Pasta
Universal Grill
Village Atelier
Villa Mosconi
Violeta's Mexican
Vittorio Cucina
Volare
White Horse Tavern
Whole Wheat
Ye Waverly
Zinno

Central Village/NoHo
(14th to Houston Sts.,
Fifth to Third Aves.)
Acme Bar & Grill
Adoré
Aggie's
Angelika Film Ctr.
Arté
Arturo's Pizzeria
Bayamo
Bimmy's
Briscola
Cafe Cento Sette
Caffe Lure
Caffe Vivaldi
Cake Bar & Cafe
California Pizza Oven
Dallas BBQ
Danal
El Rincon España
Ennio & Michael
Fez
Gonzalez y Gonz.
Gotham Bar/Grill
Great Jones Cafe
Il Cantinori
Indochine
Japonica
Knickerbocker
L'Udo
Louisiana Commun.
Marion's Cont.
Marumi
9 Jones Street
NoHo Star
Osso Buco
Pizzapiazza
Rose Cafe
Souen
Temple Bar
Time Cafe
Toast
Tutta Pasta

East Village
(14th to Houston Sts.,
East of Third Ave.)
Anarchy Cafe
Angelica Kitchen
Avenue A
Baby Jake's
Benny's Burritos

Boca Chica
Brunetta's
Burritoville
Cafe Tabac
Casanis
Castillo de Jagua
Christine's
Cloister Cafe
Col Legno
Cucina di Pesce
Dallas BBQ
Delia's
Dojo
Dok Suni
First
Frutti di Mare
Gandhi
Genji
Harry's Burritos
Hasaki
Haveli
In Padella
Iso
John's of 12th
Jules
Khyber Pass
Kiev
KK Restaurant
Lanza
La Spaghetteria
La Strada 2
Levee
Life Cafe
Little Poland
Lucky Cheng's
McSorley's
Mee Noodle Shop
Mingala Burmese
Miracle Grill
Mitali East/West
9
Odessa
103 NYC
Orologio
Orson's
Passage to India
Passport
Pedro Paramo
Pisces
Pizzeria Uno
Roettelle A.G.
Rose of India
Sahara East
Sapporo East
Second Ave. Deli
Shabu Tatsu
Stingy Lulu's
Stromboli Pizza
Sugar Reef
Sun Cafe
Takahachi
Telephone Bar
Teresa's
Three of Cups

Tibetan Rest.
Two Boots
Veniero's
Veselka
Village Crown
Windows on India
Zitella

Lower East Side
(Houston to Canal Sts.,
East of Bowery)
Katz's Deli
Ludlow St. Cafe
Sammy's

SoHo – Little Italy
(Houston to Canal Sts.,
West of Bowery)
Ahnell
Ah Umakatta
Alison
Amici Miei
Angelo's
Ballato's
Baluchi's
Barolo
Bell Caffe
Benito I
Benito II
Blue Ribbon
Boom
Broome Street Bar
Brothers BBQ
Caffe Biondo
Caffe di Nonni
Can
Casa La Femme
Cascabel
Cub Room
Cupping Room Cafe
Da Nico
Diva
Ear Inn
Fanelli
Felix
Ferrara
5 & 10
Frontière
Grotta Azzurra
Honmura An
Il Corallo
Il Cortile
I Tre Merli
Jean Claude
Jerry's
Jour et Nuit
Kaptain Banana
Kelley & Ping
Kin Khao
Kitchen Club
Kwanzaa
La Dolce Vita
La Jumelle
La Mela
L'Ecole
Le Pescadou

Le Streghe
Lucky Strike
Lupe's East L.A.
Manhattan Bistro
Manhattan Brewing
Match
Mezzogiorno
Mission Grill
News Bar
Nick & Eddie
Ñ 33 Crosby Bar
Omen
Paolucci's
Patrissy's
Pellegrino
Pietro & Vanessa
Provence
Raoul's
Savoy
SoHo Kitchen
Souen
S.P.Q.R.
Spring St. Natural
Spring St. Rest.
Taormina
Tasca do Porto
Tennessee Mtn.
Three Degrees N.
Triplets
T Salon
Vincent's
Vucciria
Zöe

Chinatown
Beijing Duck Hse.
Big Wong
Bo Ky
Canton
Chao Chow*
Golden Unicorn
Great Shanghai
Hong Fat
Hong Shoon
Hop Shing
H.S.F.
Hunan Garden
Ipoh Garden Malay.
Jing Fong
Kam Chueh
Malaysia/Indonesia
Mandarin Court
Mueng Thai
New Hong Kong City
New Viet Huong
Nha Trang
Nice Restaurant
Oriental Garden
Oriental Pearl
Pho Pasteur
Road to Mandalay
Saigon House
Seafood Palace
Tai Hong Lau
Thailand Rest.

Triple Eight
20 Mott Street
Wing Wong
Wong Kee

TriBeCa – Downtown
(South of Canal Street,
including Wall St. area)
Acappella
Amer. Renaissance
Arqua
Au Mandarin
Barocco
Bouley
Bridge Cafe
Bubby's
Burritoville
Calif. Burrito Co.
Capsouto Frères
Chanterelle
Donald Sacks
Duane Park Cafe
Ecco
Edward Moran
El Teddy's
Franklin Station
Fraunces Tavern
Gianni's
Gianpalu
Gigino
Ginger Ty
Hamburger Harry's's
Harbour Lights
Harry's Hanover Sq.
Houlihan's
Hudson Grill
Hudson River Club
Il Giglio
Jack's Place
La Barca
La Tour D'Or
Le Pactole
Lucy's Surfers
Maurya
Menchanko-tei
Montrachet
Nobu
Nosmo King
Odeon
Ottomanelli's
Paris Cafe
Pasqua Coffee
Pipeline
Pizzeria Uno
Pudgie's
Riverrun
Roebling's
Rosemarie's
Salaam Bombay
Sequoia
Sfuzzi
Sloppy Louie's
Spartina
Steamers Landing
Taliesin

T.G.I. Friday's
Thai House Cafe
Toukie's
TriBeCa Grill
Two Eleven
Walker's
Yaffa Tea Room
Yankee Clipper
Zutto

BRONX
Dominick's
Il Giardinetto
Lobster Box
Mario's

BROOKLYN

Bay Ridge
Embers
Mr. Tang's
101
101 Seafood
Paradise
Tuscany Grill

Bensonhurst
Milano
Mr. Tang's
Tommaso's

Brighton Beach
National

Brooklyn Heights
Acadia Parish
Bistro 36
Gage & Tollner
Henry's End
La Bouillabaisse
Moroccan Star
Mr. Souvlaki
Orig. Cal. Taqueria
Patsy's Pizza
Queen
River Cafe
Sam's Rest./Pizza
Teresa's
Tripoli

Carroll Gardens
Ferdinando's

Cobble Hill
Caffé Carciofo

Coney Island
Mr. Tang's
Rasputin
Totonno Pizzeria

Fort Greene
New City Cafe

Graves End
Fiorentino

Kings Plaza
Kings Pl. Diner

Manhattan Beach
Harpo
Park Slope
Aunt Sonia's
Cucina
New Prospect Cafe
Orig. Cal. Taqueria
Thai Taste
Two Boots
Prospect Heights
Garden Cafe
Williamsburg
Peter Luger

QUEENS
Astoria
Elias Corner
Jackson Hole
Karyatis
Piccola Venezia
Ponticello
Roumeli Taverna
Telly's Taverna
Bayside
Ambrosia Tavern
Boston Chicken
Pier 25A
Corona
Park Side
Elmhurst
Georgia Dinner
Harbor Seaford

Jai Ya Thai
La Fusta
Flushing
Dragon Village
Jade Palace
Joe's Shanghai
Kum Gang San
Old Roma
Forest Hills
Quartiere
Teresa's
Jackson Heights
Jackson Hts. Diner
La Portena
Kew Gardens
Pastrami King
Long Island City
Pearson's BBQ
Water's Edge
Rego Park
Goody's
Sunnyside
Dazies
Whitestone
Cooking With Jazz
STATEN ISLAND
Lum Chin
Marina Cafe
Old Bermuda Inn

SPECIAL FEATURES AND APPEALS

Breakfast
(All hotels and the following standouts)
Aggie's
Ambassador Grill
American Festival
Anglers & Writers
Bendix Diner
Big Cup
Brasserie
Caffe Bondí
Cake Bar & Cafe
Chock Full o' Nuts
City Bakery
Coming Or Going
Conservatory
Cupcake Cafe
Cupping Room Cafe
E.A.T.
Edwardian Room
Eighteenth & 8th
EJ's Luncheonette
Elephant & Castle
Ellen's Stardust
Empire Diner
Fraunces Tavern
Friend of Farmer
Good Enough to Eat
Kiev
Louie's Westside
Madison Ave. Cafe
Michael's
NoHo Star
Odessa
Pink Tea Cup
Popover Cafe
Royal Canadian
Sarabeth's
Shopsin's
Viand

Brunch
(Best of many)
Abby
Anglers & Writers
Baby Jake's
Bar Six
Barney Greengrass
Bell Caffe
Black Sheep
Bolo
Brighton Grill
Bubby's
Cafe Botanica
Cafe Con Leche
Cafe des Artistes
Cafe Luxembourg
Cafe St. John
Capsouto Frères
Carlyle
Chelsea Commons
Claire
Coconut Grill

Cornelia St. Cafe
Cottonwood Cafe
C3
Cupcake Cafe
Cupping Room Cafe
Due
EJ's Luncheonette
Elephant & Castle
Empire Diner
Food Bar
44
Friend of Farmer
Gage & Tollner
Good Enough to Eat
Grove
Gus' Place
Hudson River Club
Isabella's
Island
Jerry's
Jim McMullen
Kaffeehaus
Langan's
Le Regence
Lincoln Tavern
Ludlow St. Cafe
Main Street
Manhattan Plaza
Mark's
Match
Matthew's
Metropolis Cafe
Metropolitan Cafe
Michael's
NoHo Star
Odeon
Park Avalon
Park Ave. Cafe
Petaluma
Petrossian
Phoebe's
River Cafe
Riverrun
Sarabeth's
Serendipity 3
Sign of the Dove
Sylvia's
Symphony Cafe
Table d'Hôte
Tavern on Green
Thomas Scott's
Time Cafe
TriBeCa Grill
Trilogy Bar/Grill
T Salon
Verbena
Vince & Eddie's
Water Club
Zöe

Buffet Served
Adrienne
Ambassador Grill

196

Beit Eddine
Bombay Palace
Carlyle
Cedars Lebanon
Copeland's
Darbar
Diwan Grill
Halcyon
Jewel of India
Kinoko
L'Auberge
Le Pactole
Maurya
Mitali East/West
Palm Court
Peacock Alley
Polo
Russell's
Shaan
Shark Bar
Thai Orchid
Trionfo
Water Club
World Yacht

BYO
Afghan Kebab Hse.
Andalousia
Bella Donna
Bo Ky
Bright Food Shop
Cafe Europa
Chantale's Cajun
Cucina Stagionale
Eighteenth & 8th
Franklin Station
Harbor Seafood
Istanbul Cuisine
Jackson Hts. Diner
Jamaican Hot Pot
Kam Chueh
Khan Restaurant
Kiev
La Bouillabaisse
La Boulangere
La Chandelle
Lamarca
Moroccan Star
Moustache
Oriental Garden
Orig. Cal. Taqueria
Papa Bear
Phoenix Garden
Pho Pasteur
Pie, The
Pinocchio
Sahara East
Szechuan Kitchen
Taco Taco
Tanti Baci Cafe
Taq. de Mexico
Tibetan Kitchen
Tibetan Rest.
Tibet Shambala
Turkish Cuisine

Uncle Vanya
Zacki's PBQ
Zucchini

Coffeehouses & Desserts
(See cuisine listings of
Coffee Shops and *Pastries,*
plus the following)
Angelika Film Ctr.
Anglers & Writers
Area Code Cafe
Au Cafe
Barnes & Noble
Big Cup
Book-Friends Cafe
Cafe Cento Sette
Cafe Con Leche
Cafe Lalo
Cafe S.F.A.
Café Word of Mouth
Caffe Bondí
Caffe Via Reggio
Caffe Vivaldi
Cake Bar & Cafe
Chock Full o' Nuts
Cloister Cafe
Cooper's Coffee
Cornelia St. Cafe
Cupcake Cafe
Cupping Room Cafe
EJ's Luncheonette
Ellen's Stardust
Empire Diner
Ferrara
French Roast Cafe
Kaffeehaus
Kleine Konditorei
La Dolce Vita
Les Friandises
Lobby Lounge
News Bar
9
Palm Court
Pasqua Coffee
Rumpelmayer's
Sant Ambroeus
Sarabeth's
Seattle Bean Co.
Serendipity 3
Starbucks
Tea Box
Tea Den
T Salon
Veniero's

Dancing/Entertainment
(Check days, times and
performers for entertainment;
D = dancing)
Albuq. Eats (country/blues)
Ambassador Grill (piano)
Amer. Renaissance (piano)
Angelika Film Ctr. (jazz)
Arcimboldo (piano)
Arizona 206 (jazz)

Arturo's Pizzeria (jazz)
Assembly (piano)
Automatic Slim's (blues)
Baalbek (belly dancer)
Ballroom (cabaret)
Barbetta (piano/band)
Bayamo (mambo band)
Bell Caffe (varies)
Bill's Gay 90's (cabaret)
Birdland (jazz)
Boathouse Cafe (jazz)
Boca Chica (band)
Book-Friends Cafe (D)
Boom (bands)
Bruno Ristorante (piano)
B. Smith's (jazz/r&b)
Cafe Beulah (blues/jazz)
Cafe de Paris (piano/guitar)
Cafe Pierre (piano)
Campagnola (piano)
Carlyle (cabaret/jazz)
Carnegie Hill (jazz)
Cedars Lebanon (belly dancer)
Chez Josephine (jazz)
Cleopatra's (belly dancer)
Cloister Cafe (varies)
Coffee Shop (Brazilian)
Cornelia St. Cafe (jazz)
Cotton Club (jazz/r&b)
Cottonwood Cafe (varies)
Country Club (D/orchestra)
Court of 3 Sisters (piano)
Cupping Room Cafe (jazz)
Dakota Bar/Grill (jazz)
Danny's Grand (piano)
Dazies (piano)
Delia's (D)
Dish of Salt (piano)
Ear Inn (varies)
Ecco L'Italia (varies)
Ellen's Stardust (doo wop)
El Rincon España (guitar)
Emily's (jazz)
Empire Diner (piano)
Estia (Greek)
Fez (varies)
57, 57 (piano)
5 & 10 (jazz/r&b)
Five Oaks (piano)
Fresco (guitar)
Gage & Tollner (piano)
Garden Cafe (varies)
Gauguin (D)
Gonzalez Y Gonz. (Latin)
Harley Davidson (rock)
Honeysuckle (band)
Il Giardinetto (piano)
Iridium (jazz)
Jekyll & Hyde (theatrical)
Jezebel (piano)
J. Sung Dynasty (piano)
Jules (jazz)
Kaptain Banana (cabaret)
Karyatis (piano)

Knickerbocker (jazz)
Kwanzaa (band)
La Folie (jazz)
La Mediterranée (piano)
La Mela (guitar)
La Mère Poulard (jazz)
Le Bar Bat (band)
Le Max (piano)
L'Ermitage (piano)
Levee (band)
Lobby Lounge (piano)
Lola (varies)
Louisiana Commun. (varies)
Manhattan Brewing (band)
Mary Ann's (mariachi)
Mesa de España (guitar)
Metronome (blues/jazz)
Metropolis Cafe (jazz)
Michael's (jazz)
Milano (piano)
Mme. Romaine (piano)
Mo' Better (jazz/r&b)
Mo's Caribbean (reggae)
N (flamenco)
National (band)
New Deal (piano)
9 Jones Street (jazz)
Nino's (piano)
Nosmo King (jazz)
O'Neals' (piano)
One If By Land (piano)
Panchitos (guitar)
Paris Cafe (varies)
Park Avalon (jazz)
Perks (D)
Phoebe's (blues/jazz)
Pigalle (singer)
Rainbow Room (big band)
Rasputin (Int'l. music)
Red Tulip (band)
Regency (varies)
Rib'n & Blues (varies)
River Cafe (piano)
Roumeli Taverna (piano/guitar)
Russian Samovar (piano)
Russian Tea Room (cabaret)
Sammy's Roumanian (piano)
Sequoia (D)
7th Regiment Mess (piano)
Shark Bar (jazz/r&b)
Sign of the Dove (jazz/r&b)
Small Cafe (piano)
Stella del Mare (piano)
Sugar Reef (varies)
Supper Club (big band)
Sylvia's (jazz/r&b)
Tatou (piano/jazz)
Tavern on Green (D/jazz)
Terrace (harpist)
Tiziano Trattoria (piano)
Tommaso's (opera/piano)
Top of the Sixes (piano)
Trilogy Bar/Grill (jazz)
Triplets (varies)

Turkish Cuisine (belly dancer)
Turkish Kitchen (Turkish)
Uncle Vanya (Russian)
Victor's Cafe (piano)
Vinsanto (jazz)
Walker's (jazz)
Water Club (piano)
Water's Edge (piano)
Well's (band)
World Yacht (piano)
Yaffa Tea Room (jazz)
Ye Waverly Inn (guitar)
Zarela (Mexican)
Zephyr Grill (jazz)
Zinno (jazz)

Delivers*/Takeout

(Nearly all Asians, coffee shops, delis, diners and pasta/pizzerias deliver or do takeout; here are some interesting possibilities; D = delivery, T = takeout)
America (T)
Arqua (T)
Bice (T)
Campagna (T)
Carmine's (D)
Caviarteria (D)
Darbar (D)
Donald Sacks (D)
E.A.T. (D)
Harry's Burritos (D,T)
Hatsuhana (D)
Mad.61 (D)
Manganaro's (D)
Markham (T)
Match (D)
O'Casey's (D)
Ottomanelli's (D)
Oyster Bar (T)
Palm (T)
Petaluma (D)
Peter Luger (T)
Post House (T)
Provence (D)
Remi (D)
Russian Tea Room (T)
Sfuzzi (D,T)
Smith & Wollensky (T)
Three Guys (D)
Wilkinson's (T)
Yellowfingers (D)
(*Call to check range and charges, if any)

Dining Alone

(Other than hotels, coffee-houses, sushi bars and counter service places)
Alley's End
Alva
Asia
Between the Bread
Bloom's Deli

Brighton Grill
Cafe Botanica
Cafe S.F.A.
Carlyle
Carnegie Deli
Chez Brigitte
Chock Full o' Nuts
Christine's
Churchill's
Conservatory
Cupping Room Cafe
E.A.T.
EJ's Luncheonette
Elephant & Castle
Empire Diner
Franklin Station
Garibaldi
Gus' Place
Harley Davidson
Hatsuhana
Home
Hosteria Fiorella
Jackson Hole
Kleine Konditorei
La Boulangere
Lipstick Cafe
Mad.61
Mme. Romaine
Nobu
Piccolo Angolo
Sarabeth's
Second Ave. Deli
Sette MoMA
Stage Deli
Sushisay
Teresa's
Three Guys
T Salon
Urban Grill
Verbena
Viand
Wolf's Deli

Fireplaces

Arizona 206
Avanti
Bimini Twist
Black Sheep
Box Tree
Bruno Ristorante
Cafe Metairie
Chelsea Commons
Christer's
Churchill's
Ci Vedeamo
Cornelia St. Cafe
Cub Room
Fantino
Follonico
Friend of Farmer
Gramercy Tavern
Harbour Lights
Hunters
Jane St. Seafood
Jekyll & Hyde

Jo Jo
Jubilee
Keens Chophse.
La Boheme
La Chandelle
La Grenouille
Landmark Tavern
La Ripaille
Le Figaro
Leopard, The
Les Pyrenees
Mackinac
Marchi's
Mary's
Merchants N.Y.
Moran's
New Deal
Old Bermuda Inn
O'Neals'
One If By Land
Paolucci's
Paris Commune
Patzo
Phoebe's
Piccola Venezia
Pierre au Tunnel
Privé
René Pujol
Rosie O'Grady's
Santa Fe
Savoy
Sazerac House
7th Regiment Mess
Sign of the Dove
Sumptuary
Three of Cups
Tiziano Trattoria
"21" Club
Vittorio Cucina
Vivolo
Water Club
Water's Edge
Ye Waverly Inn

Game in Season
(The following are
recommended)
Alison
Alva
Amarcord
Ambassador Grill
Aquavit
Aureole
Barbetta
Bolo
Bouley
Campagna
Carlyle
Chanterelle
Chez Michallet
Cub Room
Daniel
Fantino
Felidia
Four Seasons

Gascogne
Giovanni
Gotham Bar/Grill
Hudson River Club
Il Mulino
Il Ponte Vecchio
Jo Jo
La Caravelle
La Cote Basque
La Grenouille
La Reserve
La Ripaille
Le Cirque
Le Perigord
Les Celebrités
Les Halles
Lutèce
Mesa Grill
Montrachet
New Deal
Park Avalon
Park Bistro
Patría
Primavera
Primola
Privé
San Domenico
Sette Mezzo
Terrace
"21" Club
Union Square Cafe

Health/Spa Menus
(Most places cook to order
to meet any dietary request;
call in advance to check; see
also Health Food, Chinese,
Indian and Thai; the following
are good bets)
Arcadia
Back Porch
Bell Caffe
Dish
Ellen's Stardust
Four Seasons
Grange Hall
Halcyon
Josephina
Josie's
Kiss
Luma
Marylou's
New World Grill
Nosmo King
Popover Cafe
Saloon
Taliesin
Time Cafe
Zephyr Grill

Hotel Dining
Algonquin Hotel, The
   Algonquin Hotel
Beekman Tower Hotel
   Zephyr Grill

Box Tree, The
  Box Tree
Cambridge Hotel
  La Mirabelle
Carlyle Hotel, The
  Carlyle
Doral Court Hotel
  Courtyard Cafe
Essex House
  Cafe Botanica
  Les Celebrités
Four Seasons Hotel
  57, 57
  Lobby Lounge
Holiday Inn Crowne Plaza
  Broadway Grill
Hotel Edison
  Edison Cafe
Hotel Lexington
  J. Sung Dynasty
Hotel Macklowe
  Charlotte
Hotel Millenium
  Taliesin
Hotel Wales
  Sarabeth's
Hyatt UN Park Plaza Hotel
  Ambassador Grill
Le Parker Meridien
  Shin's
Loews NY Hotel
  Lexington Grill
Lowell Hotel
  Post House
Mark, The
  Mark's
Marriott Marquis
  View
Mayfair Hotel
  Le Cirque
Mayflower Hotel
  Conservatory
Paramount Hotel
  Mezzanine
Peninsula Hotel
  Adrienne
Pierre Hotel, The
  Cafe Pierre
Plaza Athenee
  Le Regence
Plaza Hotel
  Edwardian Room
  Gauguin
  Oak Room & Bar
  Palm Court
  Plaza Oyster Bar
Regency Hotel
  Regency
Rihga Royal
  Halycon
Ritz-Carlton
  Fantino
Royalton Hotel
  44

Sheraton Manhattan
  Bistro 790
Sheraton Park Ave.
  Russell's
Sherry Netherland
  Harry Cipriani
St. Moritz Hotel
  Cafe de la Paix
  Rumpelmayer's
St. Regis Hotel, The
  Lespinasse
Sutton Hotel
  Small Cafe
Waldorf-Astoria, The
  Bull & Bear
  Inagiku
  Oscar's
  Peacock Alley
Westbury Hotel
  Polo

"In" Places
Alley's End
Alva
Aureole
Blue Ribbon
Bolo
Bouley
Cafe Beulah
Cafe Centro
Cafe des Artistes
Campagna
Carlyle
Casanis
Coco Pazzo
C.T.
Cub Room
Daniel
First
Flowers
Gotham Bar/Grill
Gramercy Tavern
Grange Hall
Il Mulino
Kaffeehaus
La Grenouille
Le Cirque
Le Colonial
Little Club
Mad.61
Match
Matthew's
Mesa Grill
Monkey Bar
Nobu
Park Avalon
Park Ave. Cafe
Patría
Provence
Rao's
Regency
River Cafe
TriBeCa Grill
T Salon
"21" Club

Union Square Cafe
Zitella
Zöe

Late Late – After 12:30
(All hours are AM)
Acme Bar & Grill (1)
Ahnell (1)
Albuq. Eats (1)
Allegria (2)
America (1)
Amici Miei (1)
Anarchy Cafe (4)
Andalousia (1)
Arlecchino (1)
Armadillo Club (1)
Arriba Arriba (1)
Arturo's Pizzeria (2)
Atomic Wings (4)
Avenue A (2)
Baalbek (1)
Baby Jake's (4)
Baraonda (1)
Barolo (1)
Bar Pitti (1)
Bar Six (3)
Basta Pasta (1)
Bayamo (2)
Beach Cafe (1)
Bell Caffe (4)
Benny's Burritos (1)
Bimini Twist (1)
Birdland (1)
Blue Ribbon (4)
Boom (1)
Boulevard (1)
Boxers (4)
Brasserie (24 hrs.)
Broome Street Bar (2:30)
Brothers BBQ (2)
Bruce Ho's (1)
Cafe Español (1)
Cafe Europa (2)
Cafe Lalo (4)
Caffe Rafaella (3)
Caffe Rosso (1)
Caffe Vivaldi (2)
Cantina (1)
Carnegie Deli (3)
Casa La Femme (3)
Casanis (4)
Cedars Lebanon (2)
Charley O's (2:30)
Chaz & Wilson (1)
Chelsea Commons (1)
Christo's Stkhse. (1:30)
Chumley's (1)
Clarke's, P.J. (4)
Cleopatra's (3)
Cloister Cafe (1)
Coconut Grill (1)
Coffee Shop (6)
Cornelia St. Cafe (1)
Corner Bistro (4)
Cucina di Pesce (1)

Cucina Stagionale (1)
Cupping Room Cafe (2)
Dakota Bar/Grill (1)
Dallas BBQ (2)
Danny's Grand (1)
Dish (2)
Diva (2)
Divan Kebab Hse. (1)
Dix et Sept (2)
Dojo (2)
Don Giovanni (2)
Due (1)
Ear Inn (3)
Ecco L'Italia (2)
Elaine's (2)
El Charro (1)
Elephant & Castle (1)
El Faro (1)
El Quijote (1)
El Teddy's (1)
Empire Diner (24 hrs.)
Empire Szechuan (2)
Ferrier (1)
Fez (1)
Fiesta Mexicana (1)
Figaro Pizza (3)
Finnegan's Wake (2)
First (3)
Five Oaks (12:45)
Flight 151 (2)
Florent (24 hrs.)
Flowers (1)
Flying Burrito (3)
Freddie & Pepper's's (3)
French Roast Cafe (24 hrs.)
Fujiyama Mama (1)
Gandhi (1)
Georgia Diner (24 hrs.)
Gonzalez Y Gonz. (2)
Gotham City Diner (4)
Gramercy Watering (3)
Gray's Papaya (24 hrs.)
Great Jones Cafe (1)
Halcyon (1)
Harbor Seafood (2)
Hard Rock Cafe (2)
Harley Davidson (1)
Harry's Burritos (1)
Hi-Life Bar/Grill (4)
Honeysuckle (2:45)
Hong Fat (5)
Houlihan's (1)
Hunan Balcony (1)
Il Cortile (1)
Iridium (1)
Isabella's (1)
I Tre Merli (2)
Jackson Hole (1)
Jackson Hole (4:30)
Jamaican Hot Pot (2)
Jekyll & Hyde (4)
J.G. Melon (2:30)
Juanita's (2)
Jules (2)

Kam Chueh (1)
Kang Suh (24 hrs.)
Kan Pai (2)
Kiev (24 hrs.)
Kings Pl. Diner (2)
Kom Tang Soot Bul (24 hrs.)
Kwanzaa (2)
La Focaccia (1)
La Folie (1)
La Jumelle (4)
La Metairie (1)
Langan's (1)
La Spaghetteria (1)
Lee Mazzilli's (1)
Le Pescadou (4)
Lespinasse (2)
Le Streghe (4)
Levana (1)
Life Cafe (2)
Live Bait (2:30)
Lucky Cheng's (2)
Lucky Strike (4)
Luke's Bar/Grill (3)
Mackinac (1)
Manhattan Bistro (1)
Mappamondo (1)
Markham (1)
Marti Kebab (1)
Marylou's (1)
Match (4)
Mesa Verde (1)
Mezzaluna (1)
Mezzanine (2)
Mezzogiorno (1)
Moonrock Diner (3)
Mo's Caribbean (3)
Museum Cafe (1)
Mustang Grill (1)
N (4)
Nadine's (1)
National (3)
Neary's (1:30)
Nello (1)
9 (1)
9 Jones Street (2:30)
Nirvana (1)
N.Y. Deli (24 hrs.)
Odeon, The (3)
Ollie's (2)
O'Neals' (1)
One If By Land (1)
101 (2)
103 NYC (2)
Oriental Garden (2)
Orologio (1)
Orson's (2)
Panchitos (4)
Papaya King (3)
Paris Cafe (3)
Park Avalon (1)
Passage to India (1)
Passport (1)
Patsy's Pizza (1)
Perretti Italian (1)

Pisces (1)
Pizzeria Uno (2)
Pizzeria Uno (3)
Planet Hollywood (1)
Quisisana (1)
Rainbow Room (1)
Rancho Mexican (2)
Raoul's (1)
Rascals (3)
Rasputin (2)
Red Lion (4)
Regency (24 hrs.)
Revolution (1)
Rosie O'Grady's (2)
Roumeli Taverna (1)
Royal Canadian (2)
Ruppert's (1)
Sahara East (1)
Saloon (1)
Sam's Rest./Pizza (1)
Sapporo East (12:45)
Sarabeth's (4:30)
Sardi's (1)
Seafood Palace (1)
Seattle Bean Co. (1)
Second Ave. Deli (1:45)
Serendipity 3 (1:30)
Sevilla (1)
Shabu Tatsu (2)
Shark Bar (2)
Smith & Wollensky (2)
SoHo Kitchen (2)
S.P.Q.R. (1)
Spring St. Natural (1)
Stage Deli (2)
Stingy Lulu's (6)
Stromboli Pizza (4)
Sushihatsu (3:30)
Taci Int'l (1)
Tavern on Green (12:45)
Teachers Too (1)
Telephone Bar (1:30)
Telly's Taverna (1)
Temple Bar (1)
Tequila Sunrise (1)
Thomas Scott's (1)
Three of Cups (2)
Time Cafe (1)
Toast (1)
Tony Roma's (1)
Tortilla Flats (1)
Trompe l'Oeil (1)
T Salon (1)
Tutta Pasta (1)
20 Mott Street (1)
Two Eleven (1)
Veselka (24 hrs.)
Viceroy (4)
Village Crown (1)
Vincent's (3:30)
Vinnie's Pizza (1)
Walker's (1)
Well's (4)
Westway Diner (24 hrs.)

White Horse Tavern (2)
Wolf's Deli (1)
Wollensky's Grill (2)
Woo Chon (24 hrs.)
World Cafe (1)
Yellowfingers (2)
Zip City Brewing (1)

Meet For A Drink
(Most top hotels and the
following standouts)
Algonquin Hotel
Alva
Amsterdam's
Bar and Books
Beer Bar
Bill's Gay 90's
Boathouse Cafe
Boulevard
Boxers
Broome Street Bar
B. Smith's
Cafe de Bruxelles
Cafe des Artistes
Cafe Pierre
Carlyle
Chaz & Wilson
Chelsea Commons
Chumley's
Cité Grille
Cub Room
Dakota Bar/Grill
Docks Oyster Bar
Edward Moran
El Teddy's
Fanelli
Fantino
44
Four Seasons
Gotham Bar/Grill
Gramercy Tavern
Halcyon
Harry's Hanover Sq.
Hi-Life Bar/Grill
Hudson River Club
I Tre Merli
Jezebel
JUdson Grill
Landmark Tavern
Le Bistrot Maxim
Le Colonial
Le Relais
Lespinasse/King Cole
Lincoln Tavern
Lion's Head
Lobby Lounge
Mad.61
Markham
Mark's
McSorley's
Mezzanine
Oak Room & Bar
Old Town Bar
O'Neals'
Palm Court

Peacock Alley
Pete's Tavern
Rainbow Promenade
Regency
River Cafe
Saloon
Sfuzzi
Sign of the Dove
Symphony Cafe
Temple Bar
"21" Club
Union Square Cafe
Walker's
Westside Brewing
W. 63rd St. Stkhse.
White Horse Tavern
Zip City Brewing

Noteworthy Newcomers (196)
Acappella
Ah Umakatta
Aja*
Alley's End
Alva
Amarcord
Amer. Renaissance
Annabelle
Annie Beneau
Arcimboldo
Area Code Cafe
Arté
Au Bon Coin
Baby Jakes
Bachué Café
Baluchi's
Bamiyan
Bar and Books
Bar Six
Basco
Beer Bar
Beit Eddine
Big Cup
Big Sur
Bimmy's
Blu Restaurant
Bolo
BOS
Bowery Bar*
Cafe Beulah
Cafe Cento Sette
Cafe Centro
Cafe Dara*
Cafe du Pont
Cafe Mangia e Bevi*
Cafe Noir*
Caffe di Nonni
Caffe Grazie
Caffe Lure
Cake Bar & Cafe
California Pizza Oven
Campagna
Casanis
Caterina's
Caviarteria
Chantale's Cajun

Charlton's
Chat 'n' Chew
Chock Full o'Nuts
Christer's
Chutney Mary
Cibreo*
City Crab
City Grill
Cooking With Jazz
Cooper's Coffee
C.T.
Cub Room
DaNico
Da Rosina
Demi
Diwan Grill
Dragon Village
Eros*
Evergreen Cafe
Fantino
First
First on 59th
Fish
Flowers
Flying Burrito
Franklin Station Cafe
Fresco
Fu's
Garden Cafe
Gauguin
Gianpalu
Gigino
Giovanni
Gotham City Diner
Gramercy Tavern
Harvest
In Padella
Ipoh Garden Malay.
Iridium
Jekyll & Hyde Club*
Jerry's (Columbus)
Jing Fong
Jo-An Japanese
Joe's Shanghai
Josie's
Jubilee
JUdson Grill
Julian's*
Kaffeehaus
Kelley & Ping
King's Carriage Hse.
Kum Gang San
Kwanzaa
La Folie
La Mère Poulard
L'Ardoise
La Voce
Le Colonial
Lee Mazzilli's
L'Ermitage
Les Deux Gamins
Le Select*
Le Streghe
Lex*

Lincoln Tavern
Lipizzana
Little Club
Lora*
Lotfi's Moroccan
L'Udo
Maka Nunpa*
Malaysia/Indonesia
Markham
Marlowe
Martini's
Match
Matthew's
Mavalli Palace
Merchant's N.Y.
Merenda
Metronome
Monkey Bar
Morgan Cafe
Moscow on Hudson
Mustang Grill
New City Cafe
New Hong Kong City
News Bar (SoHo)
New World Grill
9 Jones Street
Nobu
Novita*
Ñ 33 Crosby Bar
Olive Garden
Osteria al Doge
Park Avalon
Pasqua Coffee
Patría
Pearson's BBQ*
Penang Malaysian*
Phoenix Garden
Privé
Queen
Raffaele
Revolution
Rib'n & Blues
Rice & Beans
Sahara East
Salaam Bombay
Samalita's
Sasso
Seattle Bean Co.
Shaan
Shabu Tatsu (York)
Silk Restaurant
Sorelle
Soul Fixins'
Spartina
Spring St. Rest.
Starbucks
Sun Cafe
Takahachi
Tanti Baci Cafe
Taqueria de Mexico
Tasca do Porto
Tavola
Tea Box
Tea Den

Terramare Café
Three Degrees N.
Tibet Shambala
Toast
Toscana
Toukie's
Trilogy Bar/Grill
Trompe L'Oeil
Truffles
T Salon
Twins*
Uncle Nick's
Verbena
Viceroy
Virgil's BBQ
W. 63rd St. Stkhse.
World Cafe
Yaffa Tea Room
Zacki's PBQ
Zitella
Zuni
Zut!*
(*Not open yet, looks promising)

Noteworthy Closings (69)
Alcala
Andiamo
Banana Cafe
Bellini by Cipriani
Boogies Diner
Brasserie des Theatres
Brazilian Pavilion
BTI
Buckaroo's
Bukhara
Buono Tavola
Cafe
Cafe 400
Chefs Cuisiniers Club
Chelsea Central
City Cafe
Coach House
Coastal
Colors (Reopened)
Delmonico's
Eva's Cafe
Florence
Fourteen
Harlequin
Havana
Il Gattopardo
Indies
Japanese on Hudson
La Frontera
Lai Lai West
La Petite Ferme
La Topiaire
Lello Ristorante
Le Steak
Lolabelle
Luxe
Madeo
Mamma Leone's
May We
Mr. Fuji's Tropicana

Nawab
One Fifth Avenue
One Hudson Cafe
Peter Hilary's
Piccolino
Pierre's
Poiret
Positano
Prix Fixe
Raoul's on Varick
Red River Grill
Road House
Romeo Salta
Scoop
Sido Abu Salim
Silverado
Siu Lam Kung
Stephanie's
Ticino
Time & Again Restaurant
Tommy Tang's
Umeda
Valone's
Vasata
Vix Cafe
Vong and Kwong
West Broadway Restaurant
Yellow Rose Cafe
Zachary's

Offbeat
Acadia Parish
Afghan Kebab Hse.
Ah Umakatta
Andalousia
Baby Jake's
Bell Caffe
Birdland
Boca Chica
Brothers BBQ
Cabana Carioca
Casanis
Chez Brigitte
Copeland's
Dominick's
Ear Inn
Elias Corner
El Pollo
Floridita
Food Bar
Frank's
Gandhi
Honeysuckle
Jackson Hts. Diner
Jai Ya Thai
Jezebel
Joe's Shanghai
Kelley & Ping
Kiev
Kwanzaa
La Caridad
La Taza de Oro
Louisiana Commun.
Marion's Cont.
McSorley's

Mitali East/West
Mocca Hungarian
Nirvana
Pho Pasteur
Pie, The
Rao's
Rasputin
Red Tulip
Rib'n & Blues
Rolf's
Sammy's
Shabu Tatsu
Shopsin's
Stingy Lulu's
Sylvia's
Symposium
Tasca do Porto
Telly's Taverna
Thai Orchid
Toukie's
T Salon
Turkish Kitchen
Uncle Nick's
Well's
Yaffa Tea Room

Old New York
(50+ yrs.; year opened)
1716 Old Bermuda Inn
1726 One If By Land*
1763 Fraunces Tavern
1801 Bridge Cafe
1854 McSorley's
1864 Pete's Tavern
1868 Landmark Tavern
1868 Old Homestead
1870 Billy's
1871 Paris Cafe
1872 Fanelli
1879 Gage & Tollner
1880 White Horse Tavern
1885 Keens Chophse.
1887 Peter Luger
1888 Katz's Deli
1890 Clarke's, P.J.
1890 Walker's
1892 Ferrara
1892 Old Town Bar
1894 Veniero's
1896 Rao's
1902 Angelo's
1904 Lanza
1904 Vincent's
1906 Barbetta
1907 Edwardian Room
1907 Oak Room & Bar
1907 Palm Court
1908 Barney Greengrass
1908 Grotta Azzurra
1908 John's of 12th
1910 Patrissy's
1912 Frank's
1913 Oyster Bar
1917 Cafe des Artistes
1919 Grand Ticino

1919 Mario's
1920 Ye Waverly Inn
1921 Sardi's
1922 "21" Club
1923 Bill's Gay 90's
1923 Cotton Club
1924 Totonno Pizzeria
1926 Frankie & Johnnie's
1926 Palm
1926 Russian Tea Room
1927 Caffe Reggio
1927 Chumley's
1927 El Faro
1927 Fine & Schapiro
1927 Gallagher's
1927 Minetta Tavern
1929 Empire Diner
1929 Sam's Rest./Pizza
1930 Marchi's
1930 Sloppy Louie's
1931 Cafe Pierre
1931 Peacock Alley
1932 Patsy's Pizza/NY
1932 Pen & Pencil
1933 Christo's Stkhse.
1934 El Charro
1934 John's Pizzeria
1934 Papaya King
1934 Rainbow Room
1934 Tavern on Green
1937 Le Veau d'Or
1937 7th Regiment Mess
1938 El Quijote
1938 Well's
1939 Carnegie Hill
1939 Heidelberg
1940 Carnegie Deli
1940 Rumpelmayer's
1941 Mme. Romaine
1941 Sevilla
1944 Burger Heaven
1944 Patsy's
1945 Tout Va Bien

Outdoor Dining
(G = Garden; S = Sidewalk;
best of many)
Aureole (G)
Barolo (G)
Blu Restaurant (G)
Boathouse Cafe (G)
Cafe Centro (S)
Caffe Bondí (G)
Caffe Vivaldi (G,S)
Casanis (G)
Chelsea Commons (G)
Cloister Cafe (G)
Da Silvano (G,S)
El Rio Grande (G)
Gascogne (G)
Grove (G)
Manhattan Plaza (G)
Mission Grill (G)
New Deal (G)
Old Bermuda Inn (G)

O'Neals' (S)
Provence (G)
Raoul's (G)
Remi (G)
Saloon (S)
SeaGrill (G)
Sumptuary (G)
Tavern on Green (G)
Three Degrees N. (G)
Verbena (G)
Vittorio Cucina (G)
Yaffa Tea Room (S)
Ye Waverly Inn (G)

Parties & Private Rooms

(Any nightclub or restaurant
charges less at off-times;
* indicates private rooms
available; best of many)
Adrienne*
America
An American Place
Barbetta*
Barolo*
Becco*
Bill's Gay 90's*
Boathouse Cafe*
Broadway Diner
Brother Jimmy's
B. Smith's*
Carmine's
Chez Josephine*
Ci Vedeamo*
Empire Diner*
5 & 10*
Four Seasons*
Frank's*
Gabriel's*
Gallagher's*
Golden Unicorn*
Gramercy Tavern*
Hard Rock Cafe
Harley Davidson*
Honeysuckle*
Hudson River Club*
Iridium*
I Tre Merli
Japonica*
Jean Claude
Jim McMullen*
Jubilee
Keens Chophse.*
La Grenouille*
Landmark Tavern*
La Reserve*
Le Bar Bat*
Le Bernardin*
Le Cirque*
Les Celebrités*
Little Club*
Lutèce*
Main Street*
Mangia e Bevi
Manhattan Plaza*
Metronome*
Mickey Mantle's

O'Neals'*
Palio*
Palm Too*
Planet Hollywood*
Provence*
Rainbow Room*
River Cafe
Ruby's River*
Russian Samovar
Russian Tea Room*
San Domenico*
Serendipity 3*
7th Regiment Mess*
Shark Bar*
Shun Lee Palace*
Sign of the Dove*
Smith & Wollensky*
Supper Club*
Sylvia's
Symphony Cafe*
Tavern on Green*
Tavola
Tennessee Mtn.*
T.G.I. Friday's
Trattoria dell'Arte*
TriBeCa Grill*
"21" Club*
Water Club*
Water's Edge*
World Yacht*
W. 63rd St. Stkhse.*
Zip City Brewing*

People-Watching

Bice
Bolo
Bouley
B. Smith's
Campagna
Coco Pazzo
Dish
Elio's
Ferrier
44
Four Seasons
First
Flowers
Gabriel's
Gotham Bar/Grill
Jour et Nuit
La Goulue
La Grenouille
Le Cirque
Le Colonial
Le Relais
Match
Mezzanine
Monkey Bar
Nobu
Park Avalon
Russian Tea Room
TriBeCa Grill
"21" Club
Union Square Cafe
Vong

Power Scenes

Bouley
Daniel
Four Seasons
Gabriel's
Gage & Tollner
Il Mulino
Il Nido
La Cote Basque
La Grenouille
La Reserve
Le Cirque
Monkey Bar
Nobu
Palm
Park Ave. Cafe
Peter Luger
Primavera
Rainbow Room
Rao's
Regency
Sette Mezzo
Smith & Wollensky
Sparks
"21" Club

Pre-Theater Menus

(Best of many; call to check
prices, days and times; also
see pp. 19 and 20)
Ambassador Grill
Aquavit
Arcadia
Aria
Becco
Bistro 790
Bombay Palace
Cafe Botanica
Chez Josephine
Cité
Darbar
Edwardian Room
Four Seasons
Hourglass Tavern
Hudson River Club
Indochine
Jewel of India
JUdson Grill
La Caravelle
La Reserve
Le Chantilly
Le Colonial
Les Pyrenees
Levana
Nirvana
Regency
Restaurant 222
Russian Tea Room
San Domenico
Sardi's
Sfuzzi
Sign of the Dove
Tavern on Green
"21" Club
Water Club
W. 63rd St. Stkhse.

Prix Fixe Menus

(Best of many; call to check
prices and days; B=brunch;
L=lunch; D=dinner; also see
pp. 19 and 20)
Adrienne (L)
Ambassador Grill (B,L,D)
America (B)
Aquavit (D)
Arcadia (D)
Aria (D)
Arqua (L,D)
Aureole (L,D)
Becco (L,D)
Bombay Palace (L)
Bridge Cafe (B,D)
Cafe Botanica (B,L,D)
Cafe des Artistes (L,D)
Cafe Luxembourg (L,D)
Cafe Pierre (L,D)
Century Cafe (D)
Cesarina (D)
Chanterelle (L,D)
Chez Napoleon (L)
Chin Chin (L)
C.T. (D)
Cucina & Co. (D)
Daniel (L)
Darbar (L)
Docks Oyster Bar (B)
Duane Park Cafe (L)
Ferrier (L)
Four Seasons (D)
Fu's (L)
Gauguin (D)
Gotham Bar/Grill (L)
Gramercy Tavern (D)
Harry Cipriani (L,D)
Hudson River Club (L)
J. Sung Dynasty (L,D)
JUdson Grill (B,L)
Knickerbocker (B,L)
La Boite en Bois (D)
L'Acajou (L,D)
La Caravelle (L,D)
La Cote Basque (L,D)
La Grenouille (L,D)
La Maison Japon. (L,D)
La Reserve (L,D)
La Tour D'Or (L,D)
Le Bar Bat (L,D)
Le Bernardin (L,D)
Le Boeuf ala Mode (D)
Le Chantilly (L,D)
Le Cirque (L)
L'Ecole (L,D)
Lee Mazzilli's (D)
Le Max (B,D)
Leopard, The (L,D)
Le Pistou (L,D)
Le Regence (B,L,D)
L'Ermitage (L,D)
Les Pyrenees (L,D)
Les Sans Culottes (L,D)

Lespinasse (L,D)
Levana (L,D)
Le Veau d'Or (L)
Lutèce (L,D)
Mark's (B,L,D)
Mitali East/West (B,L)
Montrachet (L,D)
Nino's (L,D)
Nusantara (L,D)
Oceana (L,D)
One If By Land (D)
Our Place (L,D)
Palio (L,D)
Palm (L)
Peacock Alley (L,D)
Petrossian (B,L,D)
Phoenix Garden (L,D)
Picholine (L,D)
Pig Heaven (L,D)
Pó (L,D)
Primola (L)
Quatorze Bis (L)
Rasputin (D)
Red Tulip (D)
River Cafe (D)
Russian Tea Room (B,L,D)
San Domenico (L,D)
SeaGrill (L,D)
Sfuzzi (B,L,D)
Siam Inn (D)
Sign of the Dove (L,D)
Snaps (D)
Solera (L,D)
Sushisay (L,D)
Table d'Hôte (L)
Tavern on Green (L)
Tennessee Mtn. (B,D)
Terrace (L,D)
Tommaso's (L,D)
Toscana (L,D)
TriBeCa Grill (B,L)
Tropica (D)
Truffles (L,D)
"21" Club (L)
Two Eleven (L)
Uncle Nick's (D)
Urban Grill (D)
View (D)
Vong (L)
Voulez-Vous (B,L,D)
Water Club (B,L)
World Yacht (B,L,D)
Yankee Clipper (L,D)
Zen Palate (L,D)
Zutto (L,D)

Pubs/Bars/Sports TV*
Alley's End
Amsterdam's
Automatic Slim's*
Bar and Books
Bar Six
Beach Cafe*
Beer Bar*
Bill's Gay 90's

Billy's
Birdland
Blue Moon Mexican*
Boom
Boxers*
Bridge Cafe
Broome Street Bar*
Cafe Luxembourg
Cafe Tabac
Carmine's
Chaz & Wilson*
Chelsea Commons*
Chelsea Grill*
Chumley's*
Churchill's*
Clarke's, P.J.*
Corner Bistro*
Cottonwood Cafe*
Dakota Bar/Grill*
Docks Oyster Bar*
Ear Inn*
Edward Moran*
Fanelli*
Ferrier
Food Bar
Frank's
Gotham Bar/Grill
Gramercy Tavern
Gramercy Watering*
Heidelberg*
Hi-Life Bar/Grill
Honeysuckle*
Jean Lafitte
Jekyll & Hyde
Jim McMullen
Joe Allen*
Kiss
Knickerbocker*
Landmark Tavern*
Langan's*
Lee Mazzilli's*
Lion's Head*
Little Club
Live Bait
Lucky Cheng's
Luke's Bar/Grill*
Mad.61
Manhattan Brewing*
Marion's Cont.
Markham
Mark's
Match
McSorley's*
Memphis
Mickey Mantle's*
Mike's Bar/Grill
Miracle Grill
Monkey Bar
Mulholland Drive*
Oak Room & Bar
Old Town Bar*
O'Neals'*
Palio
Paris Cafe

Park Avalon
Patría
Pete's Tavern*
Planet Hollywood
Rao's
Rascals*
Reidy's*
Rosie O'Grady's*
Ruby's River*
Rusty Staub's*
Shark Bar
Shelby
Telephone Bar*
Trilogy Bar/Grill*
"21" Club*
Union Square Cafe
Viceroy
Virgil's BBQ
Walker's*
Westside Brewing*
White Horse Tavern*
Wollensky's Grill
Zip City*

Quiet Conversation
Adrienne
Algonquin Hotel
Alley's End
Ambassador Grill
Annabelle
Aquavit
Aria
Arté
Asia
Bar and Books
Barbetta
Book-Friends Cafe
Box Tree
Cafe Botanica
Cafe Centro
Cafe Nicholson
Cafe Trevi
Carlyle
Chanterelle
Dix et Sept
Edwardian Room
Follonico
Four Seasons
Gus' Place
Home
Honmura An
Hudson River Club
Il Monello
Il Tinello
Inagiku
Keens
Kum Gang San
La Caravelle
La Cote Basque
La Grenouille
La Reserve
Le Bernardin
Le Chantilly
Le Perigord
Le Regence

L'Ermitage
Les Celebrités
Lespinasse
Lobby Lounge
Lutèce
Manhattan Ocean
Manhattan Plaza
Matthew's
Mitsukoshi
Monkey Bar
Morton's Chicago
Nirvana
Oak Room & Bar
One If By Land
Palio
Picholine
Polo
Primavera
Regency
Russell's
Scalinatella
Seryna
Shinbashi-an
Terrace
Tse Yang
Verbena
W. 63rd St. Stkhse.

Romantic Spots
Arcadia
Aureole
Au Troquet
Bar and Books
Barbetta
Black Sheep
Bouley
Box Tree
Cafe des Artistes
Cafe du Pont
Cafe Nicholson
Cafe Trevi
Caffe Vivaldi
Casanis
Chez Josephine
Chez Michallet
Cub Room
Erminia
First
Harbour Lights
La Colombe d'Or
La Goulue
La Grenouille
La Metairie
Le Bernardin
Le Colonial
Le Refuge
L'Ermitage
Les Celebrités
Little Club
March
Mark's
Marylou's
Nick & Eddie
One If By Land
Provence

Rainbow Room
Raphael
River Cafe
Russian Tea Room
Shanghai 1933
Sign of the Dove
Sonia Rose
Tavern on Green
Temple Bar
Terrace
Village Atelier
Vivolo
Vucciria
Water Club
Water's Edge
World Yacht

Saturday – Best Bets

(B=brunch; L=lunch;
best of many)
Adrienne (L)
Aggie's (B,L)
Ahnell (B,L)
Algonquin Hotel (L)
America (B,L)
Arcadia (L)
Asia (L)
Barbetta (L)
Becco (L)
Bice (L)
Boathouse Cafe (L)
Bombay Palace (L)
B. Smith's (L)
Cafe Botanica (L)
Cafe de Bruxelles (L)
Cafe des Artistes (B)
Cafe Luxembourg (L)
Cafe Pierre (L)
Calif. Burrito Co. (L)
Canton (L)
Carlyle (L)
Carmine's (L)
Carnegie Deli (L)
Chanterelle (L)
Charlotte (L)
Chelsea Commons (L)
Chiam (L)
China Fun (L)
Cité (L)
Cité Grille (L)
Claire (B)
Coco Pazzo (L)
Cucina & Co. (L)
Dawat (L)
E.A.T. (L)
Edwardian Room (L)
57, 57 (B)
Friend of Farmer (B,L)
Gallagher's (L)
Gramercy Tavern (L)
Grange Hall (B)
Grotta Azzurra (L)
Grove (B)
Hard Rock Cafe (L)
Harry Cipriani (L)

Honmura An (L)
Hosteria Fiorella (B)
H.S.F. (L)
Il Cortile (L)
Il Monello (L)
Il Nido (L)
Japonica (L)
Jerry's (B)
Jim McMullen (L)
John's Pizzeria (L)
J. Sung Dynasty (L)
Jubilee (B)
Kaffeehaus (B,L)
La Cote Basque (L)
La Grenouille (L)
La Metairie (B)
Le Bilboquet (L)
Le Chantilly (L)
Le Cirque (L)
Le Madri (L)
Le Pistou (L)
Le Regence (L)
Le Relais (L)
Les Halles (B,L)
Lespinasse (L)
Les Pyrenees (L)
Mad.61 (L)
Mangia e Bevi (L)
Manhattan Plaza (L)
Manhattan Plaza (L)
Markham (B,L)
Mark's (L)
Match (B)
Matthew's (L)
Monkey Bar (L)
Nirvana (L)
Oak Room & Bar (L)
Palm (L)
Park Avalon (L)
Petrossian (B)
Planet Hollywood (L)
Pó (L)
Popover Cafe (B,L)
Regency (L)
River Cafe (B)
Rumpelmayer's (L)
Russian Tea Room (B)
Second Avenue Deli (B,L)
Shun Lee Palace (L)
Sign of the Dove (L)
Smith & Wollensky (L)
Sylvia's (L)
Symphony Cafe (L)
Table d'Hôte (B)
Tavern on Green (B)
Time Cafe (B,L)
Trois Jean (L)
Tse Yang (L)
20 Mott Street (L)
Uncle Nick's (L)
Union Square Cafe (L)
Viand (L)
Village Atelier (L)
Virgil's BBQ (L)

Water Club (L)
Wollensky's Grill (L)
Yellowfingers (B,L)

Sunday – Best Bets
(B=brunch; L=lunch;
D=dinner; plus all hotels
and most Asians)
Akbar (B,D)
Alison (D)
Alley's End (D)
Amsterdam's (L,D)
Aria (D)
Arizona 206 (B,L,D)
Arqua (D)
Asia (B,L,D)
Azzurro (D)
Baby Jake's (B,L,D)
Bangkok House (L,D)
Barney Greengrass (B,L)
Barocco (D)
Bar Six (B,L,D)
Ben Benson's (D)
Bice (L,D)
Bloom's Deli (B,L,D)
B. Smith's (L,D)
Cafe des Artistes (B,D)
Cafe Luxembourg (B,D)
Cafe Trevi (D)
Caffe Rosso (B,D)
Campagna (D)
Carmine's (D)
Carnegie Deli (B,L,D)
Chez Ma Tante (B,D)
Chez Michallet (B,D)
Chiam (L,D)
China Fun (B,L,D)
Chin Chin (D)
Cité (B,L,D)
Dallas BBQ (L,D)
Darbar (L,D)
Docks Oyster Bar (B,D)
First (B,D)
Gallagher's (L,D)
Good Enough to Eat (B,L,D)
Gotham Bar/Grill (D)
Gramercy Tavern (D)
Grange Hall (B,D)
Grotta Azzurra (L,D)
Hard Rock Cafe (L,D)
Harley Davidson (L,D)
Harry Cipriani (B,L,D)
H.S.F. (B,L,D)
Il Cortile (L,D)
Il Monello (L,D)
Jackson Hts. Diner (L,D)
Japonica (L,D)
Jim McMullen (B,D)
John's Pizzeria (L,D)
Jubilee (B)
Kaffeehaus (B,L,D)
Kin Khao (D)
Kwanzaa (B,D)
La Caravelle (D)
La Colombe d'Or (D)

La Metairie (B,D)
La Reserve (L,D)
Le Chantilly (D)
Le Colonial (D)
Le Comptoir (D)
Le Madri (L,D)
Le Perigord (D)
Le Relais (L,D)
Les Halles (B,L,D)
Levana (B,D)
Lola (B,L,D)
Main Street (B,D)
Manhattan Plaza (B,D)
Manhattan Ocean (D)
Markham (B,L,D)
Mary Ann's (B,D)
Match (B,D)
Matthew's (B,L,D)
Mesa Grill (B,D)
Metropolis Cafe (B,D)
Metropolitan Cafe (B,D)
Miracle Grill (B,D)
New City Cafe (D)
O'Casey's (L,D)
Ollie's (B,L,D)
O'Neals' (B,L,D)
One If By Land (D)
Orso (L,D)
Park Avalon (B,L,D)
Park Ave. Cafe (B,L,D)
Peter Luger (L,D)
Petrossian (B,D)
Phoenix Garden (L,D)
Planet Hollywood (L,D)
Popover Cafe (B,L,D)
Primavera (L,D)
Primola (D)
Quatorze Bis (B,L,D)
Rainbow Room (D)
Regency (B,L,D)
Restaurant 222 (D)
River Cafe (B,D)
Rosa Mexicano (D)
Russian Samovar (D)
Russian Tea Room (B,D)
Santa Fe (B,L,D)
Second Ave. Deli (B,L,D)
Sevilla (L,D)
Sfuzzi (B,L,D)
Shun Lee Palace (L,D)
Smith & Wollensky (L,D)
Sonia Rose (D)
Stage Deli (B,L,D)
Sylvia's (B)
Table d'Hôte (B,D)
Tavern on Green (B,D)
Time Cafe (B,L,D)
Trattoria dell'Arte (B,L,D)
TriBeCa Grill (B,D)
Uncle Nick's (L,D)
Union Square Cafe (D)
Vinnie's Pizza (L,D)
Virgil's BBQ (D)
Vong (D)

Walker's (B,L,D)
Water Club (B,D)
White Horse Tavern (B,L,D)
Wollensky's Grill (L,D)
Zoë (B,L,D)

Senior Appeal
Adrienne
Algonquin Hotel
Amarcord
Aquavit
Asia
Aureole
Au Troquet
Barbetta
Bouley
Box Tree
Cafe Botanica
Cafe des Artistes
Cafe Pierre
Cafe Trevi
Captain's Table
Carlyle
Christer's
Daniel
Darbar
Dawat
E.A.T.
Edwardian Room
Felidia
57, 57
Follonico
Four Seasons
Gabriel's
Gallagher's
Garibaldi
Gotham Bar/Grill
Halcyon
Hatsuhana
Hosteria Fiorella
Hudson River Club
Hunters
Il Monello
Il Nido
Inagiku
Jim McMullen
Jo Jo
La Boulangere
La Caravelle
La Colombe d'Or
La Cote Basque
La Grenouille
La Mangeoire
La Mediterranée
Lanza
La Reserve
Le Bernardin
Le Chantilly
Le Cirque
L'Ecole
Le Perigord
Le Regence
L'Ermitage
Les Celebrités
Levana

Lobby Lounge
Lutèce
Mad.61
Manhattan Ocean
March
Mark's
Matthew's
Mme. Romaine
Montrachet
Neary's
Nippon
Oak Room/Bar
Oyster Bar
Palm
Palm Court
Parioli Romanis.
Peter Luger
Picholine
Post House
Primavera
Primola
Rainbow Room
Raphael
Red Tulip
Remi
Restaurant 222
Rosa Mexicano
Rosemarie's
Rumpelmayer's
Russell's
Russian Tea Room
San Domenico
Scalinatella
Sette MoMA
Shun Lee Palace
Shun Lee West
Sign of the Dove
Solera
Sonia Rose
Sushisay
Tavern on Green
Tavola
Terrace
Tse Yang
"21" Club
Union Square Cafe
Vivolo
Voulez-Vous
Wilkinson's
W. 63rd St. Stkhse.

Singles Scenes
Amsterdam's
Anarchy Cafe
Arizona 206
Atomic Wings
Automatic Slim's
Baby Jake's
Barnes & Noble
Bayamo
Big Cup
Boca Chica
Boxers
B. Smith's
Cafe Tabac

Canastel's
Caribe
Chaz & Wilson
China Grill
Clarke's, P.J.
Coconut Grill
Coffee Shop
Cub Room
Dakota Bar/Grill
Delia's
Dish
Diva
Docks Oyster Bar
Edward Moran
El Teddy's
Ferrier
Fez
First
Flight 151
Flowers
Food Bar
Googies
Gramercy Watering
Harley Davidson
Hi-Life Bar/Grill
Ipanema
Isabella's
I Tre Merli
Juanita's
JUdson Grill (bar)
La Goulue
Langan's
Le Bar Bat
Le Colonial (upstairs)
Le Taxi
Levee
Little Club
Live Bait
Lucky Strike
Lucy's Surfers
Mangia e Bevi
Match
McSorley's
Memphis
Metronome
Mezzanine
Miracle Grill
Monkey Bar (bar)
Mo's Caribbean
Mulholland Drive
Old Town Bar
Park Avalon
Park Ave. Country
Patría (bar)
Planet Hollywood
Ruby's River
Ruppert's
Seattle Bean Co.
Sfuzzi
Shark Bar
Shelby
SoHo Kitchen
Steak Frites
Sugar Reef

Tortilla Flats
Toukie's
TriBeCa Grill
Walker's
White Horse Tavern
Zarela
Zoë

Sleepers
(Good to excellent
food, but little known)
Adoré
Castillo de Jagua
Chantale's Cajun
Charlton's
Ciao Europa
Cooking With Jazz
Copeland's
Cotton Club
Emily's
Fantino
Gianpalu
Gigino
Hong Shoon
Ipoh Garden Malay.
Jamaican Hot Pot
Jo-An Japanese
Kabul Cafe
Kam Chueh
Kom Tang Soot Bul
Kum Gang San
Les Friandises
Le Streghe
Lobby Lounge
Marumi
Mavalli Palace
Milano
Mueng Thai
Ñ 33 Crosby Bar
New City Cafe
New Hong Kong City
Oriental Garden
Piccolo Angolo
Ponticello
Soul Fixins'
Takahachi
Tan Go
Tanti Baci Cafe
Thomas Scott's
Well's
Wing Wong
Zitella
Zula

Teflons
(Gets lots of business, despite
so-so food, i.e. they have other
attractions that prevent
criticism from sticking)
Algonquin Hotel
America
American Festival
Amici Miei
Amsterdam's (Uptown)
Angelika Film Ctr.

Arriba Arriba
Au Cafe
Back Porch
Barking Dog
Barnes & Noble
Bayamo
Beach Cafe
Bendix Diner
Boathouse Cafe
Book-Friends Cafe
Boulevard
Boxers
Broadway Diner
Broadway Grill
Broome Street Bar
Brother Jimmy's
Burger Heaven
Cafe Tabac
Cafe Un Deux Trois
Calif. Burrito Co.
Cantina
Caribe
Charley O's
Chaz & Wilson
Christine's
Clarke's, P.J.
Coffee Shop
Dakota Bar/Grill
Dallas BBQ
Dojo
Donald Sacks
Dosanko
Edward Moran
Elaine's
Ellen's Stardust
Empire Diner
Empire Szechuan
Fanelli
Federico's
Fine & Schapiro
1st Wok
Fraunces Tavern
French Roast Cafe
Garden Cafe (MOMA)
Googies Italian
Great Am. Health
Hamburger Harry's
Hard Rock Cafe
Harley Davidson
Harry's Hanover Sq.
Hi-Life Bar/Grill
Houlihan's
Il Vagabondo
Jackson Hole
Jekyll & Hyde
Juanita's
La Fondue
Le Bar Bat
Lion's Head
Live Bait
Lucky Strike
Luke's Bar/Grill
Manhattan Brewing
Mayrose

McSorley's
Mickey Mantle's
Moran's
Mortimer's
Mo's Caribbean
Mulholland Drive
N.Y. Deli
Old Town Bar
O'Neals'
Ottomanelli's
Pasta Presto
Patzo
Pete's Tavern
Pizzeria Uno
Planet Hollywood
Pudgie's
Royal Canadian
Rumpelmayer's
Ruppert's
Saloon
Saranac
Sardi's
Sawadee Thai
Sette MoMA
Supreme Macaroni
Teachers Too
Telephone Bar
Temple Bar
T.G.I. Friday's
Tony Roma's
Tony's Di Napoli
Tortilla Flats
White Horse Tavern
World Yacht
Ye Waverly Inn
Zip City Brewing
Zucchini

Smoking Prohibited

Adoré
Ah Umakatta
Amir's Falafel
Angelica Kitchen
Angelika Film Ctr.
Barnes & Noble
Between the Bread
Blue Moon Mexican
Bo Ky
Bright Food Shop
Busby's
Cafe Con Leche
Calif. Burrito Co.
Caviarteria
Chantale's Cajun
Chanterelle
Chock Full o' Nuts
Christo's Stkhse.
Contrapunto
Cooper's Coffee
Cucina
Cupcake Cafe
East
Etats-Unis
1st Wok

Franklin Station
Freddie & Pepper's's
Friend of Farmer
Frutti di Mare
Garden Cafe
Good Enough to Eat
Harry's Burritos
Health Pub
Island Spice
Josie's
Khan Restaurant
La Boite en Bois
La Bouillabaisse
La Fondue
Lamarca
La Taza de Oro
La Vieille Auberge
L'Entrecote
Les Celebrités
Les Friandises
Levana
Lipstick Cafe
Luke's Bar/Grill
Luma
Mavalli Palace
Mazzei
Mingala Burmese
Morgan Cafe
Natalino
New Prospect Cafe
News Bar
New Viet Huong
Nicola's
Nosmo King
Nusantara
Papaya King
Park Bistro
Parma
Piccola Venezia
Piccolo Pomodoro
Rosemarie's
Sarabeth's
Seattle Bean Co
Shun Lee Palace
Sonia Rose
Souen
Szechuan Kitchen
Tacomadre
Taq. de Mexico
Tea Box
Terrace
Terramare Café
Thai House Cafe
Thomas Scott's
Tre Pomodori
Triplets
T Salon
Union Square Cafe
Viand
Vinnie's Pizza
Westside Cottage
Whole Wheat
Zacki's PBQ
Zucchini

Teas
(See also *Coffeehouses & Desserts* Index)
Adrienne
Algonquin Hotel
Anglers & Writers
Book-Friends Cafe
Café Word of Mouth
Carlyle
C3
Danal
Essex House
Four Seasons
Les Friandises
Le Train Bleu
Lowell Hotel
Mark's
Mayfair Hotel
Medici 56
Morgan Cafe
Paramount Hotel
Peacock Alley
Pierre Hotel
Plaza Athenee
Plaza Hotel
Royalton
Russian Tea Room
Sette MoMA
Tea Box
T Salon
Village Atelier
Yaffa Tea Room

Teenagers & Other Youthful Spirits
Aggie's
America
Amir's Falafel
Angelika Film Ctr.
Area Code Cafe
Arriba Arriba
Barking Dog
Barnes & Noble
Benny's Burritos
Blue Moon Mexican
Boca Chica
Bright Food Shop
Broome Street Bar
Brother Jimmy's
Cafe Lalo
Calif. Burrito Co.
California Pizza
Cantina
Carmine's
Carnegie Deli
Coconut Grill
Corner Bistro
Cottonwood Cafe
Cucina di Pesce
Cucina Stagionale
Dallas BBQ
Dosanko
E.A.T.
EJ's Luncheonette

Ellen's Stardust
El Pollo
Empire Diner
Empire Szechuan
1st Wok
Freddie & Pepper's's
Good Enough to Eat
Googies
Grotta Azzurra
Hard Rock Cafe
Harley Davidson
Hosteria Fiorella
Jackson Hole
Jerry's
Jim McMullen
John's Pizzeria
Kum Gang San
La Caridad
Lupe's East L.A.
Main Street
Manhattan Plaza
Mappamondo
Mary Ann's
Mee Noodle Shop
Mezzaluna
Mickey Mantle's
Mustang Grill
NoHo Star
Orig. Cal. Taqueria
Papaya King
Pasta Lovers
Pearson's BBQ
Pizzeria Uno
Planet Hollywood
Rosa Mexicano
Ruppert's
Sarabeth's
Second Ave. Deli
Serendipity 3
Shun Lee Cafe
Steak Frites
Sugar Reef
Szechuan Hunan
Szechuan Kitchen
Three Guys
Tortilla Flats
Tutta Pasta
Two Boots
Vinnie's Pizza

Visitors on Expense Accounts
Aquavit
Arcadia
Aureole
Bolo
Bouley
Cafe Centro
Cafe des Artistes
Carnegie Deli
Chanterelle
Chiam
Chin Chin
Christer's
C.T.

Cub Room
Daniel
Da Umberto
Dawat
Four Seasons
Gotham Bar/Grill
Gramercy Tavern
Hudson River Club
Il Mulino
Il Nido
Jo Jo
JUdson Grill
La Caravelle
La Cote Basque
La Grenouille
La Reserve
Le Bernardin
Le Chantilly
Le Cirque
Le Colonial
Le Madri
Le Perigord
Les Celebrités
Lespinasse
Lutèce
Manhattan Ocean
March
Matthew's
Mesa Grill
Monkey Bar
Montrachet
Nobu
One If By Land
Oyster Bar
Palm
Park Ave. Cafe
Patría
Periyali
Peter Luger
Petrossian
Post House
Primavera
Provence
Rainbow Room
Remi
River Cafe
Russian Tea Room
SeaGrill
Shun Lee Palace
Sign of the Dove
Smith & Wollensky
Sparks
Sushisay
Tatou
Tavern on Green
TriBeCa Grill
"21" Club
Union Square Cafe
Vong
World Yacht

Wheelchair Access

(Most places now have wheelchair access; call in advance to check)

Winning Wine Lists

An American Place
Aureole
Barbetta
Chiam
Cité
Felidia
Four Seasons
Gramercy Tavern
I Tre Merli
Le Bernardin
Le Cirque
Levana
Lutèce
Manhattan Ocean
Michael's
Montrachet
Nicola Paone
Oyster Bar
Palio
Park Ave. Cafe
Post House
Rainbow Room
River Cafe
San Domenico
Smith & Wollensky
SoHo Kitchen
Sparks
Tommaso's
"21" Club
Union Square Cafe
Wollensky's Grill

Young Children

(Besides the normal fast-food places; * indicates children's menu available)

Afghan Kebab Hse.*
Aggie's
America
Amsterdam's*
Area Code Cafe
Back Porch*
Benihana
Boathouse Cafe
Boulevard*
Broadway Diner
Brother Jimmy's*
Brothers BBQ*
Burger Heaven
Cafe Centro
Cafe S.F.A.
Cake Bar & Cafe
Calif. Burrito Co.
Carnegie Deli
Chock Full o' Nuts

City Crab*
Cowgirl Hall*
Cucina & Co.
Dallas BBQ
E.A.T.
EJ's Luncheonette*
Elephant & Castle
Ellen's Stardust
El Pollo
Embers
Empire Diner
Empire Szechuan
Freddie & Pepper's
Friend of Farmer*
Good Enough to Eat
Googies
Hamburger Harry's's
Harbour Lights
Hard Rock Cafe
Harley Davidson
H.S.F.
Jackson Hole*
Jim McMullen
John's Pizzeria
Katz's Deli
Lucky's Bar/Grill
Lupe's East L.A.
Manganaro's
Mary Ann's*
Mee Noodle Shop
Mickey Mantle's*
N.Y. Deli
O'Neals'*
Orig. Cal. Taqueria
Palm Court
Pasqua Coffee
Pig Heaven
Pizzapiazza*
Planet Hollywood
Popover Cafe*
Royal Canadian
Rumpelmayer's
Saloon
Saranac
Second Ave. Deli
7th Regiment Mess
Stage Deli*
Starbucks
Sylvia's
Tang Tang
Tennessee Mtn.*
T.G.I. Friday's
Tony Roma's*
Tortilla Flats
T Salon
Two Boots*
Vinnie's Pizza
Wolf's Deli
World Yacht
Zarela

Wine Vintage Chart
1982-1993

These ratings are designed to help you select wine to go with your meal. They are on the same 0–to–30 scale used throughout this *Survey*. The ratings reflect both the quality of the vintage and the wine's readiness to drink. Thus if a wine is not fully mature or is over the hill, its rating has been reduced. The ratings were prepared principally by our friend Howard Stravitz, a law professor at the University of South Carolina.

WHITES	'82	'83	'85	'86	'87	'88	'89	'90	'91	'92	'93
French:											
Burgundy	23	15	28	29	13	23	29	25	17	26	20
Loire Valley	—	—	18	17	13	18	25	24	17	15	18
Champagne	27	23	28	24	—	—	26	25	—	—	—
Sauternes	—	28	21	26	—	27	26	23	—	—	—
California:											
Chardonnay	—	—	—	—	—	—	26	19	27	25	28	27
REDS											
French:											
Bordeaux	29	26	28	26	16	25	27	25	18	20	23
Burgundy	19	20	28	12	21	25	26	28	21	24	22
Rhône	15	25	26	21	14	27	27	25	18	16	19
Beaujolais	—	—	—	—	—	20	25	22	24	18	23
California:											
Cabernet/ Merlot	23	14	27	25	25	15	20	25	24	23	23
Zinfandel	—	—	18	17	20	15	16	19	19	18	18
Italian:											
Chianti	16	13	27	15	—	24	—	25	—	—	—
Piedmont	25	—	26	11	18	21	26	26	—	—	19

Bargain sippers take note: Some wines are reliable year in, year out, and are reasonably priced as well. These wines are best bought in the most recent vintages. They include: Alsatian Pinot Blancs, Côtes du Rhône, Muscadet, Bardolino, Valpolicella and inexpensive Spanish Rioja and California Zinfandel. (Also: we do not include 1984 because except for Bordeaux and California reds, the vintage is not recommended.)